PIAGET'S THEORY
Prospects and Possibilities

The Jean Piaget Symposium Series
Available from LEA

SIGEL, I. E., BRODZINSKY, D. M., & GOLINKOFF, R. M. (Eds.) • New Directions in Piagetian Theory and Practice

OVERTON, W. F. (Ed.) • The Relationship Between Social and Cognitive Development

LIBEN, L. S. (Ed.) • Piaget and the Foundations of Knowledge

SCHOLNICK, E.K. (Ed.) • New Trends in Conceptual Representation: Challenges to Piaget's Theory?

NEIMARK, E.D., De LISI, R., & NEWMAN, J. L. (Eds.) • Moderators of Competence

BEARSON, D.J., & ZIMILES, H. (Eds.) • Thought and Emotion: Developmental Perspectives

LIBEN, L. S. (Ed.) • Development and Learning: Conflict or Congruence?

FORMAN, G., & PUFALL, P. B. (Eds.) • Constructivism in the Computer Age

OVERTON, W. F. (Ed.) • Reasoning, Necessity, and Logic: Developmental Perspectives

KEATING, D. P., & ROSEN, H. (Eds.) • Constructivist Perspectives on Developmental Psychopathology and Atypical Development

CAREY, S., & GELMAN, R. (Eds.) • The Epigensis of Mind: Essays on Biology and Cognition

BEILIN, H., & PUFALL, P. (Eds.) • Piaget's Theory: Prospects and Possibilities

PIAGET'S THEORY
Prospects and Possibilities

Edited by

Harry Beilin
City University of New York, Graduate School
Peter Pufall
Smith College

LEA LAWRENCE ERLBAUM ASSOCIATES, PUBLISHERS
1992 Hillsdale, New Jersey   Hove and London

Lawrence Erlbaum Associates, Inc., Publishers
365 Broadway
Hillsdale, New Jersey 07642

Library of Congress Cataloguing-in-Publication Data

Piaget's theory : prospects and possibilities / [edited by] Harry
  Beilin, Peter B. Pufall.
      p.   cm.
  Papers presented at the 20th-anniversary symposium of the Jean
Piaget Society.
  Includes bibliographical references and index.
  ISBN 0-8058-1050-1
  1. Genetic epistemology—Congresses.   2. Genetic psychology-
-Congresses.   3. Piaget, Jean, 1896-   —Congresses.   I. Beilin,
Harry.   II. Pufall, Peter B.   III. Jean Piaget Society. Symposium.
BF723.C5P555   1992
153–dc20   91-32873
                                                                        CIP

Printed in the United States of America
10 9 8 7 6 5 4 3 2

We dedicate this book to our families

Iris, Lewis, and Ian

Ann, Teresa, Miles, Matthew, and Elizabeth

As well, we acknowledge the significant contribution Lynn S. Liben has made to the scholarly quality of the Jean Piaget Symposium Series as its first editor.

As this book went to press, we learned of the untimely death of our esteemed colleague and valued friend

Michael Chapman

We are also dedicating this volume to him for his outstanding contributions to Piagetian scholarship and developmental research.

Contents

PART II: THEORY OF MIND: EXAMINING REPRESENTATION IN THOUGHT

PART III: SEEKING TRUTH AND MEANING: LOGIC AND SCIENTIFIC REASONING

PART IV: LANGUAGE, CULTURE AND THOUGHT

PART V: CONSTRUCTING SOCIETIES

Foreword

This book is the outcome of a rather special event in the history of the Jean Piaget Society: its twentieth-anniversary symposium. To my regret, I was unable to take part in the meeting, but at the request of the editors, I now have the pleasure of contributing a brief personal foreword to the present volume.

For almost half a century I had the privilege of being closely associated with Piaget's work. I was present when his scientific explorations and discoveries were made, and played a part in their realization. I cannot but believe that with the passing of the years, his *oeuvre* has lost nothing of its vigour and that its fertile promise for the future will be fulfilled.

Piaget's venture was essentially the elaboration of a scientific epistemology: As he saw it, epistemology calls for an inter-disciplinary approach, while the main instrument for its construction resides in genetic psychology. Piaget replaced Emmanuel Kant's question "How is knowledge (e.g., pure mathematics) possible?" with this other question: "How is knowledge constructed and transformed in ontogenesis?" The answer, he hoped, would reveal a process of knowledge-construction common to child development and to the sociogenesis of scientific knowledge as evinced in the history of science. When in 1929, he started teaching child psychology at the *Institut Jean Jacques Rousseau* and the history of scientific thought at Geneva University's *Faculté des Sciences,* Piaget did not go beyond a juxtaposition of the two disciplines, which allowed him to clarify aspects of one in the light of the other. In his impressive work, *Introduction à l'épistémologie génétique,* published in 1950, in the wake of numerous studies of children's growing mastery of number, physical quantity, space, time and other entities, he outlined his fundamental epistemological concepts developed both from his study of the history of scientific ideas in mathematics, physics, biology and sociology, and from genetic psychology. Finally, in *Psychogenesis and the History of Science,* written in collaboration with Rolando Garcia and published in 1983/1989, the authors placed the emphasis on the *processes* that underlie progress in knowledge.

Genetic epistemology is fundamentally constructivist and its main objective is to study the transition from less valid to more valid knowledge. A further and equally original aspect of Piaget's theory is that it is integrative and interactionist. Piaget underlined development as a process in which new acquisitions stemming from the subject's interaction with the environment integrate earlier acquisitions, "intelligence organizes the world while organizing itself." This conception contradicts both empiricism and radical nativism. In opposing reductionist theories, Piaget emphasized his interactionist convictions mainly in the study of interaction between the knowing subject and the world of physical objects as discussed in detail in *Understanding Causality* (1971/1974). Yet it should not be neglected that in some earlier work (e.g., *The Moral Judgment of the Child,* 1932; *Études Sociologiques,* 1965) Piaget set the foundation for studying interaction between individuals as a source of knowledge construction—he in fact considered the coordination of viewpoints and inter-subjectivity to be at the origin of objective knowledge.

Though it is true that genetic psychology cannot be understood or appreciated apart from its links to epistemology—and in that sense it may be called a by-product of epistemology[1]—it does not figure as a poor relation in Piaget's work. It led to a new conception of how the most general mental categories of space, time, causality and the underlying logic of action and thought, provide the basis for our endeavours to understand our universe. Piaget never intended, and certainly never claimed to be a logician, but chose and adapted certain mathematical and logical models in order to be able to analyze the construction by the child of the categories of knowledge. His search for adequate models led him to reshape his operatory logic in two directions: *Toward a Logic of Meanings* (Piaget & Garcia, 1991) which is the source of operatory logic, and towards a reformulation of propositional logic in the sense of a greater freedom from the constraints of extensional logic.

To account for the dynamics of development moving in a certain direction, Piaget elaborated a model of equilibrium and equilibration with auto-regulatory and auto-organizational mechanisms. As Michael

---

[1]American Psychological Association (see Piaget, 1976, Autobiographie. In *Revue europeenne des sciences sociales,* Nos 38-39, 1-43).

Chapman reminds us in the current volume, the origins of this idea go back to a novel entitled *Recherche* that Piaget wrote as a young man (1918). Throughout his life he continued to refine this model, which accounts for Piaget sometimes being called a cybernetician before the advent of cybernetics. He did indeed feel close to researchers such as W. S. McCullock and H. van Foerster and confirmed by L. von Bertalanffy in his conviction that developing systems are essentially open systems. Similarly, though in a different context, he saw a relationship between his theory and that of I. Prigogine.

Equilibration and auto-regulation are models for Piaget's epistemology as well as for his genetic psychology. Reflecting abstraction, a functional process linked to awareness and conceptualization, is considered to be one of the most general features of cognitive process. This process implies a reflection (as by a mirror) on a higher plane of what was established on the lower one. On the higher plane, actions are reorganized in coordination with what the subject previously constructed or is adding during reconstruction. This then becomes reflection in the sense of "thinking about." Piaget stressed the point that such reflection goes with reorganization. The first forms of reflecting abstraction occur early in life and the process becomes ever more coherent and powerful with progress and knowledge. As H. Sinclair discusses in her paper, processes of reflecting abstraction and the implications inherent in a logic of meaningful actions also appear to be at work in the transition from one-word to two- or three-word utterances produced by young children.

Piaget was creative up to the end; during the last decade of his life, he renewed his functionalistic vein, switching from research on structures to research on processes, analysing cognizance, contradictions and dialectics in terms of the subordination of mental operations to broader forms of functioning and the opening up of new possibilities and necessities.

Piaget's oeuvre gives the impression that it is complete. However, because every stage of psychogenesis opens upon future developments, his epistemological and psychogenetic conception holds great promise for the future, as is reflected in several chapters in this volume. The essay on a logic of meaning is an example of this and opens up a new field of investigation on the inferential aspects of action. The principles of self-organising open systems show their fertility in broader systems. Epistemological constructivism is reflected in linguistic studies. A new field that needs to be explored and which has been comparatively neglected up to now, is that of interpersonal relations, be it via the coordination of points of view, the dialectics of exchanges, or the formation of value systems and norms.

Instead of praising Piaget for what he accomplished, the best tribute we can pay to his memory is to go forward. With this idea in mind, together with G. Cellérier and a risk-loving research team, we have undertaken to complement the study of knowledge by that of discovery processes in the child, taking into account recent contextual evolution.

—Bärbel Inhelder

REFERENCES

Piaget, J. (1932). *The Moral Judgment of the Child.* London: Paul Kegan.

Piaget, J. (1950). *Introduction à l'épistémologie génétique.* Paris: PUF.

Piaget, J. (1965). *Etudes sociologiques.* Genève: Droz.

Piaget, J. (1974). *Understanding Causality.* New York: Norton. (Original work published 1971)

Piaget, J. & Garcia, R. (1989). *Psychogenesis and the history of science.* New York: Columbia University Press. (Original work published 1983)

Piaget, J. & Garcia, R. (1991). *Toward a logic of meaning.* Hillsdale, N.J.: Lawrence Erlbaum Associates.

1
Piaget's New Theory

Harry Beilin
City University of New York

HISTORICAL BACKGROUND

In this chapter I elaborate on what by now should be evident, that in the years following the early 1970s Piaget and his collaborators' publications moved his theory in a new direction to such a degree as to justify viewing it as a "new" theory. Three features of the new theory are discussed:

1. the shift from an emphasis on extension (and truth testing) to intension (and meaning), and a new theoretical model I refer to as *a logical hermeneutics of action,*
2. the shift from an emphasis on logical necessity to that of possibility, and its consequences for constructivist theory, and
3. the continuing emphasis on rationality and its place in current discussions of ideology.

When Piaget (1980) declared he had previously been in error in placing almost exclusive stress on extensional, truth-table logic and that a more balanced theory of meaning was needed giving greater attention to intensional logic, it appeared as though a radical and sudden transformation had occurred in his theory. It was indeed a radical change, but it was not occasioned by a sudden shift in the direction that Piaget's theory had been taking in the 10 years prior to that time. Only recently, with the posthumous translation and publication of a series of books completed near the end of Piaget's life, has the nature and magnitude of the reformulation become apparent. The changes are sufficiently striking, as already indicated, to

1

justify considering the late work as a new Piagetian theory. However, as with all transformations in Piaget's theory, and there were many, they were rarely wholly new; a case in point is the development of the theory of equilibration (see Chapman, this volume). The successive theories maintain a certain integrity over their entire history to such a degree as to make it evident that a core set of assumptions have sustained Piaget's research program with few modifications (Beilin, 1985). However, some of the changes have been of central importance, as with the new theory of correspondences and morphisms, but these have occurred in the context of an already formidable theoretical architecture so that their significance has escaped general notice.

First, I detail something of the major shift that occurred in the 1970s, that culminated in 1980 in the theory of meaning that was Piaget's final work, and then discuss other features of the new theory that are of importance to developmental psychology.

Early Functionalism

The 1920s and early 1930s were a time in which a series of debates were under way among a variety of theoretical systems in psychology. The field, by this time, had moved away from the confrontation between Wundt and Titchener's early structuralism and the functionalism of James, Angell, Baldwin, and Carr to a much more complex scene in which a number of schools sought to establish their right to the loyalties of the uncommitted (Beilin, 1983). There was faculty psychology, following in the tradition of Herbart, the German Gestalt psychologies, Freud's psychoanalysis, and the American pragmatism of Dewey, Thorndike, and Woodworth whose empiricism continued the tradition of functionalism. There was also Pavlov's conditioning theory, and the Continental functionalisms of Janet and Claparede.

Piaget's sympathy was with Claparede's functionalism, at the same time that he aggressively rejected the functionalism of associationism and connectionism that fueled American and Russian empiricism. Functionalism, in this way, continued to have a profound effect on both American and Continental psychology, particularly in the era leading up to the 1940s and 1950s. This functionalism took many forms, and its adherents shared some, if not necessarily all, of its fundamental assumptions. I have described the nature of these functionalisms elsewhere so do not repeat them now (Beilin, 1983; see also Kendler, 1987). Montangero (1985) commenting on Piaget's own theoretical development, divides it into four periods. The first period includes the five books published between 1923 and 1932; the second by the three books written in the 1930s. The principal difference between these two periods was the shift from social explanation to a theory of adaptation.

However, both periods are characterized by the emphasis on functional analysis, and contained other aspects of the functionalist agenda, such as the emphasis on process.

Structuralist Period

A marked reformulation in Piaget's theory took place in the 1940s, that continued until the 1960s. This change entailed a shift to structural analysis. The structuralist period is represented by a series of books, on which much of Piaget's later reputation is based, books that detailed the nature of logicomathematical structures underlying cognitive development. The 1960s were a period of transition, in which structural analysis was no longer stressed, but no new models of explanation were developed (Montangero, 1985). The theory from that time, on to the last works, offers an increasing return to functionalist analysis and the products of that analysis. However, I would stress that the later functionalism is quite different from Piaget's earlier functionalism, if for no other reason that it moves in tandem with Piaget's continuing structuralism, and is profoundly affected by it. What is striking in the evolution of Piaget's theory, is that during its entire course, structuralism and functionalism play either dominant or subordinate roles, but both are always present. Reference to structure appears in the early functionalist period, and function is never lost sight of in the structuralist period. In the last period, there is an intellectual struggle apparent in Piaget, to bring these two major strains in the theory into some kind of equilibrium. This final synthesis was intended to be achieved in the last of Piaget's books, that he co-authored with Rolando Garcia (Piaget & Garcia, 1991).

THE THEORY OF MEANING

Piaget's effort to develop a theory of meaning was based first on the recognition that extensional logics, even from the logician's point of view, have inherent difficulties. More importantly, from a scientific viewpoint, many do not map onto natural thought in a wholly satisfactory way. Within logic itself, the effort to overcome the paradoxes of extensional logics began in the 1950s with the reintroduction of "intension" into formal logical systems. This effort resulted, in 1975, in Anderson and Belnap's elaboration of relevance or entailment logic (see Brynes, this volume, and Piaget & Garcia, 1991).

The difficulties and paradoxes of extensional logic emerge where the truth relation between propositions (or statements) is considered. For example, if either of the terms of the disjunction $p.q \vee$ (or) $p.q \vee p.q$ is true, it follows that the implication $p \supset q$ is true, even when there is no meaning relation between p and q, that is, p does not need to imply q in what is ordinarily understood as in a meaningful way. Following on a number of equally paradoxical consequences of the nature of extensional logic, Piaget was drawn to say that it is "indispensable" to construct a logic of meaning whose major operator is a "meaning implication," which he defined as p implies q ($p \supset q$) if the meaning of q is contained in the meaning of p, and this meaning is transitive. This parallels Anderson and Belnap's conclusion that all entailments are tautologies (Anderson & Belnap, 1975). Consequently, intensional meaning embodiments, which Piaget called "inherences," correspond to extensional nestings. That is, they conform with the forms of the truth tables, and in the sense of the new proposal, such truth tables are "partial" and determined by meanings. Thus, the Piaget and Garcia proposal parallels the more formal logic of entailment based on relevance and necessity of Anderson and Belnap, although it is a psychological analogue to the logical theory and not a logical theory as such (Piaget & Garcia, 1991). The proposal, presented by Garcia (in that volume), employs truth-functional connectives in an intensional implication relation, ostensibly avoiding the fallacies inherent in pure extensional logics. Garcia holds that Anderson and Belnap's formalisms are not as coherent a system as it first appeared, in that they offer their system as a collection of ad hoc rules they consider as working hypotheses for reaching certain goals. This "highly flexible" approach to logic appeals to Garcia as a working model for genetic epistemology, when one is looking for the roots of "natural logic."

Piaget's sensitivity to developments in logic theory derive from a number of sources. In Piaget's structuralist period, the application of logicomathematical formalisms, as models to map onto developing natural thought, committed him to one form or another of logical and mathematical theory, on the assumption that the underlying structures of thought have logicomathematical form. When Piaget modified these logics to conform with demands of observed cognitive development, it led logicians to criticize Piaget's interpretation and employment of these formal logics, despite his disclaimer that what he was proposing was a psychologic and not a formal system of logic. However, sensitivity to logicians' criticisms undoubtedly motivated logicians in the Genevan circle to monitor continually the state of logical theory and to question and refine Genevan psychologic.

The greater impetus to change, appears to have come from the research itself. The initial source appears to have been Piaget's reconsideration, late in the 1960s, of the theory of causality (R. Garcia, personal communication June 2, 1990). The new work that followed on correspondences, functions, possibility and necessity, contradiction and consciousness, among others, was now interpreted in a new light. This research increasingly exposed the limitations of truth-table logics, to the point where Piaget felt a fundamental change in the theory was necessary. Piaget and Garcia emphasized that the direction developed in Genevan thinking toward intensional logic "converged" with Anderson and Belnap's relevance-entailment logic, and is not to be seen as a formalization of Piaget's operatory logic. In fact, Garcia wondered whether logical formalizations of Piaget's operatory logic was possible.

From a "logical" point of view, what Piaget's theory of meanings attempts to do, then, is integrate truth-table extensional logic with entailment-intensional logic and employ this integration as a model, if not a formalization of, operatory logical development. Historically, the effort to deal with the two aspects of logical knowledge, and of propositions specifically, goes back at least to Frege, who, in distinguishing between *Sinn* and *Bedeutung* (taken traditionally as between meaning-intension and reference or truth-extension) eventually led to Russell and Whitehead's monumental effort to purify logic by freeing it from the ambiguities of natural language. The symbolic logic they developed, which initiated a revolution in logic and philosophy, resulted in the emphasis on the truth testing of propositions to the neglect of meaning within logical form.

The attack by Wittgenstein, and others, on symbolic logic, and more generally, on the logical positivist program, has resulted in at least partial legitimization of natural language meaning in logical analysis. Piaget and Garcia, reflecting on their own efforts to develop a theory of meaning, concluded that a sharp distinction cannot be made between meaning (or intension) and truth (or extension) as was made by Frege. One might say, further, that current work in philosophy of mind and cognitive psychology is marked by the similar intent to synthesize these previously parallel but independent aspects of knowledge.

In the 1980 note declaring he had been in error in his overemphasis on extensional logic, Piaget offered the prospect that his new theory of meanings would be based on a "decanted" version of his earlier (truth-table) logic, as well as provide a new component that parallels the intensional logic of Anderson and Belnap. The theory of meaning book, published in France in 1983 (English translation, 1991) is entitled, *Toward a Logic of Meanings,* which aptly denotes the fact that the decanted version of the older theory was not developed or offered; instead, one has a programmatic statement of what such a theory should look like. Piaget's death prematurely ended the meaning project. Nevertheless, a substantial body of research was completed and a series of findings are reported on classification, seriation, collections, arithmetical operations, and more, that provide functional descriptions of how meanings precede the development of formal structures. Some striking conclusions emerge from these data and their analysis.

Considering the earlier difficulties created by Piaget's claims concerning the appearance of the 16 binary operations of propositional logic in the formal operational period, with critical reactions from logicians as well as from developmentalists, Piaget now made an even bolder claim. The data, he said, point to the very early formation of operations at the level of sensorimotor actions (well before the period of operational logic). These so-called "protological" operations, although not yet integrated into structures, are nonetheless isomorphic with one or another of the 16 binary operations of operational logic that later form the basis of groupings, and still later the INRC group. At the level of protologic, form and content are not increasingly differentiated as they are in operatory systems. The early forms of this protologic provide the first evidence of meaning (or intension) in the child's thought and provide the initial context in which the earliest elements of extensional logic are to be found.

Piaget's central thesis, now, is that at all levels, starting from the most elementary, knowledge always involves inference. Logic is first evident in the child's thought when he or she is "able to anticipate a relation between actions . . ." (Piaget & Garcia, 1991). Thus, the roots of logic appear long before language and propositional thought, in that anticipation entails inference, inference in turn, entails a logical relation, namely implication (see Perner & Astington, this volume, as a counterpoint). Consequently, a relation between actions is already a logical implication, but not in the extensional sense of requiring a determination of its truth value. Rather it is a meaning implication (i.e., an intension). Put another way, "inferences are implications between meanings (which are attributed to the properties, and to objects, and to . . . actions themselves" (Piaget & Garcia, 1991, p. 159). Meanings result from the subject's attribution of assimilation schemes to objects — objects whose properties are not simply observables, inasmuch as they always involve an interpretation of what is observed. Consistent with Piaget's concept of schemes, the meaning of an object is "what can be done" with the object — a definition that applies at the sensorimotor level as well as at the level of preoperatory (or conceptual) thought that begins with the emergence of the semiotic function. Meanings are also what can be said of objects, that is, in their descriptions, as well as in what can be thought of them, as in classifying or relating them. For actions themselves, their meaning is in "what they lead to" — in the transformations they produce in objects or situations.

What is most striking in Piaget's approach to these new data and the way they are interpreted, is that Piaget, in effect, is creating a new theoretical model, one that might well be called a *logical hermeneutics of action*. The model, as applied to the sensorimotor and preoperative periods requires a functional analysis of how subjects approach a task. An adequate model would necessarily detail the actions of the child, the objects acted on, and above all provide an interpretation of the inferences the child is making in carrying out the task. It requires an interpretation on the part of the investigator, who is attempting to characterize the meanings inherent in the situation and subsequently to identify the logical links in the system that make the meaning implications cohere. An example appears in a particular application of the method. Piaget said, in this instance,

> Above all, what is involved is an inference that amounts to saying that if certain trajectories have been accomplished, others may be possible also. This leads a number of subjects to proceed from pushing to lateral or oblique movements and eventually to drawing in the object. (Piaget & Garcia, 1991, p. 15)

In other words, where the child carries out an action that entails a directed motion, that action is only one of a series of possible motions in other directions. To exploit these other possibilities requires the child to infer that motion in other directions is possible, including those that enable the object to be pulled to oneself. In this scenario, the child is not just engaged in random movement that by trial and error brings the object to oneself, but is based on an inference-generating process linked to intensional action. Here, Piaget went beyond description and even structural explanation to an interpretive model of observed action.

This example illustrates how the introduction of systematic *interpretation* into Piaget's method, seeking for relations of implication, at first intensional and later extensional, brings Piaget's theory and method in contact with recent hermeneutical and other interpretive traditions. It is hermeneutical in that Piaget is dealing with action just as others apply a hermeneutics to texts. However, Piaget is not, as in the Nietzschean tradition, holding that all life is text, and consequently action is text. Only, that one may seek a logic of meaning in action through the (intensional) interpretation of implications in action. Piaget's hermeneutics differs from other interpretive approaches in that his goal is to explain and characterize the logical characteristics of thought, whereas for hermeneutics generally the goal is the achievement of meaning itself, ordinarily in personal, social, and historical frameworks. Piaget differs from the hermeneutical tradition (Gadamer and Ricoeur are exceptions) too in that his hermeneutics does not lead to relativism in the way texts are said to be open to multiple interpretations, each claiming legitimacy. Rather, Piaget's interpretation of the implications in action lead to universals of intensional and extensional kinds. "Different strokes for different folks" is not Piaget's motto.

Piaget and Garcia (1991), summarized their goals and achievements as follows:

1. They explain in detail how the logic of actions prepares for operatory logic, based on the new concept of *action implication*.

2. They sought to detail a stage of protologic at the level of actions that in respect to *meaning relations* is isomorphic with that of the 16 binary operations of propositional logic. (This they feel they achieved.)

3. They showed, as in the case of logical connectives, that logical relations are constructed by fragments that gradually merge into logical structures. This view, it should be emphasized contradicts the usual understanding that Piaget claims logical (i.e., structural) achievements are sudden, saltatory, and discontinuous.

4. At the level of logic, Garcia attempted to show how the logic of entailment, that combines the features of both intensional and extensional logic shows certain convergences with Piaget's logic of operations. They hoped this would lead to a "renewal" of operatory logic by rewriting the part of the logic of operations that refers to propositional logic, by incorporating a logic of meaning.

That work is yet to be done, but it is clear that the outcome foreseen was that the operatory logic of Piaget's theory would be a synthesis of meaning and truth.

CONSTRUCTIVISM AND POSSIBILITY

In parallel with the shift in emphasis from extension to intension, and truth testing to meaning, is a shift in the new theory from an emphasis on logical necessity inherent in extensional systems to the role of possibility in cognitive inference and implication. The shift has important implications for Piaget's constructivism.

A serious issue constructivist theory faces is how more powerful systems arise out of less powerful systems. Some philosophers, taking logical systems as their model, despair of the possibility, and consequently reject constructivist theories, despite the facts of species evolution and human ontogenesis. Piaget was not unaware of the issue, and insisted that his theory was designed specifically to account for "newness" or novelty in the development of knowledge. One might reject the logician's charge most simply by noting that biological and psychological forms are not logical forms and are not to be accounted for by logical theory. It is for this reason, among others, that Piaget pointed out to his logician and mathematician critics that his theory was not a logical theory and that his use of mathematical and logical models often required changes in those models to make them accord with the evidence of psychological development. Consequently, as indicated earlier, his logics were more aptly described as psychologics.

As is well known, Piaget's account of both stability and change in developing cognitive systems is in the theory of equilibration. Despite the dismay of many, who believe that the core concepts of the theory, those of assimilation, accommodation, self-regulation, and reflective abstraction, are too vague, they nevertheless play the key explanatory role in the account of how change in cognitive structure occurs. Piaget who, on more than one occasion, agreed with a questioner's objection that he had no adequate account of the nature of transitions in his stage theory, did so either because he could see its limitations and inadequacies, and/or knew that there was an improved version on its way. I am inclined to believe the latter, because the recently published volumes extend the core theory in significant ways that do much to delineate the nature of Piaget's constructivism.

Two additions hold the key to the changes: an emphasis on procedures and the delineation of the role of possibility in the development of cognitive structure. In the early 1970s, Genevans, principally under the direction of Bärbel Inhelder, undertook an exploration of strategies and procedures in the development of children's reasoning (Inhelder, Sinclair, & Bovet, 1974). The role of strategies in children's actions was not entirely new to Piaget's experiments. Even the earliest reported protocols of infants and children's actions are replete with descriptions of their strategies in approaching objects. These descriptions provided much of the material of Piaget's early functionalism. However, they were not the focus of theoretical attention. The reason, often given, was Piaget's central interest in universals in cognitive development and not in individual differences or the influence of context.

The late attention given to strategies, and more generally to procedures, has led to an important change in the theory, particularly in reshaping the conception of operations and structures and that of self-regulation (see Sinclair's chapter, this volume). Procedures, in the new conception are constituted in *procedural schemes,* and are the means for working toward a goal. They are differentiated from *presentative schemes,* those schemes that organize the properties of objects. *Operational schemes,* in the new theory are syntheses of procedural and presentative schemes. Operations are procedural in the sense that they are performed in real time, and they are like higher-order presentative schemes in that the laws of combination and organization that regulate operations are atemporal.

The earlier theory, which for convenience sake I refer to as the standard theory—the theory most people presently know (Beilin, 1989) implies that operations and structures give rise to procedures. In the new theory, logicomathematical operations with their relatively well-regulated organization, develop out of procedures that are themselves often faulty (Piaget, 1981/1987a). Whereas self-regulation involved the evolution and improvement of structures alone, now, self-regulation is seen only as procedural and not presentative, that is, as assimilative and concerned with the input to existing schemes. Schemes are not extended, as in the past theory, only by assimilation. Now, the accommodative function of schemes becomes important. As schemes are applied to new situations, accommodation exposes the possibilities in existing schemes. The introduction of new procedures in the response to new situations leads to the realization of what is possible in existing schemes, and leads further to the creation of new schemes.

The shift in the new theory, then, is toward the functions of accommodation. That is, the need to accommodate to new situations promotes the formation of new procedures. Procedures, in turn, lead to the development of new logicomathematical operations and the cycle is repeated. Equilibration, with its new set of possibilities, leads to new equilibriums (or re-equilibrations, in the Piagetian lexicon). The possibilities inherent in the construction of a new structure become the engine that drives cognitive development. But possibilities cannot be realized without procedures and procedures cannot exist without possibility. The combination of possibilities and procedural schemes leads to presentative schemes and these lead to structures. Possibility, then, serves two functions, it is, first, an instrument of equilibration, and it is the motive force in re-equilibration. It is, second, the motive force in the sense that when a new structure has been achieved, as in the combination of old structures, or as the product of the assimilation of new actions, it opens up new possibilities. This is another way of saying that two systems, each with discrete properties, when combined, creates a new system with emergent properties. This is at the heart of the constructivist thesis. But the mechanisms basic to the constructivist process are more general. The conventional analogy for justifying the constructivist thesis is to physical systems of the sort represented by sodium and chlorine, each with toxic properties, that when combined yield sodium chloride, the harmless salt that allows most animal life.

The implication in the analogy, and in the general case, is that a new system of possibilities results from the construction of a new structure. The new structure, in turn, can be put to use through procedures carried over from older structures by generalization, or are developed to fit the new structure, either by the variation of the older procedure or through a newly created one. In contrast to the older idea of the generalization of existing structures and procedures to new situations, a new structure, Piaget holds, requires the exercise of new capacities "commanding the production of variations that enable it to function" (Piaget, 1981/1987a, p. 152). Consequently, new possibilities are formed endogenously. This implies that the process of mental construction is subject-driven although such constructions do not always go smoothly. There may be disturbances or limitations that lead to efforts at compensating for these limitations. One such source of disturbance derives from objects (whether physical or logicomathematical), and thus are reality-based. The other source is in the subject himself or herself and generally, are internal obstacles to the subject's use of his or her own capacities. These are real if the subject is aware of his or her own present inability to respond to a situation; they are "virtual" if the subject does not experience them consciously. These disturbances and the mechanisms of compensation that operate to overcome them drive the transitions that take place from one level of thought to the next.

Possibilities are recognized or analyzed differently with age. They are also differentiated in respect to function, and in their structural relations (Piaget, 1981/1987a, p. 7). As functional entities they exist in different forms, as: (a) the hypothetically possible (valid solutions mixed with errors), (b) the realizable, (c) the deducible, and (d) the postulated possible. Structurally, they are (a) possibilities generated by analogies, (b) the concrete co-possibles, (c) the abstract co-possibles, and (d) the possible in its most general form, the infinite.

The relation between possibilities and operations is evident even at the earliest stages of development. When possibilities become evident, accommodative activity follows in making choices, in generating sequential procedures, and in inducing regulations. Possibilities, said Piaget, provide the raw material for the development of newly emerging operations. Possibilities also provide the source from which procedures appear that are then refined through experience. Piaget made clear that operations do not result from possibilities per se, which are diverse in content, but from an inferential act that leads to reflective abstraction and completive generalizations that themselves lead to the development of operations (Piaget, 1981/1987a).

However, there is another ingredient that goes along with possibility in the development of operations, it is necessity (Piaget, 1981/1987b). Operations are constituted from a synthesis of possibility and necessity. Procedural flexibility characterizes possibility, but necessity is characterized by self-regulation and system-bound compositions and organization. Possibilities generate differentiations; necessity yields integration.

Necessities and possibilities become progressively differentiated from reality, but it is not reality (observable facts external to the subject) itself that is the source, since reality has neither possibilities nor necessities in it. Instead, the source is in inferential capacities that result from the increasing numbers of assimilatory schemes, and their reciprocities and coordinations.

Piaget is faced with a paradoxical situation. He has always claimed that the creation of knowledge arises from the action of subject on object. Yet, even in the late formulation of the theory, he claimed that possibility and necessity are the products of the subject's autonomous activity, in that the capacities represented in both possibility and necessity do not derive from objects (that is, reality). In the past this led to criticism, particularly from Marxist materialists, that Piaget's theory is idealistic. However, he rejected this claim and further argued that the dilemma disappears by seeing the epistemic subject (the subject of universal structures) and the prior functioning psychological subject as part of reality. Thus, in the context of the new theory, the subject's actions and operations, "include reality in a network of possibilities and necessary relations" and "every real event appears as one actualization from among others that are possible within a system of logico-mathematical transformations that provide explanations." It is thus that "objects [reality] are incorporated in the subject with the help of mathematics and the subject becomes part of the object through biology" (Piaget, 1981/1987a, p. 150).

The new theory, with its emphasis on possibility and on procedures, places much greater emphasis than the past theory on the functional aspects of development in accounting for the origin of mental structure, first by stressing procedures that accompany the use of existing structures, or the use of capacities achieved by newly constructed structures. Second, the motive force and instruments of change are in the mechanisms that exploit new possibilities in the form of capacities created by structures. Further significance of the change in the theory is that it stresses that there is no end in development, in that each development represents new possibilities. Such possibilities can never be fully realized in that new contexts continually create the need for new solutions and new procedures.

Thus, Piaget's late additions extend the theory and at the same time conserve it. They extend the constructivist aspect of the theory by emphasizing the nearly unlimited possibilities in mind, and at the same time show the constraints that come from integrating the products of only some possibilities, and the procedures needed to actualize them. Thus, the developing rational mind is inherently productive, yet constrained, and we are reminded that the development of mind is subject constantly to dialectical forces, the position that Piaget increasingly came to espouse in the later theory.

The delineation of the role of possibility in the development of knowledge seems to emphasize the autonomous nature of the subject in the construction of knowledge. Yet in *Psychogenesis and the History of Science* (Piaget & Garcia, 1989) it is clear that Piaget gives an expanded role to local and historical forces in the creation of knowledge. But the way they do this is still within a subject-centered, at least, semi-autonomously constructive system. Society appears limited to influencing how "objects to be assimilated present themselves to the subject" (Piaget & Garcia, 1989). It does not directly affect the mechanisms by which subjects acquire knowledge. Society, by the way it acts on the relations between subject and object, may influence the meaning attributed to objects. However, how knowledge is acquired depends on the subject's cognitive mechanisms, not the social group's contribution. Social, environmental, and cultural models are influential only to the degree that the subject's attention is directed toward particular objects and situations, and because objects are placed in certain contexts, and not in others.

ON RATIONALITY AND IDEOLOGY

It has long been evident that Piaget's conception of the child has embodied a significant logical component. It has prompted others to refer variously, to Piaget's child "as scientist," or "as logician." It is more apt, I believe, to emphasize the theory's focus on the increasingly rational aspects of the child's thought. That is, to see the child with advancing age as relying more and more on reason. It is this quality in the theory that prompted Shweder (1984) in a quite unsympathetic account, to see Piaget as a figure of Enlightenment thinking, and to attack that view as inconsistent with the irrational and nonrational nature of much in human thinking. In the debate that has raged since World War II between views identified with Nietzsche, Husserl, Heidegger, and others, that are characterized as relativist, anti-intellectual, and nihilistic, and the alternative universalist, rationalist, and liberal views associated with Enlightenment thought, Shweder's sympathies are clearly with the former. Nevertheless, Piaget's theory is very much in the spirit of the Enlightenment. Although, to my knowledge, Piaget did not comment directly on these issues, his attack on philosophers, in *Insights and Illusions of Philosophy* (1971), who, he said, have allowed philosophy to become politicized and relativized, suggests that he would recognize the irrational and nonrational strains in human thought, yet hold that it is in the nature of the human species to overcome the irrational through the development of reason. It is no accident, I believe, that Piaget's theory rests on the notion that development proceeds toward the development of invariants in the face of transformation, or that the task of development is to overcome childhood egocentrism. Although Genevans acknowledged that egocentrism was a needlessly inflammatory term, they persist in believing that the child's inability to take all points of view into account is a condition of the child's thought that is progressively overcome through the decentering influence of rationality. Piaget did not press the social and political implications of this view. However, as Shweder holds, if one places this position in the context of liberal Enlightenment thought, then Piaget would hold that centered thought, as limited reasoning, may be maladaptive, and in need of correction in order to come to terms with social and physical reality, even though nonrational elements may play a significant role in the course of development. Karmiloff–Smith (1978) said that, even nonconservation serves a function in the development of operations.

Piaget's position in another regard is sometimes misunderstood. Radical constructivist views are at root relativistic in opening themselves up to conventionalism, the view that our conception of reality is defined by conventional or consensual agreement. This is not Piaget's constructivism. He insisted, as indicated before in his rejection of the accusation of idealism by Soviet Marxists, that his constructivism ultimately refers to an objective reality. This view, in turn, has led some others (e.g., Rotman, 1977) to see Piaget as a realist. I concur in this identification to the degree that Piaget's theory is conceived as a form of constructivist realism, neither radically constructivist nor naïvely realist. Piaget's rejection of relativism is, by implication, also evident in his appeal to universalism. He insisted, in the face of criticism that he neglects individual differences and the effects of context on performance, that although these are legitimate concerns of psychologists, they are not his. What he was interested in, instead, were those universal features of thought that function despite, or in the face, of all varieties of difference.

The emphasis, these days, in intellectual circles on the social and historical origins of thought, which manifests itself in an attack on Piaget's theory both external to, and now even in Geneva itself, highlights another feature of Piaget's Enlightenment perspective. For Piaget, the origin of thought is in an autonomous, or at the least, semi-autonomous mind. Although Piaget acknowledged the social elaboration of knowledge and the social and historical continuity of the products of human reason, they do not constitute for him the origin of thought. That source must ultimately be individual, even if the individual is engaged in a dialectical encounter with individual or collective others. Recent attempts to show that Piaget had a sociological theory and thus did not neglect the social, while true, cannot be used to enlist Piaget in the current politics of culture. Yet to Shweder, and most others, despite Piaget's dialectics and subject–object interactionism, Piaget's theory is indeed individualistic. With all the concern for objects and reality, the emphasis in the theory is on the subject's action on objects and not on objects themselves. In his notion of physical abstraction, and more importantly, in reflective abstraction, it is, again, the *subject* that constructs a conception of reality. Although, in *Psychogenesis and the History of Science* (Piaget & Garcia, 1989), Piaget paid considerable attention to social and historical trends in science, and attempted to show how socially constituted epistemological frameworks (in a manner reminiscent of Kuhn's paradigms) affect scientific discovery and progress. However, one never loses sight that Piaget held that it is individual scientists who develop theories and not collectives. Even Marx, the progenitor of the modern theory of class declared, "The doctrine that men are the products of circumstances and upbringing forgets that it is men that change circumstances" (quoted in Lewontin, 1990, p. 6).

This tension between the socially constituted and individually constituted has been the basis of much philosophical and political debate, since at least the 17th century. The American, French, and Russian revolutions were the seminal events that defined positions on this issue, and clearly reflected this tension. Theoretical issues within the social sciences, including psychology, harbor these same conflicts. The current debates in developmental psychology between contextualist theory and universalist theory are an instance of the larger conflicts, and the evidence adduced in favor of each position must be seen as ammunition in anything but an objectivist account of reality. The issue is also not one of a simple division between the political left (for contextualism) and the political right (for universalism). It is no secret that Piaget's own political views leaned toward the political left, so that the debate clearly crosses gross political divisions. But the issue here between the individual and the social will no more be decided by the revolutions of 1989 in Eastern and Central Europe than they were in France in 1789. Yet in taking a stand, Piaget's theory, if not totally and squarely imbued with liberal Enlightenment thought, certainly in its emphasis on reason and individuality is in accord with its central spirit.

The various developments in Piaget's later theory, fit well within this ideological framework. The move toward functionalism, and even the recognition of how social and historical forces affect cognition, have not deflected Piaget from the theory's underlying ideological commitment. I do not recall anyone openly arguing that Piaget was rigid and dogmatic in protecting his theory from change, although there can be little question of his determined allegiance to its general form. Thus, although there is a core commitment in Piaget's program to logicomathematical models, there is no necessary commitment to any particular model. The evidence is readily at hand in the new theory of meaning with the dethroning of truth-table (propositional) logic, even if it was not worked out as to how much would remain in the decanted version of the theory. This was not the only radical change in the theory to have occurred, particularly in the later works. The theory of correspondences is another example. In the early theory he had relied exclusively on the notion that logicomathematical thought only entails transformations. "To think is to transform" was an early Piagetian motto. This aspect of the theory is, in fact, sustained to the end. But it became clear to Piaget, sometime in the late 1960s, either from research findings themselves or from developments in mathematics and logic, or as his account usually puts it, from both, that logical thought is based as well on relations that are not transformational but static. This is the case where logical structures resulting from comparisons between object states take on the properties of morphisms and correspondences. This type of mathematical thought or natural logic is illuminated by mapping onto it a mathematical system developed by Maclane, and generally known as category theory. Taken together with the theory of functions, also derived in part from mathematical and logical theory, these two models (category theory and the theory of functions) are used to explain developments in preoperational thought (4 to 7 years) that had been neglected in the earlier specification of the theory. Thus, if one takes into account the later addition of protologics in the sensorimotor period, we see not a diminution of Piaget's commitment to the theory of the child as being increasingly rational, but the opposite. Again, despite the functionalism of the later theory, cognitive development emerges with a design of increasingly sophisticated and powerful rational forms, although Piaget's theory offers anything but a guarantee that these capacities will be used effectively. Looking to future development of Piagetian theory, it is inevitable that these models will be found wanting and better ones will take their place. What will not change, in accord with the assumptions underlying Piaget's theory, is the commitment to the idea that the development of human thought, both individually and socially, strives toward the rational, in the service of overcoming the irrational and chaotic. Although reason is not the only source of human virtues and capabilities, in it resides the only hope for the survival and betterment of the human species.

REFERENCES

Anderson, A. R., & Belnap, N. D. (1975). *Entailment: The logic of relevance and necessity.* Princeton, NJ: Princeton University Press.

Beilin, H. (1983). The new functionalism and Piaget's program. In E. K. Scholnick (Ed.), *New trends in conceptual representation: Challenges to Piaget's theory?* (pp. 3–40). Hillsdale, NJ: Lawrence Erlbaum Associates.

Beilin, H. (1985). Dispensable and core elements in Piaget's theory. *Genetic Epistemologist, 13,* 1–16.

Beilin, H. (1989). Piagetian theory. In R. Vasta (Ed.), Six theories of child development: Revised formulations and current issues. *Annals of Child Development, 6,* 85–132.

Inhelder, B., Sinclair, H., & Bovet, M. (1974). *Learning and the development of cognition.* Cambridge, MA: Harvard University Press.

Karmiloff-Smith, A. (1978). Commentary on C. J. Brainerd: The stage question in cognitive-developmental theory. *Behavioral and Brain Sciences, 2,* 188–189.

Kendler, H. H. (1987). *Historical foundations of modern psychology.* Chicago, IL: Dorsey Press.

Lewontin, R. C. (1990). Review of S. J. Gould, *Wonderful life: The Burgess shale and the nature of history. New York Review of Books, 37,* 3–7.

Montangero, J. (1985). *Genetic epistemology: Yesterday and today.* New York: CUNY, Graduate School and University Center.

Piaget, J. (1971). *Insights and illusions of philosophy.* New York: World Book.

Piaget, J. (1980). The constructivist approach: Recent studies in genetic epistemology. *Cahiers de la Fondation Archives Jean Piaget, 1,* 1–7.

Piaget, J. (1987a). *Possibility and necessity: Vol. 1. The role of possibility in cognitive development*. Minneapolis: University of Minnesota Press. (Original work published 1981)

Piaget, J. (1987b). *Possibility and necessity: Vol. 2. The role of necessity in cognitive development*. Minneapolis: University of Minnesota Press. (Original work published 1981)

Piaget, J., & Garcia, R. (1989). *Psychogenesis and the history of science*. New York: Columbia University Press.

Piaget, J., & Garcia, R. (1991). *Toward a logic of meanings*. Hillsdale, NJ: Lawrence Erlbaum Associates.

Rotman, B. (1977). *Jean Piaget: Psychologist of the real*. Ithaca, NY: Cornell University Press.

Shweder, R. A. (1984). Anthropology's romantic rebellion against the enlightenment, or there's more to thinking than reason and evidence. In R. A. Shweder & R. A. LeVine (Eds.), *Culture theory: Essays on mind, self, and emotion* (pp. 27-64). New York: Cambridge University Press.

UNDERSTANDING SELF-ORGANIZING SYSTEMS AS EQUILIBRATING SYSTEMS

2 The Structure of Knowledge and the Knowledge of Structure

Rolando Garcia
Center for Research and Advanced Studies, Mexico City

The purpose of this chapter is to present some reflections on Piagetian epistemology in the context of two of the problems posed by the development of science in this century: (a) the relation between empirical facts and formal theory and, (b) the mechanisms of self-organization in the evolution of open systems.

WHAT DO WE KNOW OF THE PHYSICAL WORLD?

Constructivism or genetic structuralism appears at a moment of historical importance for science, in particular for the crisis of classical physics. No great thinker of the stature of Piaget has been indifferent to the moments of crisis in any of the main scientific disciplines. Piaget was not himself a physicist, and reflection on this branch of science was thematized only during one of the latter epochs of the International Centre of Genetic Epistemology. However, I can say on the basis of my intense working relationship with Piaget, that his thinking was very much influenced by what was happening in physics at the beginning of this century. Furthermore, Piaget's contribution to epistemology is extremely pertinent to the understanding of some of the fundamental problems posed for science from physics. For this reason, I start by referring to the scientific revolution that took place at the beginning of this century.

Physical Intuition and the Constitution of Matter

This revolution implied a drastic change in the basic concepts of science. It was not only that some concepts were substituted by others, although this was also the case. In the Theory of Relativity, for example, "space" and "time" were replaced by "space–time" (Dugas, 1954). That seemingly superficial substitution had profound implications.

The new concept required renouncing customary ideas associated with the concepts of space and time as found in what was usually referred to as "direct intuition." Neither Newton nor his followers thought that the day would come when those intuitions were questioned. The idea of a "real" absolute space where all bodies are located had already been questioned by Leibniz (1720),[1] but his critique never came to shake Newtonian physics.

Even Heisenberg, one of the most brilliant minds of the century, had difficulties in accepting the new conceptions. In one of his autobiographical works, Heisenberg (1972) wrote of a dialogue he had in his youth with Wolfgang Pauli, in which he declared that although the mathematical frame of Einstein's theory did not cause him any problems, he found it incomprehensible "that a moving observer might understand the word 'time' differently from a stationary observer" (p. 50).

In spite of this statement, in a very short time Heisenberg himself was to become one of the principal actors of the greatest drama in the history of physics. I said "drama" because it meant the definitive renunciation of the use of our intuition in the comprehension of the constitution of matter. More than that, from this moment onward, the very notion of "understanding" would change in meaning.

In this respect I would like to refer in some detail to a dialogue between the young Heisenberg and the great Danish physicist, Niels Bohr. It is well known that Bohr enunciated a theory of the atom, still taught today in secondary schools, that the atom is conceived as a planetary system in miniature. At the center of the atom is the nucleus, containing most of the mass and surrounded by much lighter electrons (particles with a negative electric charge) that move around it as the planets around the sun. From the point of view of classical physics, such an image of the atom cannot be sustained because if the atoms were indeed thus constituted, matter would not be stable.

In 1922, Bohr was invited by Sommerfeld to Göttingen to deliver a series of lectures on atomic theory. Bohr was impressed by the questions posed by young Heisenberg, then a student, and invited him to walk with him so they could discuss the issues after the lectures. During the discussion, Heisenberg (1972) expressed his doubts concerning the conception of the atom as consisting of particles charged with electricity—the electrons—that actually

---

[1] In his polemic with Clarke, Leibniz says, "J'ai marqué plus d'une fois que je tenais l'Espace pour quelque chose de *purement relatif,* comme le Temps, pour un *ordre des Coexistences,* comme le Temps est un *ordre des Successions*" (Third Letter).

move around the nucleus. Bohr's reply merits quoting in full but I shall give only the gist of it:

> Because matter is stable, Newtonian physics cannot be correct at a sub-atomic level; at most it can give us a starting point.[2] And, for the same reason, there cannot be a visual description of the structure of the atom, since such a description — precisely because it is visual — has to be based on the concepts of classical physics, concepts which no longer enable us to apprehend phenomena. You must realize — Bohr continued — that the attempt to formulate a theory of this sort is a task that is *a priori* impossible. Because we have to say things about the structure of the atom, but we do not have a language which can make what we want to say comprehensible.

> Heisenberg insists — but what then do the images of atoms that you have discussed and even justified in your lectures of the past few days mean? What is it that you really wanted to say?

> These images — Bohr replied — have been deduced or, if you prefer, "guessed" on the basis of experimental facts; they are not the fruit of theoretical calculations. I hope that these images describe the structure of atoms *as well* — but only *as well* — as possible in the visual language of classical physics. We should realize that we cannot use this language here except as poets do. They also do not seek to represent facts in a precise manner, but hope only to create images in the spirit of their audience and to establish connections at the level of ideas. (Heisenberg, 1972, p. 65)

This dialogue between two of the greatest revolutionaries in the history of ideas is more eloquent for the epistemologist than any treatise on the situation of science in our century. Bohr's comments posed what appear to be insurmountable problems: If physical theory was to be accepted and it implies renouncing the concepts of solid matter, trajectories in space–time and causality, how could it be validated by measurements with instruments that assume these concepts? What kind of world is the world of physics if none of our basic physical intuitions is applicable to it? What kind of "knowledge" is "physical knowledge"?

Physical Theory and Mathematics: Russell and Carnap

It was Bertrand Russell, one of the great philosophers of this century, who attempted to provide an answer to these questions and to extract the

---

[2] Bohr refers here to the fact that, according to Newtonian physics, a particle with an electric charge having a cyclic motion would emit radiation and therefore would lose energy, so that all electrons should finally collapse onto the nucleus.

consequences for the theory of knowledge. In 1927, the same year that saw the culmination of the research on the structure of the atom (with the quantum theory of Heisenberg), Russell published his book *The Analysis of Matter* (1927). A volume not much read by physicists because it was very philosophical and not much read by philosophers because it contains a lot of mathematics. Russell himself provided the best summary of his theory, in a single sentence: "In *Analysis of Matter* I argued, rightly or wrongly . . . that our knowledge of the physical world is only a knowledge of structure." (Russell, 1944, p. 716). In plain terms, Russell's claim meant that physics can tell us nothing about the nature of the physical world beyond the structural relations represented in the mathematical framework of physical theories.

It should be clear that this formulation is radically different from the position inherited from the 17th century. This is clearly stated in an often quoted statement made by Galileo in his Dialogue:

> [t]he great book of the universe . . . cannot be comprehended unless one first learns to understand the language and read the letters with which it is composed. It is written in the language of mathematics and the characters are triangles, circles and other geometrical figures without which it is humanly impossible to comprehend a single word of it. (p. 471)

Galileo's position consists of showing the necessity of expressing natural phenomena (that are studied by means of observation and experimentation) in mathematical statements. Mathematics thus appears as the *language* in which the laws of nature are expressed, a language that gives them greater precision, allowed interrelationships to be clearly established and opens up the possibility of making predictions. But the laws refer to a world that is "out there," and is known *just as it is* through observation and experimentation. The tradition of Galileo was taken up and carried to its ultimate conclusion by one of the epistemologies typical of our century: logical empiricism. Its chief exponent was Rudolf Carnap.

Let us now look briefly at why neither Russell or Carnap provided a solid foundation to their epistemological theories. Russell's *The Analysis of Matter* and Carnap's work, *Der Logische Aufbau der Welt,* published in 1928, are the most relevant works to be considered.[3]

We begin with Russell. The thesis that "we only know the structure of the

---

[3] Just before I wrote the last version of this chapter, a colleague brought to my attention an important article by W. Demopoulus and M. Friedman (1985), in which this subject is analyzed in considerable detail. My criticism of these authors is that they don't pay attention to the profound epistemological differences between Russell and Carnap concerning the structural conception of physical theories. As I have indicated, Carnap follows Galileo's tradition as to the role of mathematics in empirical science. This is not Russell's position.

physical world" was demolished a year later by M. H. A. Newman (1928), a mathematician not very inclined toward epistemology, in an article published in *Mind*. Newman develops his logical argument with the utmost clarity, but I will not present it in full as what is important for the present discussion is his conclusion that Russell's theory is either trivial or false. The fundamental reason is that if we *only* know the structure of the physical world, we know nothing. Because given *any* structure, *all* sets, whatever the nature of their elements, having the same *cardinality* (the same number of elements, if they are finite sets), can be organized in a manner satisfying the structure. Therefore, if we do not know anything else, there is no basis to assert that a given structure is in fact *the* structure of *our* world.

Newman sent a copy of his article to Russell, who replied with a pathetic letter, the first paragraph of which reads as follows:

Dear Newman,   24th April, 1928

Many thanks for sending me the off-print of your article about me in Mind. I read it with great interest and some dismay. You make it entirely obvious that my statements to the effect that nothing is known about the physical world except its structure are either false or trivial, and I am somewhat ashamed at not having noticed the point for myself. (Russell, 1968, pp. 259–260)

It is clear that the Achilles' heel of Russell's theory was the word "only." To be able to say that the structure that we know is the one that corresponds to *our* physical world, we need to know something more than the structure.

Russell never mentioned Newman's objection in his later works. He was to formulate the position once again, in a slightly modified form in his reply to Nagel, found in *The Philosophy of Bertrand Russell* (1944):

The inference by which physicists pass from percepts to physical objects (which we are assuming valid) only enable us to know certain facts about the structure of the physical world as ordered by means of causal relations, compresence[4] and contiguity. Beyond certain very abstract mathematical properties, physics can tell us nothing about the character of the physical world. (Russell, 1944, p. 706)

In his last philosophical work (Russell, 1948), the theme is not explicitly mentioned, but there are indirect references that make evident changes in Russell's position. For example, in the chapter entitled "The World of Physics," he states:

---

[4] As defined by Russell (1927, p. 294), two events have a relation called "compresence" if they overlap in space–time. This concept is used by Russell to define a "point," or rather a "point-instant" as a group of events such that any two members of the group are compresent, and no event outside the group is compresent with every member of the group.

Mathematical Physics contains such an immense superstructure of theory that its basis in observation tends to be obscured. It is, however, an empirical study, and its empirical character appears most unequivocally where the physical constants are concerned. (1948, p. 27)

Another indication of change is seen in the chapter entitled "Structure," which concludes:

Considerations deriving from the importance of structure show that our knowledge, especially in physics, is much more abstract and much more infected with logic than it would seem. There is, however, a very definite limit to the process of turning physics into logic and mathematics; it is set by the fact that physics is an empirical science, depending for its credibility upon relations to our perceptive experiences. (Russell, 1948, p. 256)

Russell does not mention how these relations are established. The kind of construction he had proposed in previous works, particularly in Russell (1914), could not be sustained. In my view, he was prevented from going beyond them by his empiricism (despite the fact it did become weaker over time). Perhaps for this reason the final chapter of this last philosophical work is entitled "The Limits of Empiricism." In it he states "it must be admitted that empiricism as a theory of knowledge has proved inadequate." And he adds, perhaps as a consolation, "though less so than any other previous theory of knowledge" (1948, p. 507). I would hazard a guess that Russell arrived at the very doors of constructivism, but did not dare to enter.

Let us now look briefly at Carnap's position. Carnap (1928) makes some statements that may appear to parallel the former Russellian structuralism, and even have some "Piagetian flavour." Let us take one example:

If science is to be objective, then it must restrict itself to statements about structural properties, and . . . it can restrict itself to statements about structures, since all objects of knowledge are not content but forms and can be represented as structural entities. (Carnap, 1928, p. 107)

But the Piagetian flavor disappears when we go closely into the bases for such a statement.

Carnap's thesis, that "science only deals with the description of structural properties of objects" should be placed in the context of his more encompassing thesis that "each scientific statement can in principle be so transformed that it is *nothing but* a structure statement" (the emphasis is ours). Carnap adds a surprising and revealing assertion:

[t]his transformation is not only possible, it is imperative. For science wants to speak about what is objective, and whatever does not belong to the structure but to the material (i.e. anything that can be pointed out in a concrete ostensive definition) is in the final analysis, subjective. (Carnap, 1928, p. 29 of the Dover edition)

It is well known that in Carnap's empiricist epistemology, knowledge starts from perceptions leading to "ostensive definitions" and the problem he had to face was how the knower went from there to structural properties. His resolution led to a truly monumental construction, but it fell short of the target. It must be said that his was an honorable failure. With admirable honesty, Carnap recognized his failure and made no further attempts. In fact, in his later courses on the philosophy of physics (Carnap, 1966), no trace of this resolution remains; his empiricist convictions stayed intact, however.

Carnap and Russell were not the only ones who arrived at a structuralist conception of science from empiricist positions. The most conspicuous example within present-day philosophy of science is Quine (Hahn & Schilpp, 1986). He was a peculiar kind of empiricist, to be sure, having repudiated what he calls the "dogmas" of empiricism. The following statement, for instance, does not differ from Russell's: "Structure is what matters to a theory, and not the choice of its objects" (Quine, 1981, p. 20). Although Quine recognizes that Ramsay and Russell both held this position before he did, he points out that they referred only to theoretical objects, and adds on the same page, "I extended the doctrine to objects generally, for I see all objects as theoretical." This statement receives further clarification in another chapter: "Bodies and our knowledge of them are related only structurally and causally and not by a sharing of qualities" (Quine, 1981, p. 177).

Quine is quite aware of the roots of the difficulties faced by both Russell and Carnap in trying to carry out the program that he defines as "translation of all discourse about the external world into terms of sense data, set theory, and logic" (Quine, 1981, pp. 83–84). This is clearly indicated in the same text. Although recognizing that: "Carnap achieved remarkable feats of construction, starting with sense data and building explicitly, with full Principia techniques and Principia ingenuity toward the external world," Quine concludes, "One must in the end despair of the full definitional reduction . . . and it is one of the merits of the Aufbau that we can see from it where the obstacles lie" (Quine, 1981, p. 84). He ends up his comments with a most remarkable assertion: "The empiricist's regard for experience thus impedes the very program of reducing the world to experience" (1981, p. 85).

However, Quine like Carnap, takes ostensive definitions as the starting point of knowledge, but he makes no attempt to bridge the gaps in the

Aufbau because, he says in another essay, "the project of a rational reconstruction of the world from sense data . . . an attractive idea . . . (but) I am convinced, regretfully, that it cannot be done" (Quine, 1981, pp. 22–23).

Quine's way out is his well-known *naturalism*. Science is taken for granted and what is left of the epistemological problems faced by Russell and Carnap is displaced to the problem of how we build the *language* of science. In the chapter "Empirical Content" (1981, p. 24), Quine says:

> What sort of thing is a scientific theory? It is an idea, one might naturally say, or a complex of ideas. But the most practical way of coming to grips with ideas, and usually the only way, is by way of the words that express them. What to look for in the way of theories, then, are the sentences that express them. There will be no need to decide what a theory is of when to regard two sets of sentences as formulations of the same theory; we can just talk of the theory formulations as such.

> The relation to be analyzed, then, is the relation between our sensory stimulations and our scientific theory formulations: the relation between the physicist's sentences on the one hand, treating of gravitation and electrons and the like, and on the other hand the triggering of his sensory receptors.

So, Quine's analysis begins "by looking at the sentences most directly connected with sensory stimulation" (p. 25).

This road is not free from difficulties either (see, for instance, the essay by P. F. Strawson, 1986). But, even if successful, it is hard to reject the idea that the fundamental epistemological problems are dismissed rather than solved.

Piagetian epistemology has been able to overcome these difficulties and to offer a solution to what appeared to be an insurmountable dilemma presented by modern physics. We have been forced to renounce intuitive concepts to describe the constitution of matter. The traditional sense of "description" is not applicable to events inside the atom. We only have a mathematical theory to account for them. Yet, "structural descriptions" without empirical support, which is necessarily based on intuitive concepts, cannot single out any particular world as our world.

Genetic epistemology offers a way out of this dilemma based on the analysis of the common origins of causal relations and logic operations. Piagetian theory of causality is well known and I do not dwell on it. The structure is present at the very beginning, but it is not hanging in the vacuum. The path from action, at the sensorimotor level, as intermediary between "objects" and cognitive instruments, to physical theory is long and laborious. A reconstruction of it is far beyond the scope of this chapter.

THE VALIDITY OF PIAGETIAN EPISTEMOLOGY

This brings me to my second theme. What is the epistemological theory of Piaget? In the analysis of the characteristics and the validity of genetic epistemology there are two different questions that require particular attention:

1. The epistemological theory as an organized totality that may provide an explanation for the development of cognitive systems.
2. The basic assumptions of the theory, making it a scientific theory, in that they confer on it an empirical character, whose areas of experimentation are genetic psychology and the historical–critical analysis of the history of science.

Point (2) has been dealt with extensively in a volume on which I was fortunate enough to collaborate closely with (Piaget, 1983; Piaget & Garcia, 1989), *Psychogenesis and the History of Science.*

The first aspect, the theory as a global system or totality, is the focus of my examination of the validity of genetic epistemology. My insistence on referring to the theory as an organized totality has two reasons. The first is concerned with the name "theory." This word covers too wide a spectrum in scientific writing today, ranging from systems with a high degree of formalization to sets of opinions and ideas that attempt to explain a given and highly restricted phenomenon.

Without entering into the question of its degree of validity, I believe that it can be said that Piaget's theory constitutes a coherent body, with a high degree of integration, that appears as a system explaining the fundamental processes that intervene in the development of knowledge, both at the individual level and in the history of science.

In this sense, I call it an "organized totality" and I apply it to the thesis of Pierre Duhem, elaborated by Quine (which I agree with entirely) with regard to the validation of theories. Although he had referred to this thesis in numerous contexts, Quine formulated it in its sharpest — almost provocative — way in his well-known paper "Two dogmas of empiricism." Quine's formula is: "Our statements about the external world face the tribunal of experience not individually, but only as a corporate body" (1953, p. 41).

The thesis is clear and totally anti-Popperian in two senses. In the first place, it rejects the idea that a theory is a conjunction of statements that can be separately corroborated or invalidated, such that when one of the statements is refuted, the whole is refuted. Secondly, a theory is an organized body and when it fails in one application it is not at all obvious what it is that has failed and why it failed in this particular application.

Let me develop this second point further. *All* empirical theories have failed in some particular, seemingly critical application, even in extensive fields of application that appear to enter naturally into their domains. For example, Newton's theory of motion/gravitation cannot explain the "anomalous" movement of the smallest of the planets—Mercury—although it did permit predicting the existence of a planet unknown to humans at the time. Neither does Newtonian physics apply at a subatomic level. But these are not "proofs" that the theory is false, and that it should be discarded. What does falsification mean when these failed predictions are set side by side with our ability to send a space vehicle to Neptune based on these "laws"? The calculations as to its path and the time to be taken by the journey are all made with the tools of the solid theory that is Newtonian mechanics—and the vessel reaches Neptune, within the time period calculated!

The question that should be asked with respect to a theory—assuming it is a theory formulated in an acceptable fashion and has been successfully applied in a given number of instances—is not, therefore, whether it is true or false, but rather what is its domain of application? In which situations does it cease to be valid? What are the factors not taken into account by the theory that should be taken into account when it fails?

EQUILIBRATION THEORY AND PRIGOGINE'S DISSIPATIVE STRUCTURES

Following Quine's conception of theories, I consider genetic epistemology as a "corporate body." It is a theory about the development and evolution of *a system,* namely the cognitive system. The detailed analysis of any part of the theory would be entirely out of the scope of this chapter. Instead, I focus on what could be considered the core of Piagetian conceptions: the theory of equilibration. Again, I do not attempt any detailed analysis. My aim will rather be an evaluation of the consistency of the theory as a whole within the context of present-day ideas on the development and evolution of systems, which, like the cognitive system, are *natural systems* (that is, not the result of laboratory experiences), *complex* (that is, having heterogeneous constituents in continuous interaction with each other) and *open* (that is, in continuous interaction with the external environment).

Piaget's (1985) central ideas about the development and evolution of the cognitive system are presented in *The Equilibration of the Cognitive Structures,* with the subtitle *The Central Problem of Development.* Throughout the remainder of this chapter I refer to that problem as "equilibration," or less often "dynamic equilibrium."

I begin by recapitulating very briefly the fundamentals of the equilibration theory and then examine how it fits into a general theory of complex systems. The objective is twofold. First, I attempt to show how the main features pointed out by Piaget as being characteristic of the evolution of the cognitive system are in fact general characteristics of open systems. Secondly, I will provide some examples of the fruitfulness of making comparative analyses of the evolution of quite different open systems with the evolution of the cognitive system as depicted in Piaget's equilibration theory.

One of the fundamental tenets of Piagetian epistemology was the assertion that the development of the cognitive system was neither continuous growth nor a linear process. The existence of stages was an expression of these two facts. The cognitive system can be viewed as an open system whose dynamics are determined to a large extent by exchanges with the environment. The system evolved through periods of nearly steady-state conditions (the stages) such that the components of the system remained in dynamic equilibrium (equilibration).

New knowledge consisted of assimilating objects or events to the previous schemes and structures of the subject. Assimilation implied an *integration* of new contents (objects, events) into an existing system. The progress of knowledge thus consisted of new forms of organizing such contents. This required new coordinations and modifications of pre-existing schemes (accommodation).

Conflicts, gaps, contradictions (i.e., the impossibility of accommodation of existing schemes and structures to new contents) may ultimately result in disequilibration or destructuration of the system. Re-equilibration resulted from constructing new structures, new coordinations, new operations, which accommodate without conflict the same contents that acted as perturbations leading to the disruption of the former structure.

The theory of equilibration thus summarized was not meant to be just a metaphorical description of the stages found by Piaget in his psychogenetic researches. Far from it, it was proposed as a coherent theory of cognitive development that has enough explanatory power to account for the mechanisms that govern both the growth of knowledge and change of structure.

From early on, Piaget had the clear intuition that many features of his theory had a wider domain of applicability than the field of knowledge. He cautiously expressed this in his book on equilibration (Piaget, 1985), where he points out that "cognitive equilibria are quite different from mechanical equilibrium" and that "they differ still more from thermodynamic equilibrium . . . which is a state of rest after the destruction of structure." But he adds: "they are closer (however) to those dynamic steady-state conditions referred to by Glandsdorff & Prigogine (1971) with the exchanges that maintain a functional and structural order in an open system" (p. 10).

The subject of "similarities" between cognitive development, as described by Piaget's cognitive theory, and the self-organization of dissipative systems was taken up again in the discussions we held during the preparation of our joint publication, entitled, *Psychogenesis and the History of Science,* and in the last chapter we identified five "close analogies." Subsequent work convinced me that they were more than superficial analogies.

Let us then consider some systems with quite different natures that I would maintain, give support to the assertion of "more than superficial analogy." My presentation here was only indicative. A more detailed analysis is included in Garcia (1990).

A Laboratory Experiment Showing Successive Reorganizations of a Simple System

Long before Prigogine formulated the theory of dissipative systems, there were a number of laboratory experiments with open systems, particularly in the field of fluid dynamics, that exhibited "strange behavior" having characteristics of what we now know, after Prigogine, as "dissipative systems."

Perhaps the most impressive of such experiments were carried out by D. Fultz at the University of Chicago beginning in 1946. I had the fortune, as a student, of witnessing such an experiment. I must confess that neither we—the students—nor the professor understood at that time what was going on in the laboratory. The experiments were later the object of careful studies by Fultz and other researchers in the 1950s.

Essentially, it consisted of a rotating annulus filled with fluid. The internal border of the annulus is kept at a constant temperature, whereas the external border may be subject to a strictly controlled varying temperature so that a temperature gradient is established within the fluid. The experiment may proceed by either varying the magnitude of the temperature differential in the annulus or varying the rotation rate. Let us consider the first case.

Starting with a constant rotation and no temperature differential, the fluid acquires a laminar motion symmetrical about the rotation axis. Looking at the tank from above, the streamlines appear as closed circles. Then the temperature of the outer border is increased *in a linear and continuous manner* (constant rate). The following evolution or development if you wish, can be observed:

1. The speed of the flow will increase, but always with closed circular streamlines.

2. As the temperature gradient continues to be increased, the streamlines are disrupted. There is a transition period of disorderly motion until an unsymmetrical flow pattern develops and becomes stable.

3. After a period of time (with temperature gradients increasing *linearly and continuously*) a new disruption of the streamlines takes place. The flow is disorganized until a new stable pattern develops.

4. The same kind of events is repeated a number of times. The evolution may be described as a succession of "stages." All of them are characterized by a nearly steady, slowly drifting wave pattern. The number of waves increase from one stage to the next (from two to about five).

5. Finally the flow pattern will consist of a number of irregular eddies drifting around.

The analogies with the development of the cognitive systems referred to here are very striking in this experiment. The temptation is great to apply the same language of the equilibration theory:

1. The continuous injection of heat from the outside is the "perturbation" that the system has to "assimilate."

2. At each "stage," the assimilation takes place by a simple kind of "accommodation" of the structure consisting of an increasing speed of the fluid motion *within the same flow pattern* (same structure).

3. When the perturbation (injection of heat) increases beyond a certain threshold, no "accommodation" of the existing structure may assimilate it. The system is disequilibrated.

4. Re-equilibration takes place when a more complex structure is set in.

5. The "perturbation" (heat flow) is acting in a continuous and linear manner, but the system reacts *discontinuously* by a succession of complete reorganizations.

6. It should be pointed out that a "repetition" of the experiment would reproduce the general characteristics of the structures, but not exactly the same patterns.

Intensive research on physical, chemical, and biological systems carried out by a large number of researchers in the last few decades has shown a high degree of generality of these steps in the evolution of open systems. As a general rule in physical systems, instabilities set in when the gradients generated by external forces exceed certain values. In Garcia (1990) I maintain that in the cognitive system social factors take the place of "external forces."

The Evolution of Natural Systems of High Complexity

Since 1976, I have been doing research on *natural* systems of far greater complexity than the one just described. The accumulated experience has provided enough evidence, in my opinion, that the analogies described between the rotating fluid experiments and the cognitive system are much more than mere superficial similarities. The systems I have been dealing with share with the cognitive system the three characteristics already mentioned: They are natural, open, complex systems.

The studies have been carried out within the framework of a program called Interdisciplinary Research on Complex Systems and consisted of a number of case studies on agrarian regions of Mexico and Argentina, sponsored by the United Nations Research Institute for Social Development and the International Federation of Institutes for Advanced Study (IFIAS) (Garcia et al., 1988a, 1988b). Studies prior to these were undertaken in Africa (Sahelian region) within a program called "Drought and Man," sponsored by IFIAS (Garcia, 1981).

In all cases the systems under analysis were composed of essentially three subsystems in interaction: a physical subsystem (soil, climate, hydrology), an agroproductive subsystem (crops and their associated technology) and a socioeconomic subsystem (the agrarian community, the production relations, the acting economic forces). The evolution of such systems was analyzed with particular reference to the periods of significant changes due to modifications of "boundary conditions" such as: climatic anomalies, introduction of new crops, changing technologies, economic crises, and so on. These systems are clearly quite beyond the range of the dissipative systems analyzed by the Prigogine school.

The importance we assigned to this work was that in our study cases, contrary to the case of the fluid dynamic experiment, the center of analysis was the interaction between the physical environment and society, and in most cases, the human factor played the most important role.

At the start, there was little hope that with such extreme complexity the systems would exhibit in their evolution any of the characteristics of Piagetian equilibration theory. We even doubted that such systems might behave as "totalities" in the sense analyzed by Piaget.

It was a striking discovery to find what had been learned through equilibration theory and dissipative system theory served as guidance in our research. In fact, the interactions between the physical environment and society (in selected agrarian regions) did act as a system (a totality in the Piagetian sense). The whole system went through "stages" (i.e., periods of stabilized production, living conditions, and so on). Disequilibration took place under strong perturbations of the type indicated earlier. But then the *whole* system would be reorganized: new kinds of production and/or new technologies; new socioeconomic relations; new interactions with the physical subsystem.

The Value of Comparative Analyses

The accumulated experience with both natural systems and laboratory experiments would seem to provide enough evidence to assert that the similarities with the equilibration theory of cognitive systems are the manifestation of deep processes that determine to a large extent the functioning of all open systems. Therein the usefulness of comparative analyses; I will present one example of how Piaget's equilibration theory organizes questions germane to open systems.

In his book on equilibration, Piaget introduced the concept of *equilibration majorante* referring to the equilibration processes conceived of as "a structuration oriented towards improved equilibrium conditions" (Piaget, 1985, p. 36). And in the "Conclusion" he refers to it as "the central concept . . . in the explanation of cognitive development (in the history of sciences as well as in psychogenesis)" (Piaget, 1985, p. 170).

Piaget presented two main questions arising from this conceptualization:

1. Since, according to the definition, reequilibration involves actions having a general teleonomic character, how is the election of the objectives to be explained?
2. How to explain the mechanisms of the *"equilibration majorante* in its twin aspects of construction and increasing coherence"(p. 171).

Teleonomy and "newness" of the structures arising in reorganizations are indeed two dominant problems in equilibration theory and they are also problems central to the analysis of open systems beyond cognitive systems.

I do not enter into the analysis of the answers given by Piaget to these questions. My only purpose here was to show that the same kind of questions present themselves in the quite different types of open systems we have analyzed and *there equilibration theory appears to yield very precise answers.*

Let us consider once again the rotating fluid experiment. The function performed by the fluid is to transport the heat from the outer to the inner border. In each one of the stages we have described (starting with helicoidal motions, changing into wave patterns with an increasing number of waves) the fluid motions adopt the most efficient flow structure that transport the heat for the given temperature difference up to that moment.

At each stage the increase in temperature difference is "assimilated" by increasing the fluid speed without changing the flow pattern. As the temperature difference continues to increase, this "accommodation" mechanism does not suffice to transport enough heat, that as a consequence is then accumulated at the outer border establishing a strong temperature gradient that destabilizes the motion. The flow becomes irregular until the next pattern is established that is able to transport the heat at a higher rate leading to a new stabilized stage. This is clearly a teleonomic process and Piaget's question "How to explain the election of the objective?" is equally applicable here. How does the fluid know which structure of motion it has to adopt to do a better job of transporting the heat? The answer is simple and eliminates any suspicion of teleology. When the flow becomes unstable, the irregular, random motion opens the way to all possible flow patterns. However, most of them are unstable and only some trajectories of the fluid particles will be stable for the temperature gradient existing at that moment. These are the kind of trajectories that remain and that establish the new structure of the flow.

After this explanation we can make sense of anthropocentric or teleological expressions such as: The fluid learns by trial and error; the fluid adopts the best structure to do the job; the fluid creates new structures, and so on.

We may also go back now to Piaget's texts with some clues to uncover the meaning of some cryptic statements. In my own experience, the foregoing explanation helped me to understand, for instance, Piaget's view of how the possible fulfills its role in cognitive development (as expressed in his posthumous books on *The Possible* and *The Necessary*). In the "General Conclusions" of the volume on *The Possible,* Piaget (1981) asserts that the results reported there renewed the equilibration model "by explaining the mechanism of reequilibration by an internal dynamic, specific to the possible, and such that each possible novelty constitutes at the same time a construction and an opening" (p. 185). The stability theory of the fluid experiment provides a model, in my opinion, where this somewhat cryptic statement acquires a clear meaning.

CONCLUDING REMARKS

In the preceding parts of this chapter I attempted to present Piagetian genetic epistemology as a coherent theory deeply immersed in some of the most fundamental problems that have been the concern of science in our century. We referred to two of such problems:

1. The relation between empirical facts and mathematical theory in the interpretation of the physical world. Here, Piagetian constructivistic epistemology, with its conceptualization of a genetic structuralism, provided an answer to the questions that empiricism (whether of the Carnapian or the Russellian brands) left unsolved.

2. The increasing evidence that open systems, subject to continuous interaction with the "environment" through exchanges of matter, energy, information, and so on, evolve through a series of successive stages of self-organization, quite in line with the Piagetian theory of equilibration of cognitive structures.

I submit that no other epistemology has similar credentials as a scientific theory of the structure of knowledge and as a solid foundation for the theories with which science endeavors to explain the structure of the world.

ACKNOWLEDGMENT

The author is very grateful to Professor Peter Pufall and Professor Harry Beilin for many valuable comments that helped to improve the original version of this chapter.

REFERENCES

Carnap, R. (1968). *Der Logische Aufbau der Welt.* [The quotations are taken from the edition *The logical structure of the world.*] Los Angeles: University of California Press, Berkele. (Original work published in 1928).

Carnap, R. (1966). *Philosophical foundations of physics.* New York: Basic Books.

Demopoulus, W., & Friedman, M. (1985). Bertrand Russell's the analysis of matter: Its historical context and contemporary interest. *Philosophy of Science, 52*(4), p. 621.

Dugas, R. (1954). *La Mécanique au XVII Siècle.* Neuchatel, Switzerland: Editions du Griffon.

Galilei. (1632). *Dialogo sopra i due massimi sistemi del mondo.* (English edition: *Dialogue concerning the two chief world systems.* Berkeley, CA: University of California Press, 1953).

Garcia, R. (1981). *Nature pleads not guilty.* Oxford, England: Pergamon Press.

Garcia R., (1990). *Structural evolution of open systems: The case of cognition.* Paper presented to the Congress on Evolution and Cognition, at Bergamo, Italy, October.

Garcia, R., et al. (1988a). *Modernización en el agro: Ventajas comparativas para quien?.* Mexico City: Centro de Investigación y de Estudios Avanzados del I.P.N..

Garcia, R., et al. (1988b). *Deterioro ambiental y pobreza en la abundancia productiva.* Mexico City: Centro de Investigación y de Estudios Avanzados del I.P.N.

Glandsdorff, P. & Prigogine, I., (1971). *Thermodynamic theory of structure, stability and fluctuations.* New York: J Wiley.

Hahn, L. E. & Schilpp, P. A. (1986). *The philosophy of W. V. Quine.* The Library of Living Philosophers (Vol. 18). La Salle, IL: Open Court.

Heisenberg, W. (1972). *La partie et le tout.* Paris: Editions Albin Michel. (Original work published in German as *Der Teil und das Ganzen*)

Leibniz. (1720). The quotation is taken from Dugas (1954), who reproduces a text included in *Recueil de pièces sur philosophie, la religion naturelle, l'histoire, les mathématiques, etc., par Messrs Leibniz, Clarke, Newton et autres célèbres.* Amsterdam: De Sauzet.

Newman, M.H.A. (1928). Mr. Russell's causal theory of perception. *Mind, 37.*

Piaget, J. (1981). *L'évolution des possibles chez l'enfant.* Vol. 1 of *Le possible et le nécessaire.* Paris: P.U.F.

Piaget, J. (1983). *L'évolution du nécessaire chez l'enfant,* Vol. 2 of *Le possible et le nécessaire.* Paris: P.U.F.

Piaget, J. (1985). *The equilibration of the cognitive structures.* (Original edition, *L'Equilibration des structures cognitives,* Paris: P.U.F., 1975)

Piaget, J., & Garcia, R. (1989). *Psychogenesis and the history of science.* New York: University of Columbia Press. (Translated from *Psychogenèse et histoire des sciences,* Flammarion: Paris, 1983)

Quine, W. V. (1953). Two dogmas of empiricism. (Reprinted in *From a logical point of view.* New York: Harper & Row)

Quine, W. V. (1981). *Theories and things.* Cambridge, MA: Harvard University Press.

Russell, B. (1914). *Our knowledge of the external world.* London: G Allen & Unwin.

Russell, B. (1927). *The analysis of matter*. London: G Allen & Unwin, Dover ed., 1954.

Russell, B. (1944). Reply to criticisms. In P. A. Schilpp (Ed., *The philosophy of Bertrand Russell*. Vol. 5 of *The library of living philosophy*. Chicago: Northwestern University.

Russell, B. (1948). *Human knowledge, its scope and limits*. New York: Simon & Schuster.

Russell, B. (1968). *The autobiography of Bertrand Russell*. Vol. 2 Boston: Little, Brown.

Strawson, P. F. (1986). Reference and Roots. In Hahn L. E. & P. A. Schilpp, (Eds.), *The Philosophy of W. V. Quine*. The Library of Living Philosophers (Vol. 18). La Salle, IL: Open Court.

3 Equilibration and the Dialectics of Organization

Michael Chapman
University of British Columbia

EQUILIBRATION AND THE DIALECTICS OF ORGANIZATION

In a book published at the beginning of the 1980s, Cohen (1981/1983) concluded that Piaget's work was no longer in step with the concerns of contemporary psychology and that henceforth he should be regarded as an historical figure only. Ten years later, it is fitting to consider the question once again: not just whether to accept or reject Piaget's various ideas, but whether he continues to speak to us as a contemporary or only as a figure from the past. I argue in this chapter that he still has a vital message for psychologists, but in order to profit from that message, one must resist two temptations. The first is to accept the idea that the standard textbook version of Piaget's theory is anything like a complete picture. Without claiming to have discovered the "true" Piaget, or even that there is a true Piaget to be discovered, I would argue that aspects of his work are still insufficiently assimilated or accommodated to in developmental psychology. The second temptation is the tendency, once one has gone beyond the standard version of the theory, to dismiss criticisms of it as uninformed. This tendency arises, because the standard criticisms are directed at the standard version that one has just rejected. In fact, the problems with the theory do not disappear when it is better understood. Instead, one discovers that the problems are somewhat different (and considerably more interesting) than they appeared at first.

If the significance of a theory is measured, not in its completeness, but in the importance of the problems that it poses, then Piaget's work remains significant indeed. There can be no doubt that he left psychology with many unsolved problems and that those problems have lost none of their importance in the 1990s. This point is illustrated in this chapter with reference to the concept of equilibration, the idea that was perhaps most central to his thinking (Rowell, 1983). The importance of equilibration in Piaget's own mind is reflected in the fact that he chose the topic, "Problems of Equilibration," in addressing the first annual meeting of the Jean Piaget Society in Philadelphia in 1971 (Piaget, 1977a).

But despite the centrality of the notions of equilibrium and equilibration in Piaget's own thinking, their utility has been doubted by psychologists otherwise receptive to his work. Bruner's (1959, p. 365) characterization of the concept of equilibrium as theoretical "surplus baggage" epitomized this skepticism for many critics of Piagetian theory. The goal of this chapter is to consider the equilibration theory in the light of Cohen's question: whether it has something vital to contribute to present-day psychology, or whether in the 1990s it is of historical interest only. First, an attempt is made to reconstruct the *intuitions* that lay behind the equilibration concept by tracing its development in Piaget's thought. Then the relevance of the equilibration theory for contemporary psychology is evaluated. It is important to consider Piaget's intuitions in this matter, because his intuitions often outstripped his ability to realize them concretely.

ORIGINS OF THE THEORY

The origins of the equilibration theory in Piaget's own thinking can be traced to his autobiographical novel *Recherche,* published in 1918 when he was 22 years old. It is the story of a young Swiss Protestant youth named Sébastien who suffers what one can recognize today as an adolescent identity crisis. As described by Piaget, Sébastien's coming of age coincided with the social and historical upheaval surrounding World War I. This interpenetration of personal and social crises is reflected in the opening sentence: "While the war sustained in everyone's spirits the greatest *disequilibrium* ever suffered by thought, Sébastien concentrated within himself the pain of this tormented world" (Piaget, 1918, p. 1, italics added).

Sébastien traces the origins of this historical crisis to the opposition between the search for truth and the search for value. At one extreme, he views positivistic science as representing a commitment to truth but not to value, and at the other extreme, dogmatic religion as representing a commitment to value but not to truth. In the course of the novel, Sébastien examines the existing alternatives to these two extremes and suffers several emotional crises before arriving at a solution in the form of a *new science* of organization. In this new science, the organization of life at every level can be described in terms of certain "laws of equilibrium," which can be summarized as follows:

1. Every organization tends to conserve itself as such.
2. Each organization is open to environmental influences that modify its various parts, bringing them into conflict with the whole. A dominance of the parts over the whole at this point leads to disintegration, and a dominance of the whole over the parts leads to stagnation.
3. The whole modifies itself in order to reduce the conflict with the parts.
4. This compromise tends to evolve into a more stable form of equilibrium characterized by the mutual preservation of parts and whole. However, this higher equilibrium is never actually reached because of the novelties constantly introduced by the environment. It is therefore described as an *ideal* equilibrium toward which all real equilibria tend.

Having formulated these laws of equilibrium, Sébastien goes on to apply them to different problems: perception and personality; the structure and evolution of organisms; the form and dynamics of social organization; and most importantly, to his original problem of science and value. Real equilibria can be studied scientifically in the organization of natural processes; the directionality of these processes provides them with an inherent value. This directional value is most obvious in living organisms, insofar as the maintenance or increase of organization is inherently preferable to disintegration and death for the organism in question.

Thus, from the beginning Piaget's concept of equilibrium represented a directed process, rather than a steady state, as the term might be taken to imply. The four laws of equilibrium guarantee a continuous but never completed transformation of conflict into cooperation, and this process gives development a direction without a predetermined goal. In retrospect, one is impressed at the extent to which the ideas articulated in *Recherche* anticipated Piaget's later thinking. The point is not that Piaget's mature work was merely the expression of some youthful ideas, rather that his repeated efforts to realize the intuitions originating in this period of his life led to continued development of the ideas themselves.

In the following sections, the evolution of Piaget's thinking about equilibrium and equilibration is traced through three general phases. Inevitably, this review is highly selective, but an overview of the development of these concepts should provide one with a better sense of the intuitions that lay behind them.

EQUILIBRIUM IN THOUGHT AND ACTION

The first phase in the development of the equilibrium concept comprised Piaget's studies of children's thought and reasoning and of infant's sensorimotor intelligence during the 1920s and 1930s. This period was characterized by rather straightforward efforts to apply the ideas about equilibrium first enunciated in *Recherche* to concrete problems in psychology. For example, young children's thinking was said to be characterized by "syncretism" and "juxtaposition" (Piaget, 1923/1955, 1924/1928). *Syncretism* was described as the tendency to connect otherwise unrelated thoughts or propositions by assimilating them globally to a general scheme. Such "deforming" assimilations were said to result in a form of disequilibrium in which the whole (the general scheme) dominates the parts (the individual thoughts or propositions) in the sense that the parts tend to lose their specific identities in being assimilated to the whole. In contrast, *juxtaposition* was defined in terms of the inability to relate successive thoughts to one another for lack of any general scheme which could encompass them both. It resulted in a disequilibrium characterized by the dominance of the parts (the successive thoughts) over the whole (the coordination of those thoughts by means of a general scheme).

Both of these limitations were said to be overcome through the development of "reversibility," described as a higher form of equilibrium between parts and whole. For example, understanding the relations embodied in the equation $2 + 2 = 4$ represents an equilibrium between two different ways of viewing the same thing: as a whole collection of four objects or as two partial collections of two objects each. This equilibrium is reversible in the sense that it balances the symmetrical operations of assimilating the parts to the whole and of differentiating them as distinct elements.

Children's social and moral thinking was also interpreted according to this model of part–whole equilibrium, in this case an equilibrium between individuals and a social whole (Piaget, 1932/1965). Egocentrism was described as a disequilibrium in which the individual perspective prevailed over the coordinated perspectives of social whole; *constraint* was a disequilibrium characterized by a dominance of the whole (especially as represented by parents and other authority figures) over the individual; and *cooperation* was considered a higher form of equilibrium in which individual and group perspectives were evenly balanced. Such an equilibrium was believed most likely to occur among peers than among persons of unequal power and authority (Youniss & Damon, this volume).

Another important contribution from this period was the analogy comparing the *epistemic* relation between the subject and object of knowledge and the *functional* interaction between organism and environment. To the equilibrium between parts and wholes, Piaget now added the equilibrium between organism and environment. Both forms of equilibrium found expression in Piaget's work on the development of sensorimotor intelligence. For example, in *The Origins of Intelligence in Children* (Piaget, 1936/1963, pp. 9-12), he used the term *organization* to refer to the formation of sensorimotor totalities from the equilibrium among action schemes at each stage of development. In contrast, the term *adaptation* was used to refer to the equilibrium between organism and environment resulting from assimilation and accommodation. Still missing at this point were any general principles for describing the sensorimotor totalities formed through the reciprocal assimilation of schemes. Only when Piaget came to the development of infants' understanding of space did he find a solution to this problem. Taking a cue from the French mathematician, Henri Poincaré, he described the systems of spatial transformations which develop at each stage of sensorimotor development in terms of mathematical group theory.

STRUCTURES AS FORMS OF EQUILIBRIUM

An extension of this insight led to the second phase in Piaget's thinking about the equilibrium concept, a phase coinciding with the operatory structuralism of the 1940s and 1950s. Central to the theory at this time was the idea that logical thinking resulted from the coordination of interiorized actions (or operations) and that such coordinations could be described in terms of operatory structures of different kinds. It should come as no surprise at this point that these structures were described in terms of parts and wholes in equilibrium. In this case, the "parts" were the individual operations, and the "whole" was the total structure resulting from their possible compositions.

Consider now the equation $2a + 2a = 4a$. In this case, the terms 2a, 2a, and 4a no longer represent mere quantities, but *operations* of collecting a certain number of objects together. The plus sign represents the *composition* of two or more of such individual operations, and the structure exemplified by the equation encompasses all the operations of collecting of which the individual is capable together with the total set of their possible compositions. The *equilibrium* inherent in such structures consists, not merely in the part–whole reversibility noted previously, but in the fact that every possible composition of individual operations corresponds (and is equivalent) to a further individual operation — just as the composition of 2a and 2a is equivalent to the operation 4a.

As this example suggests, the structure exists, not as a kind of representation in children's minds, but as an ensemble of operational *possibilities* and their interrelations. It affects children's performance by constraining the possibilities available to them. Piaget once expressed this idea as follows: "In a state of psychological equilibrium, possibility . . . plays as important a causal role as real operations" (Inhelder & Piaget, 1955/1958, p. 263). In this view, the causal role characteristic of operatory structures is one of constraint, rather that of an efficient cause (Keil, 1981). This conception of operatory structures as ensembles of operational possibilities is one reason why Piagetian theory does *not* imply consistency of performance across domains of content (see Chapman, 1988, chap. 7).

One of the problems of the structuralist theory during this period was its apparent emphasis on attained *states* of equilibrium rather than on the equilibrating *processes* in which Piaget was originally interested. He addressed this problem in several essays on equilibrium as a principle of explanation in psychology during the 1950s and early 1960s (Piaget, 1952, 1959/1968a). This renewed emphasis on equilibrating processes in development was reflected in his increasing use of the term *equilibration* from this period onward.

Piaget related his efforts in this direction to von Bertalanffy's (1968) conception of "open systems," to Weiss's (1971) concept of "hierarchical systems," and to Ashby's (1947) model of self-organizing processes in the cerebral cortex. His own approach differed from theirs primarily in its emphasis on the capacity of cognitive systems to anticipate external "disturbances" and to compensate for them in advance. The major innovation of this period was the attempt to explicate equilibratory processes with a probabilistic model of *decentration,* according to which centration on isolated aspects of a problem or situation became increasingly less likely with development, and the coordination of two or more centrations became increasingly more likely. However, Piaget later abandoned this probabilistic model, and this abandonment led to the next phase in the development of the equilibration concept.

THE REFORMULATED THEORY

The period from the late 1960s until Piaget's death in 1980 was marked by a number of remarkable new developments in his work, including a "return" to evolutionary biology, a wholesale revision of his earlier work on operatory logic, studies of action, consciousness, and contradiction, as well as research on the development of children's understanding of possibility and necessity — among other things (see Beilin's chapter, this volume). For present purposes, the most important development during this period was the final reformulation of the equilibration theory in *The Equilibration of Cognitive Structures* (Piaget, 1975/1985). One of the first things a reader encounters upon opening this book is a description of three forms of equilibration. The first form is equilibration between schemes and external objects in terms of the functions of assimilation and accommodation. The second form is the equilibration among various schemes through the reciprocal assimilation and accommodation of schemes to each other. The third form is the equilibration between individual schemes and the total structures of which they are a part. The correspondence between these three forms of equilibration and the "laws of equilibrium" enunciated in *Recherche* reflects a remarkable continuity in Piaget's thinking across 60 years of active research. What is new is his attempt to specify how equilibration works in the context of some of the cognitive tasks that he had studied in the meantime.

In particular, he tried to describe more specifically how equilibration can result in essentially new and better forms of thought, a process of *reflective abstraction* in which coordinations among actions or operations at one level become the "elements" to be coordinated at the next higher level. Development from one level to the next is motivated by an attempt to compensate for "perturbations," which may include *contradictions* in the functioning of the system, and *lacunae,* or gaps in knowledge. Piaget described three stages in the compensation of such perturbations: In *alpha* reactions, perturbations are ignored or removed without any change in the system. In *beta* reactions, the system is modified as the result of past perturbations. In *gamma* reactions, *possible* perturbations are anticipated and compensated in advance of their actual occurrence, and accordingly are incorporated among the possible transformations belonging to the system. The heart of the equilibration book is an attempt to describe how these compensatory processes operate in perceptual and sensorimotor functioning and in the development of such familiar concrete operational abilities as conservation, class inclusion, seriation, and transitivity (see Kuhn, this volume, for a similar pattern of reactions in the coordination of evidence and theory).

This emphasis on system organization as a set of compensatory relations among possible transformations led Piaget to study the development of the understanding of possibilities as such. The significance of this study for his central theoretical goals is described on the first page of *Possibility and Necessity* (Piaget, 1981/1987, p. 3). There he wrote that a theory of equilibration is not sufficient for a constructivist explanation of how new forms of knowing develop, because one could always argue that the regulating mechanism itself is either innate or acquired through more or less complex learning. As an alternative, he argued that the actual development of new forms of knowing is preceded and prepared by what he termed the "opening of new possibilities." In addition to the regulations and compensations described in *The Equilibration of Cognitive Structures,* he argued in effect that the development of new forms of organization is also characterized by an increase in the possible transformations available to the system. The significance of this new idea will became apparent in later sections.

EQUILIBRATION AS SELF-ORGANIZATION

More could be said about Piaget's equilibration theory. But instead of reviewing it further, an attempt will be made to draw some conclusions from what has been summarized so far. The main conclusion is that Piaget's intuition in this matter was one of an incipient *systems theory* in which general principles of organization were articulated. More specifically, Piaget's many references to equilibria between parts and wholes (or systems and subsystems) can best be understood as an embryonic theory of *self-organizing* systems (see Garcia's chapter, this volume). It is significant in this connection that he often linked equilibration theory with other theories of self-organization, including those of Ashby (1947), Prigogine (1977; Prigogine & Wiame, 1946), and Atlan (1972). In Piaget's theory, self-organization can occur when the reciprocal interaction among systems results in the formation of a total system that begins to take on a life of its own. His basic intuition was that such self-organizing processes are inherent in organic functioning at all levels, including *cognition*. In effect, higher-order totalities formed through the interaction of lower-order totalities at every major juncture of cognitive development.

That was the intuition, but one would really like to know how good a theory it is. According to some philosophers of science (Laudan, 1977; Popper, 1979), theories can be evaluated only in relation to the problems deemed relevant to them. For Piaget, the major problems of interest were explaining the *generativity of intelligence* and the *progressive increase of rigor* observed in intellectual development. The basic idea was (a) that intelligence is generative because the new totalities formed at each stage of development are more than the sum of the parts from which they derived and (b) that cognitive development is progressively more rigorous because each stage is characterized by more highly organized totalities than the preceding stages.

The most valuable aspects of Piaget's approach are perhaps his statement of the problems to be solved and his argument for the necessity of a theory of equilibration for solving them. Most of his empirical work can be regarded as a vast documentation of the generativity and progressiveness of intellectual development, and much of his theorizing is an argument against the sufficiency of either nativism or empiricism for explaining those phenomena. If the increasing organization observed in development is neither preprogrammed within the developing subject nor imported from the outside, then the only remaining alternative is some form of dialectical constructivism (cf. Piaget, 1967/1971b, p. 212; Pascual–Leone, 1988).

But an argument for the necessity of a theory of self-organization in development is not enough. Sooner or later, one must produce the theory itself. Piaget's particular models of equilibration represent his efforts to do so, but they fall somewhat short because of their excessive abstractness. So the task of producing a concrete theory of cognitive development as a self-organizing process remains, and that theory may or may not resemble Piaget's own models very closely. Indeed, some attempts to explain development in terms of self-organization bear little resemblance to Piaget's equilibration theory (e.g., Fogel & Thelen, 1987; Valsiner, 1987).

The question I would like to consider next is whether existing theories of self-organizing systems can be of use in formulating a more concrete equilibration theory. As mentioned previously, Piaget often likened equilibration theory to other theories of self-organization, in particular, to Prigogine's (1980, chap. 4) theory of dissipative structures. Prigogine (1977) spoke at the seminar on equilibration held in honor of Piaget's 80th birthday, and on that occasion, Piaget stated that he believed himself to be "prolonging the way opened by Prigogine" (commentary in Inhelder, Garcia, & Vonèche, 1977, p. 41). Although there are some interesting parallels between the two approaches, important differences exist as well. The main similarities are stated by Piaget and Garcia (1983/1989, pp. 274–275) in the final pages of *Psychogenesis and the History of Science.* The systems described in both theories are open to exchanges with the environment, and these exchanges lead to self-organization, which stabilizes the systems in question. However, the kinds of exchanges involved differ in each case. In Piagetian theory exchanges with the environment are a product of the assimilation of the environment *by* the system, but in Prigogine's theory the major form of exchange is a dissipation of entropy generated within the system *into* the environment. The direction of exchange is different; Piaget's schemes *assimilate,* but they do not *eliminate.* For this reason, Prigogine's theory is unlikely to prove useful as a direct model for extending the equilibration theory (cf. Garcia's chapter in this volume; also Valsiner, 1987).

Similarly, any apparent parallels between Piaget's approach and cybernetic theories of self-organization (e.g., Ashby, 1947; von Foerster, 1960; Maturana & Varela, 1980) are partial at best. As noted previously, Piaget was certainly influenced by cybernetic theories (especially that of Ashby) at certain points in his development, but he parted company with them with respect to the issue of the openness versus closure of self-organizing systems. Whereas cybernetic theories tend to emphasize the closed, circular character of self-regulating feedback loops, Piaget's theory was based on a dialectic of openness and closure. In his view, a tendency toward an entropic increase in closure within a given system coexisted with the expansive "opening of possibilities," and the latter in particular was responsible for the generativity of intelligence. This dialectic was most clearly expressed in Piaget's reply to von Foerster's presentation at Piaget's 80th-birthday celebration:

> An adequate model of the construction of knowledge must fulfill two difficult to reconcile conditions: the indefinite opening on new possibilities and the conservation of the cycle of mutual implications already constructed and destined to become subsystems in subsequent expanded systems. It is thus a question of reconciling openness and closure. (Piaget, in Inhelder et al., 1977, p. 91; on this point, see also Gallagher, 1977)

Perhaps a closer parallel to Piaget's approach is Haken's (1980, 1983) theory of *Synergetics*. Like Piaget, Haken describes self-organization as resulting from the cooperation among subsystems at the level of physical reality to the biological, psychological, and sociological levels. Unlike Piaget, his theorizing is often expressed in mathematically precise form. But this precision does not necessarily aid one in knowing how to apply the theory to concrete problems in psychology. Haken writes of "order parameters" that constrain the activity of subsystems within a larger system, thereby maintaining the coherence of the whole. The problem is to know what these order parameters might refer to in the case of cognition. As Haken himself remarks, in searching for general principles of organization one risks overlooking the specific qualities of organization in systems existing in different domains or at different levels (see Haken, 1980, p. 128). The main difficulty in attempting to apply general principles of organization to cognitive development is in knowing to what specific properties of cognition those principles pertain.

In this connection, Piaget comes into his own. The structuralist aspect of his theorizing can be viewed as an attempt to articulate the specific principles of organization governing cognitive systems. For example, a central aspect of cognitive development for Piaget was the increasing capacity for anticipating events and acting on them in advance. This property of cognitive systems has not been considered in most general systems theories. An important exception is Rosen's (1985) theory of *anticipatory systems*. One of the central theorems in this theory is that the capacity of a formal (e.g., a cognitive) system to anticipate the behavior of a natural system will depend on periodic "recalibrations" of the formal (cognitive) system. In some ways, this theory would appear to resemble Piaget's notion of "re-equilibration," except that the latter is intended to explicate qualitative changes in the cognitive system itself which go beyond mere "recalibration."

One final parallel between Piaget's equilibration theory and other theories of self-organization deserves to be mentioned. Both Atlan (1972) and Brooks and Wiley (1988) have described self-organization in biological systems as an entropic process: In their respective theories, order can appear in biological systems over time if the *maximum* entropy increases at a faster rate than the *actual* entropy. Self-organization occurs as the result of increases in the possible states available to the system. This expansion of possibilities bears more than a passing resemblance to Piaget's concept of the "opening of possibilities" described earlier.

In summary, some striking parallels exist between Piaget's equilibration theory and existing theories of self-organization. However, such theories may be of limited use in developing the equilibration theory, because they often are stated too generally to encompass principles of organization specific to cognitive systems. Nevertheless, the possibility exists that concrete models of development as self-organization, once they are developed, may reflect some of the principles of organization described in those theories.

EQUILIBRATION AND INTERSUBJECTIVITY

Although the equilibration theory was intended specifically for explaining cognitive development, Piaget sometimes has been accused of overlooking important aspects of human cognition in his use of biological metaphors for cognitive processes (Broughton, 1981a; Hamlyn, 1978; Rotman, 1977). As mentioned previously, the idea that the relations between subject and object could be modeled on the interaction between organism and environment was basic to his view. This analogy has the virtue of emphasizing the interactive nature of knowing, but it also might tend to obscure the intersubjective, semiotic character of conceptual knowing. In organism–environment interaction, the other organism is a part of the *environment*. But once initiated into the human world of symbolic meanings, the knowing subject confronts the object of knowledge with a repertoire of concepts acquired through interaction with *other subjects* (see Furth, this volume).

Piaget has often been charged with having neglected "social factors" of various kinds (Broughton, 1981b; Cohen, 1981/1983). There is indeed some justice to these claims, but Piaget's position with respect to such "social factors" was not quite as naïve as his critics often allege (Chapman, 1988, chap. 7). The common notion that Piaget's described intellectual development as occurring in a social vacuum is based on a narrow reading of the theory of operativity and usually on an ignorance of his sociological writings (Piaget, 1965/1977b; see Chapman, 1986; Smith, 1982). To be sure, Piaget did not describe in any detail how cognition is affected by variations in social context, but his reticence on this score did not result because he failed to recognize the potential importance of such factors in development. For better or worse, this "neglect" of social factors in development resulted from the kinds of questions he sought to answer. One might have a good theory of the *effects* of social context on the course or rate of intellectual development without addressing the epistemological problems of explaining the generativity and rigor of intelligence.

A more serious version of this same criticism is that Piaget underestimated the importance of the social dimension with respect to the very epistemological questions in which he *was* interested (Hamlyn, 1978; Rotman, 1977; Toulmin, 1981). The problem is to describe the ways in which "social factors" are implicated in the generativity and rigor of intellectual development. In previous work on the development of children's reasoning, I have argued that conceptual knowing has an irreducibly triadic structure involving the active subject, the object of knowledge, and a cosubject or interlocutor. I called this triad the *epistemic triangle* (Chapman, in 1991a). From birth, children interact with other persons as well as with physical objects, and they discover some important differences between the two. By virtue of the similarities between their own bodily actions and those of other persons, infants find that they share many more possibilities for *reciprocal interaction* with other persons than they do with physical objects. From an early age, they engage in such reciprocal interactions in the form of the contingent behavioral exchanges that Watson (1972) called "the game" and, increasingly, in ever more sophisticated forms of *imitation*. At the same time, they acquire a sensorimotor acquaintance with the world through interacting with physical objects.

At the end of the sensorimotor period, these two forms of interactivity become coordinated with each other. The imitative exchange of gestures acquires the potential for *signifying* something beyond itself, and the sensorimotor world the capacity for *being signified*. The epistemic triangle is constructed from such a coordination of subject–object and intersubjective forms of interaction, and representational thought is the result. Although Piaget (1937/1971a, 1945/1962) described the development of both objectivity and imitation in exquisite detail, he perhaps underestimated the differences between these forms of interaction and the importance of their intercoordination in the development of cognitive representation. In describing the latter in dualistic terms as the progressive differentiation of signifier and signified (Piaget, 1936/1963), he overlooked the irreducibly triadic structure of signification (cf. Peirce, 1955) and, consequently, of the implicitly triadic structure of representational knowing.

In summary, the argument is that cognitive development involves not only equilibration between subject and object, but also equilibration between subjects. The problem then becomes one of knowing what form such intersubjective equilibration is likely to take. One way of approaching this problem is to consider the kinds of "perturbations" that result in equilibration and how they would be manifest in the intersubjective sphere. As previously mentioned, Piaget (1975/1985) described two general types of perturbations leading to equilibration: contradictions and lacunae. His examples were taken exclusively from the realm of subject–object interaction, but one imagine that similar kinds of perturbations would manifest themselves in intersubjective interaction as well.

One salient type of intersubjective contradiction is *a difference of opinion* between persons. Indeed, the word itself means "speaking against" (Latin, *contradicere*). In effect, a logical contradiction is the kind of error that a person makes in affirming two opposing propositions, literally, in "speaking against" oneself. In contrast, a *dialogical* contradiction results when the opposing propositions are uttered (and presumably believed) by different persons. One way in which such dialogical contradictions are addressed by the parties involved is through a process of *argumentation,* defined as a "social, intellectual, verbal activity serving to justify or refute an opinion . . . and being directed toward obtaining the agreement of a judge who is deemed to be reasonable" (Van Eemeren & Grootendorst, 1982, p. 1). These theorists further describe argumentation as a kind of speech act intended to *convince* other persons of a particular point of view by providing them with reasons to do so (see Kuhn's chapter, this volume).

The key feature of this definition is that differences of opinion are addressed through the generation, consideration, and weighing of *reasons* for and against the opinions in question. It is this feature that qualifies argumentation as a potential form of equilibration. In effect, argumentation is a dialectical synthesis of conflict and cooperation. It begins with the conflict between opposing opinions, but involves cooperation with respect to the procedures used to address that opposition. In engaging in argumentation, the parties involved implicitly agree to allow their differences to be decided solely by the weight of the reasons generated by each side, and not by other considerations. This rationality of argumentation is not purely cerebral; the reasons considered might well involve appeals to values shared by the participants, and the process itself implies certain norms of fairness and reciprocity. (For an effort to explicate the normative dimension of argumentative discourse, see Habermas, 1981/1984–1989.)

In Piaget's (1975/1985) equilibration theory, contradictions are overcome through the construction of negations to balance every affirmation. Argumentation deserves to be considered an example of intersubjective equilibration because it is an alternating process by which the reasons generated by one side (affirmations) are balanced by those produced by the other side (negations). This equilibratory balancing may be accomplished either by refuting the reasons advanced by one's opponent and/or by producing new positive reasons to support one's own position. In either case, the outcome of such attempts to *over*compensate the arguments of the opposing side is generally not a static equality. According to Van Eemeren and Grootendorst (1982), the "happy" outcome of argumentation occurs when one party succeeds in convincing the other of his or her own point of view by weight of the reasons adduced in its favor. However, other outcomes can also be imagined. For example, the process of examining the reasons for and against the opposing positions originally represented by the two parties could result in the construction of an entirely new viewpoint, recognized by one or both participants as superior to their respective starting positions. This outcome would be an intersubjective counterpart to Piaget's "optimizing equilibration."

Besides contradiction, the other type of perturbation recognized by Piaget (1975/1985) involved lacunae, or gaps in knowledge. This sort of perturbation results when subjects engaged in the pursuit of a goal realize that they lack one or more of the means necessary for its attainment. Such gaps in knowledge were said to be overcome through a constructive filling-in of the gap in question. Again, the examples considered by Piaget were all taken from the realm of subject–object interaction, and the question is how such perturbations might be manifest and overcome in the intersubjective sphere.

One possibility is that subjects might attempt to overcome gaps in knowledge through a process of *inquiry* or *interrogation,* that is, through addressing questions to someone presumed to possess at least parts of the knowledge that is lacking (for a theory of interrogation as a general form of knowledge seeking, see Hintikka, 1984/1989a; Hintikka & Hintikka, 1982). Such a process would be equilibratory in the minimal sense that it would tend to equalize the knowledge of the subjects in question. But if such inquiry merely results in the unilateral transfer of knowledge from one person to another, it would hardly be generative in the sense of resulting in *new* knowledge. It was precisely for this reason that Piaget (e.g., 1966) rejected the social environment as an explanation for the *origins* of knowledge. Once invented or discovered, knowledge can be transmitted from person to person or from one generation to another, but that knowledge first must be invented or discovered before it can be transmitted in this way. Moreover, the act of communication presupposes that subjects already share knowledge of some semiotic system and of whatever domains of experience to which it refers. Such knowledge obviously cannot be acquired through the same communicative processes that presuppose it to begin with.

However, inquiry can result in other outcomes besides the unilateral transmission of knowledge from one person to another. Especially if it is conducted as a *joint* activity in which subjects come to share the knowledge that each alone possesses, it potentially can lead to the construction of new knowledge that neither individual possessed before. In this sense, inquiry can be considered a form of intersubjective equilibration with "optimizing" possibilities. Indeed, it is precisely in this sense that Socratic questioning can lead to new knowledge. According to Hintikka (1989b), such interrogatory games were employed in Plato's Academy as one of the chief methods for acquiring knowledge. In this view, much of Aristotelian logic (e.g., his discussion of fallacies) can be interpreted as the codification of rules and strategies for such dialectical inquiry.

In his early work, Piaget (1923/1955, 1924/1928) studied argumentative and interrogatory communication between children and considered the encounter with other perspectives to be the major equilibratory process in cognitive development. After he developed the theory of operations, the equilibration of operations within the subject and between subject and object became more prominent in his thinking. Although he never abandoned the belief in the equilibratory coordination of perspectives, he did not explain how such intersubjective equilibration was related to subject-object and intrasubjective forms of equilibration (e.g., Piaget, 1954/1968b). One way of viewing the idea of the epistemic triangle is as an attempt to integrate Piaget's early theory of social interaction with his later theory of operativity (Chapman, 1991a; Chapman & McBride, in press).

Such an endeavor suggests new questions for theory and research—for example, how dialogical argumentation and inquiry develop and what role they play *in* development. As suggested in the preceding paragraph, answering such questions within the context of an expanded equilibration theory is likely to involve a reconsideration of Piaget's early work on communication and its relation to the development of reasoning. For example, Dorval and Gundy (1990) reformulated Piaget's (1923/1955) early model of the development of communication in dialogical terms and compared the original with the reformulated model in the context of argumentative discussion among peers. Stages in the development of argumentative discourse in the sociomoral domain were described by Berkowitz, Oser, and Althof (1987), and research on "cognitive conflict" in intellectual development was reinterpreted by Chapman and McBride (in press) in terms of the semantic relations between language and operations. Finally, dialectical inquiry was proposed as a model for the development of children's thinking by Sigel (1981).

MODELS OF DEVELOPMENT

Since the publication of Reese and Overton's (1970; Overton & Reese, 1973) seminal articles on organismic and mechanistic models in developmental psychology, Piaget generally has been considered the paradigmatic organismic theorist. But one might well ask how the view of equilibration as self-organization described in the previous sections fits into that picture. A further question is how to accommodate the semiotic character of conceptual knowing in such a conception of equilibration.

Significantly, one of the major problems addressed by theorists of self-organization had to do with the relation *between* organismic and mechanistic systems. A mechanical universe is characterized by increases in entropy or disorder with time, consistent with the Second Law of Thermodynamics. In contrast, organic growth and evolution are characterized by progressions of increasingly more ordered forms. The problem addressed by Prigogine and Wiame (1946) and other theorists of self-organization was how to reconcile the facts of biological development and evolution with the Second Law. The possibility of solving this problem in theories of self-organization has important implications for general models in developmental psychology.

In a recent chapter, Dixon, Lerner, and Hultsch (1991) described four dimensions of change on which models of development could be classified: *Mechanistic* models were said to be characterized by randomness, relativity, reversibility, and continuity of change, and *organismic* models by directedness, universality, irreversibility, and discontinuity. The question is where the theories of self-organization mentioned earlier would fit on these dimensions. In a commentary on the Dixon et al. chapter (Chapman, 1991b), I argued that they do not fit at all — at least not in any unambiguous way. Briefly, the argument is that theories of self-organization embrace both poles of each dimension simultaneously. There is a place in such theories for both randomness and directedness, relativity and universality, reversibility and irreversibility, as well as continuity and discontinuity. Accordingly, they can be classified unambiguously neither as mechanistic nor as organismic, and one is led to ask whether some new root metaphor is necessary.

In this connection, the work of Bogdanov (1919–1921/1984) is relevant. Generally known to history as a rival of Lenin for the leadership of the Bolshevik faction in prerevolutionary Russia, Bogdanov was also the founder of *Tektology,* which he described as "the general science of organization." The goal of this new science, like that of the systems theories that it foreshadowed (see Gorelik, 1975), was to describe general principles governing organizational processes at different levels and in different domains of reality. However, Bogdanov's root metaphor was not that of organism; rather it was derived from *the cooperative activity of human beings,* and this focus on cooperation is what makes him relevant for Piaget.

In Bogdanov's view, the process of organization involves (a) an initial phase of *conjunction* in which individuals come together for a common purpose, (b) a phase of *differentiation* in which their respective contributions are coordinated in a complementary way, and (c) a phase of *consolidation* in which the system contradictions generated during the second phase are addressed and, to the extent that is possible, overcome. The process as a whole he called "organizational dialectic" to distinguish it from what he termed the "formal dialectic" of Marx and Engels. This implicit critique of the founder of dialectical materialism provided Lenin (1909/1977) with the opportunity to discredit him as a reactionary Machist. However, recent scholarship suggests instead that Bogdanov's philosophy of "empiriomonism" was an attempt to go beyond classical Marxism and Machism, rather than merely a species of the latter (Grille, 1966; Jensen, 1978).

But the point is not to suggest that "organization" modeled on human cooperation should replace organism or mechanism as a general "world-hypothesis." The point is rather that theoretical metaphors should be commensurate with the *level* of organization considered. If the organization of human cognition is the phenomenon of interest, then the metaphor of cooperation may be appropriate because it presupposes each of the components of the epistemic triangle. In particular, the coordination of actions by different human agents presupposes a semiotic communicative system by which joint planning can be carried out. The intrapsychic counterpart of interpersonal cooperation is the coordination or composition of interiorized operations, an essential aspect of operational thinking in Piaget's theory (cf. Doise & Mugny, 1985). Thus, I believe that the use of human cooperation as a metaphor for understanding human cognition is eminently consistent with Piagetian theory, although it implies an increased emphasis on the role of communicative interaction in the development of operational thinking.

CONCLUSION

In summary, the argument has been that, suitably reinterpreted, Piaget's theory remains relevant for contemporary psychology. The questions he raised and his general intuitions are more relevant than his specific models. Too often the specifics of Piaget's theories have been debated without an appreciation for the particular questions they were meant to answer. Such has been the case with the equilibration theory. His questions regarding the generativity of intelligence and the progressive rigor of intellectual development have lost none of their importance in the 1990s. His intuition that these questions might be answerable through a constructivist theory of equilibration as self-organization remains a viable alternative. But his specific model of equilibratory processes itself might need to be equilibrated further. I have suggested one way in which the theory might be developed: by going beyond the analogy between subject–object relations and organism–environment interaction toward a model that explicitly includes equilibration in intersubjective interaction. This expanded field for equilibration is what was signaled in the title of this chapter by the phrase *the dialectics of organization.*

ACKNOWLEDGMENT

Preparation of this chapter was supported in part by Grant No. OGP0037334 from the Natural Sciences and Engineering Research Council of Canada.

REFERENCES

Ashby, W. R. (1947). Dynamics of the cerebral cortex automatic development of equilibrium in self-organizing systems. *Psychometrika, 2,* 135–140.

Atlan, H. (1972). *L'organisation biologique et la théorie de l'information [Biological organization and information theory].* Paris: Hermann.

Berkowitz, M. W., Oser, F., & Althof, W. (1987). The development of sociomoral discourse. In W. K. Kurtines & J. L. Gewirtz (Eds.), *Moral development through social interaction* (pp. 322–352). New York: Wiley.

von Bertalanffy, L. (1968). *General systems theory.* New York: Braziller.

Bogdanov, A. (1984). *Essays in Tektology: The general science of organization* (2nd English ed.). Seaside, CA: Intersystems. (Original works published 1919–1921)

Brooks, D. R., & Wiley, E. O. (1988). *Evolution as entropy* (2nd ed.). Chicago: University of Chicago Press.

Broughton, J. (1981a). Piaget's structural developmental psychology: III. Function and the problem of knowledge. *Human Development, 24,* 257–285.

Broughton, J. (1981b). Piaget's structural developmental psychology: IV. Knowledge without a self and without a history. *Human Development, 24,* 320–346.

Bruner, J. (1959). Inhelder and Piaget's "The growth of logical thinking." *British Journal of Psychology, 50,* 363–370.

Chapman, M. (1986). The structure of exchange: Piaget's sociological theory. *Human Development, 29,* 181–194.

Chapman, M. (1988). *Constructive evolution: Origins and development of Piaget's thought.* Cambridge, England: Cambridge University Press.

Chapman, M. (1991a). The epistemic triangle: Operative and communicative components of cognitive competence. In M. Chandler & M. Chapman (Eds.), *Criteria for competence: Controversies in the conceptualization and assessment of children's abilities* (pp. 209–228). Hillsdale, NJ: Lawrence Erlbaum Associates.

Chapman, M. (1991b). Self-organization as developmental process: Beyond the organismic and mechanistic models? In P. Van Geehrt & P. Mos (Eds.), *Annals of theoretical psychology: Vol. 7. Developmental psychology* (pp. 335–348). New York: Plenum.

Chapman, M., & McBride, M. (in press). The education of reason: Cognitive conflict and its role in intellectual development. In U. Schantz & W. Hartup (Eds.), *Conflict in child and adolescent development.* Cambridge, England: Cambridge University Press.

Cohen, D. (1983). *Piaget: Critique and reassessment.* London: Croom Helm. (Original work published 1981)

Dixon, R., Lerner, R., & Hultsch, D. (1991). The concept of development in the study of individual and social change. In P. Van Geehrt & P. Mos (Eds.), *Annals of theoretical psychology: Vol. 7. Developmental psychology* (pp. 279-323). New York: Plenum.

Doise, W., & Mugny, G. (1985). *The social development of the intellect.* Oxford, England: Pergamon Press.

Dorval, B., & Gundy, F. (1990). The development of arguing in discussions among peers. *Merrill-Palmer Quarterly, 36,* 389-410.

Van Eemeren, F. H., & Grootendorst, R. (1982). The speech acts of arguing and convincing in externalized discussions. *Journal of Pragmatics, 6,* 1-24.

Fogel, A., & Thelen, E. (1987). Development of early expressive and communicative action: Reinterpreting the evidence from a dynamic systems perspective. *Developmental Psychology, 23,* 747-761.

von Foerster, H. (1960). On self-organizing systems and their environments. In M. C. Yovits & S. Cameron (Eds.), *Self-organizing systems* (pp. 31-50). Oxford, England: Pergamon.

Gallagher, J. M. (1977). Piaget's concept of equilibration: Biological, logical, and cybernetic roots. In M. H. Appel & L. S. Goldberg (Eds.), *Topics in cognitive development: Vol. 1. Equilibration: Theory, research and application* (pp. 21-32). New York: Plenum.

Gorelik, G. (1975). Principal ideas of Bogdanov's "Tektology": The universal science of organization. *General Systems, 20,* 3-13.

Grille, D. (1966). *Lenin's Rivale: Bogdanov und seine Philosophie [Lenin's rival: Bogdanov and his philosophy].* Cologne: Verlag Wissenschaft und Politik.

Habermas, J. (1984-1989). *The theory of communicative action* (Vols. 1 & 2). Boston: Beacon. (Original work published 1981)

Haken, H. (1980). Synergetics: Are cooperative phenomena governed by universal principles? *Naturwissenschaften, 67,* 121-128.

Haken, H. (1983). *Synergetics: An introduction.* Berlin: Springer-Verlag.

Hamlyn, D. (1978). *Experience and the growth of understanding.* London: Routledge & Kegan Paul.

Hintikka, J. (1984/1989a). Questioning as a philosophical method. In J. Hintikka & M. B. Hintikka (Eds.), *The logic of epistemology and the epistemology of logic* (pp. 215-233). Dordrecht, The Netherlands: Reidel.

Hintikka, J. (1989b). The role of logic in argumentation. *Monist, 72,* 3-24.

Hintikka, J., & Hintikka, M. B. (1982). Sherlock Holmes confronts modern logic: Toward a theory of information-seeking through questioning. In E. M. Barth & J. L. Martens (Eds.), *Argumentation: Approaches to theory formation* (pp. 55-76). Amsterdam: John Benjamins.

Inhelder, B., Garcia, R., & Vonèche, J. (Eds.). (1977). *Genetic epistemology and equilibration.* Neuchâtel: Delachaux et Neistlé.

Inhelder, B., & Piaget, J. (1958). *The growth of logical thinking from childhood to adolescence.* New York: Basic Books. (Original work published 1955)

Jensen, K. M. (1978). *Beyond Marx and Mach: Aleksandr Bogdanov's "Philosophy of living experience."* Dordrecht, The Netherlands: Reidel.

Keil, F. (1981). Constraints on knowledge and cognitive development. *Psychological Review, 88,* 197-227.

Laudan, L. (1977). *Progress and its problems.* Berkeley, CA: University of California Press.

Lenin, V. I. (1977). *Materialism and empiro-criticism.* Moscow: Progress Publishers. (Original work published 1909)

Maturana, H. R., & Varela, F. J. (1980). *Autopoiesis and cognition.* Dordrecht, The Netherlands: Reidel.

Overton, W. F., & Reese, H. W. (1973). Models of development: Methodological implications. In J. R. Nesselroade & H. W. Reese (Eds.), Life-span developmental psychology: Methodological issues (pp. 65–86). New York: Academic Press.

Pascual-Leone, J. (1988). Affirmations and negations, disturbances and contradictions, in understanding Piaget: Is his later theory causal? (Review of J. Piaget, *The equilibration of cognitive structures*). *Contemporary Psychology, 33,* 420–421.

Peirce, C. S. (1955). Logic as semiotic: The theory of signs. In J. Buchler (Ed.), *The philosophical writing of Peirce*. New York: Dover.

Piaget, J. (1918). *Recherche*. Lausanne, Switzerland: La Concorde.

Piaget, J. (1928). *Judgment and reasoning in the child*. London: Routledge & Kegan Paul. (Original work published 1924)

Piaget, J. (1952). Equilibre et structures d'ensemble [Equilibrium and structures-of-the-whole]. *Bulletin de Psychologie, 6,* 4–10.

Piaget, J. (1955). *The language and thought of the child*. Cleveland: Meridian. (Original work published 1923)

Piaget, J. (1962). *Play, dreams and imitation in childhood*. New York: Norton. (Original work published 1945)

Piaget, J. (1963). *The origins of intelligence in children*. New York: Norton. (Original work published 1936)

Piaget, J. (1965). *The moral judgment of the child*. New York: Free Press. (Original work published 1932)

Piaget, J. (1966). Need and significance of cross-cultural studies in genetic psychology. *International Journal of Psychology, 1,* 3–13.

Piaget, J. (1968a). The role of the concept of equilibrium in psychological explication. In J. Piaget, *Six psychological studies* (pp. 100–114). New York: Vintage. (Original work published 1959)

Piaget, J. (1968b). Language and thought from the genetic point of view. In J. Piaget, *Six psychological studies* (pp. 88–99). New York: Vintage. (Original work published 1954)

Piaget, J. (1971a). *The construction of reality in the child*. New York: Ballantine. (Original work published 1937)

Piaget, J. (1971b). *Biology and knowledge*. Chicago: University of Chicago Press. (Original work published 1967)

Piaget, J. (1977a). Problems of equilibration. In M. H. Appel & L. S. Goldberg (Eds.), *Topics in cognitive development: Vol. 1. Equilibration: Theory, research and application* (pp. 3–13). New York: Plenum.

Piaget, J. (1977b). *Etudes sociologiques [Sociological studies]* (2nd ed.). Geneva: Librairie Droz. (Original work published 1965)

Piaget, J. (1985). *The equilibration of cognitive structures*. Chicago: University of Chicago Press.

Piaget, J. (1987). *Possibility and necessity: Vol. 1. The development of possibilities*. Minneapolis: University of Minnesota Press. (Original work published 1981)

Piaget, J., & Garcia, R. (1989). *Psychogenesis and the history of science*. New York: Columbia University Press. (Original work published 1983)

Popper, K. (1979). *Objective knowledge* (rev. ed.). New York: Oxford University Press.

Prigogine, I. (1977). Genèse des structures en physico-chemie [Genesis of structures in physical chemistry]. In B. Inhelder, R. Garcia, & J. Vonèche (Eds.), *Epistémologie génétique et équilibration* (pp. 29–38). Neuchâtel, Switzerland: Delachaux et Niestlé.

Prigogine, I. (1980). *From being to becoming*. New York: W. H. Freeman.

Prigogine, I., & Wiame, J. M. (1946). Biologie et thermodynamique des phénomènes irréversibles [Biology and the thermodynamics of irreversible phenomena]. *Experientia, 2,* 451–453.

Reese, H. W., & Overton, W. F. (1970). Models of development and theories of development.

In L. R. Goulet & P. B. Baltes (Eds.), Life-span developmental psychology: Research and theory (pp. 115–145). New York: Academic Press.

Rosen, R. (1985). *Anticipatory systems.* London: Pergamon.

Rotman, B. (1977). *Jean Piaget: Psychologist of the real.* Hassocks, England: Harvester Press.

Rowell, J. A. (1983). Equilibration: Developing the hard core of the Piagetian research program. *Human Development, 26,* 61–71.

Sigel, I. E. (1981). Social experience in the development of representational thought: Distancing theory. In I. E. Sigel, D. M. Brodzinsky, & R. M. Golinkoff (Eds.), *New directions in Piagetian theory and practice* (pp. 203–217). Hillsdale, NJ: Lawrence Erlbaum Associates.

Smith, L. (1982). Piaget and the solitary knower. *Philosophy of the Social Sciences, 12,* 173–182.

Toulmin, S. (1981). Epistemology and developmental psychology. In E. S. Gollin (Ed.). *Developmental plasticity: Behavioral and biological aspects of variations in development* (pp. 253–267). New York: Academic Press.

Valsiner, J. (1987). *Culture and the development of children's action.* New York: Wiley.

Watson, J. B. (1972). Smiling, cooing, and "the game." *Merrill–Palmer Quarterly, 18,* 323–340.

Weiss, P. A. (1971). The basic concept of hierarchic systems. In P. A. Weiss (Ed.), *Hierarchically organized systems in theory and practice* (pp. 1–43). New York: Hafner.

4 Neo-Piagetian Theories of Intellectual Development

Robbie Case
School of Education, Stanford University

Over the past 20 years, two distinct lines of investigation have been pursued, within the general theoretical framework that Piaget created. The first has been concerned with applying and extending Piaget's general theory of intellectual development to areas that he himself treated only in passing: areas such as moral development (Kohlberg, 1981), social development (Selman, 1980; Turiel, 1983), ego development (Kegan, 1982; Noam, 1988), adult development (Kuhn, this volume), language development (Sinclair-de-Zwart, 1969), and education (Elkind, 1985; Sigel, 1969). The second line has been concerned with continuing the revision (Murray, this volume) of Piaget's general theory that he initiated in his later years, with his new theory of equilibration (Piaget, 1985), and his new logic of meanings (Piaget & Garcia, 1991).

In addition to these two lines of inquiry, a third line of work has emerged which has altered Piaget's framework more substantially. What is distinctive about this third line of work is not so much its historical tie to Piaget's own research enterprise (although this tie is a strong and direct one), as its stance toward the criticisms that were leveled at that enterprise from rival epistemological and psychological traditions. Rather than merely seeking to rebut these criticisms, the individuals who have participated in this third endeavor have in some sense "made the criticisms their own." Thus, they have not only felt obliged to modify Piaget's theory more radically than he himself thought necessary, even in his later years (Beilin, this volume),[1] they

---

[1] For the points on which Piaget demurred, see Pascual–Leone (1976, 1988c).

have also felt free to borrow more extensively than he would have, from the rival traditions that generated these criticisms in the first place.

The new body of theory that has emerged as a result cannot be properly be classified as a simple extension of Piaget's work. Nor can it be classified as a revision along lines that he himself would have sanctioned. Rather, it must be seen as a hybrid, which rests on a similar set of core assumptions, and which offers an interesting set of potential solutions to the problems posed by the classical Piagetian system — but which introduces new elements into the system that genuinely transform it, and give it exciting new possibilities. Because the third line of work has these novel properties, the scholars who have contributed to its development often referred to themselves as "neo-Piagetians" (Pascual–Leone & Smith, 1969).

In the present chapter, I provide a brief introduction to, and review of, neo-Piagetian theory. My review is organized in six sections:

1. In the first, I summarize the critiques of the classic Piagetian position that were most influential in shaping the direction that was taken by neo-Piagetian theorists.
2. In the second, I describe a set of propositions that were proposed, independently, by several of these theorists, in response to these criticisms.
3. In the third, I describe the new forms of task analysis that became necessary, in order to test the propositions of the newly emerging theories.
4. In the fourth, I summarize the empirical work that was conducted, once these new forms of task analysis had been developed.
5. In the fifth, I review several lines of inquiry that are currently being conducted as the neo-Piagetian movement makes contact with intellectual movements in other areas.
6. Finally, in the sixth, I describe two new developments that may have the potential to transform neo-Piagetian theory itself, or at least alter certain of its postulates substantially.

Throughout the chapter, I use the term "neo-Piagetian" to refer to the body of theory and data that are the subject of the present review. The reader is warned, however, that the first two bodies of work mentioned in the first paragraph have recently been referred to with this same title (e.g., Beilin, 1989), and that these other bodies of work will not be covered in the present chapter.[2]

---

[2] For reviews of these other lines of work (see, Beilin, 1989, this volume; Inhelder & Piaget, 1980; Modgil & Modgil, 1982; Vuyk, 1981).

THE ORIGINS OF NEO-PIAGETIAN THEORY

Although Piaget continued to modify his theoretical system well into the 1970s and 1980s (Beilin, 1983; Chapman, 1988), the framework that constituted the starting point for most neo-Piagetian investigators was the classic one, which was completed during the mid 1960s, and which was summarized by Piaget at that time (Piaget, 1970). According to this theory, infants and children can most profitably be viewed as a young scientists, who construct ever more powerful theories of the world, as a result of applying structures of ever increasing generality and power. These structures, in turn, can most profitably be construed as systems of logical operations, which remain invariant in the face of considerable differences in surface content and cultural milieu, and which can be modeled using symbolic logic.

While empirical experience, social experience, and maturation were all acknowledged by Piaget to play some role in influencing children's construction of these structures, by far the most important role was assigned to "logico-mathematical experience" (Piaget, 1964). That is to say, by far the most important role was assigned to the universal experience of operating on the world, and then reflecting on one's own operations. It was presumed that this reflexive activity was the underlying motor of cognitive development, and that the primary criteria it brought to bear on children's thought were rational ones, such as the search for coherence, consistency, and breadth of application. It was as a result of this sort of reflexive activity, and the dynamic internal process from which it stemmed, that children's logical structures were presumed to be reworked periodically, into systems of increasing consistency and power.

Piaget's theory had a number of important strengths, which were acknowledged by investigators in a wide variety of fields. Because the theory placed such a strong emphasis on rational structures and processes, however, it was also subjected to strong criticism. This was especially true in North America, where the prevailing epistemology placed a far stronger emphasis on empirical or sociocultural factors. The epistemology that underpinned Piaget's theory has been contrasted with that of his critics along a number of dimensions (Beilin, 1983, 1989, this volume; Chapman, 1988; Overton, 1984, 1990a). From the present perspective, however, the most important features of this epistemology were (a) its explicit rejection of the classic empiricist position on knowledge and its acquisition, and (b) its tentative and rather selective endorsement of the dialectical position on knowledge and its acquisition. Each of these features led to a clash with mainstream psychology—the former with psychology as practiced in the Anglo–American community, and the latter with psychology as practiced in the Soviet community. Since neo-Piagetian theory was born in direct response to these two clashes, it is important to examine the epistemological issues that were at stake.

According to the classic *empiricist* epistemology, the process of knowledge acquisition is one in which the sensory organs first detect stimuli in the external world, and the mind then detects the customary patterns or "conjunctions" in these stimuli (Hume, 1955). North American psychologists who were influenced by this view tended to believe that children's knowledge had its origins in a growing familiarity with their external world, and the regularities that this world contains. The process of development was thus seen as a continuous one, in which children construct rules of ever increasing generality for representing and dealing with the regularities in their environment (Gibson, 1969; Klahr & Wallace, 1976; Siegler, 1978). The knowledge possessed by scientists was viewed in a similar fashion: namely, as a body of facts and laws whose origins lie in careful observation of empirical phenomena, followed by a process in which causal hypotheses are articulated and subjected to rigorous empirical scrutiny (Brainerd, 1978).

To those who endorsed this view of knowledge and its acquisition, or who were influenced by it, Piaget's theory of intellectual development appeared seriously flawed. The major substantive problems that were cited were as follows: (a) the theory postulates a psychological system that operates in an monolithic fashion, under the guidance of a set of an ill-defined "logical structures" and processes; (b) the theory assigns external, empirical observations and influences a relatively unimportant role in the formation and alteration of these structures and processes. Not only are these suggestions at variance with empiricist epistemology, they appear to be at variance with empirical data on children's development as well. Many tasks that are supposedly tests of the same underlying logical structure do not even correlate with each other (Pinard & Laurendeau, 1969). In addition, children's absolute level of performance on such tasks varies widely from one situation to the next—so widely in fact, that certain properties that are supposed to be characteristic of one stage of development (e.g., decentration during the period of concrete operations) may actually be observed at the previous stage, a good 6 years earlier. Finally, training studies have shown that it is relatively easy to influence children's understanding of logical principles, by exposing them to appropriately simplified forms of empirical experience (Beilin, 1971a, 1971b; Gelman, 1969).

For those whose epistemology had its origins in the sociohistoric tradition, the problems with Piaget's theory were different, but equally serious. According to the sociohistoric view, knowledge and thought evolve in a social and historical context, and cannot be understood without reference to the nature and dynamic tensions that are inherent in that context. Psychologists who have been influenced by this position see the origin of children's knowledge as lying in their culture, and the intellectual and linguistic tools that their culture has evolved for coping with its environment (Bruner, 1966, 1989; Cole & Bruner, 1971; Lave, 1988; McDermott, 1990; Vygotsky, 1962). While Piaget was always quick to acknowledge the importance of social factors in development, and while his model of equilibration was inherently dialectical, the fact remains that the central constructs in his system were defined in universal terms, and were seen as conforming with rational principles rather than social or linguistic ones.

When viewed from the sociohistoric perspective, then, Piaget's portrait of the young child appeared too universal, and too focused on the subject, rather than the cultural and linguistic institutions in which the subject's life is embedded. The methods that Piaget employed likewise appeared too uncritical with regard to their cultural and linguistic biases. Finally, once again, the theory did not appear to square with the available data. These data suggested (a) that different cultures pass Piagetian tasks at different ages, and reach different terminal levels (Dasen, 1972); (b) that children's response to Piagetian tasks within a culture varies widely as a function of such factors as language (Bruner, 1966; Cole & Scribner, 1974; Olson, 1986a, 1986b) and formal schooling (Cole, Gay, Glick, & Sharp, 1971; Greenfield, 1966); and (c) that the structures of Western thought themselves appear to have evolved in major ways over the last 500 years, and to be in a continued state of evolution (Keating, 1980; Olson, 1986a, 1986b).

The problems pointed out by scholars in the empiricist and sociohistoric traditions were not the only ones that influenced the direction of neo-Piagetian thought. Even among those scholars who accepted most of Piaget's underlying (rationalist) assumptions about knowledge and its acquisition, there was dissatisfaction with certain aspects of his theory. Of particular concern were (a) The absence of a sufficiently detailed treatment of stage transition: that is, the central mechanism by which children replace early forms of logical structures with more powerful ones (Pascual–Leone, 1969); (b) The absence of any treatment of "performance" factors: that is, factors which affect children's ability to apply particular structures in particular contexts (Overton, 1990b; Pascual–Leone, 1969); and (c) The absence of any account of individual differences in the developmental process (Pascual–Leone, 1969). The common theme running through this last set of criticisms was that Piaget's theory was incomplete. To present a more complete picture, it was argued, a more detailed account would have to be provided of the processes on which the structure of children's thought was dependent.[3]

---

[3] Unlike the previous critique, this last critique was one with which Piaget was in substantial agreement, and which he spent the last 15 years of his life working on himself (Beilin, 1989; Chapman, 1988).

Neo-Piagetian theory was born in response to these three general categories of criticism, that is, the criticisms raised by empiricist, sociohistoric, and rationalist scholars (Pascual–Leone, 1969). What neo-Piagetian theorists attempted to do was to *preserve* those aspects of Piagetian theory that gave it its breadth, coherence, and explanatory power, to *develop* those aspects of the theory that made it seem too static, vague, or difficult to operationalize, and to *alter* those aspects of the theory that assumed a child whose development was relatively insensitive to its physical environment, or who derived only modest intellectual benefits from its cultural and linguistic heritage.

As the neo-Piagetian movement gained sway, different neo-Piagetian theorists made different decisions regarding which elements of Piaget's theory to retain, which to develop, and which to alter, in order to accomplish the foregoing objectives (see Biggs & Collis, 1982; Case, 1978, 1985; Demetriou & Efklides, 1988; Fischer, 1980; Fischer & Ferrar, in press; Halford, 1982, 1988; Mounoud, 1986; Pascual–Leone, 1970, 1988a). They also differed in which of the foregoing objectives they saw as most central. Nevertheless, there was a good deal of commonality in the general directions they pursued. Thus, after 20 years of further writing and research, it now seems possible to specify a set of core propositions on which neo-Piagetian theorists are generally agreed, and to examine the solution that these propositions imply to the problems just described.

CORE POSTULATES OF NEO-PIAGETIAN THEORY

Postulates Retained from the Classic Piagetian System

The following traditional Piagetian postulates are ones that were retained by most neo-Piagetian theorists, in developing new or revised systems of their own.

A1. Children Assimilate Experience to Existing Cognitive Structures. Children do not simply "observe" the world around them and note its regularities. Rather, they actively assimilate this world to their existing cognitive structures.

A2. Children Create Their Own Cognitive Structures. Children's cognitive structures are not merely a product of their empirical experience. They are also a product of their own attempts to organize that experience in a coherent fashion.

A3. Children Pass Through a Universal Sequence of Structural Levels. Three or four general levels of cognitive structure can be identified in children's intellectual development. While different neo-Piagetian theorists labeled and analyzed these structures somewhat differently, they all agreed that there is a preliminary stage in which sensorimotor structures predominate, followed by two or three further stages in which children's intellectual structures become increasingly symbolic and abstract.

A4. Earlier Structures Are Included in Later Ones. The increasingly abstract structures of later stages build on, and yet transforms, those of earlier stages. Thus, for example, the higher-order conservation concepts that are possessed by elementary school children, although they are qualitatively different from those possessed by infants (Mounoud & Bower, 1974; Starkey, Spelke, & Gelman, 1983), are not unrelated to them. Rather, they are based on these concepts, and constitute a higher-order "reworking" of them.

A5. Characteristic Ages for the Acquisition of Different Structures May Be Identified. A characteristic age range may be identified for the acquisition of structures at any of the major levels specified by the theory, providing that children have been exposed to what might be termed an "optimal environment."

Postulates That Extend the Classic Piagetian System

The following postulates are ones that were not just retained, but refined and extended, by neo-Piagetian theorists.

B1. Development and Learning Must be Distinguished. Like Baldwin (1894) before him, Piaget made a distinction between development, which was said to involve a transformation or "accommodation" of a child's existing structural framework, and learning, which was said to involve the assimilation of new content to an existing structural framework (although some more minor accommodation of the framework may be necessary for this to take place). Virtually all neo-Piagetian theorists maintained some sort of distinction of this sort, and sought to explicate the processes which underlie each form of change. Thus, for example, Fischer (1980) distinguished the process of "intercoordination," which is subject to very strong developmental constraints and which can lead to a major change in children's level of cognitive functioning, from processes such as differentiation, refocusing, and chaining, which do not appear to be subject to such strong developmental constraints, and which lead instead to a greater degree of elaboration or complexity *within* an existing structural level.

Pascual–Leone (1969, 1988a), who is generally regarded as the founder of the neo-Piagetian movement, focused on the different way in which attention is involved in these two general classes of transformation. When engaged in major structural reorganization, Pascual–Leone suggested that children must actively inhibit the application of a current logical structure (L). At the same time, they must assemble a new structure, by bringing a new set of schemes to full activation and coordinating them, via mental effort (M). He called this attention-driven learning Logical or LM learning, and asserted that it is strongly dependent on development. In the second type of structural change, which does not involve this sort of focused mental effort, Pascual–Leone assumed that children merely need to apply an existing logical structure repeatedly to a variety of situations, and that this repeated activation itself will cause the existing structure to differentiate, and to incorporate new "cues" (C) in its releasing components. He called this second process LC-learning, and associated it with learning rather than development.

In the context of my own system (Case, 1985), a distinction was made between processes such as problem solving and exploration on the one hand, and processes such as consolidation and automatization on the other. The former sort of processes were presumed to lead to the formation of new cognitive structures, as existing schemes are coordinated into new patterns, via an attentionally mediated and often socially directed set of mental steps. The second set of processes were presumed to lead to the formation of stronger associations or cues among existing structural units, with the result that they can be activated more automatically. Finally it was suggested that—in order for development to take place smoothly—both sets of processes must always be at work. That is to say, the initial change in children's structures that takes place during stage transition, as a result of independent or socially facilitated exploration and problem solving, must necessarily be followed by a process in which the new structure is consolidated and automated via repeated application. Otherwise, further developmental progress is unlikely to take place.

To the reader who is unfamiliar with neo-Piagetian theory, the foregoing descriptions may appear somewhat dense. Only three points need be recognized, however, at this juncture: (a) most neo-Piagetian theories contain distinctions that derive from Piaget's original contrast between development and learning; (b) the various proposals, while different, are nonetheless compatible with each other (see also Halford, 1982; Mounoud, 1986); and (c) most of the proposals utilize the reformulated distinction they propose as a springboard from which to launch a more detailed account of the stage transition process.

B2. Developmental Restructuring Is Not System-Wide in Nature. A second neo-Piagetian notion that involves an extension of the classic

Piagetian position is actually one on which Piaget's position evolved over the years. In his best-known work, which was done in his middle years, Piaget spoke of the processes of structural transformation as though they operated on the entire system of structures in the child's repertoire (the "structure of the whole"). In his later work, however, he suggested that such processes operate on one particular class or subgroup of structures at a time (Piaget, 1985). It is this latter position that has been adopted by neo-Piagetian theorists. Thus, whether they characterize the process of development as one that entails the intercoordination of lower-level skills (Fischer, 1980), attentionally driven (LM) learning (Pascual–Leone, 1988a), or problem solving and exploration (Case, 1985), most neo-Piagetian theorists are quite explicit in asserting that the process which drives these activities operates on a small subset of schemas at a time, not on the child's entire structural repertoire. As will be indicated in the next section, they have also provided specific examples that are worked out in considerable detail, as to how these processes might actually unfold in particular physical and social contexts.

B3. A Cyclical Recapitulation of Structural Sequences May Be Identified. A third notion of Piaget's that neo-Piagetian theorists extended was the idea that there is a cyclical recursion through substages at each general stage or level of development. Once again, although this notion does exist within the classic Piagetian system (where it goes by the name of "vertical displacement" or "vertical décalage"), it is relatively undeveloped. In the context of several neo-Piagetian theories, however, the notion has been considerably strengthened, and stated in a much more stringent form. The suggestion is that there is a progression through exactly the same *number* of structural steps at each major stage, and that these steps are traversed in exactly the same *sequence* (Biggs & Collis, 1982; Case, 1978, 1985; Fischer, 1980; Mounoud, 1986).[4]

Postulates That Alter the Classic Piagetian System

The final group of neo-Piagetian postulates are ones that required a genuine alteration, rather than simply an extension, of the classic Piagetian system.

C1. Cognitive Structures Must be Redefined. In most neo-Piagetian systems, children's cognitive structures are not defined in terms that involve symbolic logic. Rather, they are defined in terms of their form, complexity, and level of hierarchical integration. This apparently simple shift in conceptualization has a number of far-reaching consequences. One conse-

---

[4] Pascual–Leone has made no commitment to this proposition; however, he has suggested that, if true, the proposition is not inconsistent with his system (Pascual–Leone, 1986).

quence is that the formal structures of Western science and mathematics (e.g., those structures that involve the partitioning of the world into variables, which are then systematically manipulated and controlled), can be seen as cultural inventions, not as universals. Another implication is that other structures, such as those involved in the visual arts or in social analysis, can be seen as playing a role in children's development that is just as important as that played by structures of a logical and mathematical nature. A third consequence is that sociocultural processes and institutions can be seen as playing a vital role in promoting children's development, particularly at higher stages. Finally, a fourth consequence is that adult thought in other cultures can be seen as different from, yet every bit as sophisticated as, that which is exhibited in the West.

C2. There Is a Shifting Upper Limit on the Complexity of Children's Cognitive Structures. There is a potential contradiction between two of the groups of postulates that have been mentioned so far: namely, those dealing with generality and those dealing with cultural, contextual, or individual specificity. On the one hand, the new forms of structural analysis that were proposed are more broadly applicable than Piaget's, and thus more general. They also yield similar age norms to those that Piaget proposed, across an even wider range of domains. On the other hand, the processes of structural transformation are held to apply more locally, and thus to be capable of yielding considerable unevenness or "displacement" in children's measured level of development. How can development simultaneously be seen as more general *and* more specific than Piaget's system implies? Stated differently, if the processes of structural transformation are of genuinely local applicability, why is there any typical age of acquisition across different sorts of cognitive structure at all?

In answer to this question, neo-Piagetian theorists have proposed a distinction between general processes which *constrain* and/or *potentiate* development, and more specific processes that operate *within* these general constraints and potentials. Although the processes of structural transformation are held to operate quite locally, and thus to give rise to considerable variation in measured developmental level, they are also presumed to be constrained by a shifting upper limit in the level at which children can function. This general constraint is seen as restricting the amount of variation that is observed in many situations, by introducing a rather literal "ceiling effect." A "floor" effect is often presumed as well, due to the fact that certain aspects of children's experience are universal (e.g., exposure to some form of caretaker, to some form of language, to some form of motor opportunity, and to some form of cultural training).

C3. Maturation Plays a Strong Role in Determining the Upper Limit on Working Memory. A third postulate held in common among most neo-Piagetian theorists is that there are specifiable biological factors that regulate the gradual shift in this upper limit. Although different theorists talk about these biological factors in different ways, their proposals are once again compatible, and quite unified in the overall view that they provide (see, for example, Case, 1985, chap. 17; in press-b; Fischer, 1987; Mounoud, 1986; Pascual–Leone, 1974, 1989a).

C4. The Attentional System Plays a Strong Role in Determining This Upper Limit.   Following the lead of Pascual–Leone (1969), and to a lesser extent McLaughlin (1963)[5] most neo-Piagetian theorists have assumed that the child's attentional capacity, or "working memory" is one of the major constraining factors on children's developing cognition: That is, attention is one of the major factors that is subject to this sort of biological influence.

C5. Individual Differences Must Be Considered Before a Full Picture of Development Is Possible.   A final proposition to which most (though perhaps not all) neo-Piagetian theorists ascribe is that individual differences play a critical role in determining the particular use to which children put their working memory, and the particular developmental pathways that their thinking follows (Case, 1992; Demetriou & Efklides, 1988; Fischer & Knight, in press; Lautrey, DeRibaupierre, & Rieben, 1987; Pascual–Leone, 1969, 1974).

Beyond the foregoing sets of propositions, different neo-Piagetian theories have diverged considerably, in accordance with the theoretical predilections of their developers. All neo-Piagetian theorists have included at least some further element from Piaget's system in their own theories, and imported other elements from elsewhere. However, the particular elements that they have retained and imported have varied widely. A detailed presentation of these differences is beyond the scope of this chapter. However, just to give a flavor of their nature, it is perhaps worthwhile to mention that certain neo-Piagetian theorists have attempted to preserve and elaborate on Piaget's notions of conflict and equilibration (Pascual–Leone, 1988a), while others have emphasized the search for consistency and reflexive abstraction (Halford, 1988; Halford & Wilson, 1980), and still others have emphasized the notions of differentiation and coordination (Case, 1988b; Fischer & Ferrar, in press). Taking off from these different points in the classic Piagetian system, then, each of the theorists cited here has worked out a detailed set of propositions concerning the nature of children's cognitive structures at different ages, and the way in which these structures are transformed, as children move from one stage or level in their development to the next.

---

[5] McLaughlin's (1963) work appears to have had the greatest influence on Halford, who used the STM values proposed by McLaughlin in his own work.

THE IMPORTANCE OF TASK ANALYSIS IN THE
NEO-PIAGETIAN RESEARCH PROGRAM

As was indicated in the previous section, most neo-Piagetian theorists place a much stronger emphasis than Piaget on the role of exogenous factors in development. They also explain the general factor in development by appeal to children's attentional or "information-processing capacity," rather than by postulating a "structure of the whole." For both these reasons, they also place a much heavier emphasis on task analysis. That is to say, they place a much greater emphasis on analyzing (a) the features of external situations that influence children's performance, (b) the goals and strategies that children adopt when they are placed in these situations, and (c) the information load that their strategies entail.

A full explication of the various systems for task analysis that have been developed by neo-Piagetian theorists would be beyond the scope of the present chapter. However, it is important to provide at least one or two examples of such analyses. As Lakatos (1962) has demonstrated, no general theory can ever be tested directly. It can only be tested in conjunction with detailed theoretical analyses of the particular phenomena that it is invoked to explain. In the case of neo-Piagetian theory, this means that none of the general propositions in the previous section can be tested directly, until a detailed analysis has been conducted of the particular situations to which the propositions are believed to apply. As will seen, these "task analyses" are in fact theoretical models in their own right, which contain their own set of postulates and simplifying assumptions.

One task that has been analyzed quite extensively, both by neo-Piagetians and by others, is Inhelder and Piaget's (1958) classic Balance Beam problem. As Siegler (1978) has demonstrated, many 6-year-olds, when asked which side of a balance will go down, respond to the question as though they were employing a rule of the form: "compute the number of weights on each side, and predict that the side with the greater number of weights will go down." By contrast, many 8-year-olds respond as though they were applying a rule with an additional feature in it: "take account of the distance of each weight from the fulcrum, whenever the number of weights on each side of the balance is equal."

In the context of classical Piagetian theory, the way in which 6-year-olds think about this problem might be explained by pointing out that this is the age at which a "logic of functions" first appears (Piaget, Grize, Szeminska, & Bang, 1977). In effect, by this age, children understand that any quantitative variable, X (in this case, the tilt of the balance), can be a direct function of another variable, Y (in this case the weight that is placed on each side). Their reasoning thus has the general form $X = f(Y)$. As we have seen, however, the notion that children's thinking can be explained in terms of a universal sequence of logical forms has certain attendant problems. How then, might this situation be modeled within the context of neo-Piagetian theory? One possible answer to this question has been provided by Furman (1981), who analyzed the Balance Beam task from the perspective of Pascual–Leone's theory. Furman's analysis of the 6-year-old strategy was as follows.

Step 1.   When children are asked the question as to which side will go down, their first step is to look at the visual display (which, let us say, has five weights on one side and four on the other), and to activate a scheme that they first acquired during the sensorimotor period, namely, that different perceptual conditions imply different actions or effects. The scheme representing this knowledge then functions as an "executive," which directs their further processing of the display, and leads them to note that the two sides do not look identical. The consequence of this perception is that the children come to the conclusion that one side or the other is likely to tilt down, because the display is not a symmetrical one. The mental activities that lead to this conclusion may be symbolized as follows:

$$M (\epsilon_1, \phi c - e, \{\phi \text{ display}\}) \relbar\joinrel\relbar\joinrel\rightarrow \phi \text{ tip}) [M:\text{demand } e + 1]$$

In this notation, ϵ stands for the child's executive scheme, which at this point is merely a representation of the instructions, $\phi^1 c - e$ stands for the sensorimotor scheme representing the knowledge that different conditions have different effects, and $\{\phi \text{ display}\}$ stands for the perceptual scheme representing the (asymmetrical) display. The regular brackets outside the entire set of symbols are meant to indicate that the children direct their mental attention (M) to the schemes within them, while the arrow indicates that a conclusion results from the overall attentional act. In this case, the conclusion is that the beam will tip to one side, which is represented by the symbol ϕ tip. The curly brackets around the display symbol indicate that this scheme is exempt from mental effort, since it is activated directly by the perceptual field. Thus the M-demand is e (the effort required to maintain the executive), plus 1 the effort required to maintain the scheme $\phi c - e$ in an active state.

Step 2.   Several milliseconds later, the expectation that is formed at the first step, namely that one side will tip down, serves to activate the child's sensorimotor knowledge that weight is relevant to the problem (since weight affects tipping, another item of sensorimotor knowledge). The same scheme also serves to direct a careful inspection of one particular side of the balance (let us say the left side), in order to obtain an estimate of its weight. Since size is the only variable that can actually be estimated visually, what results is an estimate of this variable, which is assumed to be functionally equivalent to weight. The correspondence of size and weight under most circumstances is another item of knowledge demonstrably in the repertoire of young children, as early as the sensorimotor period. Given that these items of knowledge are available, the second step in children's thinking might be formalized as follows.

$$M(\epsilon\phi \text{ tip}, \phi w \text{ (size)}, \{\phi sL\}) \text{ ----}\rightarrow \phi \text{ w(sL) [M-demand } e + 1]$$

In the foregoing notation, the general conventions are the same. The symbol, ϕ tip, represents the result that was generated in the previous step, and that is presumed to require continued activation, in order to be remembered and used at this step, where it now functions as the executive. The new scheme in the curly brackets $\{\phi sL\}$, is the one that represents the size of the 5-unit weight on the left side. The conclusion is an estimate of the size (and therefore weight) of the left-hand side, which is indicated to the right of the arrow with the symbol, ϕ w(sL). The M-demand remains at $e + 1$.

Step 3.   Now that subjects have estimated the size of the weight on the left, they continue to maintain this estimated magnitude in their field of attention, while they shift their eyes to the right and estimate the size (and hence weight) of the stack of weights on the right-hand side. If the subject cannot be certain of the results via visual inspection, he or she may count the number of units that are involved. Assuming that a careful visual inspection will yield the correct answer, however, careful gazing at the size of the stack $\{\phi sR\}$, to evaluate its weight is all that is necessary. The new mental act may be symbolized as follows.

$$M(\epsilon\phi \text{ tip}, \phi \text{ w(sL)}, \phi \text{ w(size)}, \{\phi sR\} \text{ ----}\rightarrow \phi \text{ w(sR) [M-demand } e + 2]$$

The entries in regular brackets, which continue to represent the contents of the subject's field of attention, now contain the expectation that one side will tilt, ϕ tip, coupled with an estimate of the size (and hence weight) of the left side. The actual operation that is occurring appears next, and is represented in the same fashion as in the previous step, as ϕ *w(size)* $\{\phi sR\}$. Since the appearance of the right-hand side is perceptually facilitated (hence the curly brackets), mental attention is only needed to activate the actual size estimator. The result of this estimation again appears to the right of the arrow, ϕ w(sR). The total M-demand is now e (to maintain the tipping executive in mind) + 2.

Step 4.   With the weight (via size, or number if need be) of each side now estimated, the subject next compares these two estimates, to determine which is larger. The actual operation may involve a rapid visual scanning back and forth. In any case, the mental step requires, as a minimum, a comparison operator $(\psi^6\ COMPARE)$, and the two size estimates, only one of which can be perceptually facilitated at a time. The comparison operation may be represented as follows:

M (ϕ tip, *COMPARE,* ϕ *w(wL)*, {ϕ w(sR)) -→ ϕwL heavier
[M-demand: $e + 2$]

The conclusion from this mental act, (which appears immediately to the right of the arrow), is that the weight on the left-hand side is heavier (ϕwL heavier). The M-demand remains the same, namely $e + 2$.

Step 5.   At the final step, the subject simply applies a transformation-representing scheme (called a fluent in Pascual–Leone's system) about tipping to the conclusion generated in the previous step, namely, that the left side is heavier. This transformation representing scheme is more primitive than the one being constructed, and so it is safe to assume its existence at this level of development (though Furman's pilot data prior to her analysis were available to support this assumption, as do other empirical data: e.g., Liu, 1981). The final mental act may therefore be represented as follows

M (ϕ tip, ϕ *TRANSF,* ϕ *wL heavier*) → ϕ tips left
[M-demand: $e + 2$]

Several testable conclusions may be drawn from the foregoing analysis, in conjunction with the general postulates of Pascual–Leone's theory (Case, 1974; Furman, 1981). The first and most obvious is that children with an M-power of $e + 2$,[7] regardless of their age, should be able to deploy the 6-year-old strategy, while those with a lower M-power should not. A second conclusion is that slight changes in the perceptual configuration of the task should be capable of modifying children's performance. If the configuration were changed so that any of the schemes in the foregoing model could be activated by perceptual input, for example (as would be the case if differences in size were made highly salient), then children considerably younger than 5 should be able to pass the task, since the M-demand at steps 3, 4, and 5 would be lowered to $e + 1$. A third conclusion is that changes in children's experience should also make a big difference to their performance. If children are deprived of the physical experience that is necessary to learn how weight affects the operation of a balance, for example, they should not be able to use the 6-year-old strategy, even if they have the

---

[6] The symbol ψ is used in Pascual–Leone's system to stand for an operative scheme. The symbol ϕ is used to stand for a figurative scheme.

[7] In Pascual–Leone's system, an M-power of this value is normally, but not necessarily, acquired at the age of 6.

available M-power. Alternatively, if they are given training that enables them to "chunk together," any of the separate schemes used in the mental steps for which the M-demand of the task is highest, they should find the task easier, and the passing age for task should be reduced by 2 years.

The ability to test detailed predictions regarding the effects of perceptual, experiential, and training factors constitutes a considerable strength of Pascual–Leone's theory, and of neo-Piagetian theory in general. By the same token, however, the theoretical complexity that such analyses involve also entails a number of drawbacks. A drawback on which many investigators have focused is the multiplicity of analyses that could be developed for any given task, and the consequent inability to defend any one particular analysis as the "correct" one, without a great deal of additional supporting evidence (Flavell, 1984). While this is an accurate assessment, it is not an assessment that applies uniquely to the neo-Piagetian analysis. The problem also occurs in Cognitive Science more generally, whenever a detailed attempt is made to explicate the information that subjects already possess, and the manner in which they access and transform it, in order to arrive at a solution to a novel task. Although there are some difficulties that are unique to the dilemma of parsing a task in such a fashion that a quantitative estimate of mental load can be generated, the general form of the problem remains the same. As a partial resolution to this difficulty, both Pascual–Leone and I have specified a detailed set of heuristics that can be used, in order to guide the process of task analysis (Furman, 1983, Appendix A; Case, 1974). The fact remains, however, that — just as children are capable of processing any task in more than one way — so investigators will also be capable of generating more than one model of their processing. The details of these models, and the background assumptions on which they are based, must therefore form a part of the network of predictions that are tested, in conjunction with the postulates of the general theory.

A second drawback of the foregoing sort of analysis is the length of time that it takes to develop, and to explicate. To cope with this second difficulty, I myself have developed a more compact form of task analysis, which is illustrated in Fig. 4.1. What the figure is meant to indicate is the general flow of mental events that take place as 6- and 8-year-old children focus on particular aspects of the balance beam, set themselves goals that these features occasion, and then execute a set of operations by which these goals may be realized. Within this system, the M-demand of a task can be shown to be equal to the number of goals that need be held in mind, prior to the development of a particular strategy. Thus, in the two strategies modeled, the M-demands are $e + 2$ and $e + 3$, values that accord with Pascual-Leone and Furman's (1983) analysis.

One drawback of the more compact form of analysis in Fig. 4.1 is that it can only be applied to tasks where no strong misleading or facilitating

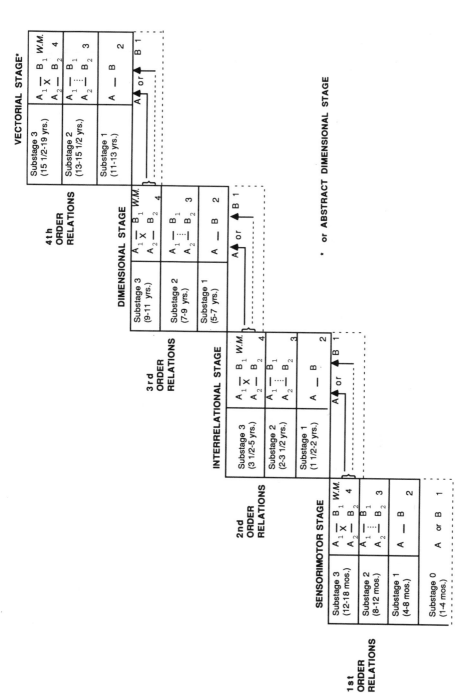

FIG. 4.1 Control structure for solving balance beam problem at two different age groups.

perceptual features are present, which restricts the utility of the analysis considerably. On the other hand, in those situations where it *can* be applied, it normally yields the same general conclusions regarding working memory load as Pascual-Leone's. Moreover it offers other advantages, which compensate for its less detailed nature, and its failure to represent perceptual effects. One of these is that it parses children's thinking into those aspects which represent the external situation, and those that represent their own goals, in a visually convenient fashion. Another is that it allows one to compare the content and structure of these features across multiple age levels, at a glance, which can lead to interesting predictions. For example, when I conducted an analysis on the full range of tasks for which detailed developmental data were available at the time (Case, 1985), what emerged was the hypothesis that the working memory demand of tasks went from one to four units within each of Piaget's classical stages, as children moved from responses that indicated no evidence of a general structure of the sort with which Piaget was concerned, to those that were normally taken as indicating possession of the structure in its full blown from.

A final use to which the analysis in Fig. 4.1 can be put is as a jumping off point toward an analysis of a more global sort. In the 6-year-old example, the general structure of children's executive control structures can be re-represented as two components: a first component (A) that is responsible for setting the overall goal and drawing a conclusion about weight and tilt, and a second component (B) that is responsible for determining relative weight, by determining relative numerosity. If one represents the coordination of these two components with a straight line, then one can assert that the global structure underlying the 6-year-old response is A–B, the global structure underlying the 4-year-old response is A or B (since they can perform either component in isolation), and the global structure underlying 8-year-old responses is $A_1 - B_1 --- A_2 - B_2$. (since 8-year-olds focus on both weight and distance). Finally, the structure underlying 10-year-old thought may be represented $A1 - B1 \times A2 - B2$, where the X stands for the new procedure used by 10-year-olds (addition or subtraction) for making tradeoffs between the two dimensions.

When these more global analyses were conducted at each age and working memory level for which balance beam data were available (or could be generated), the overall structure that emerged is the one indicated in Fig. 4.2 (Case, 1985). This more global analysis permits a bridge to be built between detailed process analyses such as Pascual-Leone's, and structural or neostructural analyses such as Piaget's, Fischer's, or Halford's. One point of contact is that, as in Piaget's theory, the hallmark of stage attainment at any level are such features as reversibility and compensation, which the notation $A_1 - B_1 \times A_2 - B_2$ is meant to capture. A second point of contact is that, as with Halford's theory, four stages emerge, with each

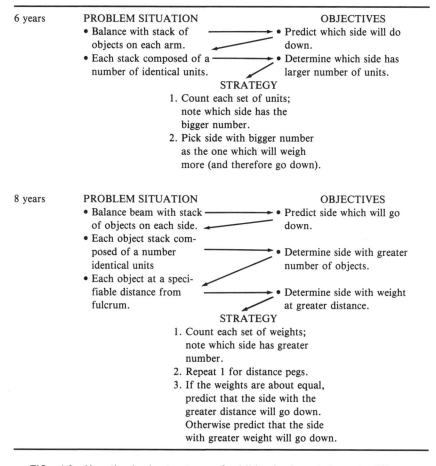

FIG. 4.2 Hypothesized structure of children's knowledge at different stages and substages of development.

treating relations of a higher order (the ages are also the same as in Halford's theory). Finally, a third point of contact is that, as suggested by Fischer's skill theory, the progression of control structures within any stage has a recursive quality. On the basis of any formal progression at one stage, therefore, it should be possible to make predictions about parallel progressions in the same content domain at earlier or later stages — this is another interesting (and novel) form of prediction.

In recent years, I have become interested in the conceptual structures that permit children to assemble control structures of the sort indicated in Fig. 4.1, since as it turns out, the same conception underlies children's responses to a far wider variety of tasks than just the balance beam. The sort of structure I have hypothesized as underlying 6-year-old thought on these tasks is the one indicated in Fig. 4.3. I will come back to this structure in later sections, and its possible significance for the development of neo-Piagetian theory. For the moment, however, I simply note that the structure in the figure constitutes one additional way of analyzing an aspect of children's response to the balance beam in the context of neo-Piagetian theory, which yields its own way of viewing the logic of functions, and its own set of predictions.

In summary, if one considers the task analyses that have been presented in this section as a group, the following general points may be made: (a) some form of task analysis is necessary, before any empirical predictions can be made on the basis of the general neo-Piagetian postulates summarized in the previous section; (b) any task analysis really constitutes a theoretical model (albeit, a rather detailed one), which entails its own set of postulates and background assumptions; (c) the different forms of task analysis that have been used by different neo-Piagetian theorists are not incompatible; to the contrary, they are complementary, as each explicates a somewhat different aspect of children's cognitive processing; (d) although there is some overlap between the different sorts of analysis (and the theories with which they have been associated) each form of analysis has its own unique strengths, and is best suited for making a particular sort of prediction.

VALIDATING RESEARCH

The following is a brief summary of the studies they have been conducted, once task analyses of the sort described in the previous section have been conducted.

As might be expected, a good number of empirical studies have been conducted to demonstrate that children's M-power or working memory grows in the fashion that is suggested by neo-Piagetian theorists (Postulate C4). Early investigators concentrated on designing new measures of this construct, using a variety of different forms of content, and predicting the absolute level of attainment children would exhibit at different ages, under conditions where attempts were made to rule out the influence of such confounding variables as chunking and mnemonic strategies (Burtis, 1982; Case, 1972, 1985, chap. 14; DeRibaupierre, Neyrack, & Spira, 1989; Parkinson, 1969, 1975; Pascual-Leone, 1970). As predicted by Pascual--Leone's theory, a linear increases in this variable was often found, particularly from age 6 to 10. In more recent studies, an attempt has been made to demonstrate the recursive set of increases in different sorts of memory capacity, which is suggested by my own and Fischer's theories.

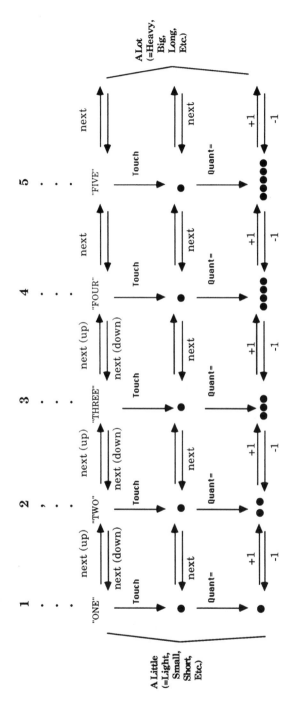

FIG. 4.3 Cognitive structure underlying 6-year-old's numerical understanding. Dotted lines indicate "optional" (i.e., nonuniversal) notational knowledge.

These studies, too, have met a considerable measure of success (see Case, 1985, chap. 12).

A second set of studies has been designed to show that the new theories, coupled with the new forms of task analysis that they introduce, can also be used to predict the sequence of developmental attainments on novel developmental tasks that are not primarily memorial in nature. The new tasks that have been developed include new tests of children's motor capabilities (Reid, 1992; Todor, 1979), their spatial capabilities, (Dennis, 1992; Morra, Moizo, & Scopesi, 1986; Halford & MacDonald, 1977), their language (Body, 1977; Case & McKeough, 1990; Johnson, Fabian, & Pascual-Leone, 1989; Johnson & Pascual-Leone, in press), and their social behavior (Bruchowsky, 1992; Fischer, Hand, et al., 1984). Novel tests of a more classic logicomathematical nature have also been designed, both for concrete operational tasks (Case, 1972; Halford, 1982; Parkinson, 1975; Pascual-Leone & Smith, 1969) and those involving formal operations (DeRibeaupierre & Pascual-Leone, 1984; Scardamalia, 1977). Finally, studies have been designed not only to demonstrate developmental changes in task performance as a function of task complexity (which all the new forms of task analysis predict), but also recursive cycles in this progression, (See Figure 4.3). These studies, too, have been successful (Bruchowsky, 1992; Case, 1985, chap. 6; Reid, 1992).

Most of the foregoing studies have used cross-sectional designs. The need for longitudinal studies has also been stressed, however, (DeRibaupierre, 1989) and several studies of this sort have already been conducted, (Goodman, 1979; Leitner, 1990; Lewis, 1989).

A third sort of study has been concerned with demonstrating the hypothesized relationship between the growth of working memory and the ability to cope with progressively more complex cognitive demands. The earliest studies in this class correlated working memory size and structural attainment within age cohorts, partialing out any residual age effects statistically (e.g., Case, 1985; Chapman, 1989; DeRibaupierre & Pascual--Leone, 1984; Groenwig, 1983; Halford, Bain, & Mayberry, 1982; McKeough, 1992; Pascual-Leone, 1988a). Other studies were designed in which children of the same age but different working memory capacities were selected for training, and predictions regarding their learning tested (Case, 1974; Daneman & Case, 1981; Scardamalia, 1977; Watson, 1984, cited in Case, 1985, chap. 14, p. 337).

For obvious reasons, the neurological/maturational factors (C3) that were postulated by neo-Piagetian theorists were not investigated as thoroughly or directly in the first studies that were designed to test their position. However, indirect evidence for some sort maturational implication in working-memory growth was acquired, by showing that children's functional working memory increases in response to practice in a fashion that is directly proportional to the speed of their processing (Case, Kurland, & Goldberg, 1982), but reaches different asymptotes at different ages, under conditions of maximum practice (Kurland, 1981). In addition, in recent years, evidence of a more direct sort has also been gathered (see the following section).

Two general categories of study have been conducted, in an attempt to show the power of neo-Piagetian theory to clarify the nature of individual differences in development.

The first sort of study attempted to show that neo-Piagetian theory can help explicate the manner in which children's cognitive development differs as a function of their particular biological or social circumstances. For upper-middle-class children suffering from congenital retardation, the general finding was that M-power and working memory develop at a slower rate than for other children, and reach a different terminal level, as does speed or operational efficiency (Rich, 1979, 1982). For any given level of speed and working memory, however, assessed developmental level remains predictable from neo-Piagetian theory. For children who do not come from Western, mainstream, high SES backgrounds, the findings were quite different. Here it was shown that measures of children's performance that entail a strong cultural learning component (including "standard" Piagetian measures), are likely to slow delay, but those that tap the development of working memory do not (Bentley, Kvalsvig, & Miller, 1990; Case, 1975; Globerson, 1983; M. Miller & Pascual–Leone, 1981; R. Miller, Pascual-–Leone, Campbell, & Juckes, 1990). This is of course what one would expect, if the neo-Piagetian differentiation between learning and development is a valid one. Finally, for children classified as "gifted," it has been shown that the rate of development is not exceptional, as measured either by tests of speed and working memory, or by more general structural assessment. What is exceptional is the children's ability to learn newmaterial *within* a developmental level (Fischer & Canfield, 1986; Globerson, 1983; Porath, 1992).

The second sort of study in the fifth category has been concerned with differences in cognitive style, and has been conducted primarily within the context of Pascual–Leone's theory. Recall that particular attention is paid in this theory to perceptual effects, and individual response to them. As a consequence, the cognitive style of field independence (and to a lesser extent, adaptive flexibility) has received particular attention. The hypothesis that individual differences in field independence should be related to children's performance on cognitive developmental tasks has been evaluated in an number of ways. In an early study, Pascual–Leone predicted the complete factorial pattern in a battery of some 40 tests of cognitive style, cognitive development, and intelligence: a considerable achievement (Pascual–Leone, 1969). In subsequent studies, he and his colleagues predicted different patterns of performance on a variety of cognitive–developmental tasks, both before and after learning, as a function of this same variable. Others also predicted the relationship of this variable and measures of working memory, mental effort, and learning (e.g., Case, 1974; Case & Globerson, 1974; Globerson, 1983, 1985; Globerson, Weinstein, & Sharabany, in press; Goodman, 1971; Parkinson, 1961, 1969; Pascual–Leone, 1989).

The foregoing studies have gone a considerable way toward answering a methodological charge that was leveled against classical Piagetian theory by empiricist scholars, and which was not mentioned in the introduction, namely, the difficulty of testing the assertions of Piagetian theory empirically, via hypotheticodeductive experiments. Of course, to say that neo-Piagetian theory has been responsive to this critique is not to say that it can as yet meet all the criteria that its critics would like. As Flavell (1984) and DeRibaupierre et al. (1989) have pointed out, for example, there are still serious problems in defining the units of working memory, and in determining how many of them are necessary to execute any given cognitive strategy. In addition, the battle as to whether development can be reduced to cumulative learning is by no means over, in spite of the attempt of neo-Piagetian theorists to define each sort of factor in a more precise fashion (see, for example, Chi & Rees, 1983; Klahr, 1988; Rumelhart & McLelland, 1987).

Notwithstanding the continuing debate between the two traditions, it seems clear that neo-Piagetian theory has come a considerable distance in responding to both the methodological and substantive aspects of the empiricist critique.

CURRENT THEORETICAL AND EMPIRICAL DIRECTIONS

Three of the most important elements that neo-Piagetian theorists introduced into the classic Piagetian system were (a) a method of analyzing the level and complexity of children's thought that is independent of its content, but which—unlike Piaget's method—does not rely on symbolic logic for doing so (Postulate C1); (b) the suggestion that each structure is constructed independently of each other structure, but that all structures are subject to a common general constraint: namely, that imposed by the attentional system (Postulates B1, C2–C4); and (c) the suggestion that there is a cyclical recursion in the process of structural assembly, at each major stage of development (Postulate B3). In the present section, I describe several lines of work that are being pursued, in an attempt to explore the implications of these new features.

Individual Differences in Intellectual Development

As long as children's internal structures are viewed as "structures of the whole," or as constituents of such structures, it is difficult to relate the study of intellectual development to the study of individual differences in cognitive functioning. All that one has is a single general dimension along which to chart children's progress. Once one reconstrues development as a series of constructions that are essentially independent, however (even though they are subject to a common general-developmental constraint) then one can imagine children's thinking as proceeding along any number of dimensions simultaneously. One can also explore the possibility (a) that each individual might have a unique developmental "profile" when their level of functioning was examined across these dimensions; or (b) that certain prototypical profiles may emerge across these dimensions, as a result of children's upbringing, talent, cognitive style, and so on. Finally, one can analyze any such patterns as may emerge empirically, using the methods of hierarchical scaling, coupled with some form of factor analysis.

As mentioned in the previous section, Pascual–Leone (1969) was the first person to adopt this general sort of theoretical and empirical approach. His original work focused on the cognitive styles of field independence/dependence and adaptive flexibility/inflexibility. In his more recent work, he has looked at the intersection of these two styles, hypothesizing that two sorts of field-independent subjects can be identified—namely, those who are flexible and those who are inflexible. Field-independent subjects who are rigid are predicted to respond in a fashion that is insensitive to field effects, even under situations where these can help them, while those who are flexible are predicted to alter their behavioral pattern of responding to the situation in an adaptive fashion.

A similar direction has been taken in the study of reflexivity/impulsivity. Drawing on the notion of an executive control structure (Case, 1985) Shafrir and Pascual–Leone (1990) have reinterpreted the classic style of reflectivity (Kagan, 1966; Shapiro, 1963) as the tendency to apply executive structures that are highly sensitive to errors. They have also suggested that reflective subjects, like those who are field-independent, may be subdivided into those who are flexible versus those who are rigid. Finally, on the basis of their theoretical analysis, they have developed a new empirical instrument for assessing reflectivity and have shown (a) that it avoids the pitfalls of earlier measures (Shafrir, 1991), and (b) that it reveals a pattern of functioning that remains constant across a wide range of cognitive situations (Shafrir, Ogilvie, & Bryson, 1990).

Utilizing a construct drawn from classical Piagetian theory, a group of neo-Piagetians in Europe has taken a similar general approach to that suggested by Pascual–Leone (Lautrey, DeRibaupierre, & Rieben, 1987;

Rieben, DeRibaupierre & Lautrey, 1983; 1990; Rieben & DeRibaupierre, 1986). The theoretical dimension in which these investigators have been interested is "digital" versus "analogical" processing, which certain theorists have suggested may be a fundamental one, possibly related to cerebral dominance. According to their (neo-Piagetian) analysis, individual differences on this dimension should lead to different developmental profiles on Piagetian tests of logical versus infralogical functioning. Among individuals those whose strength lies in analogical processing, "infralogical" functioning should develop before logical functioning, while for digital processors the reverse should be the case. Using a battery of classical Piagetian measures, and a form of analysis that combines the analysis of developmental levels with the factorial analysis of individual developmental patterns, they have found strong support for this suggestion.

In my own recent work, I have taken a similar approach with regard to the intellectual dimensions suggested by Gardner (1983). As a result of the task analyses described earlier, I hypothesized that children's functioning in the domains of quantitative, social, and spatial functioning may be underpinned by different "central conceptual structures." Within each of these domains, I proposed a progression of the sort indicated in Fig. 4.2. Using a variety of techniques, including factor analysis and instruction, my collaborators and I were able to slow that this does, in fact, appear to be the case (Case, Okamoto, Henderson, & McKeough, in press), with different individuals showing different forms of developmental profile.

In the context of Fischer's theory, a general axiom (following Lewin, 1935) is that behavior is a function of both the person and the environment. As DeRibaupierre and Dasen (1988) have pointed out, this general proposition does not indicate, a priori, what sort of dimensions of the environment or the person might be crucial. However, in his recent work, Fischer has used his theory to show that progress through his levels does take place at a different rates on different tasks, as a function of various individual difference variables. For example, children with different sorts of reading disability show different developmental profiles across tests of phonic versus semantic processing (Fischer & Knight, in press). In a similar vein, children with a history of child abuse and children with a history of shyness show a different pattern of development across tasks which ask them to act out nice versus mean themes, and integrate them (Fischer 1991).

Finally, Demetriou (1988) has administered a broad battery of Piagetian and neo-Piagetian tasks to children from a number of different age levels. Using an analytic approach that combines the analysis of developmental levels with the analysis of correlational patterns, he has extracted a number of different developmental factors, which he labels quantitative, imaginal--spatial, verbal--propositional, causal--experimental, and metacognitive--reflective. He has also developed a theoretical account of children's development along these different dimensions, using an interesting mix of constructs from classical psychometric theory, contemporary cognitive theory, and the neo-Piagetian theories summarized earlier (Demetriou, 1988).

Three common themes run through all the aforementioned studies. The first is that many of the classic psychometric "factors" also appear on developmental measures of intelligence. The second is that neo-Piagetian theory is useful in explicating these differences in a new manner. Finally, the third is that a bi-variate classification scheme, in which both stylistic and operational considerations are taken into account, appears necessary, in order to do full justice to the data. In this latter connection, it should be noted that the particular operational dimensions that are being investigated are also very similar across different groups of neo-Piagetian theorists.

Intellectual and Emotional Development

As long as children's internal structures are modeled exclusively in terms of symbolic logic, there are serious restrictions on the sort of analysis that can be conducted of children's emotional development. Either one can talk about each successive structure of development being "energized" by its own sort of affect (Piaget, 1981), or else one can talk about the sorts of situations in which children's emotions will "override" some particular logical form or another, such as syllogistic reasoning. Once one reconstrues development in an alogical fashion, however, it becomes possible to see that emotions are different from cognitions in certain ways, but are like them in many others, and thus subject to certain similar principles of development. This general idea is currently being explored by several different neo-Piagetian theorists. The position that they are developing may be summarized as follows.

Emotional responses are fundamental to the organization of children's behavior (Case, Hayward, Lewis, & Hurst, 1988; Fischer, Kenny, & Pipp, 1990; Pascual-Leone, 1988a 1991). As suggested by emotion theorists (e.g., Sherer, 1984), any emotional response has a number of closely integrated components. These include (a) a particular pattern of perceptual and/or cognitive releasers to which it is sensitive, (b) a change in arousal level and feeling state that it induces, (c) a set of general goals and motor tendencies that it primes in preparation for action, (d) a set of expressive gestures through which it signals this emerging preparedness and (e) a set of control structures which are designed to achieve this general class of goals in the various environments in which it habitually finds itself (Case et al, 1988; Fischer, Shaver, & Carnochan, 1990 Pascual-Leone 1991). At birth all the foregoing components are relatively diffuse and unintegrated. Thus, the emotions that children can experience are very limited in their range and content (e.g., positive emotions such as interest, neutral emotions such as "quiet content," and negative emotions such as distress). Like any other complex set of structures, however, emotional structures continue to become increasingly complex with age, and increasingly culturally specific (Case et al., 1988; Fischer, Shaver, & Carnochan, 1990; Pascual–Leone, 1991). Each culture also has its own rules concerning emotional display, and may provide direct or indirect instruction with regard to (a) whether those feelings are appropriate in various circumstances, and (b) how those feelings should be expressed (Fischer, Shaver, & Carnochan, 1990).

In and of themselves, the foregoing propositions are not distinctive. Indeed, they are very much in the spirit of contemporary cognitive theories in other traditions. What is distinctive about the neo-Piagetian position, however, is the proposition that the timetable with which the changes described takes place is not completely under cultural control, but rather — like any other set of developmental structures, it is subject to the general constraints imposed by the attentional system. Thus, the hypothesis is that emotional structures go through the same recursive pattern of cycles as other structures (see Fig. 4.2), and are subject to the same upper bounds (Case et al., 1988; Fischer, Shaver, & Carnochan, 1990). During the sensorimotor period, for example, it is presumed that a set differentiated "primary" emotions are assembled (e.g., anger, joy, fear, and sadness) whose complexity is similar to other sensorimotor attainments. More complex emotions (e.g., jealousy) emerge during next major stage of development for the same reason (Case et al., 1988; Fischer, Shaver, & Carnochan, 1990). Whether or not more sophisticated emotional complexes still will prove amenable to this same sort of analysis remains to be seen. However, the prospect is certainly an intriguing one.

Socio-Emotional Influences on Intellectual Development

A third line of work being conducted is closely related to the second. Once one has a means for analyzing the interplay between cognitive and emotional factors in children's development, it becomes possible to analyze the development of a class of structures that has its origins in children's positive and negative responses to their own caretakers, and which influences their emerging view of themselves, as well as the structures by which they protect themselves from inner or outer "assault." The analysis of such structures has traditionally been the exclusive province of clinical psychologists, or attachment theorists. Recently, however, several neo-Piagetian theorists have begun to take an interest in them. The following propositions are currently being explored.

As suggested both by attachment theorists (Bretherton & Waters, 1985;

Main, 1991) and object relations theorists (Kernberg, 1976; Klein, 1957; Weininger, 1984; Winnecott, 1965) children's early interaction with their primary caretakers elicits powerful emotions (Case et al., 1988; Fischer, Shaver, & Carnochan, 1990). Of particular importance are the structures for dealing with fear and/or anger. As suggested by "object relations theorists" (e.g., Klein, 1957; Winnecott, 1965; Kernberg, 1976; Weininger, 1984) children's structures for dealing with these feelings are difficult to integrate with those for dealing with more positive feelings such as joy or love. As a consequence, they can lead to "split" or "fragmented" representations of, and feelings for, the caretakers in question (Fischer & Pipp, 1984; Fischer, Shaver, & Carnochan, 1990). Under favorable social conditions, such structures become more integrated with age since, with each new stage and substage, children's capability for integrating disparate structures increases. Under less favorable situations they may remain split, and constitute the core elements for a set of structures of a defensive nature (Case, 1989, 1991b; Case et al., 1988; Fischer & Pipp, 1984). Such structures may protect the growing child from undue conflict and anxiety. However, they may also distort the child's view of the world, and prevent the child from fully enjoying certain kinds of intimate social relations, even in adulthood (Case, 1989, 1991b; Case et al., 1988). Such defensive structures exert a major impact on the developmental pathway that children follow, and likewise on the particular developmental profile they exhibit (Case, 1989; Case et al., 1988, 1988; Fischer & Pipp, 1984; Fischer, Shaver, & Carnochan, 1990). They may also influence the children's general level of intellectual attainment, or their cognitive style (Case, 1989; et al., 1988; Shafrir, 1991).

Once again, the foregoing propositions — at a general level — are very much in the spirit of the current *zeitgeist*. What gives them their distinctiveness, once again, is the potential they offer for conducting detailed task analyses of particular affective/cognitive structures, and the way in which these structures are transformed at each successive stage and substage of development (e.g., Case, 1991b; Noam, 1991).

Intellectual and Biological Development

Although Piaget acknowledged that children's development was subject to maturational influences (e.g., Piaget, 1964), the form of structural modeling he conducted did not permit him to suggest just how such maturational factors might have an impact on children's psychological structures or processes. Exactly what sort of neurological developments might be necessary, for example, in order for the INRC group to emerge, was a question that could not be posed in a meaningful fashion.

In the context of neo-Piagetian theory, the general factor in children's development is localized at least partly in the attentional system, whereas the more specific factors are localized at least partially in other systems of a more modular nature: for example, systems for constructing spatial, numerical, or social relations. Since both the attentional system and the more content-based systems are known to have neurological substrates that are topographically localized (the former in the frontal lobes, the latter in the posterior and inferior ones), it may become possible to be somewhat more specific in making suggestions about the biological underpinnings of cognitive development. The following propositions are currently being explored by investigators with an interest in this possibility.

Because the overall organization of the brain is hierarchical, and because higher levels are known to mature later than the early ones (Yakovlev & Lecours, 1967), it follows that the maturation of these later systems may constitute a precondition for children's intellectual development to take place at a normal rate, and in a normal fashion (Case, 1985; Pascual–Leone, 1988a).

Because the frontal and prefrontal systems of the cortex are known to be centrally implicated in the attentional functions that control novel behavior,[8] and because the structures that children assemble during their development are also novel, it follows that frontal lobe maturation may play an important role in children's intellectual development as well (Case, in press-b; Diamond, 1991; Fischer & Ferrar, in press; Menna, 1989; Pascual–Leone, 1988a, Pascual–Leone, Hamstra, Benson, Khan, & England, 1990). A related variable that may constrain and/or regulate the rate of children's intellectual development is the maturation of the nerve fibers that connect the frontal lobes to other regions (Fischer, 1987; Thatcher, in press).

Finally, because (a) the speed with which impulses can flow within or across different regions of the brain is dependent on a complex set of electrochemical and anatomical developments, including the deposit of myelin around long connecting fibers, and the number of dendritic connections which are available in a region, and because (b) speed of processing is one of the variables that has been cited as crucial by neo-Piagetian theorists as regulating the growth of attentional functions (Case, 1985; Kail, in press) it follows that these same sorts of changes may be promising places to look, in trying to determine what particular *sorts* of neurological changes are most likely to play the role of developmental potentiators, in the particular neurological systems that are of greatest interest (Case, 1985).

---

[8] These functions include the planning and sequential motor control that such novelty entails (Luria, 1976; Stuss,1988), and the maintenance of recently attended items of information in working memory while this planning takes place (Goldman–Rakic, 1989; Luria, 1979)

Intellectual Development in Adulthood

As long as development is construed in classic Piagetian terms, the suggestions that one can make about adult development are relatively limited. While it is clear that equilibration and reflexive abstraction are lifelong processes, it is not clear what sort of structure — if any — one could expect to build upon, and transform the logical structures of formal thought. Once development is modelled in the recursive fashion that has been suggested by neo-Piagetian theorists, however, and its ties to emotional and attentional factors specified, a number of interesting new possibilities emerge. Several propositions that are being explored are as follows:

1. Further structural progress in thought takes place during the adult years (Case, 1978, 1988b; Demetriou, 1988; Fischer, Kenny, & Pipp, 1990; Kitchener & Fischer, 1988).
2. This progress takes the form of one or more recursions through the same general sort of cycle as is traversed during childhood and adolescence (see Fig. 4.1; Case, 1978, 1988b, 1989; Kitchener & Fischer, 1988).
3. Movement within and across such cycles continues to be a function of the recursive differentiation, coordination, and integration of existing structures (Case, 1985; Fischer, 1980; Pascual–Leone, 1986, 1988b).
4. Somewhat paradoxically, the *decrement* in the power of attention that takes place between the ages of 35 to 40 may play the role of maturational potentiator that was formerly played by *increases* in the power of working memory at younger ages. The sort of decrement that has been hypothesized is in the power of working memory to prevent irrelevant intrusion into its contents or processes (Jedrzkiewicz, 1986; Pascual–Leone, 1986). Two possible side-effects of this decrement are (a) an increase in the potential range of structures that may be integrated, and (b) a failure of early defensive structures that were dependent on splitting or its derivatives (Pascual–Leone, 1988b).
5. This latter change opens up the opportunity for a restructuring of the subject's interpersonal and intrapsychic structures during their middle years, in a fashion that opens up new possibilities for a higher level of affective and cognitive integration (Pascual–Leone, 1988b).
6. When coupled with the active exercise of will, these new opportunities permit a certain wisdom about human affairs to develop that

would have been impossible at a younger age level (Pascual–Leone, 1988b).

POSSIBLE ADDITIONS OR REVISIONS

Reconceptualizing the Notion of a "Structure d'Ensemble"

As was mentioned in the introduction, Piaget's portrait of the young child was one that appeared too universal, too monolithic, and too endogenously regulated to do full justice to the empirical data: particularly the data on cross-cultural differences, intra-individual variability, and learning. While this emphasis has been corrected by neo-Piagetian theory, it is not clear that the new body of theory can as yet do full justice to the data of intra-individual *consistency* that has emerged across a broad range of subjects and cultures for certain groups of well-delimited tasks. An additional line of work along these lines offers a potential solution to this problem. The following propositions are being explored.

Although children tackle each problem situation that they encounter on its own merits, evolution has also endowed them with only five or six fundamentally different types of operation for doing so. Each of these operations has its own external "domain" to which it applies, and its own internal set of processing mechanisms by which it operates. The neurological systems that are responsible for conducting this processing correspond to the "modules" that have been identified by contemporary linguistic and neurological theorists (Fodor, 1982; Gardner, 1983).

At each stage and substage of their development, children assemble separate central conceptual structures that are relevant to each of these domains, and influence their further problem solving in them. The existence of these structures may be demonstrated empirically via a combination of developmental analysis and factor analysis (Demetriou & Efklides, 1988; Case, Okamoto, Henderson & McKeough in press), or training (Case & Griffin, 1990; Case & McKeough, 1990; Case & Sandieson, 1987). The theoretical nature of these structures may be explicated by a combination of developmental analysis and semantic modeling, of either a network (Case, 1991a) or a connectionist-(Halford, in press) sort.

Notwithstanding the modular nature of these structures, and the specificity of the operations by which they are constructed, their development remains subject to the general systemic constraints specified by neo-Piagetian theory, and therefore conforms—in its general semantic form—with the general structural progression indicated in the first figure (Case 1992; Halford, in press).

As these conceptual structures develop, children increasingly come to experience their external world as containing different "spheres" or "areas" (Demetriou & Efklides, 1988). Linguistic problems are thus experienced as having a character that is different from spatial problems, which in turn are experienced as having a different character from numerical or social problems, and so on (Case & Griffin, 1990; Case & McKeough, 1990; Case & Sandieson, 1987; Case et al., in press-a; Demetriou & Efklides, 1988; Shayer, Demetriou, & Perves, 1988).

As children develop, their interests, talents, and experience may combine to make their functioning in some of these areas more efficient than others. This is the source of the individual differences in "group factors," "specific intelligences," or "capacity spheres" that have been identified by psychometricians and other students of individual differences (Snow, Kyllonen, & Marshalek, 1984; Demetriou & Efklides, 1988; Gardner, 1983).

Reconceptualizing the Nature of Working Memory Limitations

A persistent problem with which neo-Piagetian theory has been concerned, from its inception, is the origin of the general-systemic developments on which it has focused. It has been suggested that changes in working memory are more easily seen as potentiating the quantitative changes that take place *within* developmental stages than the qualitative changes that take place *across* such stages (Biggs & Collis, 1982). It has also been suggested that the amount of variance that can be uniquely assigned to such changes is rather small (Halford & Mayberry, 1990). A final line of work that is being conducted is responsive to both these two suggestions. In a recent series of articles, Halford (in press) has suggested that the sort of quantitative capacity that is the most likely candidate for explaining transition across major stages is the number of constraints that can be satisfied by a massively "distributed" neurological system. He has also suggested that the number of constraints that must be satisfied, if the competencies of the four classic Piagetian stages are to be mastered, are 1, 2, 3, and 4 respectively. Halford's work is important not just in its own right, but because, like Pascual–Leone's early writings, it offers a potential connection to the new work on connectionism and the work on biological development that was described earlier. It also provides a good illustration of the wide range of approaches that neo-Piagetian theorists are currently considering, in their attempt to develop a more integrated view of human development. Although neoconnectionism is normally thought of as antithetical to structural theory—and indeed does depend on very different epistemological assumptions—it may well prove necessary to integrate some of these assumptions with structural ones if a deeper view of human development is to be attained (Pascual–Leone, 1969; Halford, in press; Case, 1992).

SUMMARY AND CONCLUSION

At the beginning of the present chapter, I pointed out that neo-Piagetian theory was born in response to the criticisms leveled at it by scholars from the empiricist and sociohistoric traditions, as well as criticisms that were formulated within the rationalist tradition itself. The principal empiricist criticisms were that the theory provided a view of children's development that was too monolithic, and too insensitive to external influences such as spontaneous learning or direct instruction. A related methodological criticism that was that the theory was too difficult to operationalize, and to test in a rigorous, hypotheticodeductive fashion. The principal rationalist criticisms were that the theory provided a view of the stage-transition process that was too global and incomplete, because it provided no account of performance factors or individual differences. Finally, the principal sociohistoric criticisms were that the theory provided a view of children's development that was too universal, and too focused on the subject rather than the cultural institutions in which the subject's life is embedded. A corollary was that the theory treated intellectual development as though it had no history, and only one natural endpoint: namely: the rational structures of Western scientific thought (Youniss & Damon in this volume).

The way in which the first two categories of criticism have been responded to by neo-Piagetian theorists will hopefully have been apparent, throughout the present chapter. Development is no longer seen as progressing through a single set of "structures of the whole," but as progressing along many fronts at once. The role of learning, perceptual factors, and individual differences can now also be modeled in considerable detail, as can the process of stage transition (see postulates B1, B2, C1–5). The way in which the theory has responded to the sociohistoric critique may be less obvious, however, and thus deserves a brief mention before concluding.

By abandoning the structures of Western logic as the principal form of modeling children's thought (Postulate C1) the neo-Piagetian approach opens up the way for considering Western logic as just one among many cultural inventions that children might re-create, in the course of their development. The new forms of modeling also open up the way for placing various forms of social and/or artistic endeavor—from any culture—on an equal footing with those of a more analytical nature, and for examining the historical evolution of any of these forms in a fashion that does not conflate the level of historical development of a system for representing the world (e.g., for rendering spatial perspective) with the level of intellectual activity that is required for applying or contributing to the evolution of that system.

By suggesting that social processes in general, and institutional processes that take place in the family or in school in particular, play a role which is of equal importance to more endogenous processes in promoting transition to higher levels of thought (see Postulate C5), the theory opens the way for explicating certain forms of individual and/or group difference, in a fashion that treats cultural and/or institutional life as more than an extraneous "variable," but as part and parcel of the developmental process itself (see Fiati, 1992; Case, 1991b).

By suggesting that development is a recursive process (Postulate B3), the theory at least potentially allows one to examine the possibility that children might encounter considerable internal conflict at the middle point of any stage, as they expand their representation to consider two elements, but do not yet know how to integrate them. This conflict might then be resolved toward the end of a stage, making the process of individual and social development parallel in a Hegelian sense, namely, that repeated cycles of conflict and conflict resolution might be expected (Case, 1988b).

Finally, in the detailed task analyses that it permits, indeed, requires, the theory opens up the way to understanding how certain specific intellectual tools that are cultural inventions (such as systems of enumeration), are acquired in a social and institutional context at one stage of development, but then function as independent tools of thought at the next (Case, 1985, chap. 19; Case & Threadgill-Sowder, 1990). This has long been a principal tenet of sociohistoric theory (Vygotksky, 1962), but has rarely played a central role, if it has featured at all, in the Piagetian tradition.

None of these four possibilities have been exploited fully. Nevertheless, they are at least present in the new body of theory. Moreover, as was suggested in the last section, there is at least some evidence that investigators are beginning to take advantage of them, and move in the directions that they permit (e.g. Fiati, in press). If neo-Piagetian theory does move in this direction, then it should ultimately become more congruent with, and perhaps even make some contribution to, sociohistoric theory (Case, 1988c), which holds that children only attain their full intellectual power once they have reconstructed the intellectual systems that are their cultural inheritance, and taken their place at the living tip of their culture.

In conclusion, neo-Piagetian theory is continuing to evolve in the same sort of dynamic historical context in which it had its original inception. That is to say, it is continuing to evolve in a way that is sensitive to internal problems or gaps in its present view of development, as well as problems stemming from alternative conceptions of the knowing process. While the theoretical structure that is emerging is relatively complex, the same may be said for the process of development itself. Thus, in and of itself, this should not counted as a mark against it. The ongoing dilemma that neo-Piagetian theorists will no doubt continue to face, however, is the one that they originally confronted at the beginning of their endeavor. Somehow or other, they will have to decide (a) Which postulates of their system are essential to explain the established empirical phenomena of child and adult development [and must therefore be retained]; (b) Which postulates are incomplete and must be further developed; and (c) Which new postulates must be added, in order to account for phenomena that have only recently been discovered. A final dilemma will be how to ensure that the entire process remains "progressive" (Lakatos, 1962); that is, that it proceeds in a fashion that preserves the simplicity and explanatory power of the original core theory, while guiding the search for new data and insights along productive pathways.

ACKNOWLEDGMENT

This chapter was prepared with support provided by the Spencer Foundation, whose assistance is gratefully acknowledged. The author would also like to thank Harry Beilin, Anik DeRibaupierre, Andreas Demetriou, Juan Pascual-Leone, and Peter Pufall for their comments on an earlier draft.

REFERENCES

Baldwin, J. M. (1894). Mental development in the child and in the race. New York: MacMillan

Beilin, H. (1971a). Developmental stages and developmental processes. In D. R. Green, M. P. Ford, & G. B. Flamer (Eds.), *Measurement and Piaget.* New York: McGraw-Hill.

Beilin, H. (1971b). The training and acquisition of logical operations. In M. F. Rosskopf, L. P. Steffe, & S. Taback (Eds.), *Piagetian cognitive-developmental research and mathematical education,* (pp. 81–124). Washington, DC: National Council of Teachers of Mathematics.

Beilin, H. (1983). The new functionalism and Piaget's program. In E. K. Scholnick (Ed.), *New trends in conceptual representation* (pp. 3–40). Hillsdale, NJ: Lawrence Erlbaum Associates.

Beilin, H. (1989). Piagetian theory. *Annals of Child Development, 6,* 85–131.

Bentley, A. M., Kvalsvig, J., & Miller, R. (1990). The cognitive consequences of poverty: A neo-Piagetian study with Zulu children. *Applied Cognitive Psychology, 4,* 451–459.

Biggs, J., & Collis, K. (1982). *Evaluating the quality of learning: The SOLO taxonomy.* New York: Academic Press.

Body, B. (1977). *Language development and cognitive development: A neo-Piagetian interpretation of before and after.* Unpublished doctoral dissertation, University of California, Berkeley.

Brainerd, C. J. (1978). The stage question in cognitive-developmental theory. *Behavioral and Brain Sciences, 1,* 173–182.

Bretherton, I., & Waters, E. (1985). Growing points of attachment theory and research. *Monographs of the Society for Research in Child Development, 50,* (1–2, Serial No. 209).

Bruchowsky, M. (1992). The development of empathic cognition in early and middle childhood. In R. Case (Ed.), *The mind's staircase: Exploring the structural underpinnings of children's thought and knowledge* (pp. 153–170). Hillsdale, NJ: Lawrence Erlbaum Associations.

Bruner, J. S. (1966). On cognitive growth. In J. S. Bruner, R. Oliver, & P. M. Greenfield (Eds.), *Studies in cognitive growth* (pp. 1–67) New York: Wiley.

Bruner, J. S. (1989). *Culture and human development: A new look.* Invited address to the Society for Research in Child Development, Kansas City.

Burtis, P. J. (1982). Capacity increase and chunking in the development of short-term memory. *Journal of Experimental Child Psychology, 34*, 387–413.

Case, R. (1972). Validation of a neo-Piagetian mental capacity construct. *Journal of Experimental Child Psychology, 14*, 278–302.

Case, R. (1974). Structures and strictures: Some functional limitations on the course of cognitive growth. *Cognitive Psychology, 6*, 544–573.

Case, R. (1975). Social-class differences in intellectual development: A neo-Piagetian investigation. *Canadian Journal of Behavioral Science, 7*, 244–261.

Case, R. (1978). Intellectual development from birth to adulthood: A neo-Piagetian interpretation. In R. S. Siegler (Ed.), *Children's thinking; What develops?* (pp. 37–72). Hillsdale, NJ: Lawrence Erlbaum Associates.

Case, R. (1985). *Intellectual development; birth to adulthood.* Orlando, Fl: Academic Press.

Case, R. (1988b). Dialectical cycles in the development of creative intelligence. *Journal of Social and Biological Structures. 11*, 71–76.

Case, R. (1988c). *Notes on the relevance of neo-structural theory for the study of cross cultural universals and differences in cognition.* Unpublished manuscript.

Case, R. (1989). *Situating the development of outstanding achievement in the adult life cycle.* Paper presented at the annual meeting of the Jean Piaget Society, June.

Case, R. (1991b). *The role of primitive defenses in the regulation and representation of early attachment relations.* Paper presented at the Society for Research on Child Development, April.

Case, R. (1992). *The mind's staircase: Exploring the conceptual underpinnings of children's thought and knowledge.* Hillsdale, NJ: Lawrence Erlbaum Associates.

Case, R. (in press-a). The role of frontal lobe maturation in regulating development of the executive function.

Case, R. (in press-b). Potential contributions of research in the Piagetian tradition to the planning of curriculum and instruction. In M. Carretero, M. Pope, R. J. Simons, & J. I. Pozo (Eds.), *Learning and Instruction. European research in an international context* (Vol. 3). Oxford: England: Pergamon Press.

Case, R., & Globerson, T. (1974). Field independence and mental capacity. *Child Development, 45*, 772–778.

Case, R., & Griffin, S. (1990). Child cognitive development: The role of central conceptual structures in the development of scientific and social thought. In C. A. Hauert (Ed.), *Advances in psychology: Developmental psychology.* Amsterdam: North Holland.

Case, R., Hayward, S., Lewis, M., & Hurst, P. (1988). Toward a neo-Piagetian theory of cognitive and emotional development. *Developmental Review, 8*, 1–51.

Case, R., Kurland, M., & Goldberg, J. (1982). Operational efficiency and the growth of short term memory. *Journal of Experimental Child Psychology, 33*, 386–404.

Case, R., & McKeough, A. (1990). Schooling and the development of central conceptual structures: An example from the domain of children's narrative. *International Journal of Educational Psychology, 8*, 835–855.

Case, R., Okamoto, Y., Henderson, B., & McKeough, A. (in press). The role of central conceptual structures in the development of children's quantitative and social thought. In W. Edelstein & R. Case (Eds.), *The New structuralism in Cognitive Developmental Theory and Research.* Basel: S. Karger.

Case, R., & Sandieson, R. (1987). *General developmental constraints on the acquisition of special procedures (and vice versa).* Paper presented at American Educational Research Association, Baltimore.

Case, R., & Sandieson, R. (1988). A developmental approach to the identification and teaching of central conceptual structures in middle school science and mathematics. In M. Behr & J. Hiebert (Eds.), *Research agenda in mathematics education: Number concepts and operations in the middle grades.* Hillsdale, NJ: Lawrence Erlbaum Associates, pp. 236–270.

Case, R., & Threadgill-Sowder, J. (1990). The development of computational estimation: A neo-Piagetian analysis. *Cognition and Instruction, 7,* 79–104.

Chapman, M. (1988). *Constructive evolution.* Cambridge, MA: Cambridge University Press.

Chapman, M. (1989). Concrete operations and attentional capacity. *Journal of Experimental Child Psychology, 47,* 236–258.

Chi, M. T. H., & Rees, E. R. D. (1983). A learning framework for development, *Contributions to Human Development, 9,* 71–107.

Cohler, B. J. (1990). Developmental perspectives on the psychology of the self in early childhood. In A. Goldberg (Ed.), *Advances in self psychology.* New York: International University Press.

Cole, M. Gay, J. A., Glick, J. A., & Sharp, D. W. (1971). *The cultural context of learning and thinking.* New York: Basic Books.

Cole, M., & Bruner, J. S. (1971). Cultural differences and inferences about psychological processes. *American Psychologist, 26,* 867–876.

Cole, M., & Scribner, S. (1974). *Culture and thought.* New York: Wiley.

Daneman, M., & Case, R. (1981). Syntactic form, semantic complexity and short term memory as factors affecting children's ability to acquire new linguistic structures. *Developmental Psychology, 17,* 367–377.

Dasen, P. (1972). Cross-cultural Piagetian research. A summary. *Journal of Cross-Cultural Psychology, 17,* 367–378.

Dasen, P., & DeRibeaupierre, A. (1988). Neo-Piagetian theories: Cross cultural and differential perspectives. In A. Demetriou (Ed.), *The neo-Piagetian theories of cognitive development: Toward an integration.* Amsterdam: North Holland.

Demetriou, A. (1988). *The neo-Piagetian theories of intelligence: Toward an integration.* Amsterdam: North Holland.

Demetriou, A., & Efklides, A. (1988). Experiential structuralism and neo-Piagetian theories: Toward an integration. In A. Demetriou (Ed.), *The neo-Piagetian theories of intelligence: Toward an Integration.* Amsterdam: North Holland.

Dennis, S. (1992). Stage and structure in the development of children's spatial representations. In R. Case (Ed.), *The mind's staircase: Exploring the conceptual underpinnings of children's thought and knowledge* (pp. 229–245). Hillsdale, NJ: Lawrence Erlbaum Associates.

DeRibaupierre A. (1989). *Transition mechanisms in cognitive development: The longitudinal perspective.* Oxford, England: Pergamon, pp. 297–317.

DeRibaupierre, A., Neyrack, I., & Spira, A. (1989). Interactions between basic capacity and strategies in children's memory. *European Bulletin of Cognitive Psychology 9,* 471–504.

DeRibaupierre, A., & Pascual-Leone, J. (1984). Formal operations and M power: A neo-Piagetian investigation. *New Directions in Child Development, 24,* 1–43.

Diamond, A. (1991). Neuropsychological insights into the meaning of object concept development. In S. Carey & R. Gelman (Eds.), *The epigenesis of mind: Essays on biology and cognition.* Hillsdale, NJ: Lawrence Erlbaum Associates.

Elkind, D. (1985). *The hurried child.* Reading, MA: Addison–Wesley.

Fiati, T. (1992). Cross-cultural variation in the structure of children's thought: A comparison of children's numerical, social and spatial development in four different educational and ecological environments. In R. Case (Ed.), *The mind's staircase: Exploring the conceptual underpinnings of children's thought and knowledge* (pp. 319–343). Hillsdale, NJ: Lawrence Erlbaum Associates.

Fischer, K. W. (1980). A theory of cognitive development: The control and construction of hierarchies of skills. *Psychological Review, 87,* 477–531.

Fischer, K. W. (1987). Relations between brain and cognitive development. *Child Development, 58,* 623–633.

Fischer, K. W. (1989). *Individual differences in developmental sequence and the effects of personal import.* Paper presented in the symposium on the challenges and constraints of structuralism at the biennial meeting of the International Society for the Study of Behavioral Development. Jyvaskyla, Finland.

Fischer, K. W., *Individual Differences in developmental sequence and the effects of personal import.*

Fischer, K. W., & Canfield, R. L. (1986). The ambiguity of stage and structure in behavior: Person and environment in the development of psychological structure. In. I. Levin (Ed.), *Stage and structure: Reopening the debate* (pp. 246-267). New York: Plenum.

Fischer, K. W., & Ferrar, M. J. (in press). Generalizations about generalization: How a theory of skill development explains both generality and specificity. In. A. Demetriou, M. Shayer & A. Efklides (Eds.), *The modern theories of cognitive development go to school* (pp. 137-172). London: Routledge & Kegan Paul.

Fischer, K. W., Hand, et al. (1984). Putting the child into socialization: The development of social categories in the preschool years. In L. Katz (Ed.), *Current topics in early childhood education, 5,* 27-72. Norwood, NJ: Ablex.

Fischer, K. W., Kenny, S. L., & Pipp, S. L. (1990). How cognitive processes and environmental conditions organize discontinuities in the development of abstractions. In. C. N. Alexander, E. J. Langer, & R. M. Oetzel (Eds.), *Higher stages of development* (pp. 162-187). New York: Oxford University Press.

Fischer, K. W., & Knight, C. (in press). Cognitive development in real children: Levels and variations. In Edelstein, W., & Case, R. (Eds.) *Challenges and constraints of Structuralism.* Basel; S. Karger

Fischer, K. W., & Pipp, S. (1984). Processes of cognitive development: Optimal level and skill acquisition. In R. Sternberg (Ed.), *Mechanisms of cognitive development.* New York: Freeman.

Fischer, K. W., Shaver, P. R., & Carnochan, P. (1990). How emotions development and how they organize development. *Cognition and Emotion, 4,* 81-127.

Flavell, J. H. (1984). Discussion. In R. J. Sternberg (Ed.), *Mechanisms of cognitive development* (pp. 188-209). New York: Freeman.

Fodor, J. (1982). *The modularity of mind.* Cambridge, MA: MIT Press.

Furman, I. (1981). *The development of problem solving strategies: A neo-Piagetian analysis of children's performance in a balance task.* Unpublished doctoral dissertation, University of California, Berkeley.

Gardner, H. (1983). *Frames of mind: The theory of multiple intelligences.* New York: Basic Books.

Gelman, R. (1969). Conservation acquisition: A problem of learning to attend to relevant attributes. *Journal of Experimental Child Psychology, 7,* 167-187.

Gibson, E. (1969). *Perceptual development.* New York: Appelton Century Crofts.

Globerson T. (1983). Mental capacity and cognitive functioning: Developmental and social class differences. *Developmental Psychology, 19,* 225-250.

Globerson, T. (1985). Field dependence/independence and mental capacity: A developmental Approach. *Developmental Review, 5,* 261-273.

Globerson, T., Weinstein, E., & Sharabany, R. (in press). Teasing out cognitive development from cognitive style: A training study. *Developmental Psychology.*

Goldman-Rakic, P. (1988, June). *Working memory and the frontal lobes.* Paper presented at the Toronto General Hospital.

Goodman, D. R. (1971). *Cognitive-style factors and linguistic performance with ambiguous sentences.* Unpublished M.A. thesis, York University, Toronto.

Goodman, D. (1979). *Stage transition and the developmental trace of constructive operations: An investigation of a neo-Piagetian theory of cognitive growth.* Unpublished doctoral dissertation, York University, Toronto.

Greenfield, P. M. (1966). On culture and conservation. In J. S. Bruner, R. Oliver, & P. M. Greenfield (Eds.), *Studies in cognitive growth.* New York: Wiley, pp. 1-67.

Groenwig, G. (1983). *The development of comprehension: Some linguistic and cognitive determinants of sentence verification.* Unpublished doctoral dissertation, University of Toronto

Halford, G. S. (1982). *The development of thought.* Hillsdale, NJ: Lawrence Erlbaum Associates.

Halford, G. S. (1988). A structure mapping approach to cognitive development. In A. Demetriou (Ed.), *The neo-Piagetian theories of cognitive development: Toward an integration.* Amsterdam: North Holland.

Halford, G. S. (in press). Analogical reasoning in cognitive development. *Human Development.*

Halford, G. S. & McDonald, C. (1977). Children's pattern construction as a function of age and complexity. *Child Development,* 48, 1016-1100.

Halford, G. S., Bain, J. D., & Mayberry, M. T. (1982, July). *Working memory and representational processes.* Paper presented to the 10th symposium on attention and performance, Eindoven.

Halford, G. S., & Mayberry, M. T. (1990). *The development of memory and processing capacity.* Unpublished manuscript.

Halford, G. S., & Wilson, W. H. (1980). A category theory approach to cognitive development. *Cognitive Psychology,* 12, 356-411.

Hume, D. (1955). *An inquiry concerning human understanding.* New York: Bobbs Merrill. (First published in 1748)

Inhelder, B. & Piaget, J. (1958) *The growth of logical thinking from childhood to adolescence.* New York: Basic Books

Inhelder, B., & Piaget, P. (1980). Procedures and structures. In D. R. Olson (Ed.), *The social foundations of language and thought: Essays in honor of Jerome S. Bruner.* New York: Norton.

Jedrzkiewicz, J. A. (1986). *Adult development and mental effort: A neo-Piagetian experimental analysis.* Unpublished M.A. thesis, York University, Toronto.

Johnson, J., Fabian, V., & Pascual-Leone, J. (1989). Quantitative hardware stages that constrain language development. *Human Development,* 32, 245-271.

Johnson, J., & Pascual-Leone, J. (in press). Developmental levels of processing in metaphor interpretation. *Journal of Experimental Child Psychology.*

Kagan, J. (1966). Reflection-impulsivity: The generality and dynamics of conceptual tempo. *Journal of Abnormal Psychology,* 71, 17-24.

Kail, R. (in press). Developmental change in speed of processing during childhood and adolescence. *Psychological Bulletin.*

Kant, I. (1966). *Critique of pure reason.* New York: Doubleday. (First published in 1796)

Keating, D. P. (1980). Thinking processes in adolescence. In J. Adelson (Ed.), *Handbook of adolescent psychology,* pp. 211-246.

Kegan, R. (1982). *The evolving self.* Cambridge, MA: Harvard University Press.

Kernberg, O. (1976). *Object relations theory and clinical psychoanalysis.* New York: Aranson.

Kitchener, K. W., & Fischer, K. W. (1988). A skill approach to the development of reflective thinking. In D. Kuhn (Ed.), *Developmental perspectives on teaching and learning thinking skills.* Basel, Switzerland: S. Karger.

Klahr, D. (1988). Information processing approaches to cognitive development. *Annals of Psychology.*

Klahr, D., (1989). Information-Processing Approaches. *Annals of Child Development.* 6. 133-185.

Klahr, D., & Wallace, J. G. (1976). *Cognitive development: An information processing view.* Hillsdale, NJ: Lawrence Erlbaum Associates.

Klein, M. (1957). *Envy and gratitude: A study of unconscious sources* London: Tavistock.

Kohlberg, L. (1981). *Essays on moral development.* San Francisco: Harper & Row.

Lakatos, I. (1962). Falsification and the methodology of scientific research programmes. In I. Lakatos & A. Musgrave (Eds.), *Criticism and the growth of knowledge.* New York: Cambridge University Press.

Lautrey, J., DeRibaupierre, A., & Rieben, L. (1987). Operational development and individual differences. In E. DeCorte, H. Lodewigks, R. Parmentier, & P. Span (Eds.), *Learning and instruction.* Oxford, England: Lewen University Press & Pergamon Press.

Lave, J. (1988). *Cognition and practice.* New York: Cambridge University Press.

Leitner, K. L. (1990). *Cognitive and affective development in the second year of life: A neo-Piagetian and object relations perspective.* Unpublished doctoral dissertation, University of Toronto.

Lewin, K. (1935). *A dynamic theory of personality.* New York: McGraw–Hill.

Liu, P. (1981). *An investigation of the relationship between qualitative and quantitative advances in the cognitive development of preschool children.* Unpublished doctoral dissertation, University of Toronto.

Louis, M. D. (1989). *Cognition-emotion interactions in infancy: The development of individual differences.* Unpublished doctoral dissertation, University of Toronto.

Luria, A. R. (1979) *The making of mind.* Cambridge, MA: Harvard University Press.

Main, M. (1991). *Metacognitive knowledge, metacognitive monitoring, and attachment.* Paper presented at the biennial meeting of the Society for Research in Child Development, Seattle, April.

McDermott, R. (1990). The acquisition of a child by a learning disability. In J. Lave & S. Chaiklin (Eds.), *People in action.* New York: Cambridge University Press.

McKeough, A. (in press). A neo-structural analysis of children's narrative, and its development. In R. Case (Ed.), *The mind's staircase: Exploring the structural underpinnings of children's thought and knowledge* (pp. 171–188). Hillsdale, NJ: Lawrence Erlbaum Associates.

McLaughlin, G. H. (1963). Psychologic: A possible alternative to Piaget's formulation. *British Journal of Educational Psychology, 33,* 61–67.

Menna, R. (1989). *Working memory development: An E.E.G. investigation.* Unpublished master's thesis, University of Toronto.

Miller, M. S., & Pascual-Leone, J. (1981). *Disconfirming Jensen experimentally: Intellectual versus executive-structural deficiency in underperforming low SES children.* Paper presented at the Society for Research in Child Development, Boston.

Miller, R., Pascual-Leone, J., Campbell, C, & Juckes, T. *Learning and development: A neo-Piagetian cross-cultural analysis.* Durban, South Africa: University of Natal.

Modgil, S., & Modgil, C. (1982). *Jean Piaget: Consensus and controversy.* New York: Praeger.

Morra, S., Moizo, C., & Scopesi, A. M. (1986). Working memory (or the M-operator) and the planning of children's drawing. *Journal of Experimental Child Psychology, 46,* 41–73.

Mounoud, P. (1986). Similarities between developmental sequences at different age periods. In I. Levin (Ed.), *Stage and structure: Reopening the debate.* Norwood, NJ: Ablex.

Mounoud, P., & Bower, T. G. H. (1974). Conservation of weight in infants. *Cognition, 3,* 29–40.

Noam, G. G. (1988). The self, adult development, and the theory of biography and transformation. In D. K. Lapsley & F. C. Power (Eds.), *Self, ego, and identity-integrative approaches.* New York: Springer–Verlag.

Noam, G. G. (1991, April). *Self and relationships in adolescent developmental psychopathology.* Paper presented at the biennial meeting of the Society for Research in Child Development SRCD, Seattle.

Olson, D. R. (1986a). Interpreting text and interpreting narrative: The effects of literacy on hermeneutics and epistemology, *Visible Language, 20,* 302–317.

Olson, D. R. (1986b). Mining the human sciences: Some relations between humanities and epistemology. *Interchange,* 119–171.

Overton, W. (1984). World views and their influence on psychological theory and research: Kuhn-Lakatos-Landon. In H. W. Reese (Ed.), *Advances in child development and behavior.* New York: Academic Press.

Overton, W. F. (1990a). The structure of developmental theory. In P. van Geert & L. P. Mos (Eds.), *Annals of theoretical psychology.* New York: Plenum.

Overton, W. F. (1990b). Competence and Procedures: Constraints on the development of logical reasoning. In W. F. Overton (Ed.), *Reasoning, necessity and logic: Developmental perspective.* Hillsdale, NJ: Lawrence Erlbaum Associates.

Parkinson, G. M. (1961). *Adaptive flexibility, field dependence, and two Piagetian tasks as independent variables in mirror tracking experiments.* Unpublished honors thesis, University of British Columbia, Vancouver, Canada.

Parkinson, G. M. (1969). *The recognition of messages from visual compound stimuli: A test of a quantitative developmental model.* Unpublished master's thesis, York University, Toronto.

Parkinson, G. M. (1975). *The limits of learning: A quantitative investigation of intelligence.* Unpublished doctoral dissertation, York University, Toronto.

Pascual-Leone, J. (1969). *Cognitive development and cognitive style: A general psychological integration.* Unpublished doctoral dissertation, University of Geneva.

Pascual-Leone, J. (1970). A mathematical model for the transition rule in Piaget's development stages. *Acta Psychologica, 32,* 301–345.

Pascual-Leone, J. (1974). *A neo-Piagetian process-structural model of Witkin's psychological differentiation.* Paper presented at the symposium on cross cultural studies of psychological differentiation at the meetings of the Internal Association for Cross Cultural Psychology, Kingston, Ontario.

Pascual-Leone, J. (1976). On learning and development, Piagetian style: A critical historical analysis of Geneva's research programme. *Canadian Psychological Review, 17,* 270–288.

Pascual-Leone, J. (1986). Reflections on life span intelligence, consciousness, and ego development. In C. N. Alexander, E. J. Langer, & R. M. Oetter (Eds.), *Higher stages of development: Adult growth beyond formal operations.* New York: Oxford University Press.

Pascual-Leone, J. (1988a). Organismic processes for neo-Piagetian theories: A dialectical causal account of cognitive development. In A. Demetriou (Ed.), *The neo-Piagetian theories of cognitive development: Toward an integration.* Amsterdam: North Holland.

Pascual-Leone, J. (1988b). *An essay on wisdom: Toward organismic processes that make it possible.* Unpublished manuscript. Department of Psychology, York University, Toronto.

Pascual-Leone, J. (1988c). Affirmations and negations, disturbances and contradictions, in understanding Piaget: Is his later theory causal? *Contemporary Psychology, 33,* 420–421.

Pascual-Leone, J. (1989a). An organismic process model of Witkin's field-dependence–independence. In T. Globerson & T. Zelniker (Eds.), *Cognitive style and cognitive development.* Norwood, NJ: Ablex.

Pascual-Leone, J. (1989b). Commentary. *Human Development, 32,* 357–378.

Pascual-Leone, J., & Goodman, D. (1979). Intelligence and experience: A neo-Piagetian approach. *Instructional Science, 8,* 301–367.

Pascual-Leone, J., Hamstra, N., Benson, N., Khan, I., & England, R. (1990). *The P300 event-related potential and mental capacity.* Paper presented at the fourth international symposium on evoked potentials Toronto.

Pascual-Leone, J., & Smith, J. (1969). The encoding and decoding of symbols by children. A new experimental paradigm and a neo-Piagetian theory. *Journal of Experimental Child Psychology, 8,* 328–355.

Piaget, J. (1964). Development and learning. In R. E. Ripple & V. Rockcastle (Eds.), *Piaget rediscovered.* Ithiaca, NY: Cornell University Press.

Piaget, J. (1970). *Science of education and the psychology of the child.* New York: Orion Press.

Piaget, J. (1981). *Intelligence and affectivity: Their relationship during child development.* Palo Alto, CA: Annual Review Monographs.

Piaget, J. (1985). *The equilibration of cognitive structures: The central problem of intellectual development.* Chicago: University of Chicago Press.

Piaget, J. & Garcia, R. (1991). *Toward a logic of meaning.* Hillsdale, NJ: Lawrence Erlbaum Associates.

Piaget, J. Grize, J. B., Szeminska, A., & Bang, V. (1977). *Epistemology and psychology of functions.* Dordrecht, the Netherlands: Reidel.

Pinard, A. & Laurendeau, M. (1969). "Stage" in Piaget's cognitive–developmental theory: Exegesis of a concept. In D. Elkind & J. H. Flavell (Eds.), *Studies in cognitive development.* New York: Oxford University Press.

Porath, M. (1992). Stage and structure in the development of children with various types of "giftedness." In R. Case (Ed.), *The mind's staircase: Exploring the conceptual underpinnings of children's thought and knowledge* (pp. 303–318). Hillsdale, NJ: Lawrence Erlbaum Associates

Reid, D. T. (1992). Horizontal and vertical structure: stages and substages in children's motor development. In R. Case, *The mind's staircase: Exploring the conceptual underpinnings of childrens thought and knowledge* (pp. 247–266). Hillsdale, N.J.: Lawrence Earlbaum Associates.

Rich, S. (1982). *Cognitive restructuring in children: The prediction of intelligence and learning.* Unpublished doctoral dissertation, Ontario Institute for Studies in Education, University of Toronto, Toronto.

Rieben, L., DeRibaupierre, A., & Lautrey, J. (1983). La developpment opératoire de l'enfant entre 6 et 12 ans: Elaboration d'un instrument d'evaluation. Paris: Editions du CNRS.

Rieben, L., DeRibaupierre, A., & Lautrey, J. (1990). Structural invariants and individual modes of processing: On the necessity of a minimally structuralist approach of development for education. *Archives de Psychologie, 58,* 29–53.

Rieben, L., & DeRibaupierre, A. (1986). Une definition structuraliste des formes an developpement cognitif, un projet chimérique? *Archives de Psychologie, 54,* 95–123.

Rumelhart, D. E., & McLelland, J. C. (1987). Learning the past tenses of English verbs: Implicit rules or parallel distributed processing? In B. MacWhinney (Ed.), *Mechanisms of language acquisition.* Hillsdale, NJ: Lawrence Erlbaum Associates.

Scardamalia, M. (1977). Information-processing capacity and the problem of horizontal décalage: A demonstration using combinatorial reasoning tasks. *Child Development, 48,* 28–37.

Selman, R. (1980). *The development of interpersonal understanding: Developmental and clinical analyses.* New York: Academic Press.

Shafrir, U. *Response to Failure, Strategic Awareness, and Learning.* Unpublished manuscript, Ontario Institute for Studies in Education (O.I.S.E), Canada.

Shafrir, U., Ogilvie, M., & Bryson, M. (1990). Attention to errors and learning: Across-task and across-domain analysis of the post failure reflectivity measure. *Cognitive Development, 5,* 405–425.

Shafrir, U., & Pascual-Leone, J. (1990). Post failure reflectivity/impulsivity and spontaneous attention to errors. *Journal of Educational Psychology, 82,* 378–387.

Shapiro, D. (1963). *Neurotic styles.* New York: Basic Books.

Shayer, M., Demetriou, A., & Perves, M. (1988). The structure and scaling of concrete operational thought: Three studies in four countries. *Genetic, Social, and General Psychology Monographs, 114,* 307–376.

Sherer, K. R. (1984). Emotion as a multicomponent process: A model and some cross-cultural data. In. P. Shaver (Ed.), *Review of personality and social psychology, 5,* 37–63. Beverley Hills, CA: Sage.

Sigel, I. E. (1969). The Piagetian system and the world of education. In D. Elkind & J. Flavell (Eds.), *Studies in cognitive development*. Oxford: England: Oxford University Press.

Siegler, R. S. (1978). The origins of scientific reasoning. In R. S. Siegler, (Ed.), *Children's thinking: What develops?* Hillsdale, NJ: Lawrence Erlbaum Associates.

Sinclair-de-Zwart, H. (1969). Developmental psycholinguistics. In D. Elkind & J. H. Flavell (Eds.), *Studies in cognitive development: Essays in honor of Jean Piaget.* New York: Oxford University Press.

Snow, R. E., Kyllonen, P. C., & Marshalek, B. (1984). The topography of ability and learning correlations. (pp. 47-109). In R. Sternberg (Ed.), *Advances in the Psychology of Intelligence, 2,* Hillsdale, NJ: Lawrence Erlbaum Associates.

Starkey, P. D., Spelke, E. S., & Gelman, R. (1983). Detection of intermodal numerical correspondence by human infants. *Science, 222,* 179-181.

Stuss, D. T., (in press). Biological and psychological development of frontal executive functions. *Brain and cognition.*

Thatcher, R. W. (in press). Maturation of the human frontal lobes, physiological evidence for staging. *Developmental Neuropsychology.*

Todor, J. I., (1979). Developmental differences in motor task integration: A test of Pascual-Leone's theory of constructive operators. *Journal of Experimental Child Psychology, 28,* 314-322.

Turiel, E. (1983). *The development of social knowledge: Morality and convention.* Cambridge, MA: Cambridge University Press.

Vuyk, R. (1981). *Overview and critique of Piaget's genetic epistemology 1965-1980* (Vols. 1 & 2). New York: Academic Press.

Vygotsky, L. S. (1962). *Thought and language.* Cambridge, MA: MIT Press. (first published in Russian in 1934)

Weininger, O. (1984). *The clinical psychology of Melanie Klein.* Springfield, ILL: Charles Thomas.

Winnecott, D. W. (1965). *The maturational processes and the facilitating environment.* New York: International Universities Press.

Yakovlev, P. I., & Lecours, A. R. (1967). The myelenogenetic cycles of regional maturation of the brain. In A. Minkowski (Ed.), *Regional development of the brain in early life.* Oxford, England: Blackwell.

II

THEORY OF MIND: EXAMINING REPRESENTATION IN THOUGHT

5 Perspectives on Perspective Taking

John H. Flavell
Stanford University

It recently struck me that for most of my 35 years in the field I have been studying the development of one form or another of perspective taking. My research in this area was initially inspired and guided by Piaget's work, and it continues to bear the marks of his thinking to this day. In this chapter I begin by summarizing briefly some of Piaget's ideas about perspective taking, and then chronicle my own work on the problem. I have to confess that my presentation will be egocentric, and in two different ways. On the one hand, it will mostly be a description of my own work in the guise of a tribute to Piaget's. On the other hand, after all these years of thinking about perspective taking, I find I am no longer sure which ideas about it are Piaget's and which ones are my interpretations or extensions of his. (Like all of Piaget's creatures, I am an incorrigible assimilator.) However, I console myself with the thought that, if one has to be egocentric, perspective taking is the right topic and Piaget's is the right perspective to confuse with one's own.

PIAGET ON PERSPECTIVE-TAKING DEVELOPMENT

If I have understood him correctly, Piaget's central claim in this area was that children begin development by being cognitively "egocentric" (Piaget, 1926, 1928; see also Elkind, 1967; Flavell, 1963; Flavell, Botkin, Fry, Wright, & Jarvis, 1968; Morss, 1987). By this he meant that they initially do not know that there are such mental entities in the world as conceptual, perceptual, and affective perspectives or points of view. As a consequence, they of course cannot know that they themselves have such perspectives vis-à-vis external objects and events, or that others do, or that their own perspective may differ from those of others, or that they may be unwittingly responding in terms of their own perspectives when asked to respond in terms of another person's. Piaget also considered as egocentric children who have some awareness that perspectives exist but who are not skilled at discriminating their own from another person's. Piaget thought that children gradually become more knowledgeable about perspectives and more skillful in perspective taking through experiencing disputes and other perspectival differences with others, especially peers. Such experiences forcibly confront children with the existence of viewpoints different from their own, and gradually make them aware of their own perspectives as well as those of others (Chapman, Kuhn as well as Youniss & Damon, this volume).

Although Piaget believed that children generally become less egocentric with age, he did not think that older children and adults are wholly nonegocentric in their thinking. On the contrary, he believed that individuals of any age will be prone to egocentric, single-perspective thinking when first operating at a new cognitive–developmental level or in a new and untried cognitive domain (Elkind, 1967; Inhelder & Piaget, 1958; Piaget, 1962). Among the examples of this he cited were adolescents just beginning to apply their formal-operational thinking skills to the larger social and political world and beginning teachers trying to communicate with their students. In such instances of low expertise, there is apt to be an egocentric failure to "decenter" from the nonexpert's own perspective in order to consider other possible ones.

Piaget's ideas about egocentrism have been criticized by others (e.g., Ford, 1979; Morss, 1987; Waters & Tinsley, 1985). However, although I agree with some of these criticisms, I continue to find the basic concept fascinating and tried to elaborate it further in this passage from my textbook on cognitive development:

> Unlike, say, nonconservation of number, I believe we are "at risk" (almost in the medical sense) for egocentric thinking all of our lives, just as we are for certain logical errors. The reason lies in our psychological designs in relation to the jobs to be done. We experience our own points of view more or less directly, whereas we must always attain the other person's in more indirect manners. Our own points of view are more cognitively "available" to us than another person's (Tversky & Kahneman, 1973). Furthermore, we are usually unable to turn our own viewpoints off completely when trying to infer another's. Our own perspectives produce clear signals that are much louder to us than the other's, and they usually continue to ring in our ears while we try to decode the other's. It may take considerable skill and effort to represent another's point of view accurately through this kind of noise, and the possibility of egocentric distortion is ever-present. For example, the fact that

you thoroughly understand calculus constitutes an obstacle to your continuously keeping in mind my ignorance of it while trying to explain it to me; you may momentarily realize how hard it is for me, but that realization may quietly slip away once you get immersed in your explanation. Interestingly, the "other" can be oneself in another time and condition, rather than a different person. . . . For example, it can be hard to imagine yourself feeling well and happy next week if you feel terribly ill or unhappy today. Taking the perspective of yourself, when that perspective is different from your current one, can sometimes be as hard as taking the perspective of another person. Thus, we can no more "cure" ourselves of our susceptibility to egocentrism than we can cure ourselves, say, of our difficulties in understanding two simultaneously presented messages. Both cases represent a human information-processing limitation with respect to a certain class of cognitive task. (Flavell, 1985, p. 125)

This idea about taking one's own perspective as well as those of others seems important. One reason is that how well or poorly we do this within-self perspective taking can make a huge difference to our lives. For example, one would seem likelier to attempt suicide when feeling depressed if one could not represent oneself as feeling better later — despite evidence that one has always felt better subsequent to previous bouts of depression. All of us find this sort of perspective taking difficult, but some are undoubtedly better at it than others. Similarly, it is enormously important that we be accurate rather than inaccurate in predicting how we will think and feel if we make a major change in our lives — marry, divorce, change jobs, retire, and so on. Here again the very fact that we continuously think and feel in accordance with our present perspective may interfere with our ability to predict accurately how things will seem to us in the contemplated new perspective. It is the same when we try to recapture past perspectives. Again, our present perspective may subtly color and distort our attempted reconstruction of our past perceptions, thoughts, and feelings (cf. Taylor, 1988, pp. 222–223). Thus, although it is undeniably important for our well being to predict with reasonable accuracy the perspectives of other people, it can be even more important to do the same with our own future and past perspectives.

Piaget had more to say about the nature and development of perspective taking than I have summarized in the foregoing. I will refer to additional Piagetian contributions as I describe the lines of my and my coworkers' research that these contributions helped to spawn.

FLAVELL AND COWORKERS ON PERSPECTIVE-TAKING DEVELOPMENT

The 1950s and 1960s

Most of Piaget's empirical research in the area of perspective-taking focused on two topics: spatial–perceptual perspective-taking (Piaget & Inhelder,

1956) and verbal communication (Piaget, 1926). In the spatial research he found a marked improvement with age in children's ability to infer how spatial displays would look to other observers who viewed them from different positions. For example, one famous series of studies made use of a scale model of three mountains, photographs of the model taken from various positions around it, and a doll observer who viewed the model from various of these positions. The subjects were about 4–11 years of age. The younger subjects made a variety of errors indicative of poor perceptual perspective-taking skills. Some kept selecting the photograph depicting their own view of the mountains regardless of where the doll was placed—an egocentric error, Piaget thought. Others seemed to think that a number of different photographs could all represent what the doll saw from a given position. With age, children became increasingly aware that only one photograph could depict a particular point of view and that how the display looks changes regularly with changes in the viewer's position. Children also became increasingly skilled at predicting the details of the observer's view, for example, correctly identifying which mountain would appear behind or rightward of another from the observer's perspective. In the communication research Piaget found that before 7 or 8 years of age children tended to communicate egocentrically, that is, without taking account of what their listener needs to know and tailoring their message accordingly. As Piaget put it, the younger child "always gave us the impression of talking to himself, without bothering about the other child. Very rarely did he succeed in placing himself at the listener's point of view" (Piaget, 1926, p. 115).

In the late 1950s my coworkers and I began an extensive series of developmental studies in this area which were eventually reported in a monograph entitled *The Development of Role-taking and Communication Skills in Children* (Flavell et al., 1968; see also Flavell 1966, 1974). The principal inspiration of these studies was the research by Piaget that has been described here. To illustrate this influence, like Piaget, we tested children's ability to adapt their communication to their listener's perspective and their ability to infer how object displays looked to others who viewed them from different positions. In these studies we administered a wide variety of perspective-taking and related communication tasks of our own creation to children ranging in age from 3 to 17. The following description of a few of our tasks will illustrate the nature of these studies.

In one of our conceptual perspective-taking tasks, the subject is shown an ordered series of seven pictures, which, in comic-strip fashion, illustrate the following story: A boy walks along, sees a dog pursuing him, climbs an apple tree in order to escape the dog, and eats an apple while waiting for the dog to leave. After the subject has narrated the story (an easy task for all subjects), the experimenter removes three of the pictures, leaving a four-picture sequence that would suggest a quite different story to someone who had seen only those four pictures, namely: A boy walks along, sees an apple tree, and climbs it in order to get an apple. A second experimenter then enters the room and the subject is told that this person has never seen any of these pictures before. The subject is then asked to predict the story that the second experimenter would tell on the basis of seeing just those four pictures. We expected that the younger subjects in this study (7–8-year-olds) might have difficulty suppressing their own perspective, based on the original, seven-picture story, when asked to infer the second experimenter's. The results confirmed this expectation. Almost 60% of the younger children either just repeated their original seven-picture story or else "spoiled" their correct, four-picture story by intruding seven-picture story elements in response to subsequent questioning. For example: "Why does Mr. X think that the boy wanted to climb the tree?"—"So the dog don't get him. . . ."

With another task we were able to show developmental changes across middle childhood and adolescence in a more complex, recursive form of perspective taking. In this form the subject thinks about what another person might be thinking about the subject's own thinking (e.g., "He thinks that I think that he thinks. . . ."; see also Miller, Kessel, & Flavell, 1970). Still other tasks unearthed some beginning abilities in preschool children to predict how a stimulus would look, feel, or be liked by someone whose perceptual perspective or preferences differed from their own. We returned to the study of preschoolers' perspective-taking abilities in the 1970s and 1980s, as I will show.

There were also a number of tasks that required subjects to infer the perspective of another person in order to tailor a communicative message to that person's informational needs. As in our perspective-taking tasks we made sure that the other person's perspective was different from the subject's, so that just "saying what comes naturally" from the subject's own perspective would not produce an adequate message. In one of these communication tasks subjects in Grades 2–11 first learned to play a game and then were instructed to tell an adult listener how to play it. For half the subjects at each grade level, the adult listener was blindfolded, and for the other half, sighted; in addition, a subgroup of the 2nd- and 8th-grade subjects described the game to both types of listeners. The blindfolded listener's needs for explicit verbal information were obviously much greater than those of the sighted listener, who could see at a glance what the game materials consisted of, could easily follow the subject's gestural references to this or that game object, and so on. Our main prediction was that the difference between children's messages to the two listeners would increase with age, reflecting the older children's greater sensitivity to the differing communication-reception perspectives of the two listeners and the need to take these perspectives into account when telling them how to play the game. The results confirmed this prediction. To illustrate, in the

8th-grade group the mean number of different words per message was substantially higher in the messages directed to the blindfolded listener than in those directed to the sighted listener. In contrast, in the 2nd-grade group the two means were identical, indicating that these subjects did not vary their messages much as a function of the listener's communicative needs. The communicative consequences of failing to keep the listener's perspective in mind were most vividly illustrated in the performance of a few of the youngest subjects, who blithely spoke of picking up "this" and putting it "over there," and the like, when trying to explain the game to the blindfolded listener. In other communication tasks we found similar developmental differences in children's ability to communicate effectively to a small child, and to a group of listeners with different informational requirements; to communicate nonredundantly; to persuade as well as to inform; and to detect communicative inadequacies in a message constructed by someone else.

The studies reported in the "role-taking and communication" monograph (Flavell et al., 1968) did not provide us with as much in the way of deep insights or grand theory as we had hoped they would; as will be shown, we did a bit better in later years with a two-level theory of percept knowledge development. However, these early studies did provide us with what still seems a useful conceptual analysis of what children need to develop in this area (Flavell, 1974). We identified four knowledge or skill components that they needed to acquire, referred to as *Existence, Need, Inference,* and *Application.* The *Existence* component refers to the children's knowledge that there are such things as mental states—thoughts, percepts, emotions, and so on. The absence of any *Existence* knowledge would constitute Piagetian egocentrism at its most profound. The *Need* component means children's tacit or explicit recognition that certain situations call for an effort on their part to obtain knowledge about another person's mental states. The *Inference* component refers to the actual ability to obtain this knowledge about the other person's perspective, by the use of inference or some other process. Finally, the *Application* component refers to the ability to apply this perspectival knowledge to the situation at hand. To illustrate the use of this conceptual scheme, we would say that subjects in the blindfolded-listener study need to: (a) Know that this listener has message-comprehension abilities and disabilities (Existence); (b) know that they need to find what these are in order to communicate with this listener effectively (Need); (c) know how to find out what they are (Inference); (d) know how to apply what they find out in fashioning an adequate verbal message to him (Application). A child might have some components but not others in a given situation—for example, know how to assess the other person's perspective (Inference) but not realize that such assessment would be useful (Need). This scheme does not seem to go counter to Piaget's in any important way, but it does add some distinctions within "perspective-taking ability" that he apparently did not make.

The 1960s and 1970s

During the late 1960s and 1970s my work focused increasingly on the nature and development of what eventually became known as "metacognition," roughly defined as knowledge and cognition about cognitive phenomena. I arrived at this topic by a curious route that went from private speech to memory strategies to metamemory to metacognition in general. Unlike the role-taking and communication work, the work on metacognition was thus not greatly influenced by Piaget's research. I later came to see it as related to Piagetian ideas and to perspective taking, however.

I was initially interested in studying the development of private speech, not memory strategies. However, the private speech I chanced to select for study was semicovert verbal rehearsal of to-be-remembered object names (Flavell, Beach, & Chinsky, 1966; Keeney, Cannizzo, & Flavell, 1967). My students and I discovered several things of interest in these initial studies. First, younger elementary schoolchildren seldom spontaneously rehearsed the names they were to remember, whereas older ones usually did. Second, younger children could easily be induced through brief instruction to rehearse, and when they did rehearse their recall improved markedly. Finally, when given the option on later trials of either rehearsing or not rehearsing, they often stopped rehearsing.

These findings intrigued us so much that we abandoned the private speech project and started investigating the development of memory strategies instead. At first we studied only the development of storage strategies — that is, the kinds of mnemonically oriented data processing that individuals do now because they know they will have to retrieve those data later (Flavell, 1970). Examples are verbal rehearsal and deliberate clustering of to-be-remembered items. Later we also studied the development of retrieval strategies — that is, the resourceful moves people may make when actually trying to recover things from memory storage, whether they had previously known they would be doing that (intentional memory) or not (incidental memory). An example of a retrieval strategy would be to attempt a systematic and exhaustive search through the "place" — in the head or in the world — where the to-be-recalled items are thought or known to reside. To illustrate this retrieval strategy, subjects in a study by Keniston and Flavell (1979) were unexpectedly given the incidental recall task of remembering which 20 letters of the alphabet had been presented to them earlier. We found a marked increase with age in the tendency to begin by unsystematically recalling a few, easily retrievable letters but then, when that strategy stopped working, to proceed systematically through the entire alphabet, recognizing the previously presented (target) letters as they were encountered.

As this research progressed it became apparent that the development of memory strategies might be part of a larger developmental domain, namely, that of knowledge concerning the nature of the self and others as learners and rememberers, knowledge about the diverse learning and memory tasks people confront, and knowledge of the strategies people can use to cope with these tasks. We began to refer to this knowledge about memory as "metamemory" (Flavell, 1971) and set about studying its development (see Flavell & Wellman, 1977). In the most ambitious of these studies, Kreutzer, Leonard, and Flavell (1975) interviewed children of grades K, 1, 3, and 5 concerning a wide variety of memory phenomena and showed dramatic increases in all sorts of metamemory across this age period. As examples, we found that older children were likelier than younger ones to have an intuitive knowledge of such memory phenomena as retroactive interference, savings in relearning, and the superiority of gist recall over rote recall. However, even the younger subjects displayed impressive knowledge of some memory phenomena. For example, they knew that they sometimes forget things, and that a good way not to forget to bring things to school is to put them where you will be sure to see them in the morning. In a subsequent study, Gordon and Flavell (1977) discovered that by about age 7 children have acquired an explicit understanding that thinking of one thing may bring to mind another, related thing—in effect, the concept of a retrieval cue. Likewise, Speer and Flavell (1979) found that children of about this same age also know that it is generally easier to recognize items that had previously been stored in memory than to recall them. The following response by a third grader to the question "What do you do when you want to remember a phone number?" illustrates the potential richness of children's metamemory:

> Say the number is 633-8854. Then what I'd do is—say that my number is 633, so I won't have to remember that, really. And then I would think now I've got to remember 88. Now I'm 8 years old, so I can remember, say, my age two times. Then I say how old my brother is, and how old he was last year. And that's how I'd usually remember that phone number. {Is that how you would most often remember a phone number?} Well, usually I write it down. (Kreutzer et al., 1975, p. 11)

We eventually came to regard metamemory as but one part of the larger domain of *metacognition,* broadly and somewhat loosely defined as any knowledge or cognitive activity that takes as its object, or regulates, any aspect of any cognitive enterprise. The following account of our ideas about metacognition is a lightly edited version of that given in my cognitive development text (Flavell, 1985).

The key concepts in our conceptualization of this domain are *metacognitive knowledge* and *metacognitive experience*. Metacognitive knowledge refers to the part of your acquired world knowledge that has to do with cognitive matters. It is the knowledge and beliefs you have accumulated through experience and stored in long-term memory that concern the human mind and its doings. Some of this stored knowledge seems more declarative ("knowing that") than procedural ("knowing how")—for example, your declarative knowledge that you have a rather poor memory. Other metacognitive knowledge seems more procedural than declarative—for example, your procedural knowledge of how and when to supplement that poor memory by the use of shopping lists and other external memory aids. Metacognitive knowledge can be roughly subdivided into knowledge about *persons, tasks,* and *strategies.* The person category includes any knowledge and beliefs you might acquire concerning what human beings are like as cognitive processors. It can be further subcategorized into knowledge and beliefs about cognitive differences within people, cognitive differences between people, and cognitive similarities among all people—that is, about universal properties of human cognition. An example of the within-people subcategory might be your knowledge that you are better at psychology than physics. An example of the between-people category could be your belief that your parents are more sensitive to the needs and feelings of others than many of their neighbors are (a belief about others' social–cognitive skills). The cognitive-universals subcategory is the most interesting of the three. It refers to what you have come to know or believe about what the human mind in general is like—any person's mind (note the similarity to current ideas about theory of mind development in the last two sections of this chapter). For instance, you know that people's short-term memory is of limited capacity and highly fallible. Similarly, you are aware of the important fact that sometimes people understand, sometimes they do not understand, and sometimes they understand incorrectly, or misunderstand. You also know that what you cannot recall now you may be able to recall later and that what you can recall now you may not be able to recall later. More generally, you have learned that the human mind is a somewhat unpredictable and unreliable cognitive device, although still a remarkable one. People the world over undoubtedly acquire considerable metaknowledge of this subcategory and make important use of it in managing their lives. Try this thought experiment to convince yourself of its usefulness: Imagine how well you would fare as an adult in any human society if you were incorrigibly ignorant of the fact that you and other people sometimes misunderstand or forget things.

The task category has two subcategories. One subcategory has to do with the nature of the information you encounter and deal with in any cognitive task. You have learned that the nature of this information has important effects on how you will manage it. For example, you know from experience that complex and unfamiliar information is liable to be difficult and time consuming for you to comprehend and remember. The other subcategory concerns the nature of the task demands. Even given the exact same information to work with, you have learned that some tasks are more difficult and demanding than others. For example, you know that it is easier to recall the gist of a story than its exact wording.

As for the strategy category, there is much you might have learned about what means or strategies are likely to succeed in achieving what cognitive goals—in comprehending X, remembering Y, solving problem Z, and so on. For instance, if someone asks you what a person might do to memorize a phone number you could no doubt tell him or her that the person might try rehearsing it (declarative knowledge about rehearsal as a memory strategy). And, of greater practical importance, if actually faced with the task of memorizing a phone number you would probably automatically, from long habit, start rehearsing it (overlearned procedural knowledge of when and how to use rehearsal as a memory strategy). You also probably have at least procedural knowledge of more sophisticated cognitive strategies, such as the strategy of spending more time studying more important or less-learned material than less important or better-learned material.

Finally, the bulk of your metacognitive knowledge actually concerns combinations of, or interactions among, two or three of these three categories. To illustrate knowledge of an interaction between strategy and task, you would undoubtedly select a different preparation strategy if your task were to give a talk on some topic than if you only needed to follow a talk on that topic given by someone else.

Despite its exotic and high-sounding name, "metacognitive" knowledge is not qualitatively different from other kinds. On the contrary, there are several ways in which metacognitive knowledge seems similar to other kinds of knowledge. Like much other knowledge, a given bit of metacognitive knowledge may be declarative, procedural, or some of both. As with other knowledge acquisitions, metacognitive knowledge is probably accumulated in a slow and gradual fashion through years of experience in the "domain" of cognitive enterprises. Also like the other stored knowledge, it is frequently activated automatically and nondeliberately through recognition and response processes that detect and appropriately respond to familiar cognitive situations. Much as the chess expert automatically recognizes a familiar chessboard situation and automatically retrieves from memory a set of possible responses, so too, you may recognize and respond appropriately to a familiar type of cognitive situation. You may categorize and respond to it as a situation that is going to be very difficult and time consuming to get through, as one that is basically easy but needs careful attention to detail, as one that you will not be able to solve without outside help, as one that needs clearer specification, and so on. Like the chess expert, you may have learned through years of experience to recognize and react appropriately to a large number of input patterns relevant to the conduct, course, and outcome of cognitive enterprises. Finally, just like your knowledge about other things, your knowledge about cognitive enterprises can have various shortcomings. A given segment of your metacognitive knowledge may be insufficient, inaccurate, not reliably retrieved, and used when appropriate, or otherwise flawed. Thus, although metacognitive knowledge is an important kind of knowledge, it is not a mysterious, qualitatively different kind.

Metacognitive experiences are cognitive or affective experiences that pertain to a cognitive enterprise. Fully conscious and easy-to-articulate experiences of this sort are clear cases of this category but less fully conscious and verbalizable experiences should probably also be included in it. Metacognitive experiences can be brief or lengthy, simple or complex in content. For instance, you may sense only a momentary flicker of uncertainty or puzzlement, or you may obsess at considerable length about whether you *really* understand what your friend is like, "deep down." Metacognitive experiences may also occur at any time before, during, or after a cognitive endeavor. For example, you may think that you did very well on the first half of the final exam but feel pessimistic about how you are going to do on the second half. As these examples suggest, many metacognitive experiences have as their ideational content where you are in a cognitive enterprise and what sort of progress you have made, are making, or are likely to make. They seem especially likely to occur in situations that would be expected to engender careful, conscious monitoring and regulation of one's own cognition. Examples include novel roles or situations in which you have to feel your cognitive way along, step by step, and those weighty decision problems for which the penalty for cognitive missteps is high. Trying to decide whether to marry someone, for instance, may entail both a lot of cognition and a lot of rumination about the quality of that cognition (metacognitive experiences).

Metacognitive experiences can serve a variety of useful functions in ongoing cognitive enterprises. For instance, the sudden realization that you are not understanding what you have just been reading may instigate any of several adaptive actions: As examples, you may reread the passage, rethink what you already understand (or *thought* you understood), read ahead to see if something further on clarifies the muddle, enlist someone else's help, or try to modify your task objective in such a way as to reduce the importance of the problem. Metacognitive experiences are presumably informed and shaped by whatever relevant metacognitive knowledge you have acquired. For example, when you were a young child you may not have clearly understood what your metacognitive experiences of noncomprehension signified, nor what you should do about them when they occurred. There is, in fact, research evidence to suggest that young children do not adequately attend to such experiences and do not fully appreciate their meaning and behavioral implications (Flavell, 1985, pp. 260–263). As an adult, you possess the metacognitive knowledge necessary to properly interpret and act upon them. Conversely, metacognitive experiences must also contribute information about persons, tasks, and strategies to one's developing store of metacognitive knowledge: The ideas and feelings you experience when engaged in cognition must contribute to your knowledge about cognition just as the ideas and feelings you experience while watching or playing, say, tennis must contribute to your knowledge of tennis. Finally, it seems likely that metacognitive knowledge, metacognitive experience, and cognitive behavior are constantly informing and eliciting one another during the course of a cognitive task (see Flavell, 1985, p. 108).

The concept of metacognition has at least two ancestors in Piaget's work. One dates from the 1920s (Piaget, 1928), when Piaget claimed that young children's egocentrism prevents them from being able to introspect or treat their own thought processes as an object of thought. For example, he found that they were unable to reconstruct a chain of reasonings which they had just passed through; although they could think, they could not think about their own thinking. The other is, of course, his concept of formal operations. Formal-operational thinking is clearly metacognitive in nature because it involves thinking about such cognitive entities as propositions, hypotheses, and imagined possibilities. Piaget also did additional theorizing about self-reflection in later years (e.g., Piaget, 1976; see Kuhn, this volume).

During the 1970s I returned to two developmental topics I had first investigated in the 1950s and 1960s (Flavell et al., 1968), but this time conceptualized as instances of metacognitive development. One was the development of knowledge about comprehension and communication and the other the development of knowledge about perception. The latter dealt with visual perspective taking and was heavily influenced by Piaget's work. Research on both topics continued into the 1980s.

In our initial studies of metacognition concerning comprehension and communication (Flavell, Speer, Green, & August, 1981) we showed that 6-years-olds differed in theoretically important ways from 8-year-olds in their response to communicatively inadequate (e.g., ambiguous) instructions. First, they were less likely than the older children to show signs of noticing these inadequacies (e.g., pauses, puzzled looks). Second, even when they did show such signs, they were less likely than the older children to recognize their meaning and implications, namely, that the instructions were unclear and that, in consequence, they may have failed to carry them out successfully.

Subsequent studies confirmed and elaborated these findings, providing a variety of additional evidence concerning unexpected difficulties young children have in analyzing the communicative adequacy of simple spoken and written messages. In particular, these studies showed that young children have considerable difficulty in thinking about and analyzing the message per se ("the very words" of the message), in isolation from and independently of the cognition and behavior of the person who produced the message and the person who received it. For example, if the recipient of a communicatively inadequate instruction acts as if it were adequate, young children are less likely than they otherwise would be to detect its inadequacy; in contrast, the evaluations of older children and adults are unaffected by the recipient's behavior (Singer & Flavell, 1981). Similarly, young children are likelier than older ones to confuse what the message producer meant to communicate with what the message taken by itself actually does communicate (Beal & Flavell, 1984). We also showed that it is easier for young children to analyze and evaluate the communicative adequacy of a message if it can be read as well as heard, perhaps because a written message is more easily interpreted as a thing in itself, differentiable from its author's intended meaning and its audience's interpretation of it (Bonitatibus & Flavell, 1985).

I recall spending much of the summer of 1971 puzzling over Piaget and Inhelder's (1956) and our (Flavell et al., 1968) findings on perceptual perspective taking. The evidence showed that some perceptual perspective-taking tasks were much harder than others. Some were within reach even of preschoolers whereas others were challenging even for adolescents. What accounted for this difference in difficulty? One important factor was obviously task complexity. In the more difficult tasks the subject had to infer what parts of a multi-object array would appear directly or diagonally to the right, left, front, and rear of what other parts from the other observer's point of view—no mean feat of spatial computation. Moreover, as Piaget and Inhelder (1956) argued, knowing how to compute exactly how such complex arrays would appear to the other observer required some understanding of projective spatial relations. I came to suspect, however, that qualitative differences between younger and older children's meta-cognitive knowledge about perception might also be partly responsible for differences in task difficulty. This intuition eventually became the theory that there are two principal developmental stages or levels of Existence-type knowledge about visual percepts, to which I gave the clever titles "Level 1" and "Level 2" (Flavell, 1974, 1978, 1985).

At later-developing Level 2, according to this theory, children clearly understand the idea of people having different perspectives or views of the same display. Level 2 children can represent the fact that although both they and another person see the very same thing—"same" qua thing—from different station points, the other person nonetheless sees it a bit differently, or has a somewhat different visual experience of it, than they do. Level 2 knowledge thus is essentially the kind all of us had assumed we were studying beginning with Piaget and Inhelder (1956). At earlier-developing Level 1, children understand that the other person need not presently see something (again, qua thing) just because they do. Conversely, they also recognize that the other person may currently see something they do not. However, they do not yet conceptualize and consciously represent the fact of perspective-derived differences between their and the other person's visual experience of something both people both currently see. Level 1 children know that others also see things and that they and others need not see the same things at any given moment. They may also be able to infer exactly what things others do and do not see, given adequate cues. Thus, they are clearly not profoundly and pervasively egocentric in the Piagetian sense; they definitely do have some Existence-type knowledge about visual perception. Level 2 children possess this same knowledge and ability, of course, but are additionally aware that the same things may look different to others viewing them from a different position. They may also be able to infer approximately how these things appear from that different position, again given adequate cues. We have made direct tests of the theory by comparing the same children's performance on Level 1 and Level 2 tasks, and have also explored the nature and development of various sorts of Level 1 and Level 2 knowledge and skills. Because these studies focus directly on children's perspective-taking abilities, I will summarize them in some detail.

The first tests of the theory were made by Masangkay et al., (1974). In their tasks, the child and the experimenter faced each other across a small table. To assess Level 1 knowledge, a card with a picture of a cat on one side and a picture of a dog on the other was held vertically between the two and the child was asked to indicate which animal the experimenter sees. The 3-year-olds had no difficulty whatever in looking at the cat, say, but nonegocentrically reporting that the experimenter sees the dog. To assess Level 2 knowledge, a picture of a turtle was placed horizontally such that the turtle appeared upside down from one side of the table and right side up from the other. Although the 3-year-olds always correctly reported how the turtle appeared to them (thereby demonstrating that they understood the meaning of "right side up" and "upside down"), only about a third of them consistently attributed the opposite orientation to the experimenter. In contrast, a group of 4-year-olds performed virtually without error on both tasks.

Flavell, Everett, Croft, and Flavell (1981) carried out three studies in hopes of providing confirming evidence for the distinction and to further clarify the nature of Level 2 perspective-taking ability. In Study 1, 3-year-olds were asked to solve two Level 1 and two Level 2 perspective-taking problems. In the Level 1 tasks, the children were asked whether the experimenter saw (a) the cat or the dog, when a card with a drawing of a cat on one side and a dog on the other was held vertically between the child and the experimenter; and (b) the turtle's feet or the turtle's back, when a card with a drawing of a turtle on it was placed on the table between the child and the experimenter and bisected vertically by a card, so that the turtle's back was visible from one side of the table and its feet from the other. In Level 2 tasks the children were asked (a) whether the same turtle (without bisecting card) appeared right side up or upside down to the experimenter; and (b) whether a worm appeared to the experimenter to be lying on a red blanket or a blue blanket, when a card with a drawing of a worm between two blankets was placed on the table between child and experimenter. The results provided unequivocal support for the proposed distinction: All the children correctly solved both Level 1 tasks, whereas no child correctly solved both Level 2 tasks.

In Study 2, 3-year-olds were given three Level 2 tasks: (a) the turtle task from Study 1, (b) the same turtle with the requirement to say whether it appeared to the experimenter to be standing on its feet or lying on its back, and (c) a picture book task, in which the child was asked whether the experimenter was looking at the picture "the right way" (right side up) or "the wrong way" (upside down). The latter two tasks were intended to simplify the situation for the children by giving them verbally specified distinctive features to refer to (Task b), and by asking them the Level 2 questions in the context of a naturalistic, everyday situation (Task c). The results provided strong support for the stability and uniformity of Level 2 perspective-taking ability; only about one-third of the children passed each task, with—somewhat counterintuitively—no differences in mean performance among the three tasks. In these two studies, as in Masangkay et al. (1974), the children could correctly report how the stimuli appeared to them.

In Study 3, children who failed the Level 2 tasks in Study 2 were retested on Level 2 Tasks a and b. They were then provided with a variety of experiences designed to facilitate solution of the problem, for example, being taken around to the experimenter's side of the table and shown that the turtle appeared upside down from there. Immediately following these experiences, the children were again tested on Tasks a and b. The experiences did not prove sufficient to induce Level 2 processing.

These studies suggested that there is a real and robust difference between Level 1 and Level 2 perspective-taking abilities. Furthermore, relevant experience does not readily induce Level 2 thinking in Level 1 children, even when that experience consists of literally supplying them with the correct answer to the question.

As to Level 1 knowledge and skill, the research evidence shows that children have acquired a surprisingly rich repertoire of them by 2.5–3 years of age (Churcher & Scaife, 1982; Cox, 1980; Flavell, 1978; Flavell, Everett, Croft, & Flavell, 1981; Flavell, Shipstead, & Croft, 1978, 1980; Hobson, 1980; Hughes, 1975; Hughes & Donaldson, 1979; Lempers, Flavell, & Flavell, 1977). Let S = the child, O = another person, X = the visual target (a real or depicted object), and A = any large object interposed between O and S such as to block O's vision of S. By the age of 2.5–3 years, children act as if they know implicitly that the following four conditions must hold if O is to see X (Flavell, 1978; Lempers et al., 1977): (a) at least one of O's eyes must be open; (b) O's eyes must be aimed in the general direction of X; (c) there must be no vision-blocking A on the line of sight between O and X; (d) what S sees and does not see with regard to O, X, or A has no bearing on what O sees; that is, the child's percept cognition is fundamentally nonegocentric when dealing with Level 1, "what-is-seen" type problems.

Tacit knowledge of these four facts permits children of this age to *produce, prevent,* and *diagnose* object seeing by the other person. They can produce or engender the seeing of X by O by pointing to or verbally designating X, by getting O to open his or her eyes and face X, by moving or reorienting X so that it is in O's line of sight, and by repositioning either A or X so that A no longer blocks O's seeing of X. They can prevent O's seeing of X by moving X behind A, or A in front of X, and by getting O to close his or her eyes or turn away from X. Finally, they can diagnose or assess whether or not O currently sees X by noting whether or not the foregoing seeing conditions obtain. Thus, the research evidence indicates that children of this age are nonegocentric showers (e.g., they will orient a picture so that O, but not they, can see it), nonegocentric hiders (e.g., they will place an object where they, but not O, can still see it), and nonegocentric percept assessors (e.g., they know that their bodies are still visible to O when their own eyes, but not O's, are closed).

Our theory proposes that Level 2 children know, first, that a visual display will normally look different to another person who views it from a different perspective, and second, roughly how it will look to that person, given adequate cues. Knowledge of the first, "that" type could be described as Level 2 rules, with processes leading to information of the second, "how" type described as Level 2 computations. Because we were more interested in the development of general knowledge about visual perception than in the acquisition of spatial–perspectival computational skills, we tried to measure Level 2 rule knowledge and use unconfounded by computation ability.

In a study by Flavell, Flavell, Green, and Wilcox (1981), children of 4.5, 5, and 5.5 years of age were tested for their knowledge of three spatial perspective-taking rules: (a) any object will appear the same to the self and another person if both view it from the same position; (b) a heterogeneous-sided object (in this study, a tangle of wire) will appear different to the two observers if they view if from different sides, and (c) a homogeneous-sided object (a cylinder) will appear the same to the two if they view if from different sides. The data suggested that at least rules 1 and 2 undergo development during this age period and that 5.5-year-olds have a good grasp of all three rules. Flavell, Omanson, and Latham (1978) obtained evidence suggesting that older children not only possess rules 1 and 2 but will also consciously and deliberately use them in solving concrete perspective-taking problems (see also Salatas & Flavell, 1976). In a study by Flavell, Flavell, Green, and Wilcox (1980), children of ages 3, 3.5, and 4.5 years were tested for a different form of Level 2 knowledge about visual perception, namely, that an observer stationed closer to a small object will be able to see it better than an observer stationed farther away on roughly the same line of sight, whereas they will be able to see it equally well if stationed side by side at the same distance from it. The data suggested that this knowledge undergoes considerable development during the preschool period, with many 4.5-year-olds seemingly possessing it in the form of a general rule. Finally, Pillow and Flavell (1986) showed that 4-year-olds are more aware than 3-year-olds of how the apparent size and shape of an object changes with changes in its distance and orientation with respect to the observer. This is further evidence for a developing attentiveness during the preschool years to the way things appear perceptually.

The 1980s

Recall our claim that young children with only Level 1 knowledge about perception can represent *whether* X is visually accessible to O but not *how* X appears to O when it *is* visually accessible to him or her. During the early 1980s we began to think that this cognitive limitation might be part of a more general failure to understand that the selfsame visible object or event can be mentally represented in more than one way, within S or O individually as well as between S and O. When the different representations belong to two different people, we are dealing with ordinary between-person perspective taking. When the different representations belong to the same person, we are dealing with a less familiar, within-person form of perspective taking. One example of this within-person form, cited in my initial discussion of egocentrism, would be trying to imagine oneself feeling happy while in the throes of feeling sad. Another example would be distinguishing between how an illusory stimulus appears to you at this moment and the different way it really is — that is, the appearance–reality distinction. This line of thinking led us to expect that older preschool children would prove to be better than younger ones at distinguishing between how something appears and how it really is (a form of within-person perspective taking) for much the same reason that they are better at distinguishing between how something appears to them and how it appears to another person (between-person perspective-taking) — namely, because both tasks demand Level 2 knowledge about perception. Thus it was that we began an extended program of developmental research on the appearance--reality distinction (Flavell, 1986, 1988; Flavell, Flavell, & Green, 1983; Flavell, Green, & Flavell, 1986).

In these studies we have used variations of the following procedure to assess young children's ability to think about appearance versus reality. First we pretrain briefly on the meaning of the distinction and associated terminology by showing the children (for example) a Charley Brown puppet inside a ghost costume. We explain and demonstrate that Charley Brown "*looks like* a ghost to your eyes right now" but is "*really* and *truly*" Charley Brown, and that "sometimes things look like one thing to your eyes when they are really and truly something else." We then present a variety of illusory stimuli and ask about their appearance and their reality. For instance, we first show the children a very realistic-looking fake rock made out of a soft sponge-like material and then let them discover its identity by manipulating it. We next ask, in random order: (a) "what is this *really, and truly?* Is it *really, and truly* a sponge or is it *really, and truly* a rock?" (b) "when you look at this with your eyes right now, does it *look like* a rock or does it *look like* a sponge?" Or we show the children a white stimulus, move it behind a blue filter, and similarly ask about its real and apparent color.

Our studies have shown that 3–4-year-old children presented with appearance–reality (AR) tasks of this sort usually either answer both questions correctly, suggesting some ability to differentiate appearance and reality representations, or else give the same answer (reporting either the appearance or the reality) to both questions, suggesting some conceptual difficulty with the distinction; incorrect answers to both questions occur only infrequently. There is a marked improvement with age during the preschool years in the ability to solve these AR tasks. Some illusory stimuli tend to elicit appearance answers to both questions *(phenomenism),* whereas others tend to elicit reality answers to both *(realism).* If the task is to distinguish between the real and apparent properties of color, size, and shape, phenomenism errors predominate. Thus, if an object that is really white or small or straight is temporarily made to look blue, big, or bent by means of filters or lenses, young children are likely to say the object really *is* blue, big, or bent. If, instead, the task is to indicate what object(s) or event is present, really versus apparently, realism errors tend to predominate. For example, the fake rock is incorrectly said to look like a sponge rather than a rock; an experimenter who appears from the child's viewing position to be reading a large book, but who is known by the child really to be drawing a picture inside it, is incorrectly said to look like he or she is drawing rather than reading. Indeed, Taylor and Flavell (1984) found that significantly more phenomenism errors occurred when stimuli were described to children in terms of their properties (e.g., "white" vs. "orange" liquid) than when the very same stimuli were described in terms of identities ("milk" vs. "koolaid"). We do not know yet exactly why the appearance usually seems to be more cognitively salient for young children in these property tasks and the reality more salient in the object/event identity tasks, although we have proposed some possible explanations (Flavell, Flavell, & Green, 1983). Young children also have difficulties with the appearance–reality distinction when the appearance is auditory or olfactory rather than visual (Flavell et al., 1986).

Three lines of evidence indicate that young children's difficulties with the AR distinction are nontrivial, deep-seated, genuinely intellectual ones.

1. Young children of the same age from different countries perform about equally poorly on the same AR tasks: children from the United States and People's Republic of China in the case of real versus apparent color, size, and object identity (Flavell, Zhang, Zou, Dong, & Qi, 1983); children from Great Britain, United States, and Japan in the case of real versus apparent emotions (Harris & Gross, 1988). These results suggest that their difficulties with the distinction are robust and substantial enough to survive at least some major differences in language, culture, and child-rearing practices.

2. We have attempted to uncover any nascent, fragile AR competence young children might have by using less demanding, easier-seeming tests of this competence (Flavell, Green, & Flavell, 1986; Flavell, Green, Wahl, & Flavell, 1987). Most of these attempts have failed, however. For example, we tried to ask 3-year-olds for an object's real color in a color AR task without using a "really and truly" question—arguably too difficult a question for young children (Flavell, Green, Wahl, & Flavell, 1987). With the child watching all proceedings, the experimenter placed, say, a white card under a blue color filter so the card looked blue. Then, with the card still under the filter, the experimenter detached a precut piece from the card, put the piece into a closed hand, removed the closed hand from behind the filter, placed on the table that white piece and a blue piece of the same size and shape, and then simply asked the child, "Which is the piece I just took out of the card?" This question is similar to the standard reality question ("Is this card really and truly blue or really and truly white?"), but does not require understanding of the possibly troublesome expression "really and truly" and does not require a verbal response. Nevertheless, our young subjects did not find it any easier than the standard question (in fact, in one study they actually found it significantly *harder*). That is, they frequently responded by pointing to the blue piece, the one that matched the card's

present apparent color rather than its real color, just as they frequently responded to the standard reality question by saying "blue." In fact, our only "success" in making visual AR tasks easier is our recent finding (Flavell, Green, Wahl, & Flavell, 1987) that 3-year-olds perform somewhat better on color AR tasks if visual evidence, suggesting what the object's real color is, remains available during questioning. For example, they find it easier to say that a white object held behind a green filter is really and truly white if the white handles used to hold the object extend out laterally beyond the edges of the filter, and therefore continue to look white instead of green. The handles may help by reminding the children of what the object's real color is. Consistent with the results of training studies (see No. 3), however, there was no evidence that their experience in this easier task condition taught them anything lasting about appearance versus reality representations. Furthermore, memory aids failed to benefit AR performance in a second study.

3. Flavell, Green, and Flavell (1986) and Taylor and Hort (1990) tried to teach the distinction between real and apparent color to 3-year-olds who performed poorly on standard color AR tasks. Braine and Shanks (1965) attempted to do the same with the distinction between real and apparent size. None of these attempts was successful. Thus, all three lines of evidence suggest that young children's difficulties with the distinction between appearance and reality are very real indeed.

There is much that would seem familiar to Piaget in our appearance-reality work. As indicated previously, when children err on our tasks they usually do so by encoding the stimulus in only one way. As Piaget would probably say, they either "center" only on the appearance and fail to "decenter" to consider also the reality, or they do the opposite. In addition, the concepts of "phenomenism" and "realism," used to describe, respectively, this narrow "centration" on only the appearance or only the reality, are also taken from Piaget's writings. Finally, he could justly claim to have been the first to study children's ability to distinguish appearance and reality in his famous studies of conservations. As Braine and Shanks (1965) argued some years ago, the child cannot solve Piagetian conservation problems without some ability to make an appearance-reality distinction, because these problems require the ability to ignore misleading perceptual appearances that suggest that nonconservation rather than conservation obtains. Thus, the errors that children made on conservation tasks are essentially "phenomenism" errors — errors resulting from an exclusive concentration on the appearance.

Our research on children's knowledge about perception and appearance--reality is part of a larger body of work that has sprung up during the 1980s on the development of children's knowledge about the mind or, as some conceive of it, their developing "theory of mind" (Astington, Harris, & Olson, 1988; Harris, 1989; Perner, 1991; Wellman, 1990). Thus, there is a resurgence of interest in a topic that Piaget first explored in the 1920s and that others studied in the 1950s, 1960s, and 1970s under such rubrics as "social cognition" and "metacognition." Researchers in this area have been studying such topics as: (1) Young children's knowledge about percepts, beliefs, intentions, desires, emotions, and other mental states; (2) Their ability to infer the perceptual, conceptual, and affective perspectives of others; (3) Their grasp of the distinctions between real and mental, real and pretend, real and apparent (the appearance–reality distinction), what is said and what is meant, and what is seen and how that which is seen is mentally represented. Furthermore, there is a growing sense that many of these acquisitions may be developmentally related. Some develop at about the same age and appear to reflect the same newly acquired insight into the nature of mind. Some emerge in fixed sequence, suggesting an orderly developmental succession of such insights.

A number of us have recently tried to characterize the course of development in this domain (e.g., Perner, 1991; Wellman, 1990; various chapters in Astington et al., 1988). The connections–representations account that my coworkers and I have recently formulated (Flavell, 1988; Flavell, Green, & Flavell, 1990) is an elaboration of our earlier Level 1-Level 2 theory; it also owes a great deal to the thinking of other researchers in this area. According to our account, by approximately 3 years of age—at Level 1, in the earlier theory—most children have learned that they and other people can be epistemically related or *cognitively connected* to things in the external world in a variety of different ways. An example of a cognitive connection is seeing something. Children of this age know that they can become cognitively connected to something by seeing it; they also understand that they may not see it—that they may not be connected to it in this way at a given moment. They further understand that they may be cognitively connected, or not connected, to things in many other ways as well. That is, they understand at least roughly what it is to do most of the following: hear or not hear something, taste it, smell it, feel it by touching it, know it, think of or about it, dream of or about it, picture or imagine it, pretend with it, want it, hope for it, intend to do something with it, and have specific feelings and emotions regarding it—like it, fear it, be angry at it, and so on. This account does not claim that all such cognitive connections are understood equally early or equally well nor does it explain developmental *décalages* among them. It only suggests that some knowledge about most such connections is an early acquisition.

We also credit 3-year-olds with some understanding that: (a) cognitive connections can change over time; (b) they are largely independent of one another; (c) their own connections are independent of those of other people; (d) connections entail inner, subjective experiences. As examples of (a) they are capable of realizing that they dreamed of X last night but are not dreaming of it now, and that they see Y now but did not see it a minute ago. As examples of (b) they understand that they can hear something either with or without also seeing it, think about it with or without simultaneously perceiving it, and so on. To illustrate (c) they are capable of recognizing that another person may perceive, guess, want, dislike, and so on, something that they do not or vice versa; thus we believe that their conception of these connections (but not necessarily of other mental entities, see later) is fundamentally nonegocentric rather than egocentric. As to (d) recent research (e.g., Dunn, Bretherton, & Munn, 1987; Wellman, 1990) suggests that young children can distinguish to some extent between the subjective acts and experiences of seeing, feeling, etc., something and that objective something itself. That is, it seems likely that they tend to interpret perceptions, feelings, and the like mentalistically rather than behavioristically—as experiences that take place inside themselves and other people (Lillard & Flavell, 1990). When they see another child cry, for instance, they are likely to assume that the child is experiencing unpleasant inner feelings, just as they do when they themselves cry. Similarly, when they see a person look at or listen to something, they are likely to represent that person as having the phenomenological experience of seeing or hearing it (Novey, 1975).

Despite these impressive developmental accomplishments, most researchers in this area agree that children of this age still have only a limited understanding of *mental representations*. They tacitly believe, as adults generally do, that each object or event in the world has only one nature— one "way that it is"—at any given point in time. It cannot be two or more very different, mutually contradictory and incompatible things at the same time; rather, it can only be one thing—namely, how it "is" (with "is" not differentiated in their thinking from "seems to them at that moment"). Unlike adults, however, they do not clearly understand yet that people may for one reason or another "seriously" represent that thing very differently from the way it "is" (seems to them), that is, describe it very differently other than when pretending, joking, dreaming, lying, or the like (for a possible explanation of the "seriously" qualification, see Perner, 1988, 1991; see also Furth, this volume). Young children do not clearly understand that it is possible to represent seriously (model, depict, construe, etc.) a single thing with its single nature in several different ways—ways that would be mutually contradictory if they described the object itself rather than people's mental representations of it. Thus, they do not clearly see that even though something may actually be only one thing or one way out there in the world at any given moment, it can actually be more than one thing or one way up here in our heads, in our mental representations of it. Consequently, they will tend to reject as simply wrong or incomprehensible any description of something that seems to them to contradict "the way it is at that moment." In particular, they will tend to do so even when that description is generated by a seriously held but incorrect mental representation of the thing, for example, a belief that is false because based on inadequate evidence.

This account suggests, therefore, that children of this age are to some degree cognizant of cognitive connections to things—seeing them, liking them, and so on—but not of the fact that things can be mentally represented seriously (nonplayfully) in very different ways. How might such children respond to tasks or situations that require cognizance of contradictory-seeming mental representations? The tasks we have used to assess children's understanding of the appearance–reality distinction provide one illustration. Suppose we present the children with, say, the sponge that looks like a rock. Suppose further that, after manipulating it they decide the object is a sponge, not a rock. For them, therefore, it "is" just one thing—a sponge. We then ask them our appearance and reality questions. Adults interpret these questions as questions about the two very different, incompatible-seeming ways this one object can be mentally represented, namely, as a rock in its visual appearance and as a sponge in its enduring reality (texture, compressibility, function, etc.). We mentally tag each representation for the cognitive perspective or stance that gave rise to it—for its epistemic credentials, so to speak. In this case, we tag one as "what it looks like it is" and the other as "what it really is." However, because young children lack adequate understanding of mental representations they should tend to interpret the two questions simply as two differently-worded requests for the object's single-identity-in-the-world and should therefore give the same answer to both questions—"sponge." Similarly, if they had decided instead that the object was a rock, they should answer "rock" to both questions. Recall that, consistent with this analysis, their most common error pattern is indeed to give the same answer to both questions.

Children of this age have also been shown to have difficulty with other tasks that appear to require an understanding of contrasting mental representations. For example, they have trouble understanding false belief and changes in belief (e.g., Astington & Gopnik, 1988; Astington et al., 1988; Hogrefe, Wimmer, & Perner, 1986; Moses & Flavell, 1990; Perner, 1991; Wellman, 1990; Wimmer & Perner, 1983). These studies show that if a 3-year-old subject initially thinks that, say, a candy box contains candy and then subsequently discovers that it actually contains pencils, the subject will incorrectly assert that: (a) a naïve observer will think it contains pencils; (b) the subject also initially thought it contained pencils, prior to learning the truth. That is, many 3-year-olds can neither recall their own previous false beliefs nor attribute false beliefs to others. Again, the idea that someone could *seriously* (i.e., other than in pretend play or fantasy) represent something as being other than it "is" is poorly understood at this age. Similarly, we have already seen that they also perform poorly on Level 2 visual perspective-taking tasks. For example, recall that they have difficulty understanding that a depicted turtle which they view in normal, right-side-up orientation or "standing on his feet" appears upside down or "lying on his back" to another person who views it from the opposite side of the table. Again, the problem seems to be a failure to differentiate how something "is" (seems to them) from how people might experience or represent it. For them, "what is there" is a turtle standing on its feet, and therefore it makes no sense to attribute to another person a mental representation of it as being a turtle lying on its back. In addition, there is correlational evidence that within an age group the same young children who perform well (or poorly) on appearance–reality tasks likewise tend to perform well (or poorly) on false belief tasks and Level 2 visual perspective-taking tasks (Flavell, Green, & Flavell, 1986; Gopnik & Astington, 1988). This evidence is at least consistent with our and other researchers' hypothesis that an improved understanding of mental representations mediates good performance on all three tasks.

Young children also have trouble with several other tasks that would seem to require this same understanding. In early word learning children are often reluctant to accept a second name for an object, for example, "cat" for the animal they know only as "kitty" (Clark, 1987; Markman, 1989). Perhaps the new name is interpreted as a claim that the animal is something other than a kitty. They have trouble with hypothetical statements, especially about how things might have been in the past (Kuczaj, 1981). Perhaps past hypotheticals, such as Kuczaj's "What would have happened if your mommy drank some coffee last night?" (it having just been established that she had not really done so) are hard for them to interpret properly because they are construed simply as incorrect descriptions of a previous, known reality. They find it difficult to understand scale models (DeLoache, 1989; Dow & Pick, 1990), perhaps because these models have to be construed as representations of what they model in addition to being construed as objects in their own right. Finally, Piaget long ago showed that they have difficulty seriating objects by size and in understanding that such series are transitive (Flavell, 1963, p. 193). Piaget attributed this difficulty to their failure to conceive of each object in the series as simultaneously being both smaller than its neighbor on one side and larger than its neighbor on the other side. A partial cause of this failure might be their inability to understand how an object could be thought of as "smaller" if they had just encoded it as "larger" (because "larger" is what it "is" for them), or "larger" if they had just encoded it as "smaller."

In marked contrast, 3-year-olds appear to have little difficulty with tasks that seem to require only knowledge about cognitive connections. I have already described how well they manage Level 1 visual perspective-taking problems. In Level 2 problems the issue is *how* an object that both the child and another person view from different positions *looks* or appears to the other person, for example, right side up versus upside down, or as this sort of object versus that. In Level 1 problems the question is only *what* object the other person *sees* from his or her viewing position. There is no issue in these latter problems of how the other person mentally represents that object, but only of whether the person is or is not visually connected to it. There is also evidence that 3-year-olds have some understanding that at any given moment an observer can be cognitively connected to an object in one way but not in another (Flavell et al., 1990; Yaniv & Shatz, 1988), for example, be able to hear but not see the object. As to other cognitive connections, Wellman and Woolley (1990) have recently shown that even 2-year-olds have some understanding of people's desires. They also cite work by others suggesting some early awareness that people have emotions, goals, motives, and intentions. Consistent with the present developmental account, they hypothesize that children initially acquire a "desire psychology," and only later a "belief-desire psychology" that allows them to understand false belief and other mental representations (Wellman, 1990).

What accounts for the developmental transition from only understanding connections to also understanding representations? The following are some possibilities (Flavell, 1988, Flavell, Flavell, & Green, 1987; Flavell, Green, & Flavell, 1990; see also Astington & Gopnik, 1990; Gopnik, 1990; Perner, 1991; Wellman, 1985, 1990). An age-dependent increase in information-processing capacity might make the transition possible, as Halford (in press) has recently suggested. Children might find it easier to at least consider the possibility that the same thing could be mentally represented in different ways as it becomes easier for them to hold two or more such representations in mind at the same time. Consistent with this possibility, Flavell et al. (1987) found that 3-year-olds perform better on color AR tasks if visual evidence of the object's real color remains available during questioning. For instance, they are likelier to say that a white object held behind a green filter is really and truly white if the white handles used to hold the object extend out laterally beyond the edges of the filter, and therefore, still appear white rather than green to them. The handles may aid by helping the child keep in mind what the object's natural color is. On the other hand, such capacity increases could scarcely be a sufficient cause of the transition. For example, 3-year-olds who assert that, say, a white object behind a red filter both looks red and really is red are usually aware that the object will look white again when the filter is removed (Flavell et al., 1986; Flavell et al., 1987). Thus even when both real and apparent color seem to be available to them cognitively, 3-year-olds will often refuse to attribute both to the object at any one point in time. In fact, even 5-year-olds, who normally perform well on AR tasks, will often give an appearance answer to a reality question if the question specifies the present reality, for example, "*Right now, for real,* is this object blue (apparent color) or white (real color)?" (Flavell, Flavell, & Green, 1989). Processing limitations could hardly explain these errors by 5-year-olds.

Young children also have experiences that seemingly could help them learn about mental representations, again assuming that they are cognitively ready to profit from them. In their pretend play they have repeated experiences representing things as other than what they really are and observing their playmates do the same. Perhaps these play experiences help sensitize children to the possibility of nonplayful conflicting representations in other situations (Flavell et al., 1987). Similarly, they learn other relevant-seeming contrasts between reality and something else — real versus toy, real versus depicted, real versus fake, and real versus apparent (Woolley & Wellman, 1990). Gopnik (1990) has suggested that noticing changes in their own beliefs over time, as new information comes their way, may also help. That is, noticing that one's mental representation of something has changed even though the something itself has not, might be a developmentally formative experience for the prepared mind; it is the conceptual equivalent of walking around a visual display and noting how different it looks from different perspectives. In addition, other people must frequently make salient to the child differences between the child's mental model of reality (e.g., beliefs about it) and their own or those of others. The child says a toy is his or hers; a playmate strenuously objects, saying that it is his or hers. The child thinks something is good; someone else says it is bad. Many parents often call young children's false beliefs and other cognitive missteps to their attention, point out differences between different people's perspectives, and otherwise help them realize that the same thing can be mentally represented in more than one way. There is evidence that children hear a lot of talk about mental events from parents and older siblings from an early age, and that earlier maternal talk about mental events predicts later child acquisition of mental terms (Dunn et al., 1987). Finally as Gopnik (1990) has cogently argued, a theory of mind that includes no concepts of conflicting mental representations should inevitably lead children who hold this theory to make many wrong predictions about others people's behavior. For example, they should habitually default to the prediction that another person will act in accordance with their own beliefs and expectations, not the person's own. According to Piaget's equilibration model, a theory of that kind would be particularly ripe for developmental change.

Here as elsewhere in cognitive development, however, a complete explanation will have to specify the developmental role of innate and maturing capabilities within the child as well as potentially formative experiences. There is evidence that autistic children tend not to progress beyond an understanding of some cognitive connections (e.g., Level 1 knowledge about vision), despite the fact that these formative experiences are presumably also available to them (Baron–Cohen, 1989; Leslie & Frith, 1988). They clearly lack whatever basic capabilities are needed to benefit from these experiences. This and other evidence has led Leslie (1991) to suggest that normal development in this area is powered by an innate or early-maturing "theory of mind module" — an "engine of development," which is seriously impaired or lacking in autistic children.

Our connections-representations developmental account has a Piagetian cast to it in that it emphasizes qualitative rather than quantitative changes with age in the child's knowledge about the mind. Knowing that people mentally represent or model the world is, at least on the face of it, qualitatively different from not knowing that, and only knowing about cognitive connections. Other theorists in the "theory of mind" area are also postulating qualitative changes with age in the child's knowledge (e.g., Forguson & Gopnik, 1988; Perner, 1988, 1991; Wellman, 1990). Also, reminiscent of Piagetian stage-wise development is the already-cited finding that children's performance on appearance–reality, false–belief, and Level 2 perspective-taking tasks are positively correlated, suggesting the development of a single underlying competency that mediates mastery of all three. In addition, we have seen that it is not easy to induce, either through training or the use of easy tasks, understanding of Level 2 perspective taking or appearance–reality problems in 3-year-olds who do not understand them spontaneously. Recent evidence suggests that this may also be true of false–belief tasks (Flavell, Flavell, Green, & Moses, 1990; Moses & Flavell, 1990; for a dissenting view, see Chandler, Fritz, & Hala, 1989). My coworkers and I get the impression when testing young 3-year-olds that most of them are simply not "maturationally ready" to understand our questions about mental representations, and that the best we can do is just wait for them to grow a little older. It is, indeed, very like the impression one is likely to have when trying vainly to get a young preschooler to conserve or seriate: There is just not enough there yet on which to build. Finally, this account is Piagetian in yet another way. I began this chapter by describing Piaget's belief that young children do not know that they and other people have conceptual, perceptual, and affective perspectives. I think he might accept as roughly synonymous with this belief our and others' claim that they do not know that people mentally represent the world. I suspect that he gave little thought to a still earlier period of development in which they first lack and later acquire knowledge about lower-level cognitive connections.

CURRENT PERSPECTIVES ON PERSPECTIVE TAKING

Psychologists' perspectives on perspective-taking development—my own and others'—have naturally changed considerably since Piaget's seminal studies and our early follow-up efforts. The current perspective is broader, and we "center" on different things than in the past. The nature of the change in perspective can be suggested by listing some of the main questions that preoccupy contemporary investigators in this area (see also, for example, Astington & Gopnik, 1991; Astington et al., 1988; D'Andrade, 1987; Frye & Moore, 1991; Perner, 1991; Wellman, 1990; Whiten, 1991).

1. What is the "folk psychology" or "naïve theory of mind" of the typical adult in our culture? That is, what is our workaday model of people's mental entities (beliefs, desires, etc.) and of their relationships to perceptual input, to one another, and to behavioral output? It is apparent that this question is much broader than our initial ones concerning the development of perspective-taking skills.

2. To what extent are we justified in thinking of what we possess in this area as a "theory," rather than, say, a collection of isolated concepts or rules?

3. Where, how, and how much do we use this theory (or whatever it is) in our daily lives?

4. Do adults the world over possess basically the same theory, or are there important intercultural differences in theory?

5. What about intracultural differences? Do all normal laypersons from the same culture end up with identical theories of mind? How do the theories of mind of cognitive scientists, normal laypersons, and nonnormal laypersons (e.g., autistic, psychotic, or mentally retarded adults) compare?

6. What about other species? For example, do chimpanzees show evidence of possessing any elements of a theory of mind?

7. What is the sequence of developmental steps in the child's acquisition of the normal layperson's theory? Which elements of the adult theory do children acquire first, which elements later, and which elements later still? For example, do they think of people as compliant agents before they think of them as conscious experiencers, and think of them as conscious

experiencers before they think of them as mental representers? Similarly, do they conceive of the mind differently at different ages? For example, do they first tacitly construe it as a Lockean mind that passively takes in information as is and only later as a Piagetian mind that actively constructs and interprets?

8. A question discussed briefly in the preceding chapter section: How will we explain whatever course of development we finally describe? What role might such factors as the following play in the child's construction of a theory of mind: inborn or early-maturing "metarepresentational" (Leslie, 1991) abilities, an increase with age in information-processing capacity, awareness of and reflection on one's own mental states, the acquisition of mental state terms, and various forms of assistance by parents, siblings, peers, and others?

9. How will we integrate the recent work on theory-of-mind development with the earlier work on metacognitive and social–cognitive development? All three bodies of work concern the child's naïve psychology but they have tended to focus on different age groups and different phenomena.

It is clear from the foregoing that what Piaget began almost a lifetime ago has grown into a large and complex area of developmental inquiry. But that is a familiar story. Here as in so many other areas, he was the prophet of genius and we his grateful followers.

ACKNOWLEDGMENTS

Excerpts from this paper were presented at the 20th annual symposium of the Jean Piaget Society, Philadelphia, June 2, 1990.

REFERENCES

Astington, J. W., & Gopnik, A. (1988). Knowing you've changed your mind: Children's understanding of representational change. In J. W. Astington, P. L. Harris, & D. R. Olson (Eds.), *Developing theories of mind*. New York: Cambridge University Press.

Astington, J. W., & Gopnik, A. (1991). Theoretical explanations of children's understanding of the mind. *British Journal of Developmental Psychology, 9*, 7–31.

Astington, J. W., Harris, P. L., & Olson, D. R. (Eds.). (1988). *Developing theories of mind*. New York: Cambridge University Press.

Baron–Cohen, S. (1989). Are autistic children behaviorists? An examination of their mental–physical and appearance–reality distinctions. *Journal of Autism and Developmental Disorders, 19*, 579–600.

Beal, C. R., & Flavell, J. H. (1984). Development of the ability to distinguish communicative intention and literal message meaning. *Child Development, 55,* 920-928.

Bonitatibus, G. J., & Flavell, J. H. (1985). Effect of presenting a message in written form on young children's ability to evaluate its communication adequacy. *Developmental Psychology, 21,* 455-461.

Braine, M. D. S., & Shanks, B. L. (1965). The conservation of a shape property and a proposal about the origin of the conservations. *Canadian Journal of Psychology, 19,* 197-207.

Chandler, M., Fritz, A., & Hala, S. (1989). Small scale deceit: Deception as a marker of 2-, 3-, and 4-year-olds' early theories of mind. *Child Development, 60,* 1263-1277.

Churcher, J., & Scaife, M. (1982). How infants see the point. In G. Butterworth & P. Light (Eds.), *Social cognition: Studies of the development of understanding.* Chicago: University of Chicago Press.

Clark, E. V. (1987). The principle of contrast: A constraint on language acquisition. In B. MacWhinney (Ed.), *Mechanisms of language acquisition: Proceedings of the 20th Annual Carnegie Symposium on Cognition 1985.* Hillsdale, NJ: Lawrence Erlbaum Associates.

Cox, M. V. (1980). Visual perspective-taking in children. In M. V. Cox (Ed.), *Are young children egocentric?* New York: St. Martin's Press.

D'Andrade, R. (1987). A folk model of the mind. In D. Holland & N. Quinn (Eds.), *Cultural models in language and thought.* New York: Cambridge University Press.

DeLoache, J. S. (1989). The development of representation in young children. In H. W. Reese (Ed.), *Advances in child development and behavior* (Vol. 22). New York: Academic Press.

Dow, G. A., & Pick, H. L. (June, 1990). *Young children's use of models and pictures as spatial representations.* Poster presented at the 2nd annual meeting of the American Psychological Society, Dallas.

Dunn, J., Bretherton, I., & Munn, P. (1987). Conversations about feeling states between mothers and their young children. *Developmental Psychology, 23,* 132-139.

Elkind, D. (1967). Egocentrism in adolescence. *Child Development, 38,* 1025-1034.

Flavell, J. H. (1963). *The developmental psychology of Jean Piaget.* Princeton, NJ: Van Nostrand.

Flavell, J. H. (1966). Role-taking and communication skills in children. *Young Children, 21,* 164-177.

Flavell, J. H. (1970). Developmental studies of mediated memory. In H. W. Reese & L. P. Lipsitt (Eds.), *Advances in child development and behavior* (Vol. 5). New York: Academic Press.

Flavell, J. H. (1971). First discussant's comments: What is memory development the development of? *Human Development, 14,* 272-278.

Flavell, J. H. (1974). The development of inferences about others. In T. Mischel (Ed.), *Understanding other persons.* Oxford, England: Blackwell.

Flavell, J. H. (1978). The development of knowledge about visual perception. In C. B. Keasey (Ed.), *Nebraska symposium on motivation* (Vol. 25), Lincoln: University of Nebraska Press.

Flavell, J. H. (1985). *Cognitive development* (2nd ed.). Englewood Cliffs, NJ: Prentice-Hall.

Flavell, J. H. (1986). The development of children's knowledge about the appearance-reality distinction. *American Psychologist, 41,* 418-425.

Flavell, J. H. (1988). The development of children's knowledge about the mind: From cognitive connections to mental representations. In J. W. Astington, P. L. Harris, & D. R. Olson (Eds.), *Developing theories of mind.* New York: Cambridge University Press.

Flavell, J. H., Beach, D. H., & Chinsky, J. M. (1966). Spontaneous verbal rehearsal in a memory task as a function of age. *Child Development, 37,* 283-299.

Flavell, J. H., Botkin, P. T., Fry, C. L., Wright, J. W., & Jarvis, P. E. (1968). *The development of role-taking and communication skills in children.* New York: Wiley.

Flavell, J. H., Everett, B. A., Croft, K., & Flavell, E. R. (1981). Young children's knowledge about visual perception: Further evidence for the Level 1-Level 2 distinction. *Develop-*

mental Psychology, 17, 99–103.

Flavell, J. H., Flavell, E. R., & Green, F. L. (1983). Development of the appearance–reality distinction. *Cognitive Psychology, 15,* 95–120.

Flavell, J. H., Flavell, E. R., & Green, F. L. (1987). Young children's knowledge about the apparent–real and pretend–real distinctions. *Developmental Psychology, 23,* 816–822.

Flavell, J. H., Flavell, E. R., & Green, F. L. (1989). A transitional period in the development of the appearance–reality distinction. *International Journal of Behavioral Development, 12,* 509–526.

Flavell, J. H., Flavell, E. R., Green, F. L., & Moses, L. J. (1990). Young children's understanding of fact beliefs versus value beliefs. *Child Development, 61,* 915–928.

Flavell, J. H., Flavell, E. R., Green, F. L., & Wilcox, S. A. (1980). Young children's knowledge about visual perception. Effect of observer's distance from target on perceptual clarity of target. *Developmental Psychology, 16,* 10–12.

Flavell, J. H., Flavell, E. R., Green, F. L., & Wilcox, S. A. (1981). The development of three spatial perspective-taking rules. *Child Development, 52,* 356–358.

Flavell, J. H., Green, F. L., & Flavell, E. R. (1986). Development of knowledge about the appearance–reality distinction. *Monographs of the Society for Research in Child Development, 51*(1, Serial No. 212).

Flavell, J. H., Green, F. L., & Flavell, E. R. (1990). Developmental changes in young children's knowledge about the mind. *Cognitive Development, 5,* 1–27.

Flavell, J. H., Green, F. L., Wahl, K. E., & Flavell, E. R. (1987). The effects of question clarification and memory aids on young children's performance on appearance–reality tasks. *Cognitive Development, 2,* 127–144.

Flavell, J. H., Omanson, R. C., & Latham, C. (1978). Solving spatial perspective-taking problems by rule versus computation: A developmental study. *Developmental Psychology, 14,* 462–473.

Flavell, J. H., Shipstead, S. G., & Croft, K. (1978). Young children's knowledge about visual perception: Hiding objects from others. *Child Development, 49,* 1208–1211.

Flavell, J. H., Shipstead, S. G., & Croft, K. (1980). What young children think you see when their eyes are closed. *Cognition, 8,* 369–387.

Flavell, J. H., Speer, J. R., Green, F. L., & August, D. L. (1981). The development of comprehension monitoring and knowledge about communication. *Monographs of the Society for Research in Child Development, 46,*(5, Serial No. 192).

Flavell, J. H., & Wellman, H. M. (1977). Metamemory. In R. V. Kail & J. W. Hagen (Eds.), *Perspectives on the development of memory and cognition.* Hillsdale, NJ: Lawrence Erlbaum Associates.

Flavell, J. H., Zhang, X. D., Zou, H., Dong, Q., & Qi, S. (1983). A comparison between the development of the appearance–reality distinction in the People's Republic of China and the United States. *Cognitive Psychology, 15,* 459–466.

Ford, M. (1979). The construct validity of egocentrism. *Psychological Bulletin, 86,* 1169–1188.

Forguson, L., & Gopnik, A. (1988). The ontogeny of common sense. In J. W. Astington, P. L. Harris, & D. R. Olson (Eds.), *Developing theories of mind* (pp. 226–243). New York: Cambridge University Press.

Frye, D., & Moore, C. (1991). *Children's theories of mind.* Hillsdale, NJ: Lawrence Erlbaum Associates.

Gopnik, A. (1990). Developing the idea of intentionality: Children's theories of mind. *Canadian Journal of Philosophy, 20,* 89–114.

Gopnik, A., & Astington, J. (1988). Children's understanding of representational change and its relation to the understanding of false belief and the appearance–reality distinction. *Child Development, 59,* 26–37.

Gordon, F. R., & Flavell, J. H. (1977). The development of intuitions about cognitive cueing. *Child Development, 48,* 1027–1033.

Halford, G. S. (in press). *Children's understanding: The development of mental models.* Hillsdale, NJ: Lawrence Erlbaum Associates.

Harris, P. L. (1989). *The child's concept of emotion.* Oxford, England: Blackwell.

Harris, P. L., & Gross, D. (1988). Children's understanding of real and apparent emotion. In J. W. Astington, P. L. Harris, & D. R. Olson (Eds.), *Developing theories of mind.* New York: Cambridge University Press.

Hobson, R. P. (1980). The question of egocentrism: The young child's competence in the co-ordination of perspectives. *Journal of Child Psychology and Psychiatry, 21,* 325-331.

Hogrefe, G. J., Wimmer, H., & Perner, J. (1986). Ignorance versus false belief: A developmental lag in attribution of epistemic states. *Child Development, 57,* 567-582.

Hughes, M. (1975). *Egocentrism in preschool children.* Unpublished doctoral dissertation, University of Edinburgh.

Hughes, M., & Donaldson, M. (1979). The use of hiding games for studying the coordination of perspectives. *Educational Review, 31,* 133-140.

Inhelder, B., & Piaget, J. (1958). *The growth of logical thinking from childhood to adolescence.* New York: Basic Books.

Keeney, T. J., Cannizzo, S. R., & Flavell, J. H. (1967). Spontaneous and induced verbal rehearsal in a recall task. *Child Development, 38,* 953-966.

Keniston, A., & Flavell, J. H. (1979). The nature and development of intelligent retrieval. *Child Development, 50,* 1144-1152.

Kreutzer, M. A., Leonard, C., & Flavell, J. H. (1975). An interview study of children's knowledge about memory. *Monographs of the Society for Research in Child Development, 40,*(1, Serial No. 159).

Kuczaj, S. A., II (1981). Factors influencing children's hypothetical reference. *Journal of Child Language, 8,* 131-137.

Lempers, J. D., Flavell, E. R., & Flavell, J. H (1977). The development in very young children of tacit knowledge concerning visual perception. *Genetic Psychology Monographs, 95,* 3-53.

Leslie, A. M. (1991). The theory of mind impairment in autism: Evidence for a modular mechanism of development? In A. Whiten (Ed.), *Natural theories of mind: Evolution, development and simulation of everyday mindreading.* Oxford, England: Blackwell.

Leslie, A. M., & Frith, U. (1988). Autistic children's knowledge of seeing, knowing, and believing. *British Journal of Developmental Psychology, 6,* 315-324.

Lillard, A. S., & Flavell, J. H. (1990). Young children's preference for mental state versus behavioral descriptions of human action. *Child Development, 61,* 731-741.

Markman, E. M. (1989). *Categorization and naming in children: Problems of induction.* Cambridge, MA: MIT Press.

Masangkay Z. S., McCluskey, K. A., McIntyre, C. W., Sims-Knight, J., Vaughn, B. E., & Flavell, J. H. (1974). The early development of inferences about the visual percepts of others. *Child Development, 45,* 357-366.

Miller, P. H., Kessel, F. S., & Flavell, J. H. (1970). Thinking about people thinking about people thinking about . . .: A study of social cognitive development. *Child Development, 41,* 613-623.

Morss, J. R. (1987). The construction of perspectives: Piaget's alternative to spatial egocentrism. *International Journal of Behavioral Development, 10,* 263-279.

Moses, L. J., & Flavell, J. H. (1990). Inferring false beliefs from actions and reactions. *Child Development, 61,* 929-945.

Novey, M. S. (1975). *The development of knowledge of others' ability to see.* Unpublished doctoral dissertation, Harvard University, Cambridge, MA.

Perner, J. (1988). Developing semantics for theories of mind: From propositional attitudes to mental representation. In J. W. Astington, P. L. Harris, & D. R. Olson (Eds.), *Developing theories of mind.* New York: Cambridge University Press.

Perner, J. (1991). *Understanding the representational mind.* Cambridge, MA: Bradford Books/MIT Press.

Piaget, J. (1926). *The language and thought of the child.* New York: Harcourt, Brace.

Piaget, J. (1928). *Judgment and reasoning in the child.* New York: Harcourt, Brace.

Piaget, J. (1962). *Play, dreams and imitation in childhood.* New York: Norton.

Piaget, J. (1976). *The grasp of consciousness: Action and concept in the young child.* Cambridge, MA: Harvard University Press.

Piaget, J., & Inhelder, B. (1956). *The child's conception of space.* London: Routledge & Kegan Paul.

Pillow, B. H., & Flavell, J. H. (1986). Young children's knowledge about visual perception: Projective size and shape. *Child Development, 57,* 125–135.

Salatas, H., & Flavell, J. H. (1976). Retrieval of recently learned information: Development of strategies and control skills. *Child Development, 47,* 941–948.

Singer, J. B., & Flavell, J. H. (1981). Development of knowledge about communication: Children's evaluations of explicitly ambiguous messages. *Child Development, 52,* 1211–1215.

Speer, J. R., & Flavell, J. H. (1979). Young children's knowledge of the relative difficulty of recognition and recall memory tasks. *Developmental Psychology, 15,* 214–217.

Taylor, M. (1988). The development of children's understanding of the seeing–knowing distinction. In J. W. Astington, P. L. Harris, & D. R. Olson (Eds.), *Developing theories of mind.* New York: Cambridge University Press.

Taylor, M., & Flavell, J. H. (1984). Seeing and believing: Children's understanding of the distinction between appearance and reality. *Child Development, 55,* 1710–1720.

Taylor, M., & Hort, B. C. (1990). Can children be trained to make the appearance–reality distinction? *Cognitive Development, 5,* 89–99.

Tversky, A., & Kahneman, D. (1973). Availability: A heuristic for judging frequency and probability. *Cognitive Psychology, 5,* 207–232.

Waters, H., & Tinsley, V. (1985). Evaluating the discriminant and convergent validity of developmental constructs: Another look at the concept of egocentrism. *Psychological Bulletin, 97,* 483–496.

Wellman, H. M. (1985). The child's theory of mind: The development of conceptions of cognition. In S. R. Yussen (Ed.), *The growth of reflection in children.* San Diego: Academic Press.

Wellman, H. M. (1990). *The child's theory of mind.* Cambridge, MA: Bradford Books/MIT Press.

Wellman, H. M., & Woolley, J. D. (1990). From simple desires to ordinary beliefs: The early development of everyday psychology. *Cognition, 35,* 245–275.

Whiten, A. (Ed.) (1991). *Natural theories of mind: Evolution, development and simulation of everyday mindreading.* Oxford, England: Blackwell.

Wimmer, H., & Perner, J. (1983). Beliefs about beliefs: Representation and constraining function of wrong beliefs in young children's understanding of deception. *Cognition, 13,* 103–128.

Woolley, J. D., & Wellman, H. M. (1990). Young children's understanding of realities, nonrealities, and appearances. *Child Development, 61,* 946–961.

Yaniv, I., & Shatz, M. (1988). Children's understanding of perceptibility. In J. W. Astington, P. L. Harris, & D. R. Olson (Eds.), *Developing theories of mind.* New York: Cambridge University Press.

6 The Child's Understanding of Mental Representation

Josef Perner
University of Sussex

Janet Wilde Astington
Institute of Child Study, University of Toronto

This chapter briefly describes some key findings on children's under-standing of the mind. We use this opportunity to discuss the larger issues within which this kind of research is conducted. We focus first on the question what *representation* is and the *theory view of mind,* because these topics show the philosophical influences on the field and the potential contrasts to Piagetian theory. We then consider the implications of this view and its relation to various Piagetian concerns.

This research explores the development of children's understanding of the mind (their own and other people's) and has come to be known as "Children's Theory of Mind." More specifically it focuses on the changes that take place in children's understanding of the mind between about 3 and 5 years. This period is recognized by most researchers in the field (e.g., Astington, Harris, & Olson, 1988), although not all (e.g., Chandler, 1988), as one where important changes take place that center around age 4. Several different proposals have been made for what the deeper intellectual changes are that underlie the observed changes around this age, for instance:

1. Understanding the mind as representational (Flavell, 1988, and in the current volume; Forguson & Gopnik, 1988; Perner, 1988; Wellman, 1990);
2. Understanding the causal role of mental states (Leslie, 1988), in particular, their causal origin in perception (Wimmer, Hogrefe, & Sodian, 1988b);
3. Advance in the ability to simulate other people's minds or one's own past mental states (Harris, 1989; Johnson, 1988).

We will focus only on the first position in any detail. A defense of this position against the alternatives can be found in Perner (1991-b, chaps. 8 & 11).

UNDERSTANDING THE MIND AS REPRESENTATIONAL

The question of when children start to view the mind as representational raises some basic questions about what constitutes representation in general and mental representation in particular. If we want to evaluate claims that children at a particular age acquire an understanding of the mind as representational then we should first get clear on the question what it means for something to be a representation.

What Is "Representation"?

One could suggest that Piaget's writing might provide a clear answer to this question since he discussed the issue of mental representation extensively in the context of how children develop mental representation at the end of the sensorimotor stage. Unfortunately, Piaget was concerned with how to differentiate representational thinking from perceptual processes. However, as Mandler (1983) has emphasized, there is a wider meaning of "representation," as it is used in cognitive science, which includes all forms of knowing. Our question is what the common feature is of all instances that fall under this wider notion. For an answer we look in the philosophy of mind.

The notion of representation is familiar to us from things such as pictures, photos, maps, models, and language. Pictures and linguistic expressions differ vastly in how they represent and in how they acquire their representational capacity. Nevertheless, there is one important commonality: They all are *about* something else. A photo of, say, the philosopher Nelson Goodman's black horse is not just a piece of glossy paper but is a photo *of* Goodman's black horse. The same holds true in the linguistic domain; the sentence "This is Goodman's black horse" is not just a sequence of letters but is *about* that black horse.

This property of being *about* something else is also considered to be one, if not the, basic characteristic of the mind, as Brentano (1874/1955, pp. 124–125) put it: "In the imagination something is imagined . . . in desire something is desired, and so on." This commonality between mind and external representations such as pictures and sentences provides the intuitive basis for cognitive psychology, which tries to explain the mind as a system of representations (e.g., Fodor & Pylyshyn, 1988).

So, the essential property of any representation is that it is *about* something else, which is called the *representational content*. This is captured in the following scheme:

representational medium ----[representational relation]---- > representational content

e.g., paper --------------------[depicting]--------------------> black horse

which, in Piagetian terminology amounts to the distinctions among *"significant," "signification,"* and *"signifié"* (Piaget & Inhelder, 1966, p. 42). Despite its simplicity, this scheme can serve us to highlight several important points.

Terminology. Notice that we did not use the word "representation" at all in the diagram. If we had, the most natural use would be to use representation to refer to the photo, that is, the piece of paper (the representational medium), which depicts the black horse, and not the black horse depicted in the photo (the representational content of the photo). It may seem superfluous to dwell on such a seemingly obvious point. Unfortunately, normal language use is not so clear. Sometimes the word representation is used to refer to content. This usage is particularly likely when nonexisting entities, such as a unicorn, are depicted. When asked about the existence of the unicorn one might answer that it does not exist at all, it is just a representation, since its existence is confined to being in the picture. However, although the unicorn, indeed, does not exist independently of the picture, we must realize that it is not the same as the picture. Hence, the use of representation to refer to the picture as well as the unicorn is ambiguous. Failure to distinguish these two distinct uses of the word has caused much confusion in philosophy (see, e.g., Lehrer, 1986) and in recent developmental writings about metarepresentation (see Perner, 1991-b).

In other words, by the term "representation" we mean the piece of paper (or representational medium), which because of its peculiar properties has a representational relationship to something else, for example, Goodman's black horse (or a unicorn). Similarly in the case of the mind we refer by representation to those neuronal states that by their peculiar properties stand in a representational relationship to something else. We do not use representation to refer to what these neuronal states represent (their representational content).

The conflation of representational medium with representational content is also tempting in the case of mental representations. Since we are largely in the dark about their physical specification, they are purely hypothetical entities, whose shape and location we know nothing about. The only specification we have of them is in terms of what they represent (their content). Because they have no independent physical specification it is tempting to conflate them with their content, as it is similarly tempting to confuse the unicorn with its picture, because the unicorn has no independent existence apart from being shown in the picture (but notice that despite the lack of independent existence there must be some difference between the unicorn and the picture of the unicorn, for one cannot be replaced by the other without change of meaning: "This picture shows a unicorn" is not the same as "this picture shows a picture of a unicorn").

One most important question in all this is the question about what these "peculiar properties" are that turn some pieces of paper and some neural processes into representations. This question has a long history in the philosophy of mind and cognitive science, which has recently been the focus of intense debate. Fortunately we can bypass this question, since one can understand that something is a representation without understanding the processes that turn something into a representation. We are content to provide references to some of the recent works discussing this issue that we found helpful: Dretske (1988), Fodor (1984, 1987, 1990), Millikan (1984), Cummins (1989), Dennett (1987). We also point out that Piaget's proposition that mental representations originate from internalizing bodily imitation, is not discussed in this literature. One reason is that the deeper question is where representations get their content from. Piaget's answer is not really a solution, begging the original question by deferring it to the question of where imitatory behavior get its content. In our view, Piaget's position is not adequate because imitatory behavior implies a mind that confers content (what it is supposed to be an imitation of) on it.

The Sense–Reference Distinction.   Even though we cannot give a satisfactory answer to the question about what makes something a representation of something else, we can state one more essential feature of representations, namely that the representational relation is not a simple relation. Representations do not just represent something, they always represent *something as something* (or something as being a certain way). This distinction between *representing* and *representing-as* was made by Goodman (1976) in his analysis of depiction. Dretske (1988) pointed out that this distinction corresponds to Frege's (1892/1960) earlier distinction between *sense* and *reference* in the context of the meaning of definite descriptions.

Goodman introduced this distinction with the example of a photo of his black horse on which his horse came out as just a tiny, gray speck in the distance. Hence, although it is truly a photo of his black horse it does not depict it *as* a black horse. One of Frege's famous examples was the definite descriptions "The Morning Star" and "The Evening Star," both of which denote the planet Venus *(referent),* yet differ in their meaning because one describes Venus *as* the star shining in the evening and the other *as* the star shining in the morning. And that part of their meaning in which they differ, Frege called their *sense.*

Misrepresentation.   One important consequence of distinguishing reference and sense is that one can conceive of the possibility of misrepresentation. Cases of misrepresentation occur when something represents something (referent) not as it really is but as being different (sense). For instance, should Goodman's black horse come out as brown on the photograph, due to bad lighting conditions, then the photograph would misrepresent his black horse (referent) as a brown horse (sense).

Although the sense/reference distinction is inherent in any kind of representation, cases of misrepresentation bring it out most clearly. Sense, how the thing is represented, does not match reality, how the thing really is (hence, how it should be represented). For this reason, misrepresentation has become a touchstone for any theory of representation (e.g., Fodor, 1984; Dretske, 1986). Understanding misrepresentation is therefore a good indicator for understanding representation. It is probably not pure coincidence that some of the core findings in the Theory of Mind literature, which gave rise to the claim that children do not understand the mind as representational before the age of about 4, involve cases of misrepresentation. Before 4, most children find it hard to understand that someone can entertain a false belief. For example, if a person puts some chocolate in a cupboard from which it is moved during his or her absence, he or she mentally misrepresents the chocolate's real location as being an empty cupboard (Perner, Leekam, & Wimmer, 1987; Wimmer & Perner, 1983). Children of this age find it equally hard to differentiate between appearance and reality (Flavell, Flavell, & Green, 1983); for instance, they do not understand that the appearance of a piece of sponge, which is painted to look like a rock, can misrepresent the sponge as being a rock.

To reiterate, the essential property of any representation is that is it *about* something else — its representational content. Furthermore, the relation by which the representation is related to the content is not a simple one. Representation always represents something as being a certain way; in our earlier example, the representation *of* the black horse represents it *as* a black horse, or more critically, in the case of misrepresentation, the representation *of* the black horse represents it *as* a brown horse. For children to understand the mind as representational, they must understand these characteristics of mental representation.

EXAMINING PIAGET'S THEORY IN THE CONTEXT OF THEORY OF MIND

In the remainder of the chapter we will examine some of the empirical support for the view that children do not develop this sort of understanding until about 4 years of age. We will also consider whether children younger than 4 understand the mind, and if they do, how. Most importantly, we will compare our interpretations with Piagetian interpretations of the same data. Although the topic of investigation, children's understanding of mind and social interaction, is very Piagetian (see the chapters by Chapman, Furth, Kuhn, and Youniss & Damon in this volume), the theoretical basis of research in Theory of Mind is anchored in perspectives on philosophy of mind that antedate Piaget's work, and in certain respects put the field on an anti-Piagetian footing. Although we are emphasizing the differences between experimental work in Theory of Mind and Piagetian research, other authors have commented on their similarities, and in a broader perspective Theory of Mind is indeed related to Piagetian research. Miller (1989) characterizes Theory of Mind research as neo-Piagetian because it postulates stage-like change, albeit within the specific domain of the mind. Astington and Gopnik (1991-b) have drawn parallels between the Theory of Mind view and a Piagetian one: Theories are like schemata, and the process of theory formation is akin to the Piagetian concept of equilibration (i.e., assimilation and accommodation). However, Astington and Gopnik point out that the Theory of Mind and Piagetian views differ in the sort of ways that we will be discussing here. Indeed, there are some potentially quite interesting differences between Piagetian and theory-of-mind interpretations of certain developmental phenomena. We will focus on the following issues:

1. Does hypothetical reasoning (as in pretense) require an understanding of representation?
2. Is there any understanding of the mind that is not representational understanding?
3. How does the theory view of mind explain the phenomenon of egocentrism and the development of role-taking abilities?
4. What are the implications of the theory view of mind for the phenomenon of childhood realism that Piaget described?
5. What are its implications for moral realism?

Representation and Hypothetical Reasoning (The Case of Pretense)

The possibility of misrepresentation as an essential part of representation makes it clear that an understanding of representation requires the ability to engage in hypothetical thinking. To understand misrepresentation means that one understands that the representation is supposed to represent something as it is but in fact represents it as it isn't. To understand this one has to be able to represent mentally something as it isn't, which is a rudimentary form of hypothetical thinking, representing the world as different from how it really is, how it could be.

This observation has important consequences for our interpretation of pretend play. Since pretense occurs considerably earlier (in the second year of life) than reliable understanding of misrepresentation (about 4 years of age) one is compelled to interpret the significance of pretense as a reflection of the emerging ability to entertain thoughts about how the world isn't and *act as-if* the world were like that. For instance, in one of Piaget's (1945/1962, p. 96) well-known examples, Jacqueline pretended that a piece of cloth was her pillow. She put her head down on it in pretend sleep but uttered a "no-no" in recognition of the fact that her behavior was out of the ordinary.

One possible interpretation of Jacqueline's behavior is that she engaged in rudimentary hypothetical reasoning: "This object in my hands could be my pillow (though it is, of course, just a piece of cloth)" and then acted as-if that object were indeed her pillow. This interpretation of what went on in Jacqueline's head is compatible with the position that Jacqueline had no notion of representation at this tender age. Although the ability to engage in hypothetical reasoning is a prerequisite for later understanding of what it means to represent, nevertheless, entertaining the thought that something could be something else (the cloth could be the pillow) does not require understanding that something can be used to represent something else (the cloth represents the pillow).

This interpretation is, of course, diametrically opposed to that given by Piaget (1945/1962, p. 97). He interpreted his daughter's behavior as symbolical, that is, that Jacqueline treated her toy as representing her pillow and her "no-no" as an indication that she was aware of what she was doing. Piaget's claim that Jacqueline at 1 year and 3 months understood her behavior as using one thing as a representation of another is naturally incompatible with the view that children do not understand anything as a representation of something else until about 4. However, in our view, young children's ability to pretend and to understand pretense in others can be explained without assuming that such young children understand representation.

There has been remarkably little empirical investigation of young children's understanding of pretense in the Theory of Mind research area, although there is great interest in the phenomenon and awareness of its theoretical importance. Leslie (1988) and Perner (1988) point out that 3-year-olds' inability to attribute a false belief to another person, or to understand that an object is really a sponge, though it looks like a rock, could not be due to their inability to represent alternative models of the world, as Wimmer and Perner (1983) had originally proposed. This is because the 2-year-old, in pretending that a banana is a telephone, is already constructing an alternative model of the world and acting as-if the world were that way. While true as far as this analysis goes, it does not go far enough. As we have pointed out, constructing an alternative model, which shows the banana as a telephone, and even acting accordingly, does not require an understanding of representation. It does not require a mental representation of how one's model represents the banana as a telephone, as Leslie (1987, 1988) suggests in using the term "metarepresentation." Nor does it require a mental representation of the banana being used as a representation of a telephone, as is suggested by Piaget's analysis of pretense.

Our analysis would predict that 3-year-olds would understand pretense before misrepresentation in comparable situations. In false belief tasks, children are asked to predict what someone will do or think, whereas the data on their understanding of pretense come from naturalistic studies of pretend play, where children are not explicitly asked to make predictions about anything. However, children in fact do so, because in playing with another, they predict what the other will do in the pretend scenario. Even 2-year-olds can coordinate their activity with others in this way (Dunn & Dale, 1984).

Other investigators have shown that 3-year-olds understand pretense in experimental situations, but do not understand misrepresentation in a similar situation. For example, Flavell, Flavell, and Green (1987) showed that 3-year-olds could distinguish between the pretend and real identities of objects, but not between apparent and real identities (as in the sponge rock task), even when the same objects are used in the two conditions. Gopnik and Slaughter (1991) showed that 3-year-olds could remember their own earlier pretenses but not their own earlier false beliefs, although what was pretended and believed were different in the two conditions.

Wimmer and Perner (1990) made a precise comparison of 3-year-olds' understanding of their own pretending or misrepresenting in identical situations. In one case the children knew that a box that appeared to contain chocolates actually contained a toy car, but they pretended it contained chocolates and jokingly said that to a puppet when he asked them what was in the box. In the other case they mistakenly told the puppet that the box contained chocolates because they thought it did, not having seen inside it, and they later discovered that it actually contained the toy car. In both cases they were then asked to remember what they had told the puppet was inside the box. In the case where they had been mistaken, they misremembered what they had said and thought they had told the puppet there was a car in the box. This is because 3-year-olds cannot understand representation and therefore cannot differentiate between the content (chocolates) and the referent (car) of their mistaken statement in answer to the puppet's question about what was in the box. On the other hand, in the case where they had been pretending, they had no difficulty remembering that they had said to the puppet that there were chocolates in the box. In this case they never thought their answer was describing the actual content of the box. At the time they answered the puppet's question, they knew they were describing a situation different from the real one, they were constructing some hypothetical, as-if, situation, and later, they had no difficulty remembering that.

Further, our analysis would predict that there would be some change in children's understanding of pretense after 4 years of age, when it can be understood representationally, if it need be. However, this may be hard to demonstrate. Perhaps Malvestuto–Felice's (1986) findings are relevant here: 2-year-olds can follow instructions to pretend actions that they cannot actually perform, for example, pretend to go to sleep, but not actions they can perform, for example, pretend to clap your hands—then they just do it.

The Nonrepresentational Mind?

As we have already seen, a central issue in Theory of Mind research concerns what it means for children to understand the mind as representational, and more controversially, what it could mean to say that children understand the mind but not as representational. The question here is what kind of understanding of the mind younger children have if they cannot grasp the concept of mental representation before the age of about 4. One possible answer is: none. This would be the natural implication to draw for cognitive psychologists who equate mind with mental representation. If you can't understand mental representation then you must be a behaviorist who denies the existence of mind altogether. This may well have been the implicit lesson many people in the field had drawn from the early data, or at least appear to have drawn in Chandler's (1988) caricature of the "consensus" view. It was also the view taken about autistic children who, like 3-year-old children, failed to understand false belief (e.g., Baron–Cohen, Leslie, & Frith, 1985, 1986), which was explicitly addressed in the title of a paper: "Are autistic children behaviourists?" (Baron–Cohen, 1989).

A middle ground between characterizing children as behaviorists or as cognitive psychologists who understand the mind as a system of mental representations seems needed. This middle ground accepts evidence that younger children understand a great deal about the mind and that even babies cannot be denied some understanding, but does not assume infants have a "theory of mind" as Bretherton, McNew, and Beeghly-Smith (1981) suggested. Flavell (1988) for instance, speaks of "cognitive connections." The young child, failing to understand that people entertain mental representations, sees people as *cognitively connected* to things in the world and real events. The limiting factor of cognitive connections seems to be that people can only be connected to actually existing things and states of the world, whereas mental representations provide an understanding that people can want, think about, and so on, nonexisting things and events. In a similar vein Wellman (1990, chap. 8) suggested that 2-year-olds are limited to a conception of "simple desires" that allows them to understand that people try to obtain actually existing objects but prevents them from conceiving of desires for nonexisting objects.

Perner (1991-b, chap. 11) pointed out that young children's understanding of the mind cannot be limited to connections to really existing situations, since, for instance, they knowingly engage in joint pretend play from at least the age of 2 onwards (e.g., Dunn & Dale, 1984). What something is pretended to be is, almost by definition, something that it is *not really*. Similarly any conception of desire that is limited to the already existing is not just simple but useless, since it allows only for desires to obtain something one has already got (existing state of affairs). Even the very young are not limited to the *actual existing* in their understanding of human desires and thoughts. Perner (1988, 1991-b), therefore, speaks of young children as "situation theorists." As situation theorists they can understand desire and pretense, and some aspects of belief (short of being able to differentiate between "thinking-of" and "thinking-that," see Perner, 1991-a), which require them to represent alternative situations but do not require them to see these alternative situations as representations. They can understand people as being related to various situations, which may be real, or hypothetical, or outright counterfactual (as in pretense). This gives children a potentially very powerful theory of behavior of which they will hardly ever realize the full potential. Nevertheless, this situation theory has its principled limitations. Without a notion of mental representations it is difficult to understand cases of misrepresentation (false belief, appearance–reality distinction) and how mental states are created and how they affect action (an inability emphasized by Leslie, 1988, and by Wimmer et al., 1988-b).

Theory Versus Egocentrism and Role Taking

The label "theory" for this research area is not totally unwarranted. Wellman (1990, chap. 5) lists several reasons why it is advantageous to look at children's growing understanding of the mind as the acquisition of a theory. In addition, the label "theory" commits the field to a particular position within philosophy of mind (e.g., Churchland, 1984). It is this aspect of "theory" that puts it in opposition to Piaget's notion of *egocentrism* (at least in its popularized version) and the neo-Piagetian research on *role taking*.

An important question in the philosophy of mind is what determines the meaning of our language about the mind, that is, verbs such as *thinking, believing, knowing,* and *wanting.* The Cartesian answer, which enjoys the backing of common sense, is that we know each mental state through our direct introspective experience. We know what it means to "know something," "to believe something," "to want something" because we experience those mental states daily in ourselves. One difficult problem for this position (highlighted by Wittgenstein) is the *problem of other minds,* that is, since we cannot experience the inner states of our fellow humans, how do we know that they, too, are endowed with such mental states?

The major alternative to the Cartesian position is the "folk theory" position (e.g., Churchland, 1984; Dennett, 1978). According to this view mental terms of our language do not get meaning through introspection but as theoretical concepts that are part of a theory for explaining and predicting human behavior. Mental states have the status of hypothetical constructs. They are not directly observable, need to be inferred, and provide advantages for predicting behavior. Hence, Premack and Woodruff (1978) conclude in their article "Does the chimpanzee have a theory of mind?" that anyone (person or animal) able to attribute mental states should be credited with a *theory* (but see Perner, 1991-b, for some reservations concerning this liberal use of "theory").

As Wimmer (1989; Wimmer & Hartl, 1991) and Gopnik (1990; Astington & Gopnik, 1991-a) point out, these two opposing philosophical positions have interesting, testable developmental implications. If the mind, as Descartes implied, is transparent to itself, then children should have little difficulty understanding their own minds. The principal developmental difficulty should lie in trying to figure out other people's minds. This, in fact, seems to be exactly the agenda of neo-Piagetian research on role (or perspective) taking. Indeed, role taking only works if the Cartesian position is right. For what use would it be to try and figure out another person's state of mind by putting oneself in his or her shoes, that is, by asking, "what would I see/feel/know . . . if I were in his or her position?" if one had no understanding of what one would experience in his or her position?

Wimmer (1989) and Gopnik (1990) pointed out that recent evidence on children's understanding of their own beliefs and knowledge is incompatible with the Cartesian position. Gopnik and Astington (1988) reported that 3- and even some 4-year-olds have equal difficulty in remembering their own mistaken belief as they have in attributing such a belief to another person. For example, if they discover that a box (e.g., a well-known candy box) has unexpected contents (e.g., pencils) they not only predict that their friend who has not seen inside the box will think it has pencils in it (Perner et al., 1987), but they cannot remember what they themselves thought was in the box when they first saw it. Moreover, Wimmer, Hogrefe, and Perner (1988-a) found that children of this age find it as difficult to explain the source of their own knowledge (Gopnik & Graf, 1988) as it is to use information about another person's informational source in making a judgment about that person's state of knowledge. This evidence, Wimmer

(1989) suggested, favors the "folk theory" position in the philosophy of mind, since from that perspective one would expect children to encounter about equal difficulty understanding other people's minds as understanding their own minds (see Johnson, 1988; Harris, 1989, 1991, for a defence of the role-taking, or "simulation" approach).

Perner (1991-b, chap. 11), furthermore, argued that there is also a tacit Cartesian presupposition underlying Piaget's popular notion of "egocentrism," insofar as it is supposed "to encourage [the child] to accept [his own view] . . . as the only one possible . . . [and] turn it into a kind of 'false-absolute'." (Piaget & Inhelder 1948/1956, p. 194). If the theory position is right, then children may still have difficulty understanding differences in perspective, but should not have a particular tendency to prefer their own view. So it is interesting that what was thought to be evidence for that kind of egocentrism needed reinterpretation under the onslaught of better experimental control. Children's alleged tendency to pick their *own* view in the classic Three-mountain Problem (Piaget & Inhelder, 1948/1956) turned out to be a preference for a *good* view of the mountains (Liben & Belknap, 1981; Light & Nix, 1983, who then prefer the term "intellectual realism") and evidence for conceptual egocentrism in children's knowledge attributions (Marvin, Greenberg, & Mossler, 1976; Mossler, Marvin, & Greenberg, 1976) does not remain tenable when additional control conditions are used (Wimmer et al., 1988-a; see Perner, 1991-b, chap. 11, for an overview).

Childhood Realism

We have argued that at around 4 years of age children come to understand the mind as representational, and that children younger than this have a fairly sophisticated mentalistic theory of behavior. How do these claims fit with Piaget's description of childhood realism? Piaget said that before age 6, children have no appreciation of mental life at all; they are adualists who are completely unable to distinguish between mental and real phenomena. They make no distinction between mental entities, such as thoughts and dreams, and real physical things. For example, they associate thinking with speaking; when Piaget asked them, "What do we think with?" they replied, "With the mouth." Similarly, they gave realist answers to the question, "Where do dreams come from?" They thought dreams came from the night, from lamps, from the sky; they thought the dream was in the room with them and some of them thought that others would also see the dream if they were in the room. That is, childhood realism endows mental entities, such as thoughts and dreams, with physical characteristics such as a public existence and a place in the world. Children who are realists in this way cannot distinguish between things and thoughts about them. Piaget said that "the child cannot distinguish a real house, for example, from the concept or mental image or name of the house" (Piaget, 1926/1929, p. 55).

Henry Wellman and his colleagues challenged this conclusion (Wellman & Estes, 1986), demonstrating that children between 3 and 5 can distinguish between real things and mental entities, such as thoughts, memories, and dreams. Shown a picture of a boy who has a cookie and a boy who is remembering, or thinking, or dreaming about a cookie, children could say which boy could see, touch, eat, or share the cookie, and they could say that the first boy's cookie was real, and the second boy's cookie was not real. In an extensive series of studies (see Wellman, 1990, chap. 2) it was shown that children in this age range could distinguish mental entities, including mental images, from physical things, even potentially confusing things such as smoke, sounds, and photographs. In a particularly convincing study, 3-year-olds were able to distinguish between a mental image of an object, for example a cup, and a real cup hidden in a box, and understood that they could transform the image but not the real object (e.g., turn the cup upside down) just by thinking about it. The children were also able to provide reasonable explanations of their judgments.

It seems clear from Wellman's studies that children younger than 6 are not the adualists Piaget claimed they were. Wellman suggested that he was able to reveal young children's competence because he asked simple, direct questions about specific mental entities, rather than general questions about abstract mental entities, questions that sometimes presupposed an ontology the adult did not really hold, such as "Where do dreams come from?" In an interesting comparison of his data with Laurendeau and Pinard's (1962) replication of Piaget's findings, Wellman (1990, chap. 2) showed that when the explanation data he had collected were coded according to the Laurendeau and Pinard scheme, many of the children, especially the 3- and 4-year-olds, were classified as realists. Wellman claims that his results provide a better picture of the young child's competence, because his studies compared children's judgments and explanations of both mental *and* real entities, and showed that they were sensibly different. Piaget as well as Laurendeau and Pinard, on the other hand, relied solely on children's ability to produce verbal explanations only of mental phenomena, and interpreted children's figurative explanations (e.g., dreams are pictures) too literally.

From our point of view, we would expect 4- and 5-year-olds to distinguish the real and the mental world, since they understand the mind as representational. But what about 3-year-olds? How do we explain their success on Wellman's tasks? The results are not problematical for Wellman because he says that 3-year-olds have a representational theory of mind. Although Wellman uses his data as evidence of children's ability to distinguish between representations and reality, his questions were essentially questions about mental contents (recall our earlier discussion of the terminological confusion surrounding the word "representation"). It may be that 3-year-old situation theorists can answer questions about mental content on the basis of their ability to represent hypothetical situations, that is, they can talk about a thought-of cup. They do not need to understand anything about representation in order to do this. Sometimes the children in Wellman's studies, especially 3-year-olds, confused talk about the mental entity with talk about the physical entity, although even the 3-year-olds could correct such errors if they were asked directly which entity they were talking about (the real cup on the table in front of them or the thought-of cup in their mind). It seems not surprising that children were sometimes confused in this way because language is ambiguous and largely depends on context to sort out what "space" (i.e., real, thought, time) one is talking about.

Thus, 3-year-olds' ability to distinguish between real and mental entities depends on their understanding the content of their images, thoughts, memory, and so on, as "imagined situations," that is, as real or counterfactual situations with particular properties. They do not have the ability, however, to understand their mental images, thoughts, and memories *as representations*. The distinction between these two abilities may reflect the one that Wellman makes when he says that 3-year-olds are ontological dualists but epistemological realists, that is, they can distinguish mental contents from real entities, but they have no understanding that the mental contents are created by being mentally represented. It is also similar to the distinction Astington and Gopnik (1991-a) make when they say that 3-year-olds understand that people have mental products in their minds, but they do not understand the representational process; that is, they do not understand that people represent things in mind. Thus, by conceptualizing 3-year-olds as situation theorists, we can explain their ability to distinguish the content of their thoughts from real things without having to credit them with an understanding of representation.

Moral Reasoning

Piaget (1932/1977) also found elements of realism in young children's moral judgments, for example, in how they assigned blame to misdeeds. He told children pairs of stories, each describing a child's actions, and then asked them to say in which story the child was more naughty. Piaget found that until the age of 7 children's judgments reflected "moral realism." They judged acts as good or bad by considering their material consequences, not the actor's intentions (see Youniss & Damon's chapter in this volume for another perspective on intentionality). Thus a large amount of damage done while trying to help was considered naughtier than a small amount of damage done while playing. The change to making subjective judgments, where the story characters' intentions were considered, came gradually, between 7 and 9. These studies provoked a great deal of interest and criticism. Subsequent researchers, using a variety of methods to increase the salience of the actors' intentions and to simplify the task of making a judgment, showed that 5- or 6-year-olds could use information about intentions to make judgments about accidental damage.

Piaget also told children pairs of stories in which a character who had no intention to deceive actually said something quite untrue, and another character who did intend to deceive said something mildly untrue. Again, children younger than 7 did not consider intention in making a judgment of who was naughtier. Thus an honest mistake, or an exaggeration caused by fear, received more blame than an intentional misrepresentation of the facts. Young children considered how far the statement deviated from the truth, not the speaker's intention to deceive. Moreover, they called all factually incorrect statements *lies,* even when there was no intention to deceive, as when a speaker was simply mistaken.

In a series of carefully controlled experiments, Wimmer, Gruber, and Perner (1984) showed that Piaget was half right. Children do apply the term *lie* in the way Piaget said. Until 6- or 7-years old, they consider all untrue statements to be lies, whatever the intentions of the speaker, and in the contrived circumstance where someone intends to deceive but is himself misinformed and so accidentally tells the truth, they say the speaker did not lie, though some children said he didn't but wanted to. However, Wimmer et al. showed that even though they use the term *lie* in this way, children as young as 4 do consider intentions in making moral judgments. The studies used false belief stories acted out with dolls and toys; for example, a story in which a boy puts some chocolate in one place, goes out to play, and then returns to look for the chocolate which, during his absence, has been moved to a new location. The children were asked where the boy would look for the chocolate and then before he can look his sister appears and asks him where the chocolate is. Wimmer et al. contrasted two cases, one where the boy wants her to find it and the other where he doesn't want her to. In the first case the boy does not intend to deceive his sister, but he thinks the chocolate is still in the place where he put it so he tells his sister something false. In the second case the boy does intend to deceive his sister, because he doesn't want her to find the chocolate, but he accidentally tells the truth, he tells her it's in the place where it's been moved to, even though he thinks it's still in the place where he put it. The striking finding is that even 4-year-olds rewarded the first boy with gold stars for being nice to his sister, and punished the second boy with black marks for being nasty to his sister (even though this boy actually *said* the place where the chocolate was). Clearly the children based their moral judgment on the boys' intentions. However, when they were asked if the boy had lied, they said the first one had lied, and not the second, that is, the one who had no intention to deceive but who actually uttered a false statement was the one who lied, in the 4-year-olds' eyes. Wimmer et al. conclude that young children are not moral realists, as Piaget said they were. They do take intention into account and make subjective judgments, but they are "lexical realists"—their use of the word *lie* is determined by the facts of the matter in the world.

Why do children respond differently, and make judgments based on intention for these stories and not for the ones Piaget used? The difference may be that in order to convey the distinction between a lie and a mistake one needs to have a clear case of false belief, as in the stories that Wimmer et al. used. It was clear that children understood the speaker's false belief because they responded correctly to the question where the boy would himself look for the chocolate. Piaget, on the other hand, had no way of checking that his stories, correctly understood by adults, were understood in the same way by children.

Not all intentionally false statements are lies. A person may intend to say something false without intending to deceive anyone—it may be said sarcastically, jokingly, or as a fantasy caused by fear or desire; this last seems to be the case in a number of Piaget's stories. What differentiates such statements from a lie is a "second-order" intention, so-called because it is an intention about a belief. A lying speaker wants the listener to believe what he or she says; a joking speaker, for example, doesn't want the listener to believe it. Leekam (1991) told children pairs of stories in which she manipulated the second-order mental states involved. She made the contrast between these two cases obvious by asking children a question that included the explicit contrast: "One of these boys wanted his mother to know . . . and one didn't want his mother to know. . . . Which boy wanted his mother to know?". She showed that again children as young as 4 are able to make the distinction between these two cases when they are asked which of the two speakers wants the listener to know the truth, and also when they are asked which speaker is joking or which one is lying. That is to say, young children recognize the distinctions among mistakes, lies, and jokes. Moreover, although they wrongly assign the lexical term *lie* to mistakes, they do not call jokes *lies,* but correctly apply the term *joke.*

The explicit contrast Leekam made between the lying and joking speaker is implicit in some of Piaget's story pairs; for example, the boy frightened by a dog who tells his mother it was as big as a cow, was probably not intending her to be deceived, whereas the boy who said his teacher had given him good marks when she hadn't may have been intending to deceive the mother in order to be rewarded, as indeed he is at the end of the story. Again Piaget had no way of checking that children had correctly understood the contrast implicit in the two stories. When this contrast between speakers' second-order mental states is made explicit, even quite young children are able to make appropriate judgments.

CONCLUSION

These discussions of pretend play, egocentrism, childhood realism, and moral reasoning, indicate how theoretical analysis within Theory of Mind research impinges on basic Piagetian theory. Furthermore, we have shown that, having a quite independent theoretical basis, Theory of Mind research comes into basic conflict with Piagetian interpretations of the same developmental phenomena. Finally, we have shown that one should certainly not mistake Theory of Mind as just a brand of research in social cognition that happens to investigate children's understanding of particular aspects of the mind especially thoroughly.

REFERENCES

Astington, J. W., & Gopnik, A. (1991-a). Developing understanding of desire and intention. In A. Whiten (Ed.), *Natural theories of mind: Evolution, development and simulation of everyday mindreading* (pp. 39–50). Oxford, England: Basil Blackwell.

Astington, J. W., & Gopnik, A. (1991-b). Theoretical explanations of children's understanding of the mind. *British Journal of Developmental Psychology, 9,* 7–31.

Astington, J. W., Harris, P. L., & Olson, D. R. (Eds.). (1988). *Developing theories of mind.* New York: Cambridge University Press.

Baron–Cohen, S. (1989). Are autistic children "Behaviourists"? An examination of their mental–physical and appearance–reality distinctions. *Journal of Autism and Developmental Disorders, 19,* 579–600.

Baron–Cohen, S., Leslie, A. M., & Frith, U. (1985). Does the autistic child have a "theory of mind"? *Cognition, 21,* 37–46.

Baron–Cohen, S., Leslie, A. M., & Frith, U. (1986). Mechanical, behavioural and intentional understanding of picture stories in autistic children. *British Journal of Developmental Psychology, 4,* 113–125.

Brentano, F., von (1955). *Psychologie vom empirischen Standpunkt* Band 1. (Herausgegeben von O. Kraus.) Hamburg: Felix Meiner. (Original work published 1874)

Bretherton, I., McNew, S., & Beeghly–Smith, M. (1981). Early person knowledge as expressed in gestural and verbal communication: When do infants acquire a "theory of mind"? In M. E. Lamb & L. R. Sherod (Eds.), *Infant social cognition* (pp. 333–373). Hillsdale, NJ: Lawrence Erlbaum Associates.

Chandler, M. (1988). Doubt and developing theories of mind. In J. W. Astington, P. L. Harris, & D. R. Olson (Eds.), *Developing theories of mind* (pp. 387–413). New York: Cambridge University Press.

Churchland, P. M. (1984). *Matter and consciousness: A contemporary introduction to the philosophy of mind.* Cambridge, MA: MIT Press/Bradford.

Cummins, R. (1989). *Meaning and mental representation.* Cambridge, MA: MIT Press/Bradford.

Dennett, D. C. (1978). *Brainstorms.* Montgomery, VT: Bradford.

Dennett, D. C. (1987). *The intentional stance.* Cambridge, MA: MIT Press/Bradford.

Dretske, F. (1986). Misrepresentation. In R. J. Bogdan (Ed.), *Belief* (pp. 17–36). Oxford, England: Clarendon Press.

Dretske, F. (1988). *Explaining behavior: Reasons in a world of causes.* Cambridge, MA: MIT Press/Bradford.

Dunn, J., & Dale, N. (1984). I a daddy: 2-year-olds' collaboration in joint pretend with sibling and with mother. In I. Bretherton (Ed.), *Symbolic play* (pp. 131–158). New York: Academic Press.

Flavell, J. H. (1988). The development of children's knowledge about the mind: From cognitive connections to mental representations. In J. W. Astington, P. L. Harris, & D. R. Olson (Eds.), *Developing theories of mind* (pp. 244–267). New York: Cambridge University Press.

Flavell, J. H., Flavell, E. R., & Green, F. L. (1983). Development of the appearance–reality distinction. *Cognitive Psychology, 15,* 95–120.

Flavell, J. H., Flavell, E. R., & Green, F. L. (1987). Young children's knowledge about the apparent–real and pretend–real distinctions. *Developmental Psychology, 23,* 816–822.

Fodor, J. A. (1984). Semantics, Wisconsin style. *Synthese, 59,* 231–250.

Fodor, J. A. (1987). *Psychosemantics: The problem of meaning in the philosophy of mind.* Cambridge, MA: MIT Press/Bradford.

Fodor, J. A. (1990). *A theory of content.* Cambridge, MA: MIT Press/Bradford.

Fodor, J. A., & Pylyshyn, Z. W. (1988). Connectionism and cognitive architecture: A critical analysis. *Cognition, 28,* 3–71.

Forguson, L., & Gopnik, A. (1988). The ontogeny of common sense. In J. W. Astington, P. L. Harris, & D. R. Olson (Eds.), *Developing theories of mind* (pp. 226–243). New York: Cambridge University Press.

Frege, G. (1960). On sense and reference. In P. Geach & M. Black (Eds.), *Translations from the philosophical writings of Gottlob Frege,* (2nd ed., pp. 56–78). Oxford, England: Basil Blackwell. (Original work published 1892)

Goodman, N. (1976). *Languages of art.* Indianapolis: Hackett.

Gopnik, A. (1990). Developing the idea of intentionality: Children's theories of mind. *Canadian Journal of Philosophy, 20,* 89–114.

Gopnik, A., & Astington, J. W. (1988). Children's understanding of representational change and its relation to the understanding of false belief and the appearance–reality distinction. *Child Development, 58,* 26–37.

Gopnik, A., & Graf, P. (1988). Knowing how you know: Young children's ability to identify and remember the sources of their beliefs. *Child Development, 59,* 1366–1371.

Gopnik, A., & Slaughter, V. (1991). Young children's understanding of changes in their mental states. *Child Development, 62,* 98–110.

Harris, P. L. (1989). *Children and emotion: The development of psychological understanding.* Oxford, England: Basil Blackwell.

Harris, P. L. (1991). The work of the imagination. In A. Whiten (Ed.), *Natural theories of mind: Evolution, development and simulation of everyday mindreading* (pp. 283–304). Oxford, England: Basil Blackwell.

Johnson, C. N. (1988). Theory of mind and the structure of conscious experience. In J. W. Astington, P. L. Harris, & D. R. Olson (Eds.), *Developing theories of mind* (pp. 47–63). New York: Cambridge University Press.

Laurendeau, M., & Pinard, A. (1962). *Causal thinking in the child.* New York: International Universities Press.

Leekam, S. (1991). Jokes and lies: Children's understanding of intentional falsehood. In A. Whiten (Ed.), *Natural theories of mind: Evolution, development and simulation of everyday mindreading* (pp. 159–174). Oxford, England: Basil Blackwell.

Lehrer, K. (1986). Metamind: Belief, consciousness and intentionality. In R. J. Bogdan (Ed.), *Belief* (pp. 37–59). Oxford, England: Clarendon Press.

Leslie, A. M. (1987). Pretense and representation: The origins of "theory of mind." *Psychological Review, 94*, 412–426.

Leslie, A. M. (1988). Some implications of pretense for mechanisms underlying the child's theory of mind. In J. W. Astington, P. L. Harris, & D. R. Olson (Eds.), *Developing theories of mind* (pp. 19–46). New York: Cambridge University Press.

Liben, L. S., & Belknap, B. (1981). Intellectual realism: Implications for investigations of perceptual perspective taking in young children. *Cognitive Development, 52*, 921–924.

Light, P., & Nix, C. (1983). "Own view" versus "good view" in a perspective-taking task. *Child Development, 54*, 480–483.

Malvestuto-Felice, G. R. (1986). *The development of the understanding of the intentional predicates "pretend" and "imagine."* Unpublished doctoral dissertation, University of Toronto.

Mandler, J. M. (1983). Representation. In J. H. Flavell & E. Markman (Eds.), *Manual of child psychology: Cognitive development* (4th ed., Vol. 3, pp. 420–494; P. H. Mussen, General Ed.). New York: Wiley.

Marvin, R. S., Greenberg, M. T., & Mossler, D. G. (1976). The early development of conceptual perspective taking: Distinguishing among multiple perspectives. *Child Development, 47*, 511–514.

Miller, P. H. (1989). *Theories of developmental psychology* (2nd ed.). New York: Freeman.

Millikan, R. (1984). *Language, thought and other biological categories.* Cambridge, MA: MIT Press/Bradford.

Mossler, D. G., Marvin, R. S., & Greenberg, M. T. (1976). Conceptual perspective taking in 2- to 6-year-old children. *Developmental Psychology, 12*, 85–86.

Perner, J. (1988). Developing semantics for theories of mind: From propositional attitudes to mental representation. In J. W. Astington, P. L. Harris, & D. R. Olson (Eds.), *Developing theories of mind* (pp. 141–172). New York: Cambridge University Press.

Perner, J. (1991-a). On representing that: The asymmetry between belief and intention in children's theory of mind. In D. Frye & C. Moore (Eds.), *Children's theories of mind* (pp. 139–155). Hillsdale, NJ: Lawrence Erlbaum Associates.

Perner, J. (1991-b). *Understanding the representational mind.* Cambridge, MA: MIT Press/Bradford.

Perner, J., Leekam, S., & Wimmer, H. (1987). Three-year-olds' difficulty with false belief: The case for a conceptual deficit. *British Journal of Developmental Psychology, 5*, 125–137.

Piaget, J. (1929). *The child's conception of the world* (J. & A. Tomlinson, Trans.). London: Routledge & Kegan Paul. (Original work published 1926)

Piaget, J. (1977). *The moral judgement of the child* (M. Gabain, Trans.). Harmondsworth, England: Penguin. (Original work published 1932)

Piaget, J. (1962). *Play, dreams, and imitation in childhood* (C. Gattegno & F. M. Hodgson, Trans.). New York: Norton. (Original work published 1945)

Piaget, J., & Inhelder, B. (1956). *The child's conception of space* (F. J. Langdon & J. L. Lunzer, Trans.). London: Routledge & Kegan Paul. (Original work published 1948)

Piaget, J., & Inhelder, B. (1966). *La psychologie de l'enfant.* Paris: Presses Universitaires de France.

Premack, D., & Woodruff, G. (1978). Does the chimpanzee have a theory of mind? *Behavioral and Brain Sciences, 1*, 515–526.

Wellman, H. M. (1990). *The child's theory of mind.* Cambridge, MA: MIT Press/Bradford.

Wellman, H. M., & Estes, D. (1986). Early understanding of mental entities: A reexamination of childhood realism. *Child Development, 57*, 910–923.

Wimmer, H. (1989, April). *The Cartesian versus the theory view of mind: Developmental evidence.* Paper presented at the biennial meeting of the Society for Research in Child Development, Kansas City.

Wimmer, H., Gruber, S., & Perner, J. (1984). Young children's conception of lying: Lexical realism–moral subjectivism. *Journal of Experimental Child Psychology, 37,* 1–30.

Wimmer, H., & Hartl, M. (1991). The Cartesian view and the theory view of mind: Developmental evidence from understanding false belief in self and other. *British Journal of Developmental Psychology, 9,* 125–138.

Wimmer, H., Hogrefe, G. J., & Perner, J. (1988-a). Children's understanding of informational access as source of knowledge. *Child Development, 59,* 386–396.

Wimmer, H., Hogrefe, J., & Sodian, B. (1988-b). A second stage in children's conception of mental life: Understanding informational accesses as origins of knowledge and belief. In J. W. Astington, P. L. Harris, & D. R. Olson (Eds.), *Developing theories of mind* (pp. 173–192). New York: Cambridge University Press.

Wimmer, H., & Perner, J. (1983). Beliefs about beliefs: Representation and constraining function of wrong beliefs in young children's understanding of deception. *Cognition, 13,* 103–128.

Wimmer, H., & Perner, J. (1990). *Young children's memory for false statements: Separating sense from reference.* Unpublished manuscript, University of Salzburg, Austria.

III SEEKING TRUTH AND MEANING: LOGIC AND SCIENTIFIC REASONING

7 Meaningful Logic: Developmental Perspectives

James P. Byrnes
University of Maryland

Developmental psychologists who study children's reasoning are faced with the task of supplying theoretical models to explain children's reasoning performance. After the cognitive revolution of the 1960s, these models often took the form of mental structures or rules (Gardner, 1985). For example, in order to explain why an adolescent correctly predicts that a balance will remain level, given a certain configuration of weights, cognitive developmentalists have appealed to structures such as "formal operations" (Inhelder & Piaget, 1958), or to rules such as "If the weights are the same and the distances are the same, it will stay level" (cf. Siegler, 1976). A similar trend occurred in the domain of developmental psycholinguistics in which knowledge of grammatical rules was attributed to children (e.g., Bloom, 1970; Braine, 1963; McNeill, 1966).

Developmental psychologists often turned to the fields of logic and linguistics for insight into how to construct models of language and thought. This was a reasonable thing to do, given that logicians and linguists had grappled intensively with the structure of thought and language for many years. In the case of language, McNeill (1966) and Bloom (1970) adopted Chomsky's (1957, 1965) transformational grammar as a model of children's linguistic knowledge. In the case of reasoning, Inhelder and Piaget (1958) and Wason and Johnson–Laird (1972) adopted truth-functional logic as a standard. Somewhat later, Braine (1978) abandoned truth-functional logic in favor of Gentzen's (1935/1964) natural logic. Many theorists, then, assumed that the models developed by logicians and linguists were good descriptions of the structure of knowledge and began gathering data in order to determine whether children and adults

163

have the logical and linguistic competence specified by these models. In essence, truth-functional logic and transformational grammar became *normative* for psychologists because these models were considered to be good descriptions of how one *should* reason or use language.

In the case of reasoning, however, data began to amass that demonstrated that the responses of adolescents and adults were at odds with the responses specified by truth-functional logic (e.g., Wason & Johnson--Laird, 1972). In other words, most adolescents and adults gave a different response than that predicted from truth-functional logic. This was particularly true when task items were devoid of meaningful content. For example, consider the following syllogism: "If there is a D on one side of a card, there is a 7 on the other side of the card. There isn't a D on one side. Is there a 7 on the other side?" For such problems, most subjects respond "No." However, truth-functional logic specifies that the correct response is "can't tell." When one substitutes more meaningful content such as "if someone is drinking beer then that person is at least 21," the correct responses increase dramatically. Since logic was designed to be a content-free model of universal truths (Quine, 1950), one could interpret variations in performance as a result of content in one of two ways: (a) adolescents and adults are incapable of reasoning logically, or (b) truth-functional logic is not a good model of human reasoning. These two competing interpretations formed the basis of a controversy that was waged for many years (see Cohen, 1981, for a sampling of the debate).

In the last several years, there has been a growing number of cognitive developmentalists who have agreed that truth-functional logic is not the most appropriate model of human reasoning and have tried to propose alternative models (e.g., Byrnes, 1988a; Falmagne, 1990; Keating, 1990; Overton, 1990; Ricco, 1990; Scholnick & Wing, 1990). Before describing these approaches, I shall first describe a problem that I believe makes adopting the truth-functional model or any other purely formal model problematical. In subsequent sections, I will judge the adequacy of new models partly on the basis of whether they avoid this pervasive problem.

THE FORMALISM FALLACY

To get a sense of what the formalism fallacy is, consider the following three events: (a) an apple falls from a tree; (b) one billiard ball hits another; and (c) wind blows a leaf along the ground. Physicists (i.e., Newtonians) attempted to find formal similarities among these events and developed theoretical constructs to explain them. In each case, there is some force *(F)* that acts upon an object that has a certain amount of mass *(M)*, and causes it to move with increasing speed (*A* for acceleration). Physicists were able to capture the similarities across these situations with the theoretical statement "Force = Mass × Acceleration." This statement was further simplified into a mathematical formula: $F = ma$. This formula allows physicists to make predictions and to communicate with each other in a form that is simple and efficient.

Of course, no physicist would claim that the contentless formalism, $F = ma$, exists in the world in a disembodied form waiting to become instantiated in multiple ways by specific forces and masses such as those in the list of three events just given. This would seem to be an absurd proposal that few would accept.

However, consider the description of linguistic competence depicted in Fig. 7.1.

In the late 1960s, many psychologists argued that the rewriting of rules 1-3 of Chomsky's early formulations (Chomsky 1957, 1965) underlie a native speaker's comprehension and production of well-formed utterances. Importantly, these rules are purely formal in the sense that the complex symbols "DET," "N" in the terminal strings of the phrase structure tree are *uninterpreted;* that is, they have no meaning until a lexical insertion stage occurs in which meaningful lexemes are substituted for the complex symbols listed in the terminal string. These rules are generative in that these three rules can generate an infinite number of well-formed utterances that are formally identical to sentences (1) and (2) in the figure, but are semantically distinct. And yet, these rules would also produce the nonsensical sentence (3). To avoid such nonsensical outcomes, psychologists adopted Chomsky's (1965) notions of *constraints* and context-sensitive frames that are built into the lexicon. For example, the entry "Bite" is marked for animacy. This animacy restriction would preclude and block the insertion of "bite" after the inanimate "rock."

Consider next the formalization of conditional inferences found in several accounts of propositional reasoning (e.g., Braine & Rumain, 1983). Adolescents and adults are frequently encountered engaging in *modus ponens* inferences such as (1) and (2) shown in Table 7.1. The formalism (inference schema) at the top represents that which is common across all such inferences and is considered to be generative in the same way that Chomsky's rewriting rules have been interpreted to be. However, again we have the problem illustrated in (3) in which nonsensical content inserted into this inference schema results in a valid but nonsensical conclusion. The philosophers Anderson and Belnap (1962) suggested placing a *relevance constraint* on such schemata such that only "if" statements in which the antecedent and consequent were related through a relevance relation could enter a formal proof involving a *modus ponens* inference (Ricco, 1990).

Each of these examples, then, illustrate the same four-step sequence: (a) a set of behaviors is observed; (b) the theorist captures the structural

Rewriting Rules

   Rule 1: S ---> NP + VP

   Rule 2: NP --> Det + N

   Rule 3: VP --> V + NP

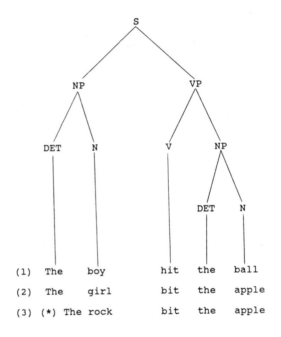

		DET	N	V	DET	N
(1)	The		boy	hit	the	ball
(2)	The		girl	bit	the	apple
(3)	(*) The	rock		bit	the	apple

Constraints: (bite, +V, + ___ NP, +animate,...)

FIG. 7.1.   Generative grammar rules.

similarities of the behaviors with a formalism; (c) the formalism is attributed to the mind in a contentless form; and (d) constraints have to be built into the system to avoid the insertion of inappropriate content.

What can account for the discrepancy between the behavior of physicists and that of psychologists? Most would agree that attributing the formalism $F = ma$ to a leaf or a billiard ball would be illogical, but many readily attribute formalisms such as "S --> NP + VP" or "If p then q; p therefore q" to humans. It is not simply a matter of rule-governedness because the world can certainly be characterized as rule-governed. How is it that we have "mistaken the model for the mind" in the case of humans?

Lakoff (1987, pp. 219–228) describes some of the historical reasons for

TABLE 7.1.   Logical Inference Schema

IF *P* THEN *Q*; *P*
$$\overline{}$$
Q

(1) If it is raining then the grass is wet. It is raining, therefore the grass is wet

(2) If it is Tuesday, then I have class. It is Tuesday, therefore I have class.

(3) If vinegar is acid, then some men have beards. Vinegar is acid,
    therefore some men have beards.

---

the insertion of logical models in the mind and why this is not a valid enterprise, but these will not be pursued here. I think the primary problems have arisen from the tendency of psychologists to fail to recognize a difference between the role of models in psychology and the role of models in logic or linguistics. Chomsky formalized the machinery of English grammar and argued that transformational grammar was a good model if it produced any and all well-formed sentences of English and no ill-formed sentences (all on its own) (Chomsky, 1965, pp. 33–47). Logicians such as Frege and Russell engaged in a similar sort of behavior. They wanted logic to account for all of the axioms of mathematics independent of particular mathematical problems. Notwithstanding the important work of linguists and logicians, their techniques can have little bearing on *how the mind* works. On the one hand we have adults reasoning correctly and children easily learning their native tongue. They usually do not produce the nonsensical inferences and sentences listed in the figures. On the other hand psychologists introduce many complex constraints and build these into the (innate) hardware. This being so, current notions regarding the role of formalisms in the mind appear to be seriously misguided.

Does this mean that we should avoid "rules in the head" proposals as Skinner or Connectionists argue? Reviewing the arguments for attributing rules to the human mind (but not to inanimate objects) may be helpful for answering this question. These arguments are summarized in Table 7.2. First, we have the fact that rules are considered to be causally related to human behavior. They operate within the human mind somehow to affect behavior. This can be contrasted to explanations in physics where causes typically exist outside of objects. The next four explanations regarding productivity, two types of systematicity, and compositionality are due to Fodor and Pylyshyn (1988). Their arguments for the productivity of thought are as follows:

The representational capacities of [rich representational systems] are, by assumption, unbounded under appropriate idealization; in particular, there

TABLE 7.2.   Reasons for Attributing Rules

General: (1) Causes are judged to be internal in the case of humans (animate objects).

Fodor & Pylyshyn (1988):
    (2) The productivity of thought
    (3) The systematicity of cognitive representation
    (4) The compositionality of representations
    (5) The systematicity of inference

Slobin (1979):
    (6) The regularities of behavior (weak evidence)
    (7) Extension of regularities to new instances (stronger evidence)
    (8) A normative sense of a rule (stronger still)
    (9) The ability to detect vioations of a rule (stronger still)
    (10) Stating the explicit rule

are indefinitely many propositions which the system can encode. However, this unbounded expressive power must presumably be achieved by finite means. The way to do this is to treat the system of representations as consisting of expressions belonging to a generated set. (p. 33)

Their arguments for the systematicity of cognitive representation are illustrated by considering the systematicity of language comprehension and production:

> What we mean when we say that linguistic capacities are *systematic* is that the ability to produce/understand some sentences is *intrinsically* connected to the ability to produce/understand certain others. . . . Our point is that you can learn *any part of a phrase book without learning the rest.* . . . You don't find, for example, native speakers who know how to say in English that John loves the girl but don't know how to say in English that the girl loves John. (p. 37)

Their arguments for the compositionality of representations are illustrated with reference to the semantics of the lexicon. They suggest that it would be strange for people to understand the meaning of "John loves the girl" without being able to understand the meaning of "the girl loves John" since they have the same lexical components (as well as the same syntactical rules). Their arguments for the systematicity of inference are illustrated with reference to logical inferences. They suggest that it would be strange to attribute an inference to people of the form "*P & Q & R;* therefore *P*" but not attribute to them the inference "*P & Q; therefore P.*" The sum of their arguments are nicely illustrated in the following:

> What's deeply wrong with Connectionism [or a similar nonrule based approach] is this: Because it acknowledges neither syntactic nor semantic

structure in mental representations, it perforce treats them not as a generated set but as a list. But lists, qua lists, have no structure; any collection of items is a possible list. . . . So as far as Connectionist architecture is concerned, there is nothing to prevent minds that are arbitrarily unsystematic. (p. 49)

These arguments and those of Slobin (1979) are sufficiently compelling to suggest retaining the notion of rules in the functioning of the human mind. What is perhaps ironic is that Fodor and Pylyshyn acknowledge three levels of the cognitive architecture: physical, syntactical, and semantic. In their account, syntax or form is dissociated from semantics or content and as such, the Fodor/Pylyshyn proposal still requires the notion of constraints. Fodor and Pylyshyn, however, make no provision for the possibility of inappropriate content being fed into the syntactical machinery. One way to salvage their view is to suggest that in real-time processing, semantics *always precedes* syntax. That is, we know what we want to say or want to infer and this is fed into the syntactical machinery, which computes the appropriate, meaningful output. In this view, there is no need for constraints because the syntactical component is not expected to work all by itself.

To summarize, there are two major reasons for assuming that truth-functional logic fails as a model of human reasoning performance. The first reason is empirical: Predictions deriving from truth-functional logic are often incorrect. The second reason is logical: By attributing an abstract, contentless formalism to the mind one falls prey to the formalism fallacy. One rectifies both problems by incorporating *meaningful content* into one's model of mind. In particular, studies have shown that meaningful content of a certain type greatly improves performance on reasoning tasks (e.g., Byrnes & Overton, 1986; Ward, Byrnes, & Overton, 1990). Additionally, avoiding the formalism fallacy requires making meaningful content an *integral part* of the model, not a tangential component. In what follows, I review some recent proposals that have attempted to incorporate meaning into developmental models of mind.

DEVELOPMENTAL PERSPECTIVES ON MEANINGFUL LOGIC

There have been two main proposals regarding the role of meaning. The first set of arguments stem from Piaget's most recent writings in which he argued that the original, truth-functional model of formal operations might be inadequate for characterizing adolescent reasoning (Piaget, 1980, 1986, 1987; Piaget & Garcia, 1991). Adherents to the second proposal argue that logical reasoning skill is learned while using language in context. I shall describe each of these proposals in turn. In each case, I present the theoretical underpinnings of a proposal first and the empirical support for it second.

The Logic of Meanings and Entailment

Theoretical Underpinnings. Piaget recently argued that the original model of formal operations might be inadequate for characterizing adolescent reasoning because it was based on truth-functional logic (e.g., Piaget & Garcia, 1991). In these writings, he suggested replacing truth-functional logic with a logic of entailment as specified by Anderson and Belnap (1962) (Beilin, this volume; Ricco, 1990).

The heart of the matter concerns Piaget's contention that any adequate model of thinking in children or adolescents must characterize both *intensional* and *extensional* relations (Apostel, 1982; Chapman, 1988). Simply put, intensional relations are "representation-to-representation" relations. An example would be the inclusion relation between a subclass and superordinate class (i.e., X is a *kind of Y*). Each of the subclass, superordinate class, and inclusion relation are mentally represented. In the case of classes, intensional properties are qualitative in that they allow a differentiation between the members and nonmembers of a class. Extensional relations, on the other hand, are "representation-to-world" relations. An example would be the reference relation between a category label (e.g., "dog") and the objects in the world to which this label can be appropriately applied. The extension of a class, then, represents its quantification. Whereas Piaget's model of concrete operations characterizes both the intension and extension of categories (Inhelder & Piaget, 1964), the original model of formal operations in *entirely extensional;* that is, logical concepts such as conditional implication (i.e., "if p then q") are defined by the truth values of the component propositions "p" and "q" (Byrnes, 1988a; Piaget, 1972). Defining the meaning of a proposition by truth values, however, makes meaning entirely based on the accuracy of the reference relation between a proposition and some state of affairs in the world.

The problems of a purely extensional logic have been well known since the time of Frege (1952), when he made his famous distinction between "sense" (intension) and "reference" (extension). In a purely extensional account, sentences such as "The present king of France is bald" can have no meaning because there is no actual person to which this sentence can be applied. Hence, it is neither "true" nor "false." But the sentence does seem to have meaning anyway. Further problems were revealed when *modus ponens* inferences were used by logicians to derive certain obviously absurd theorems (Byrnes, 1990; Ricco, 1990) and when a truth-functional account was applied to the meaning of "if . . . then" statements. In the truth-functional account, an "if p then q" statement is true (i.e., has meaning) if any or all of the following conjunctions are true: "*p* and *q*," "not-*p* and *q*" and "not-*p* and not-*q*." So a statement such as "if it is a dog, then it is a mammal" is true if we encounter a dog that is a mammal, a nondog that is a mammal (e.g., a cat), or a nondog that is not a mammal (e.g., a lizard). However, under this *material implication* interpretation, the sentence "If acid is vinegar, then some men have red beards" is also true because of the truth values of its conjunctions. What is missing in this truth-functional account is the meaning that is derived from intensional relations. For the "dog" statement, meaning is derived from the class inclusion relation that exists between clauses. For a causal statement, intensional meaning would derive from a causal relation that exists between events in the clauses. For the vinegar statement, however, no intension relation exists. Hence, it is judged to be meaningless.

As was his penchant, Piaget often looked to the domains of logic and mathematics when he was in need of new models of mind. Aware as he was of the limits of a purely extensional logic (e.g., Piaget, 1962), he consulted the domain of logic again to see how logicians themselves tried to deal with the problems presented by truth-functional logic. Historically, truth-functional logic was supplanted by various modal logics that emphasized *possibility* and *necessity* rather than truth per se (Hughes & Cresswell, 1968; Pieraut–LeBonniec, 1980). These logics were called "intentional" because they tried to capture the meaning omitted from extensional accounts. One can see why Piaget turned to these logics as a solution.

Because "if . . . then" conditionals seemed to lie at the heart of many problems, modal logicians developed the notion of *entailment* to reduce the possibility of either absurd theorems being derived or meaningless, but "true" sentences being constructed. In the case of a conditional, an entailment relation exists between clauses when the case "*p* and not-*q*" is judged to be *impossible* (not just merely false). For example, in the statement, "If someone is a bachelor, then he is an unmarried adult male," the second clause could not be false if the first clause were true; that is, someone *has to be* an unmarried adult male if he is a bachelor. Because exceptions to this are impossible, the first clause is said to entail the second. On the other hand, entailment does not exist between clauses for the statement, "If I get tenure, I will be less depressed" because it could empirically turn out that the speaker does get tenure but remains depressed anyway. As Ricco (1990) notes, entailment relations often exist for statements in which what is said in the second clause is part of, or is *implicit in,* the first clause. In the bachelor example, the second clause is part of the definition of the first clause. True entailment is quite rare, of course, because the majority of meaningful "if" statements are more like the "tenure" statement than like the "bachelor" statement (Ward et al., 1990).

Whereas modal logics seemed initially promising to logicians, it was soon found that entailment defined formally (e.g., "*P* entails *Q* iff -pos(*p* & not-*q*)") leads to different, though equally troublesome theorems and statements when one substitutes certain meaningful content for the symbols in the formal definition (Pieraut–LeBonniec, 1980). This led Anderson and Belnap (1962) to place a "relevance" restriction on content: The content of the first clause must have relevance to the content of the second clause. Piaget (1986, 1987) apparently felt that Anderson and Belnap's entailment logic was a more suitable model for characterizing adolescent reasoning than the original truth-functional model.

For some readers, Piaget's shifting to a relevance-based entailment logic might seem to indicate a major change in his theory. Ricco (1990) argues, however, that this shift is not as radical as it may seem. Truth-functional logic is *contained within* modal logic (Hughes & Cresswell, 1968). For example, one defines the possibility of some proposition *"p"* (e.g., "it is raining") by saying that either *"p"* or its opposite *"not-p"* (e.g., "it is not raining") is *true* in some state of affairs (e.g., right now). So possibility and necessity are really about the truth and falsity of propositions in various contexts or "possible worlds." Because modal logics account for all of the issues that a truth-functional logic does and then some, modal logics are said to be *more powerful* in the Godelian sense (Hughes & Cresswell, 1968). Hence, just as concrete operations are not replaced by formal operations but subsumed within the latter, truth-functional logic is subsumed within modal logic. If this analogy is sound, however, Piaget's adoption of an entailment logic as a model does represent a significant "qualitative change" in my opinion. Beilin (this volume) likewise considers the adoption of an entailment logic to be a radical change in the theory. Nevertheless, few realize that Piaget saw problems with a purely formal truth-functional account as early as 1962 (Byrnes, 1988b; Piaget, 1962).

The issue remains, however, as to how entailment and other meaningful relations are constructed by the child. In several places in his later work, "meaning" was partly identified with the "reasons" children supply for phenomena (Piaget & Garcia, 1974; Pieraut–LeBonniec, 1990; Ricco, 1990). Children's understanding of causality is a paradigmatic case. If children's knowledge of causality is limited to detecting covariance relations among events, Piaget argued that they do not genuinely understand causality (Piaget & Garcia, 1974; Piaget, Grize, Szeminska, & Bang, 1977). On the other hand, if children can provide reasons for *why* one event brings about another, then they can be said to understand causality. The same can be said for any other relation besides causality including categorical and numerical relations (Pieraut–LeBonniec, 1990). This idea is quite similar to the current work on "theories" (e.g., Carey, 1985; Gelman & Coley, in press; Keil, in press). Keil, for example, argues that children's categorical knowledge begins as a network of correlational relations. These correlations among concept nodes eventually become replaced by meaningful, theory-based explanations as children gain expertise.

Coincident with Piaget's emphasis on entailment and meaning was his emphasis on *signifying implication* (Overton, 1990; Piaget, 1986, 1987; Piaget & Garcia, 1991; Ricco, 1990). In a signifying implication, one object, action, or event has meaning for another object, action, or event. These objects, actions, or events may be part of immediate sensorimotor experience or may be represented. An early example of a signifying implication is an infant's understanding that if an attractive toy is on a blanket that is within reach, he or she can obtain the toy by pulling on the blanket. Hence, "toy on blanket" ("p") implies "toy can be obtained" ("q"). This implication would be an early form of entailment if the child believes that the case "the toy is on blanket, but it cannot be obtained" ("p and not-q") is impossible.

As a means of describing the importance of the notion of signifying implication in recent Piagetian thinking, Overton (1990) placed the issue in the larger context of another of Piaget's more recent emphases: the relation between structures and procedures (Inhelder & Piaget, 1980). Piaget defined "structures," as those cognitive entities that have form and content (Byrnes, 1988a; Piaget, 1972) and exhibit transformations, wholeness, and self-regulations (Piaget, 1970). A paradigmatic case would be the concrete operation of "primary addition of classes" (e.g., $A + A' = B$). Piaget defined "procedures" as goal-directed behaviors in which certain behaviors serve as the means for attaining a goal (Inhelder & de Caprona, 1990). An good example of goal-directed behavior would be a child combining a "pushing" scheme with "grasping" scheme in order to find a hidden object. Of course, procedures can be performed mentally as well (e.g., mental arithmetic).

Inhelder and Piaget (1980) argue that there are several important differences between structures and procedures that have an impact on their relationship. First, procedures are inherently temporal or sequential in that they transform objects in order to attain goals. In contrast, structures are derived by abstracting across transformations in order to form atemporal systems. Second, procedures are chained sequentially or contingently in order to achieve a goal and are not typically integrated. In contrast, structures tend to be integrated into each other. Third, an understanding of why a procedure works is not essential; its success in achieving results is key. On the basis of results, procedures are modified. Fourth, diversification (i.e., differentiation) is the rule for procedures. They become more varied with time because each problem often has its own solution. In contrast, unification (i.e., integration) is the rule for structures. Finally, Inhelder and Piaget argue that structures and procedures relate in dynamic cycles in which structural knowledge is built up as a result of trying to understand why a procedure was effective. That is, structures are developed as a child tries to supply "reasons" for the success of certain procedures. On the other hand, structures must be present in order for new procedures to be constructed (Inhelder & Piaget, 1980; Overton, 1990). For example, the procedure used on a seriation task of repeatedly selecting the largest stick remaining would only be constructed by a child who comprehends the notion of relative size. For Piaget, this concept is provided by the concrete operations (i.e., structures) having to do with relations of order (Byrnes, 1988a).

The meaningful relations inherent in signifying implications result first from the reciprocal assimilation of sensorimotor and representational schemes (Piaget, 1986). An example of a reciprocal assimilation is a child fusing a "pulling" scheme together with a "grasping" scheme in order to attain a goal. Once such an integration among these schemes has taken place, they are related through a signifying implication relation. This integration of schemes continues on the representational level (Overton, 1990) where a child integrates, say, individual images of someone performing separate actions. As the child tries to find "reasons" for the results of action sequences (i.e., procedures), higher-order structures in the form of concrete operations are developed. When the child reaches the level of concrete operations, he or she integrates categories through reciprocal assimilation. When this occurs, a subclass is said to "imply" or "entail" a superordinate class. For this reason, the statement "if it is a dog, then it is a mammal" expresses an entailment relation. Finally, through the process of reflective abstraction which operates over signifying implications and inclusion relations, a full propositional logic is constructed (Voelin--Liambey & Berthoud–Papandropoulou, 1977). Thus, when reciprocal assimilation produces "within-stage" integrations, signifying implications are made possible. In addition, there are analogous forms of meaningful implications or entailments at each level of development, the highest of which is the propositional version described by logicians.

As Overton (1990) points out, there is nothing contradictory about Inhelder and Piaget's (1980) dual emphasis on structures and procedures. A structuralist orientation and a functionalist orientation are compatible and complementary if the same stance on physical realization possibilities is maintained in each orientation. Piaget's structuralism emphasizes a system of meanings that arise out of the embodied experiences of an individual (Overton, 1990). A compatible functionalism would, then, have to emphasize human physiology and activity. There are, of course, other varieties of functionalism, such as *machine functionalism,* which take the Turing Machine or Lycan's "Tin Foil" man as models of mind (Dennett, 1987; Lycan, 1987; Overton, 1990). Because adherents to these forms of functionalism argue that the same basic "program" can be carried out in a variety of physical instantiations (e.g., the human brain, a computer, etc.), they are incompatible with Piaget's biological functionalism (Overton, 1990). Thus, Overton argues that is it not inconsequential that a computer and human carry out a procedure differently at the both the *algorithmic* and *hardware* levels (cf. Marr, 1982). That is, functional equivalence (cf. Newell & Simon, 1972; Pylyshyn, 1984) is not enough; the embodied experiences must be similar.

Empirical Support.   Even though Piaget's entailment logic proposal is relatively new, its credibility has been strengthened by recent empirical findings (e.g., Ward et al., 1990; Pieraut–LeBonniec, 1990). Ward et al. (1990), for example, directly based their study of conditional reasoning on this revised theory and found a high degree of support. In particular, they found that using semantic content that was merely familiar did not substantially enhance conditional reasoning performance unless entailment relations existed between clauses. For example, subjects performed significantly better on familiar statements which expressed entailment (e.g., "If it is a diamond, then it is hard") than on familiar statements which do not express entailment (e.g., "if it is hard, then it is a diamond"). Of course, many additional studies still need to be conducted.

Before moving on to the second proposal, it is necessary to point out that a theorist who finds Piaget's new proposals appealing would still fall prey to the formalism fallacy if he or she were to simply attribute an Anderson--Belnap entailment logic to an individual's mind. That is, it is erroneous to assume that a contentless formalism of the entailment logic type exists in the mind and guides behavior. Rather, one should assume that actual, meaningful knowledge exists and that this knowledge is organized in a particular way. It is the *organization* that yields entailment (e.g., the inclusion of one actual category into another), not some disembodied entailment logic.

The Linguistic Source of Logic

Theoretical underpinnings.   Rather than considering the structure of knowledge to be the source of meaning, several theorists have recently considered natural language to be the source of logical reasoning skill. Falmagne (1990), for example, argues that logical relations are an inherent part of linguistic meaning, as well as an inherent part of nonlinguistic aspects of performance such as conceptual relations or the environmental context. It is in the process of using language in context that children come to understand these relations. She has suggested that Barwise and Perry's (1983) theory of *Situation Semantics* is a possible model of how logic is acquired through language use because it includes a detailed account of both linguistic and nonlinguistic aspects of meaning (Falmagne, 1990). Moreover, Barwise and Perry's account shows how a situated agent must be present in order for meaning to be derived from a situation. Furthermore, it emphasizes two notions that are compatible with the psychological work on event knowledge (e.g., Nelson, 1986): classes of situations and event-types.

In order get a sense of the potential utility of Situation Semantics, it is helpful to describe its key aspects. At a very general level, Situation Semantics combines elements of set theory, possible worlds semantics (e.g., Stalnaker, 1984), Gibson's (1979) ecological theory of perception, and Dretske's (1981) account of the "flow of information." However, Situation Semantics differs from possible worlds semantics in important ways. Instead of getting at the meaning of a statement by considering all of the possible worlds in which the statement would be true, the approach is one of considering: (a) the conditions under which a sentence can be used to *convey information,* and (b) what information the sentence conveys under those conditions (Barwise, 1986, 1989). A key idea is that a situation s of type S can carry information about another situation s' of type S'. For example, a situation involving smoke (s) often signals a situation involving fire (s'), and a situation involving someone saying "Have a cookie" (s) often signals a situation where a cookie is handed to the listener (s'). The notion of the "flow of information" refers to the dynamic character of human experience in which situations are linked together within informational chains, with humans embedded within these chains. So, instead of considering all possible factual and counterfactual worlds, one need only consider *parts* of the one real world, that is, situations.

Barwise and Perry (1983) refer to the informational relations between situations as *constraints* and formally represent the constraint between situations of type S and situations of type S' as S = > S'. Such constraints can be: (a) *necessary* relations such as that between being a woman and being human, or between "2 + 2" and "4"; (b) *nomic* relations such as the natural laws studied by physicists (e.g., gravity); or (c) *conventional* constraints that arise out of the conventions that hold between communities of living beings such as those inherent in human languages. Whereas necessary relations are unconditional and ubiquitous constraints because they are always true regardless of context, nomic and conventional constraints are conditional in that they are not true in all contexts and can be violated (Barwise & Perry, 1983).

In order to derive meaning and information from contexts, humans have to be "attuned" to the constraints between situations (Barwise, 1989; Barwise & Perry, 1983). That is, information is out there in the real world to be had, and humans become attuned to reality when their mental states are constrained in the same way. For example, assume that there is a constraint between two environmental situations of the form S = > S', and let the mental state corresponding to S be symbolized #S, and that corresponding to S' be symbolized #S'. Assume also, as Barwise and Perry do, that mental states are situations of a particular kind. Attunement exists when #S => S, #S' => S', and #S => #S' (Barwise, 1989). Barwise and Perry (1983) elaborated on these notions to develop a *relational theory of meaning* which "looks at the meaning of a sentence as providing a constraint between two proper parts of the world, the utterance and the described situation. That, in a nutshell, is what situation semantics is all about" (Barwise, 1989, p. 91).

In order to understand how Situation Semantics characterizes linguistic meaning, we need to consider the distinction between the meaning of a sentence and its *interpretation* in context. The meaning of a sentence such as "I am sitting" is "a relation that holds between an utterance u and a situation e just in case there is a location l and an individual a such that in u, a is speaking at l and in e, a is sitting at l" (p. 19). More specifically, the meaning is the constraint between the set of all the situations of type u and the set of all the situations of type e. The specific situation described on a specific occasion when a statement is made with this sentence is its interpretation. So interpretations "fix" and extend the meaning of a sentence in a particular context. An important outcome of the distinction between the meaning of a sentence and its interpretation is what Barwise and Perry call the *efficiency of language:* "the fact that expressions, whether simple or complex, can be recycled, can be used over and over again in different ways, places, and times and by different people, *to say different things*" (p. 32). Competent speakers of a language exploit situational uniformities, conditional, and unconditional constraints in order to make a single sentence mean a variety of things. For the sake of brevity, I will not examine how speakers exploit constraints and situations, but rather, refer the interested reader to elaborate treatments in Barwise and Perry (1983) and Barwise (1986).

In addition to linguistic meaning, Situation Semantics has been applied to inference and knowledge, though in less detail. For Barwise (1989), "a sound inference is one that has the logical structure necessary to serve as a link in an informational chain" (p. 56). However, inference does not always require language (p. 149) or other types of mental representation (Barwise & Perry, 1983, p. 270). For example, Barwise suggests that inferring the outside temperature from the way people are dressed does not require language. Even when inference does involve language, however, it is not a formal language that makes no reference to content or the embedding context. Rather, it is a situated language that involves both contents and context (Barwise, 1989, p. 146). As for knowledge, Barwise and Perry (1983) state that "some beliefs contain information for the agent, some don't. The former constitute knowledge, the latter don't" (pp. 225–226). So again, there is information to be had in the environment and if the agent becomes attuned to this information, they have knowledge.

Given this account of Situation Semantics and Falmagne's research program, it is clear why she proposed that Situation Semantics could be potentially used as a tool for examining how children learn language and logical relations in context. Certainly, the notion of event-types can be grounded in well-established psychological theories of event representations (e.g., Nelson, 1986) and the treatment of interpretations in context could be fruitful for determining how children learn the meaning of logical connectives like "if."

I would point out, however, that Lakoff (1987) provides cogent criticisms of the extreme objectivist aspects of Situation Semantics because of its emphasis on information that is "out there" in the real world. Also, Fodor (1986) labels the theory "behaviorist" and criticizes it for failing to include an inferential component that is sensitive to the syntactical form of arguments. Barwise (1989) responded to these criticisms by arguing that both Fodor and Lakoff have misunderstood the theory, and by arguing that Fodor's overly formal account of inference is incorrect. Notwithstanding these rejoinders, I might add that Barwise (1986) has apparently contradicted himself by using a realist theory to account for *counterfactual* conditionals. If there is only one real-world and mental representations reflect this, how is counterfactual reasoning possible? Lakoff (1987) makes a similar point regarding metaphor and other creative aspects of thought. Additionally, the theory is silent on how categorization of objects relates to situations since Situation Semantics takes objects and properties to be unanalyzed primitives. Finally, it does not elaborate on how important constraints between mental states such as causal relations are represented.

Empirical Support.   As was the case with the new Piagetian proposal, there is not much in the way of empirical support for Linguistic Source proposals because they are relatively new. There is, however, Scholnick and Wing's (1990) study of conversation-based inferences. They analyzed two corpora for evidence of deductive reasoning within conversations among children and adults and extracted 3,600 "if" sentences from these corpora. They discovered that in about 10% of these cases, children produced a second statement which, in effect, completed an inference. Five kinds of inferences were coded:

1. *Modus ponens* inferences, in which one speaker says something like "If it is raining, we won't go" (i.e., if p then q) and the listener says something like "It is raining so we're not going."

2. *Modus tollens* inferences in which the listener denies the antecedent because the consequent is false (e.g., "We're going so I guess it isn't raining").

3. *Indeterminate* inferences which reflect an understanding of the asymmetry of "if" statements (e.g., commenting that "We might not go anyway even if it isn't raining").

4. *Biconditional* inferences that suggest a lack of understanding of the asymmetry of "if" because the negated counterpart of the first "if" statement is uttered right after it (e.g., "If it doesn't rain, then we'll go").

5. *Contradictions* in which the listener essentially denies the entailment relation expressed by the speaker's "if" statement (e.g., "But last time we went when it *was* raining!").

Scholnick and Wing found that even 3- and 4-year-olds produced at least one instance of each of the five inference-types. The majority (90%) of their completed inferences, however, were *modus ponens,* contradictions, and biconditionals. An analysis of the content of their utterances was quite revealing. Most of the children's utterances described actions in the "if" clause as well as in the second clause. These actions predominantly concerned social rules and intentionality. Moreover, when children were speakers, they predominantly referred to their own actions and intentions as opposed to the actions of other people or objects.

Scholnick and Wing's study, then, demonstrates that preschoolers possess surprising deductive inference-making competencies. Even though children typically did not set up and complete their own premise chains, they clearly must possess knowledge structures that give them insight into the logic of the premise content expressed by someone else.

Nevertheless, in order for Linguistic Source proposals to have merit, it has to be shown that the completion of inferences within conversations causes children to acquire logical reasoning skill. At the very least, there must be correlational evidence that children who frequently complete conversational inferences acquire logical reasoning skill earlier than children who do not. More credible evidence would come from experiments that induce or train children to complete inferences. If those children given such training show improved skill on logical reasoning tasks whereas untrained children show no improvement, then the linguistic use proposal would gain solid empirical support.

CONCLUSIONS

In this chapter I have argued that any purely formal model of reasoning is likely to fail for both empirical and logical reasons. Piaget and several other theorists recently recognized the problems of a purely formal model and have advanced new models in which meaning plays a central role. Both of the proposals presented seem reasonable, and neither one really contradicts the other. In fact, the "correct" account probably includes elements of both proposals. Nevertheless, one may well ask whether these proposals will have an impact on the field.

These proposals will have an impact if multiple subgroups of researchers adopt them as models of adolescent and adult thinking. Only a few studies have been conducted and they only scratch the surface. Unlike most of the research of the last 20 years, which was motivated to show how the old Piagetian model of adolescent reasoning is inadequate, research based on the new models will be highly progressive; that is, it will likely be geared toward confirmation of novel hypotheses rather than disconfirmation of an old model. As Ward et al. (1990) argue, for example, only the new Piagetian model can currently make predictions about entailment relations and knowledge organization. Most other models of knowledge only describe associative links among pieces of knowledge. Similarly, the incorporation of event representations into the logical reasoning literature would certainly yield novel predictions. In brief, I suggest that the adoption of either the Piagetian or Linguistic Source proposals would represent a genuine paradigmatic shift with respect to the nature of adolescent thinking.

On the other hand, both proposals will be short-lived if researchers who adopt them fall prey to the formalism fallacy. That is, if either an entailment logic or Barwise and Perry's formalisms are attributed to the mind, disconfirming evidence will again amass which shows low performance on reasoning tasks. One avoids making the formalism fallacy by limiting one's structuralism to the assumption that knowledge is structured (i.e., organized) in a particular way and this organization affects reasoning performance. A theorist may go beyond this by simply describing this organization using a formalism, but a theorist goes too far by attributing a contentless formalism to the mind.

ACKNOWLEDGMENT

I wish to thank Peter Pufall and Harry Beilin for excellent comments on a prior draft of this chapter. The inspiration for many of the ideas contained in this chapter comes from a symposium on meaningful logic that took place during the 20th anniversary meeting of the Jean Piaget Society. The participants of this symposium included Robert Ricco, Willis Overton, Rachel Falmagne, Ellin Scholnick, and myself.

REFERENCES

Anderson, A. R., & Belnap, N. D. (1962). The pure calculus of entailment. *Journal of Symbolic Logic, 27,* 19–52.

Apostel, L. (1982). The future of Piagetian logic. *Revue Internationale de Philosophie, 142–143,* 567–611.

Barwise, J. (1986). Conditionals and conditional information. In E. C. Traugott et al. (Eds.), *On conditionals* (pp. 112–127). Cambridge, MA: Cambridge University Press.

Barwise, J. (1989). *The situation in logic.* Stanford, CA: Center for the Study of Language and Information.

Barwise, J., & Perry, J. (1983). *Situations and attitudes.* Cambridge, MA: MIT Press.

Bloom, L. (1970). *Language development: Form and function in emerging grammars.* Cambridge, MA: MIT Press.

Braine, M. D. S. (1963). The ontogeny of English phrase structure: The first phase. *Language, 39,* 1–14.

Braine, M. D. S. (1978). On the relation between the natural logic of reasoning and standard logic. *Psychological Review, 85,* 1–21.

Braine, M. D. S., & Rumain, B. (1983). Logical reasoning. In P. Mussen (Ed.), *Handbook of child psychology* (Vol. 3, pp. 266–340). New York: J Wiley.

Byrnes, J. P. (1988a). Formal operations: A systematic reformulation. *Developmental Review, 8,* 66–87.

Byrnes, J. P. (1988b). What's left is closer to right: A response to Keating. *Developmental Review, 8,* 385–392.

Byrnes, J. P. (1990). Translation and annotation of B. Matalon's "Étude genetique de l'implication." In W. F. Overton (Ed.), *Reasoning, necessity and logic* (pp. 87–110). Hillsdale, NJ: Lawrence Erlbaum Associates.

Byrnes, J. P., & Overton, W. F. (1986). Reasoning about certainty and uncertainty in concrete, causal, and propositional contexts. *Developmental Psychology, 22,* 793–799.

Carey, S. (1985). *Conceptual change in childhood.* Cambridge, MA: MIT Press.

Chapman, M. (1988). *Constructive evolution: Origin and development of Piaget's thought.* New York: Cambridge University Press.

Chomsky, N. (1957). *Syntactic structures.* The Hague, The Netherlands: Mouton.

Chomsky, N. (1965). *Aspects of the theory of syntax.* Cambridge, MA: MIT Press.

Cohen, L. J. (1981). Can human irrationality be experimentally demonstrated? *Behavioral and Brain Sciences, 4,* 317–331.

Dennett, D. (1987). *The intentional stance.* Cambridge, MA: MIT Press.

Dretske, F. (1981). *Knowledge and the flow of information.* Cambridge, MA: MIT Press.

Falmagne, R. J. (1990). *Situations, statements and logical relations.* Paper presented at the 20th annual symposium of the Jean Piaget Society, Philadelphia, June.

Fodor, J. (1986). Information and association. *Notre Dame Journal of Formal Logic, 27,* 307–323.

Fodor, J. A., & Pylyshyn, Z. W. (1988). Connectionism and cognitive architecture: A critical analysis. *Cognition, 28,* 3–71.

Frege, G. (1952). *Translations from the writings of Gottlob Frege* (P. Geach & M. Black, eds.). Oxford, England: Blackwell.

Gardner, H. (1985). *The mind's new science: The history of the cognitive revolution.* New York: Basic Books.

Gelman, S. A., & Coley, J. D. (1991). Language and categorization: The acquisition of natural kind terms. In S. A. Gelman & J. P. Byrnes (Eds.), *Perspectives on thought and language: Interrelations in development* (pp. 146–196). Cambridge, England: Cambridge University Press.

Gentzen, G. (1935/1964). Investigations into logical deduction. *American Philosophical Quarterly, 1,* 288–306.

Gibson, J. J. (1979). *The ecological approach to human perception.* Boston: Houghton Mifflin.

Hughes, G. E., & Cresswell, M. J. (1968). *An introduction to modal logic.* London: Methuen.

Inhelder, B., & de Caprona, D. (1990). The role and meaning of structures in genetic epistemology. In W. F. Overton (Ed.), *Reasoning, necessity, and logic.* Hillsdale, NJ: Lawrence Erlbaum Associates.

Inhelder, B., & Piaget, J. (1958). *The growth of logical thinking from childhood to adolescence.* New York: Basic Books.

Inhelder, B., & Piaget, J. (1964). *The early growth of logic in the child.* New York: Basic Books.

Inhelder, B., & Piaget, J. (1980). Procedures and structures. In D. R. Olson (Ed.), *The social foundation of language and thought* (pp. 19–27). New York: Norton.

Keating, D. P. (1990). Structuralism, deconstruction, reconstruction: The limits of reasoning. In W. F. Overton (Ed.), *Reasoning, necessity and logic* (pp. 299–320). Hillsdale, NJ: Lawrence Erlbaum Associates.

Keil, F. C. (in press). Theories, concepts, and the acquisition of word meaning. In S. A. Gelman & J. P. Byrnes (Eds.), *Perspectives on language and thought.* Cambridge, England: Cambridge University Press.

Lakoff, G. (1987). *Women, fire, and dangerous things.* Chicago: University of Chicago Press.

Lycan, W. G. (1987). *Consciousness.* Cambridge, MA: MIT Press.

Marr, D. (1982). *Vision.* Cambridge, MA: MIT Press.

McNeill, D. (1966). Developmental psycholinguistics. In F. Smith & G. Miller (Eds.), *The genesis of language: A psycholinguistic approach* (pp. 15–84). Cambridge, MA: MIT Press.

Nelson, K. (1986). *Event knowledge: Structure and function in development.* Hillsdale, NJ: Lawrence Erlbaum Associates.

Newell, A., & Simon, H. A. (1972). *Human problem solving.* Englewood Cliffs, NJ: Prentice-Hall.

Overton, W. F. (1990). Competence and procedures: Constraints on the development of logical reasoning. In W. F. Overton (Ed.), *Reasoning, necessity, and logic.* Hillsdale, NJ: Lawrence Erlbaum Associates.

Piaget, J. (1962). Introduction. In E. W. Beth et al. (Eds.), *Implication, formalisation, et logique naturelle.* Paris: Presses Universitaires de France.

Piaget, J. (1970). *Structuralism.* New York: Harper & Row.

Piaget, J. (1972). *Essai de logique operatoire: Deuxième edition du traite de logique.* Paris: Dunod.

Piaget, J. (1980). The constructivist approach: Recent studies in genetic epistemology. *Cahiers de la Fondations Achives de Jean Piaget, 1,* 1–7.

Piaget, J. (1986). Essay on necessity. *Human Development, 29,* 301–314.

Piaget, J. (1987). *Possibility and necessity: The role of necessity in cognitive development.* Minneapolis: University of Minnesota Press.

Piaget, J., & Garcia, R. (1974). *Understanding causality.* New York: Norton.

Piaget, J., & Garcia, R. (1991). *Toward a logic of meanings.* Hillsdale, NJ: Lawrence Erlbaum Associates.

Piaget, J., Grize, J. B., Szeminska, A., & Bang, V. (1977). *Epistemology and the psychology of functions.* Dordrecht, the Netherlands: Reidel.

Pieraut-LeBonniec, G. (1980). *The development of modal reasoning: Genesis of necessity and possibility notions.* New York: Academic Press.

Pieraut-LeBonniec, G. (1990). The logic of meaning and meaningful implication. In W. F. Overton (Ed.), *Reasoning, necessity, and logic.* Hillsdale, NJ: Lawrence Erlbaum Associates.

Pylyshyn, Z. W. (1984). *Computation and cognition*. Cambridge, MA: MIT Press.

Quine, W. V. O. (1950). *Methods of logic*. New York: Macmillan.

Ricco, R. B. (1990). Necessity and the logic of entailment. In W. F. Overton (Ed.), *Reasoning, necessity and logic: Developmental Perspectives* (pp. 45–65). Hillsdale, NJ: Lawrence Erlbaum Associates.

Scholnick, E. K., & Wing, C. S. (1990). *Speaking deductively: Conversation as a context for inference*. Paper presented at the 20th annual symposium of the Jean Piaget Society, Philadelphia, PA.

Siegler, R. S. (1976). Three aspects of cognitive development. *Cognitive Psychology, 8*, 481–520.

Slobin, D. I. (1979). *Psycholinguistics* (2nd ed., pp. 53–55). Glenview, IL: Scott, Foresman.

Stalnaker, R. C. (1984). *Inquiry*. Cambridge, MA: MIT Press.

Voelin-Liambey, D., & Berthoud-Papandropoulou, I. (1977). Problémes d'inclusions et d'implications. In J. Piaget et collaborateurs (Eds.), *Recherches sur l'abstraction reflechissante* (Vol. 1: *L'abstraction des relations logico-arithmetiques*, pp. 81–113). Paris: Presses Universitaires de France.

Ward, S. L., Byrnes, J. P., & Overton, W. F. (1990). Organization of knowledge and conditional reasoning. *Journal of Educational Psychology, 82*, 832–837.

Wason, P. C., & Johnson-Laird, P. N. (1972). *Psychology of reasoning: Structure and content*. Cambridge, MA: Harvard University Press.

8 Piaget's Child as Scientist

Deanna Kuhn
Teachers College, Columbia University

I am pleased to contribute a chapter to this particular volume, as I see myself as representative of a particular generation of North American scholars whose work builds on Piaget's — extending beyond it, certainly, and perhaps even contradicting it in respects, and yet each of us in this group has done work that would not — could not — have been done without the foundation that Piaget's thinking provided.

To capture its essence is, of course, difficult. The two most fundamental dimensions of a theory of human development are mechanism and end point, and of these, end point is perhaps most fundamental. For Piaget, this end point was the "second-order" operation of thinking about one's own thought. Whether or not we go on to differentiate further kinds of higher-order thinking, I believe Piaget was right about the crucial significance of treating one's own thought as itself an object of thought. But I also believe that we have yet to appreciate fully what that significance is — what difference achieving this capacity makes in people's lives. Exploring this significance is one of the goals of this chapter.

Like a number of other developmental theorists, Piaget attempted to convey end point by means of metaphor — the child as a developing philosopher, or logician, or, most often and most compelling — a developing scientist. The implications and significance of this metaphor I also want to explore.

THE NATURE OF SCIENTIFIC THOUGHT

Piaget went beyond the child as scientist metaphor in proposing the genetic hypothesis that was in many ways a cornerstone of his lifework — the hypothesis of a parallelism between the evolution of scientific thought in the child and in the culture, one attributable to a common mechanism by means of which each occurs. It is worth noting that in proposing his genetic hypothesis, Piaget faced a more formidable undertaking than he would have had he been introducing the hypothesis today.

At the time Piaget first proposed his ideas, analysis of the evolution of scientific thought in the culture was a professional specialization stringently defined by the philosophers of science who engaged in it. Central to the method was Reichenbach's (1938) now-classical distinction between the contexts of discovery and justification. The epistemological method, termed "rational reconstruction," dealt only in the domain of justification and entailed analysis of the logical validity and truth status of scientific theories. The questions it addressed were independent of the actual *doing* of science. Issues of how scientific theories originate and develop — and hence the actual thought processes of scientists — were delegated to the context of discovery, a realm of conceivable interest to behavioral scientists. But it was the epistemologist's role to assess the status of these theories as knowledge, and the two tasks were treated as quite distinct, as the genesis of a belief was regarded as irrelevant with respect to the analysis of its validity (Houts, 1989). To introduce into this climate the claim that the thinking of little children bears any connection to the rational analysis, or reconstruction, of scientific theories was indeed a bold, even courageous, move.

Today, the climate is very different. From the extreme of the positivist program of rational reconstruction, over the course of just a few decades the view has become widely accepted that it is impossible to study the evolution of knowledge apart from the cognitive processes of human knowers. On the philosophical side, we now have "naturalistic" epistemologists who allow for the role of empirical observations as an integral part of attempts to understand knowledge (Heyes, 1989). On the psychological side, we now have a blossoming psychology of science, with its proponents beginning to explore all of a variety of ways in which psychological study illuminates the attempt to understand the progress of science (Gholson, Shadish, Neimeyer, & Houts, 1989). Were Piaget introducing his hypothesis today, then, he would have a more receptive audience, one that largely already appreciates the valid intersection of psychological and philosophical questions.

Yet, paradoxically, the historical development just described may in fact have the consequence of making Piaget's project all the more challenging. No longer would the proposal be taken as one of a formal parallelism involving two radically different, unconnected domains. Instead, we now have the real possibility of something much different. Once the proposition is accepted that science is not a set of facts or ideas disembodied from the human thinking that gave rise to them, the way is paved to truly link child and scientist. The possibility becomes clear of identifying a common subject — one and the same person — who begins life as a child and develops into the scientist who, with others, will advance scientific thought in the culture. This possibility, however, brings with it its own set of challenges.

Once we establish a link between the thinking of children and scientists, we must be sure that we can transcend the uninformative circularity of simply characterizing the one developmental evolution in terms of the other. The fact that the evolution of scientific thought in the culture is brought about by scientists whose own thinking developed from its childhood origins should not cause the parallel to collapse into meaningless circularity. Instead, it is this very connection that gives it its meaning and potential. But to avoid circularity and achieve this potential, we must seek to identify just what the connections are between the thought of the child, the lay adult, and the scientist. It is significant, and reassuring, to note that at least by the time of his later book with Garcia, published in 1983, it is in just these terms that Piaget himself cast the problem: "Our point of departure is that there is *continuity* in the development of the cognitive system, from the child to the average adult (one not educated in science) to the scientist" (Piaget & Garcia, 1989, p. 263).

The challenge remains, however, to identify these links in, concrete, explicit terms, and once we try to do so, it is really not so clear just what they are. The problem poses itself especially starkly when we try to insert the third, and crucial, member of the trio that is to provide the needed continuity — the lay adult. The lay adult serves as the critical intermediary who can connect the child and the scientist to one another. The link between child and adult is easy enough to see, but in what sense can we find the scientist in the ordinary person and the ordinary person in the scientist?

To answer this question, we need to ask another one: What does scientific activity consist of? We need at least a guiding characterization here, if we hope to identify an analogous activity in scientists and average people. Now, the dominant descriptor in this respect has been science as *exploration*. Indeed, much of Piaget's writing about infants and young children is consistent with this descriptor. Piaget portrays the central developmental task as exploration of one's world and one's potential actions on it. It is on this basis that the child constructs meanings that are attributed to both self and world. Yet, alternative descriptors are possible and indeed I will make the case in this chapter for one that I think is in many respects preferable. Let us first identify some problems with science as exploration.

Science as Exploration

Science as exploration appears to fit both scientist and child fairly well — its virtue perhaps. But in what way can exploration serve to characterize the activity of average adults, the crucial intermediary in our chain? Indeed the problem is evident before adulthood—even before the end of childhood and certainly by adolescence. I can convey it best perhaps in personal terms. As one who has the experience of simultaneously parenting a young child and an adolescent, I am struck by how readily the term fits in one case and how difficult it is to apply in the other. I can literally observe my young son busily engaged in exploring the world around him—finding out how things work and constructing all sorts of experiments to test their limits, the products of which are often presented as a morning greeting to his father and me as we open first one eye and then another, struggling to interpret just what today's early morning laboratory session has yielded. I am hard pressed, in contrast, to identify what a comparable activity might be in my teenaged daughter. As she literally flies by in the morning from her bedroom to front door with at best a hasty exchange of good-byes, she admittedly provides less behavior to interpret, but I don't think that is where the problem lies. What has happened to the exploration that was so plain to observe during her childhood years?

Do children in fact lose their scientific natures, to be reconstructed again only among the scant few who will embark on scientific careers? The dismal picture with respect to science achievement in our schools is consistent with this view, and indeed we can hear it expressed explicitly by those concerned with educating our youth in science:

> Children are born scientists. From the first ball they send flying to the ant they watch carry a crumb, children use science's tools—enthusiasm, hypothesis, tests, conclusions—to uncover the world's mysteries. But somehow students seem to lose what once came naturally. (Parvanno, 1990)

I am going to argue that if we look at scientific thinking more deeply, this view of the development of scientific thinking is wrong in two respects. No, it doesn't come naturally, but, then, once you get it, you don't lose it. But to understand scientific thinking in this way, we need an alternative to viewing science as exploration. The alternative I propose is science as *argument*. My objective, recall, is to link the thinking activity of scientists and ordinary people, and so I'll need to argue for the aptness of this characterization for both groups.

Science as Argument

I shall make a briefer case as regards the professional scientist, since others have laid this ground well. Science is a social activity. It advances through thought processes that occur between persons, not just within them (Westrum, 1989). In seeking to redress epistemologists' dismissal of the context of discovery, psychologists seeking to understand the evolution of scientific thought may have made the opposite error, focusing on the creative insights achieved by the lone scientist, to the exclusion of the social exchange which is the arena in which these ideas are articulated, questioned, clarified, defended, elaborated, and indeed very often arise in the first place. From the positivist conception of science as absolute and accumulative, we have come to recognize that there will be no scientific method capable of detaching science from controversy, from argument — an advance in which Thomas Kuhn (1962) played a foundational role.

The legal model of advocacy may be both apt and accurate. Most often, major scientific questions are couched in terms of two, or sometimes three or four, competing theories. The process is one of debate, with individuals typically playing advocacy roles. To participate, an individual scientist must analyze the evidence and its bearing on the different theories as a means of argument to the scientific community in support of his or her favored view. But, furthermore, this analyzing and weighing process of argument is, in interiorized form, almost certainly an important part of what goes on in the private thought of the individual scientist.[1] To participate, an individual scientist must analyze the evidence and its bearing on the different theories as a means of argument to the scientific community in support of his or her favored view. But, furthermore, this analyzing and weighing process of argument is, in interiorized form, almost certainly an important part of what goes on in the private thought of the individual scientist.

Now where do we find anything like these same activities in the lives of average adolescents and adults? In the arguments they have with one another, certainly. But, as I've just claimed is the case for the scientist, such arguments also take an internal form. The idea that "children's thinking tends to replicate the procedural logic of the social communications in which they participate," as Damon (1990) puts it, has been put to great advantage in understanding young children's thinking, as well as their social behavior, but the same correspondence I believe needs to be probed in the case of the more complex thinking of adolescents and adults — whether we regard it in the Vygotskian framework of an interiorization from social to mental planes or more in the Piagetian framework of a correspondence between the two planes.

My claim, then, is that we can find scientific thinking in average adolescents and adults if we conceive of it as argument. I want to go on to describe research I have done to explore the nature of such thinking. First, however, it is important to clarify that scientific thinking so construed will diverge somewhat from, but is by no means incompatible with, Piaget's

---

[1] See Casti (1989) for an interesting examination of major scientific questions in an explicit advocacy form.

view of the child as a developing scientist. Some of the ambiguity discussed earlier has arisen from the fact that Piaget drew on the child as scientist metaphor in two different ways—what we can think of as a functional and a structural sense. The functional sense corresponds to science as exploration. But Piaget also drew on the metaphor in a structural way to refer to the later evolution of a mode of thought used by scientists—one in which thinking is "formalized" into propositions that can then be reflected on and evaluated. We return to these dual senses of scientific activity, and how they might be reconciled, in the concluding part of this chapter.

In understanding the latter, structural sense in which the mature thinker takes on the status of scientist (the metaphor of scientist as a developmental end point), a persistent problem has been that just as we are hard-pressed to identify scientific exploration in the activities of average people, neither do they appear to do anything like formal hypothesis testing. A further complication to emerge is the fact that formal thinking appears to be very much influenced by what it is that is being thought about.

In undertaking to study the layperson's formal or scientific thinking as argument, we have endeavored to stay within the realm of activities and thinking that might occur naturally in people's lives. In addition, it is their own personal theories that we ask them to reason about. Yet, as we shall see, we come back squarely to Piaget's view in identifying thinking about one's own thought as the essence underpinning the competencies we examine.

THINKING AS ARGUMENT

With only a few exceptions, psychologists have not studied thinking as argument. Argument has tended to be regarded as the province of philosophers, with psychologists characteristically approaching thinking as problem solving. And yet it is in argument that we may find the most significant way in which reasoning figures in the lives of average people. Thinking as argument is implicated in all of the beliefs people hold, the judgments they make, and the conclusions they come to.

To examine thinking as argument, we must first establish a distinction, and then an identity, between two kinds of arguments. The dictionary definition of an argument in the first sense is "a course of reasoning aimed at demonstrating the truth or falsehood of something." Simply for purposes of identification, I shall refer to an argument in this sense as a *rhetorical* argument. In everyday usage, we more commonly regard an argument in its second sense as a dialogue between two persons who hold opposing views. Each offers justification for his or her own view, and, at least in a skilled argument, each attempts to rebut the other's view by means of counterargument. I shall refer to an argument in this sense as a *dialogic* argument.

Though connections are rarely made between these two kinds of arguments, they in fact bear a close relationship to one another, as the preceding discussion has suggested. In a dialogic argument, at a minimum one must recognize an opposition between two assertions—that, on surface appearance at least, both are not correct. One must then relate supporting and refuting evidence to each of the assertions, and, ideally, if the argument is to move toward resolution, one must be able to weigh supporting and refuting evidence in an integrative evaluation of the relative merit of the opposing views.

What is less often noted is that these same skills are in fact entailed in a rhetorical argument in more implicit form, though the rhetorical argument may on the surface appear less complex cognitively. An argument in support of an assertion is an empty, indeed superfluous, argument unless one can conceive of an alternative to what is being asserted—an opposing assertion. Once two or more contrasting assertions are in place, cognitively speaking, the further challenge poses itself of relating evidence to them. Presumably, it is a weighing of positive and negative evidence that has led one to espouse the favored assertion over its alternatives. Indeed, it is just such a weighing process that is implicit when we speak of a *reasoned* argument. Thus, any reasoned argument in support of an assertion implicitly contains a full dialogic argument.

This identity between rhetorical and dialogic arguments provides a framework for exploring the nature of the less externally observable rhetorical argument. Are the elements of the dialogic argument evident when we probe the thinking underlying people's beliefs and opinions? And is the presence or absence of these elements revealing of the quality of people's thinking?

To investigate these questions (D. Kuhn, 1991), we asked people their opinions, or, more formally, their causal theories, on three topics:

1. What causes prisoners to return to crime after they are released?
2. What causes children to fail in school?
3. What causes unemployment?

These topics were chosen as ones that people have occasion to think and talk about. They are also ones about which people are able and willing to make causal inferences without a large base of technical knowledge. They nevertheless involve phenomena the true causal structure of which is complex and uncertain.

Subjects in this work were chosen to represent average people across the life-span, beginning with adolescents (9th graders), and including young adults in their 20s, middle adults in their 40s, and older adults in their 60s. Within each age group, as well as males and females, we examined people of two different education levels—generally, those who had high school versus at least some college education (these differences were prospective among the adolescent group). We also included a group of experts of three different types—experienced parole officers, regarded as having domain expertise in the return-to-crime topic; experienced teachers, regarded as having domain expertise in the school-failure topic; and philosophers (specifically, PhD candidates working on their dissertations in the Columbia University philosophy department), whom we regarded as having expertise in reasoning itself.

I will not dwell on the theories themselves, since they were not our main concern. It is important to note, however, that people tended to hold these theories with certainty—from one-half to three-quarters (across topics) claimed that they were sure or very sure that their theories were correct. So, in eliciting their theories, we were asking people questions to which they felt they had answers.

Rather than the theories themselves, our interest was in the *arguments* people offer to support their theories. Following the framework of the dialogic argument, we asked subjects first for evidence for their theories, and then probed them regarding alternative theories, counterarguments, and rebuttals. Finally, we presented some evidence of our own related to the topic and asked them to interpret it. We began simply, asking the question, "How do you know that this is the cause?", followed by a number of probing questions along this same line. People also answered this question quite readily. No one said, "I don't know why I think so. I just think it's the cause."

Now, what kind of evidence could we expect laypeople with no special knowledge or interest in these topics to offer? In fact, for each topic, roughly 40% (averaged across topics) offered what we classified as genuine evidence. What we call genuine evidence is by no means evidence that is conclusive, nor even compelling, nor even necessarily very convincing evidence. Rather, it is simply evidence that (a) is differentiated from the theory, which we will see is an important criterion, and (b) bears on its correctness.

In Table 8.1 are summarized the different kinds of genuine evidence we observed. I shall not go through them in detail, but they provide an idea of what genuine evidence looked like, in subjects' own language. About half refer to covariation—variation in the alleged cause corresponds to variation in the outcome, but some other familiar kinds of reasoning appear as well, such as counterfactual reasoning, discounting, and analogy.

TABLE 8.1. Genuine Evidence

I. Covariation evidence	
Ia. *Correspondence.* Evidence notes simply a correspondence between antecedent and outcome.	(20Cms) [family problems] Well, if someone makes a study of cases of students where failures, dropouts . . . students who drop out of school . . . and sees where they have family problems, perhaps that would be solid evidence to prove what I believe.
Ib. *Covariation.* The idea of covariation becomes explicit and incorporates both comparison and quantification.	(60Cfs) [lack of parental support] Let's say the reading scores that are being published right now, and it somehow has a reflection on the [geographical] area they are in. The good ones are being in areas where parents take an interest, and the bad ones appear where there are many single-parent families, where perhaps they don't even have a home. (TCmc) [unemployment] You could probably take a survey and find out the percentage of people who get jobs who have been convicts. I'm sure it's very low.
Ic. *Correlated change.* Change in the outcome co-occurs with change in the antecedent.	(TCfs) [drugs] I guess people who have drugs and might not be doing so great in school, and so if they knew they took drugs they could see what happened when they weren't on drugs and, you know, prove it or whatever.
II. Evidence external to the causal sequence itself	
IIa. *Positive*	(40Nfc) [bad environment] It is not uncommon to hear that when someone is arrested that they have had previous charges in the same place for a similar crime. (What does this show?) I think it does show that it is in fact true that it's the environment.
IIb. *Negative* (counterfactual)	(40Nmc) [prison's failure to rehabilitate] Their habit patterns. All outward appearances in every case that I have known or even heard of has not changed. If they had had their head properly shrunk, everything about them would have changed, from their haircut right on through.
III. Indirect evidence	
IIIa. *Analogy* (particular to particular)	(20mc) [return to a familiar way of life] I think if you look at it in terms of, well, an occupation, whether crime could be an occupation or not . . . most people generally stay in an occupation their whole life, and it's very hard for them to change.
IIb. *Assumption* (general to particular)	(20Cmc) [desire for material rewards] People that don't have things . . . I mean, everybody wants things, especially in this country. This is a consumer society. People want to accumulate things, and that's not true of everywhere. People just want basic things, and if you don't have them, and you don't know how to get them, then you can take them.
IIIc. *Discounting* (elimination of alternatives)	(40Nfc) [unemployment] Well, I don't believe that anyone is just born that way . . . that they like crime, that they like going to prison. So if they could get a good job, I don't believe anyone would turn to crime.
IIId. *Partial discounting* (discounting of alternative factor at one level or end of its range of operation only)	(40Cfs) [family background] The background of the parent is something important, because you find some very intelligent children with IQs of 140. And yet they have no family with background. You put them in a very expensive school, they cannot sustain themselves.

What I want to focus on here are the remaining roughly 60% of responses that were classified as unsuccessful, beginning with those in a category we called nonevidence. Nonevidence took a number of forms, but the most striking was that in which the phenomenon itself is taken as sufficient evidence that it is produced by the cause the subject advocates. For example, Joe, a subject in his 20s, for the school-failure topic indicates poor nutrition as cause. He responds to our question "What *evidence* would you give to show this?" as follows:

> The points that they get in school. The grades that they get in school show. . . . *(What would that show?)* That they are lacking something in their body. That the kids who were failing lack something in their body.

So, in other words, the very fact of the outcome presumes the cause.

Joe's is clearly an example of nonevidence. Let us consider another response that is somewhat harder to classify. Kathryn, a teenager, offers the theory that prisoners return to crime because they prefer life in prison. We query her as follows:

> *(How do you know that this is the cause?)* I think because if they commit crime they're getting attention. They'll be—the prisoner, you know, in prison—they'll be taken care of, they'll be given food and all this, and they get attention. They come out and everybody, you know. . . . he was a prisoner, so that they stay away from him; they're scared and everything. So they decide that the only way they're going to be, that they'll have attention or they're going to be cared for is if they're in prison.

> *(If you were trying to convince someone else that your view is right, what evidence would you give to try to show this?)* The evidence I would give is that when they are in prison, they're secure. They're sure that, you know, no one's going to hurt them. Well, they're not sure no one's going to hurt them, but, you know, they know they're secure. They've got a place to eat, a place to sleep. But if they come out into the world and, you know, with unemployment and people not wanting to take anybody in that was an ex-con or something, when people reject them because of their past, they're sure to go back into the crime just to go back to their jail cell and stay in it.

> *(Can you be very specific, and tell me some particular facts you could mention to try to convince the person?)* Well, some facts could be that when they're in there, they'd want to make friends with other cons and stuff like that, and when they're out here, they've got to start all over again, and it's real hard for people who committed a mistake, for other people to accept that they've paid for it and everything. And then when they're out here people reject them and they look at them, you know, like they're scared of them. They don't want to stay in the world if they think everywhere they go people are going to be

looking at them and feeling, you know, real insecure when they're around. So they'd rather be where people, you know, they're all the same.

How should we characterize Kathryn's response? Is this evidence that she is offering for her theory? We classified it as pseudoevidence, which we define simply as a scenario, or script, depicting how the phenomenon might occur. The defining characteristic that distinguishes pseudoevidence from genuine evidence is that pseudoevidence can't be sharply distinguished from the theory itself. Hence, responses to "What causes X?" don't differ sharply from responses to "What evidence can you give to show that this is the cause of X?" In Kathryn's case, she makes an intuitively convincing case for the *plausibility* of the cause she specified leading to the outcome, yet without providing any genuine evidence that this cause is in operation in instances of the phenomenon. Her own words establish that, for her, the function of evidence is to establish such plausibility: "The evidence I would give is that when they are in prison they're secure." This "evidence" does not establish that "preference for prison life" *is* the cause of the phenomenon; rather, it enhances its plausibility as a possible cause.

At its most minimal, pseudoevidence simply illustrates the causal sequence. At its best, it enhances the plausibility of the causal sequence, as Kathryn's pseudoevidence does. "Good" pseudoevidence might heighten our interest in testing a causal theory, but it can't tell us whether the theory is correct. In fact, since pseudoevidence can never conflict with a theory, it cannot really be considered evidence at all. It is more appropriately regarded as part of the theory.

Can subjects who offer only pseudoevidence envision the possibility that this is *not* what happens? Following the framework of the dialogic argument, this is the question we looked at next, by asking subjects to generate an alternative theory. In response to our question ("A person whose view is different from yours—what might they say is the cause?"), some subjects generate an alternative theory without difficulty. Others generate what appears to be an alternative but then immediately agree with it—"That could be part of it, too"—in effect incorporating the alternative cause into their own theory. Such subjects are unable to conceive of anything that is *not* a cause. Other subjects try unsuccessfully to generate an alternative, producing something very like their own theory. Still other subjects simply decline:

I don't know what someone else would say. I have no idea.

Or,

I don't know what they would say. I'd really have to get someone else's point of view. Cause I imagine my thoughts run in this direction and that's about it.

Or,

> I don't know what they might say is the reason. I don't think I'm wrong.

Or, significantly, the hypothetical other's view is simply assimilated to one's own.

> I think they'll say the same thing I'd say. I think that the majority think the way I do.

The percentage of subjects who are able to generate alternative theories averaged across topics is about 60%, higher than the 40% who generate genuine evidence, but, importantly, there is a significant association between the two, one that makes clearer the meaning of pseudoevidence. In not generating alternatives, those subjects who rely on pseudoevidence do not call upon this pseudoevidence to perform the very function it cannot — address the correctness of a theory, relative to all the others with which, if the subject conceived of the possibility, it could compete.

Subjects who generate neither genuine evidence nor alternative theories thus take their theories for granted, simply as statements about the way the world is. They don't reflect on their theories as objects of cognition — as claims needing to be evaluated in the light of alternatives, as well as evidence. To truly evaluate one's own theory, then, one must not only reflect on it as an object of cognition, but reflect on it relative to its alternatives. It is only by considering alternatives — by seeking to identify what isn't — that one can begin to achieve any certainty about what is.

To evaluate a theory against alternatives implies that it could be true or false, that is, indicates an acceptance of its falsifiability. It is this question of falsifiability that we looked at in the study of counterarguments: "What could someone say to show that you were wrong?" Do subjects comprehend the evidence that would falsify their theory, were they to encounter it? The success rate here is about 50% (see Table 8.2 for a summary of the various forms of successful counterarguments). Despite the critical role that falsifying cases play in examining a theory, many of our subjects show considerable resistance to the very idea. As one of them put it rather plaintively, "If I knew the evidence that I'm wrong, I wouldn't say what I'm saying." Many of those who did attempt a counterargument simply offered an alternative theory as a counterargument, for example, "They would say it's not the parents, it's the school that causes kids to fail." Such counterarguments, of course, leave the original theory unexamined.

Finally, rebuttals are critical because they complete the structure of argument, integrating argument and counterargument. Only 25% of subjects (averaged across topics) achieve an integrative rebuttal (see Table 8.3 for a summary of the various forms of successful integrative rebuttals).

TABLE 8.2.   Successful Counterarguments

I.	Noncovariation arguments	
Ia.	*Arguments against causal sufficiency.* Antecendent is present and outcome fails to occur.	(60Nms) [lack of family support] He could possibly point out to me that here is a kid who succeeded while the family was let's say drunkards or separated and there was no inspiration at home.
Ib.	*Arguments against causal necessity.* Antecedent is absent and outcome still occurs.	(40Cms) [lack of family support] I think they would have to prove it with hard fact, that would show that not just one child but a large cross-section of the population was failing and, you know, the parents were very heavily involved.
Ic.	*Arguments against causal sufficiency and necessity.*	(40Cms) [family problems] They could point out examples, specific examples that particular children failed and their family situation was very . . . what we consider a strong, stable family situation. They could also conversely point out a child doing well but yet the family is fragmented.
II.	**Discounting arguments**	
IIa.	*Full discounting.* Existence of the antecedent is denied.	(60Cms) [poor educational system] The fact that they are really consistently introducing and carrying out a practical program, an intelligent program, a progressive program in the schools.
IIb.	*Partial discounting.* The antecedent is denied for some subset of cases.	(TNms) [negative attitude toward school] He would show me some other students who have these . . . have good marks, and ask them why do you study hard. And they will say because the school is good.

Others offer a simple rebuttal, in which they simply offer a counterargument to the alternative theory, again leaving the original theory unexamined. And some simply argue by assertion, for example, "If they said it's the school, I'd say no, it's the parents," leaving both original and alternative theories unexamined. And some simply decline, like Lois, who says, "I don't think I'd even try. (Why not?) He wants to believe it, that's fine. I'm not argumentative."

As Lois's reply hints, underlying subjects' argumentive reasoning are implicit theories of knowledge and knowing. Our findings regarding subjects' epistemological theories are summarized in Table 8.4. Our findings resemble in many ways those of others who have investigated naïve epistemological theories. What is most interesting about our findings is the rich insight we get into subjects' epistemological stances from just the three questions we asked (shown across the top of Table 8.4; assignment to epistemological level was based on just these questions about expertise, with the questions about proof shown in the fourth column merely corroborative). About 50% of our subjects (averaged across topics) are classified as absolutists, who regard knowledge as certain and accumulative, a rather remarkable percentage in view of the topics involved—fully half of our adolescent and adult population think that complex questions such as why

TABLE 8.3.   Integrative Rebuttals

I.   Rebuttals of counterarguments

Ia. *Qualitative rebuttal.* The counterargument is rebutted on qualitative grounds that undermine its force, thereby restoring force to the original theory.

(40Cms) [poor home environment] *(What evidence might this person give to try to show that you were wrong?)* Evidence that shows that their early environment was not the way I said it was in cases of failures — for instance, that the people were wealthy or that the situation was other than the way I said it. But I think there are subtle forms of deprivation. The fact that sombody is wealthy does not mean that they pay attention to their children or set a good example.

Ib. *Quantitative rebuttal.* The instances that constitute the counterargument are alleged to be of low frequency.

(40Cfc) [return to same environment] Every once in a while you hear of someone who really did better themselves while they were in prison. They went to school or they wrote a book or whatever, but that's one in a million, is my guess.

II.   Rebuttals involving alternative theories

IIa. *Arguments against causal sufficiency of the alternative theory.* The alternative casue is not sufficient to produce the outcome, as long as the original cause is absent.

(40Cms) [lack of motivation] [alternative theory: "enticements" of earning money and taking drugs] In terms of what you might call enticements of life, I would revert back to my basic premise that if you have the desire for learning and value learning, then even if you might to some degree take up the other enticements, you'd still maintain enough interest in learning to not fail.

IIb. *Arguments against causal necessity of the alternative theory.* The outcome occurs in the absence of the alernative cause, as long as the original cause is present.

(40Cfc) [lack of motivation] [alternative theory: "joining gangs" and poor home life] Well, I could show that there are students who are failing and they're not in gangs and they have a fine home life, but they just don't seem to try for some reason.

IIc. *Arguments against relative importance of the alternative theory.* The alternative cause may be contributory but to a lesser extent that the original cause.

(60Nmc) [innate character] [alternative theory: poor environment] While environment plays an important part, I think even more important is the importance of that innate quality of goodness.

IId. *Arguments that attempt to reconcile original and alternative theories.* Original and alternative causes are linked into a single causal chain.

(60Nmc) [lack of economic opportunity] [alternative theory: "antisocial" personality] I've heard arguments where they said certain people are basically antisocial. But there again you come right back to what made them antisocial, and you come back with they never had the real opportunities to get into the mainstream of today.

prisoners become repeat offenders can be answered with complete certainty. Another 35% are multiplists, or relativists, who note that experts disagree and infer therefore that nothing is certain and all opinions therefore of equal validity. In a word, so as not to discriminate, one must be indiscriminate. Both absolutists and multiplists thus leave the knowing

TABLE 8.4. Epistemological Theories

	Do experts know for sure what the cause is?	Would it be possible for experts to find out for sure if they studied this problem long and carefully enough?	How sure are you of your view, compared to an expert?	Questions about proof
Absolutist Knowledge is objective, certain, and simply accumulates.	(20Nms) If they're experts, they know.	(40Cfs) Yes, if they have all the facts to draw conclusions.	(60Nfc) Not as sure. There again, I have to get my statistics and do some research and have some facts, which, as I say, I haven't thought about it. I mean, I have my feeling and thoughts, but I don't have the facts.	(40Cms) (Is there anything you could say or do to prove that this is the cause?) I'm probably very susceptible to, you know, acceptance of almost any proof on that. I think if somebody took a study from some place like a university like Yale or Columbia, or somebody of that nature, it would be believed.
Multiplist Knowledge is subjective, dictated only by personal tastes and wishes of the knower.	(TCfc) I don't think anybody knows for sure really, because there really isn't one right answer. There's not one right answer really for anything.	(60Nms) I don't think anything is sure. Things change. Just because an expert says something. There are so many experts, and that goes for doctors too. They have been wrong in so many instances. they are always changing.	(TCfs) The same. My opinion can stand just as high as theirs.	(TCfs) (Would you be able to prove this person wrong?) No, you can't prove an opinion to be wrong. (Why not?) Because an opinion is something which somebody holds for themselves. You can't change their opinion or alter it. They have their own opinion. (40Cfs) (Could someone prove that you were wrong?) They could prove I'm wrong if they can give me good examples, but I can still hold my opinion.
Evaluative Knowledge is an open-ended process of evaluation and judgment.	(20Cms) Well, I think they're close. I mean, nothing's for sure, but I'm sure they have good ideas about why people fail.	(40Cmc) I don't know if it's provable. In other words, the situation is such that we probably are going to get to a point where it is still a matter of judgment which opinion would be right or wrong.	(20Cms) Confronted by an expert, I might be less sure than I am, because he can marshal all kinds of evidence and argue in an entirely different manner. I'm arguing from just a personal kind of perspective. But, by the same token, I would be reluctant to change my position unless a substantially varied, lucid and documented argument were presented to me.	(40Cmc) (Would you be able to prove this person wrong?) Perhaps to my satisfaction, not necessarily to his. I think it's more a matter of convincing by arguments, and whatever, than it is by any indisputable proof that you are wrong.

process out of their judgments. Only 15% fall into the evaluative category, in which knowing is regarded as a process that entails thinking, evaluation, and argument.

As the final aspect of this research, we presented evidence of our own regarding two of the topics and asked subjects to evaluate it. The evidence for the crime topic is shown in Table 8.5. We included evidence of two forms, underdetermined (appearing first) and overdetermined. Underdetermined evidence in effect simply restates the phenomenon in the context of a specific instance, with few clues as to its cause. Overdetermined evidence, in contrast, explicitly refers to three broad families of causes, without favoring any of them. I will not discuss the evidence evaluation results in detail, and, instead, simply summarize their implication by noting that subjects commonly assimilated both kinds of evidence to their own theories. "This pretty much goes along with my own view," was the prototypical response, and, again, subjects expressed high certainty regarding these evaluations. If evidence is simply assimilated to a theory, any ability to evaluate its bearing on the theory is of course lost. More broadly, with this loss comes loss of the ability to maintain a differentiation between what

TABLE 8.5.   Evaluation of Evidence

Underdetermined evidence (crime topic)

Pete Johnson is someone who has spent a good portion of his adult life in prison. He was first convicted of a crime at age 14, when he took part in the theft of a newspaper stand. He began serving his first prison sentence at age 18, after being convicted on several charges of auto theft and robbery. He remained in a medium-security state prison until the age of 20. After he was released on parole, he returned to live with his mother in the same neighborhood where he had grown up and began to look for a job. After 3 months out of jail, he took part in the robbery of a grocery store. He was caught and convicted and returned to prison. Since then, Pete has served 3 more prison sentences for different crimes, with only brief periods out of prison between sentences.

Overdetermined evidence (crime topic)

A study was done of 25 prisoners who were about to be released from prison. All had served more than one prison sentence; some were in prison for the third or fourth time. All had been in prison for the past 3 years or longer, mostly for crimes of armed robbery.

A social worker investigated the prisoners' life histories. All had unhappy early lives with many personal and family problems. None had good school records. They tended to be uninterested in school, to do poorly, and to drop out without finishing. Almost all became involved in crime at an early age.

A government official did a study of their prison life. The prison was badly overcrowded; each prisoner shared a cell with two or three others. Because of crowded conditions, prisoners were able to have periods of exercise and outdoor recreation only infrequently. No prisoner received job training.

Another social worker followed their lives outside prison during the 6 months following their release. The majority had been unable to find jobs since they had been released. Some applied to training programs, but there were long waiting lists with only a few openings. Many hadn't found suitable housing.

derives from one's own thought and what derives from external sources, and hence control of the interaction of theories and evidence in one's own thinking.

Results across subject groups in this research are easily summarized. Skill levels show no significant differences by sex. Nor do significant differences appear across age groups. However, we observe consistent, and sizable, differences by education group, at every age level. For example, from 16% to 29% of all noncollege subjects (across topics) generate genuine evidence, compared with 53%-66% of college subjects.

The other important result is that we observe significant, but by no means total, generality of skills across the three topics. Although many subjects exhibit a skill on some topics and not others, the numbers exhibiting the skill for all topics or no topics are significantly greater than would be expected by chance, if performance across topics were independent. This outcome is of course critical, because it suggests that we have identified forms of thinking that transcend the particular content in terms of which they are expressed. However imperfectly, we are tapping something about the *way* people think. The expertise results support this claim. The philosophers reasoned well overall, as expected, but the domain expertise of the others did not influence reasoning ability. Parole officers reasoned no better about the crime topic than they did about the other topics, nor did teachers reason better about the school topic. Again, the form of reasoning appears to transcend the content.

The variability we observe in argumentive reasoning skills among average adolescents and adults is perhaps the single most important finding of this research, with some people displaying these skills readily and without difficulty and others scarcely at all. It is of course particularly significant that these skills are associated with education at all age groups, despite the fact that the skills involved are not an explicit part of the school curriculum at any age level. Most interesting is the fact that the skill differences appear among teens, when the education differences are only prospective, and we see no further development in skill when we might most expect and hope for it—between the early high school and college years. Neither the number of subjects showing mastery of the simplest argumentive skills, nor the number who attain the most complex skills, such as integrative rebuttal, increases significantly from the adolescent to the young adult groups.

Together, these findings suggest that it is some very broad, general kinds of experience associated with education—not all of which takes place inside school—that are responsible for these differences. Within school, it is possible that academic experience encourages the attitude that assertions need to be justified and alternatives considered. But whatever these benefits are, they are conferred early, certainly by the end of junior high school, and we see no further development in this respect.

The idea that acquiring the ability to think well should be a mission of education represents a thriving enterprise right now. But critical to, and largely missing from, this enterprise, are precise, empirically grounded definitions of just what it means to think well, and, by implication, to be an educated person. In this respect, and even though we can speak only in terms of covariates rather than causality, the research that I have described makes some contribution toward defining what it means, cognitively speaking, to be an educated person — or, to put it more specifically, what is meant by characterizing an educated person as one who thinks well.

To convey this definition in a sentence or two, we can contrast two kinds of knowing, although they are in fact poles of a continuum on which most knowing lies. At one pole, knowing prevails in the comfortable ignorance of the knower never having considered that things could be otherwise. At the other pole, knowing is an ongoing, effortful *process* of evaluation, one that the everpresent possibility of new evidence and new arguments leaves never completed.

Central to this process is reflection on one's own thinking — metacognition in its most basic and important sense. Beneath its surface is the structure of argument that has been examined in this chapter. It is this structure that must be in place for someone to hold reasoned beliefs or make reasoned judgments, which we can think of as the building blocks of educated thinking. And it is this structure that must be in place to competently interpret new evidence bearing on one's beliefs, and hence be in control of the interaction of theory and evidence in one's own thinking.

It is at this latter pole of the continuum I have portrayed that the thinking of average people assumes the crucial characteristics of scientific thinking — thinking that examines and reflects on assertions, as objects of cognition, evaluating these assertions relative to their alternatives and the available evidence. Our results make clear that not all people achieve such thought to its full potential. Yet, it is in the kinds of competent argumentive thinking that have been described here, I believe, that we can identify formal or scientific thinking, or at least the potential for such thinking, in the thinking that ordinary people do.

SCIENCE AS EXPLORATION REVISITED

Before concluding, I would like to connect the work that has been described here to earlier work in which, instead of seeking to identify what is formal or scientific about the thinking ordinary people do, we explicitly ask ordinary people to think in scientific ways (D. Kuhn, Amsel, & O'Loughlin, 1988). Like scientists, subjects are asked to investigate a domain and draw conclusions about the causal relations that exist there. We have examined behavior in a number of different domains, but I will use as an example the racecar domain that Leona Schauble designed for her dissertation (Schauble, 1990). It consists of a computerized racetrack and cars having different features (e.g., color, engine size, presence or absence of a muffler); the subject can construct cars and use them in road tests that the subject designs and carries out. The subject is asked to investigate what features of the cars make a difference in their speed.

Results of this work make it very clear that scientific investigation does not "come naturally." Consonant with our earlier study of self-directed scientific investigation (D. Kuhn & Phelps, 1982) and in sharp contrast to the performance of several professional scientists to whom we presented the task, fifth- and sixth-grade subjects had difficulty designing informative experiments and readily made invalid inferences based on the experiments they did conduct. Only 31% of all experiments and 38% of all inferences were coded as valid. Most subjects did gradually discover simple effects (though not more complex curvilinear and interactive effects) despite their generally poor procedures, though subjects with better procedures discovered them faster.

A second thing that this work makes clear is that becoming a competent scientist is not just a matter of acquiring the formal hypothesis-testing strategies of investigation and inference on which Inhelder and Piaget (1958) focused their empirical study. The design of our research allows us to observe how subjects' initial theories about the effects of the cars' features influence the discovery process. Though it declined over time in our microgenetic studies, this influence is considerable. Studying it has led us to the conclusion that the major challenge subjects face is not one of developing appropriate experimentation strategies but of developing the ability to coordinate their existing theories with new evidence they generate. Interestingly, Klahr and his coworkers (Dunbar & Klahr, 1989; Klahr & Dunbar, 1988; Klahr, Fay, & Dunbar, 1991), who are also studying children's scientific reasoning, give little attention to Piaget and cast their work in an explicit information-processing framework. Yet they see the child's task in a similar way to the one I have just proposed. In their terms, the child must coordinate a search of "two problem spaces"—the space of hypotheses and the space of instances, or experiments. What Klahr's framework may not highlight sufficiently is that it is the child's own personal theories that are both the starting and finishing point of investigative activity. It is in this process of coordination of one's own theories and evidence, I believe, that we can see development (see D. Kuhn, 1989).

In our work, while the extent to which subjects' theoretical beliefs distorted their interpretation of evidence declined over time, this progression could not be characterized as one in which subjects gradually set aside their own theories in order to attend to and interpret the evidence. Instead, we found a close interlocking of theory and evidence. Rather than setting aside theories, which were often wrong, and simply interpreting the evidence before them, subjects typically replaced their original theories with new ones, most often before acknowledging the corresponding pattern in the evidence. What subjects seemed unwilling to do was to interpret evidence of the effectiveness or ineffectiveness of a feature until they had a compatible theory in place that made sense of that evidence. So, for example, in the logbooks that were provided for subjects to record information, in contrast to the professional scientists and college students we observed, who for the most part systematically recorded particular constellations of features and their observed outcomes, in 11-year-old Jamie's logbook we find the assertions, "With big wheels it will go slower because it takes more time for the wheels to go around" and "A tailfin would make a difference because it has more weight for the wheels to turn around." Like our subjects in the argument research who generate pseudoevidence in support of their theories, these children do not clearly differentiate evidence from a plausible theory that can assimilate it.

And over time, we can observe the prolonged struggle children have in reconciling their beliefs with disconfirming evidence. Randy, for example, starts with the incorrect belief that the muffler affects the speed. After a long period during which he conducts experiments that are not capable of disconfirming this belief, at the sixth session he designs and correctly interprets a valid experiment showing that a car with and a car without a muffler yield the same speed. "No, the muffler doesn't matter," he concludes. "I just had a feeling it might help to push it along." But he then goes on to comment on a third car he included in his road test, one that achieved the maximum speed and happened to have a muffler. Here, Randy tells us, the muffler might have helped just a little bit.

CONCLUSIONS

In both the preceding context and in the argument research described earlier, what children or adults need to be able to do is to distance themselves from their own beliefs to a sufficient degree to be able to evaluate them, as objects of cognition. And it is here, of course, that we have Piaget's thinking about one's own thought. Inhelder and Piaget (1958) perhaps regarded the formal operational reasoning skills they studied in too "formal" a way, that is, as operating in a uniform manner irrespective of the subject's own beliefs about the content being reasoned about (D. Kuhn, 1989). Yet the concept of reflective knowing that has been the focus of this chapter—the capacity to think about one's theories, rather than only with them—is a concept not only closely allied to Inhelder and Piaget's construct of formal operations; it is one close to the core of Piaget's entire theoretical system.

A number of science educators in recent years have indicated that Inhelder and Piaget's construct of formal operations has turned out to be not as useful to them as they once thought it would be. More disturbing is the suggestion by Linn (1986) that a new, more information-processing-like construct has greater promise—"metareasoning," defined as the ability to reason about one's own reasoning. I hope to have maintained greater historical perspective, and I believe that I appreciate the connection of the framework I have proposed to Piaget's, as the preceding remarks suggest. It is in probing what it really means to think about thought that I believe the research I have described makes a contribution, and it is here, I think, that important work remains to be done.

There is one other respect in which we can connect the ideas I have proposed to Piaget's thinking. Still another way in which Piaget talked about developmental end point was in terms of the achievement of a maximum equilibrium between individual and environment. The equilibrium Piaget had in mind was not the more commonly referred to biological or social equilibrium, but rather one between an individual's *cognitive* functions and an external world. (See Chapman in this volume for a historical discussion of equilibration.) But just what does it mean for cognitive functions to be in equilibrium with the environment? A key to understanding this kind of equilibrium may lie in the concept of control. I suggested earlier that it is the argumentive structure involved in reflecting on and evaluating one's own beliefs that must be in place in order for an individual to be able to interpret competently new evidence bearing on these beliefs and hence be in control of the interaction of theory and evidence in one's own thinking. Individuals who possess such control can differentiate what comes from their own thought and what comes from external sources. The beliefs of an individual who does not possess this control come into contact with external evidence only in an unstable, unequilibrated manner. New evidence is either ignored or distorted, to protect the individual's belief at all costs. Or the individual is unduly swayed by it, leaving beliefs totally dominated by transitory, unpredictable external influence over which the individual exercises no control. In contrast, each new piece of evidence does not dominate or destroy reasoned beliefs. Reasoned beliefs are sensitive to new evidence but are not dominated by it.

Finally, three different connections have been made in this chapter, each of which requires some concluding comments. The first is the connection between the intuitive science in which each of us engages and the professional science to which only a few devote their lives. The model of competent argumentive reasoning that has been portrayed here is not intended as a characterization of how theories and evidence interact and how knowledge and understanding progress in the development of scientific thought over the course of history. These are complex, controversial questions that philosophers of science have debated for decades. While the present work probes only very simple reasoning competencies of individuals in isolation, it does identify a set of reasoning competencies that are clearly minimum fundamental prerequisites for entry into scientific dialogue. Indeed, in the community of scientific discourse, they are taken for granted—assumed to be in place among all who participate. They are shared expectations regarding the nature of such discourse. The research described in this chapter makes clear that these competencies should not be taken for granted as universal human attributes. Instead, they are cognitive achievements that are fully attained and practiced by only a small segment of the human population.

A second connection that should be clarified is that between science as exploration and science as argument. Piaget, of course, would endorse both conceptions, and this reflects the fact that the two do not in fact contradict one another. The exploratory behavior that infants and children display "naturally" is indeed worth supporting and nurturing in all of the ways we know how. The most gifted science educators, such as Duckworth (1990), seem even to be capable of resurrecting it in adults in whom it has lay dormant for years. My point here, and it is one with which Piaget would agree, is that by itself, it is not enough. There is more that we are trying to do, or should be trying to do, than keeping alive a "natural curiosity." The natural curiosity that infants and children show about the world around them needs to be enriched and directed by the tools of scientific thought.

The final connection that I would like to comment on is that between argument in its social and dialogic forms. This connection has important educational implications (D. Kuhn, 1991). Social dialogue offers a way to externalize the internal thinking strategies we would like to foster within the individual. This externalization serves not only the research objective of analysis but also the practical objective of facilitation. Dialogic argument holds the potential for transforming mindless opinions into reasoned ones. The diversity of the social world enhances and corrects individual thought, a fact that holds true for the whole range of human discourse from the simplest of everyday conversations to the evolution of scientific theories. Piaget made much of the correspondence between the mental and social planes in children, but he had less to say about this correspondence in the case of the more complex forms of thinking achieved by adolescents and adults. The idea that higher-order thinking needs equally to be viewed in a social context I think represents a promising avenue both for us as researchers in understanding it and as educators in promoting it (see Youniss & Damon as well as Chapman in the present volume).

And it is in its social context that such thinking assumes its greatest significance. Scientific thinking is typically compartmentalized, regarded as accessible and relevant to only a narrow, specialized segment of people. In sharp contrast, when we regard scientific thinking as argument, its significance for all of society is clear. It is essential for participation in a democratic society. To be in control of their own thinking is perhaps the most important way in which people both individually and collectively take control of their lives.

REFERENCES

Casti, J. (1989). *Paradigms lost: Images of man in the mirror of science.* New York: William Morrow.

Damon, W. (1990). Social relations and children's thinking skills. In D. Kuhn (Ed.), *Developmental perspectives on teaching and learning thinking skills. Contributions to human development* (Vol. 21). Basel, Switzerland: Karger.

Duckworth, E. (1990). Opening the world. In E. Duckworth, J. Easley, D. Hawkins, & A. Henriques (Eds.), *Science education: A minds-on approach for the elementary years* (pp. 21–59). Hillsdale, NJ: Lawrence Erlbaum Associates.

Dunbar, K., & Klahr, D. (1989). Developmental differences in scientific discovery strategies. In D. Klahr & K. Kotovsky (Eds.), *Complex information processing: The impact of Herbert A. Simon (Proceedings of the 21st Carnegie–Mellon Symposium on Cognition).* Hillsdale, NJ: Lawrence Erlbaum Associates.

Gholson, B., Shadish, W., Neimeyer, R., & Houts, A. (Eds.). (1989). *Psychology of science: Contributions to metascience.* New York: Cambridge University Press.

Heyes, C. (1989). Uneasy chapters in the relationship between psychology and epistemology. In B. Gholson, W. Shadish, R. Neimeyer, & A. Houts (Eds.), *Psychology of science: Contributions to metascience* (pp. 115–137). New York: Cambridge University Press.

Houts, A. (1989). Contributions of the psychology of science to metascience: A call for explorers. In B. Gholson, W. Shadish, R. Neimeyer, & A. Houts (Eds.), *Psychology of science: Contributions to metascience* (pp. 47–88). New York: Cambridge University Press.

Inhelder, B., & Piaget, J. (1958). *The growth of logical thinking from childhood to adolescence.* New York: Basic Books.

Klahr, D., & Dunbar, K. (1988). Dual space search during scientific reasoning. *Cognitive Science, 12,* 1–48.

Klahr, D., Fay, A., & Dunbar, K. (1991). *Developmental differences in experimental heuristics.* Unpublished manuscript, Carnegie–Mellon University, Pittsburgh.

Kuhn, D. (1989). Children and adults as intuitive scientists. *Psychological Review, 96,* 674–689.

Kuhn, D. (1991). *The skills of argument.* New York: Cambridge University Press.

Kuhn, D., Amsel, E., & O'Loughlin, M. (1988). *The development of scientific thinking skills.* Orlando, FL: Academic Press.

Kuhn, D., & Phelps, E. (1982). The development of problem-solving strategies. In H. Reese (Ed.), *Advances in child development and behavior* (Vol. 17). New York: Academic Press.

Kuhn, T. (1962). *The structure of scientific revolutions.* Chicago: University of Chicago Press.

Linn, M. (1986). Science. In R. Dillon & R. Sternberg (Eds.), *Cognition and instruction* (pp. 155–204). Orlando, FL: Academic Press.

Parvanno, C. (1990). (chairman of the division of natural sciences at SUNY, Purchase) quoted in the article, "Hands on," by Janet Elder, in Education Life, *New York Times,* special supplement, Jan. 7.

Piaget, M., & Garcia, R. (1989). *Psychogenesis and the history of science.* (Trans. Helga Feider). New York: Columbia University Press.

Reichenbach, H. (1938). *Experience and prediction.* Chicago: University of Chicago Press.

Schauble, L. (1990). Belief revision in children: The role of prior knowledge and strategies for generating evidence. *Journal of Experimental Child Psychology, 49,* 31–57.

Westrum, R. (1989). The psychology of scientific dialogues. In B. Gholson, W. Shadish, R. Neimeyer, & A. Houts (Eds.), *Psychology of science: Contributions to metascience* (pp. 370–382). New York: Cambridge University Press.

IV LANGUAGE, CULTURE, AND THOUGHT

9 Changing Perspectives in Child Language Acquisition

Hermina Sinclair
Université de Genève

As suggested by the title of this chapter, I begin by sketching how my collaborators and I changed the orientation of our child language studies. In addition, this chapter is concerned with some of the ways children change their perspective on language, focusing on different aspects at different ages or in different contexts of verbal activity. Finally, I indulge in some theoretical speculations concerning linguistic structure and Piaget's operatory logic.

My first study was more psychological than linguistic and was designed to answer the question whether the development of certain basic notions investigated by Piaget and Inhelder, such as concepts of conservation, was accompanied by a change in children's use of certain descriptive terms for the comparison of quantities: There is such a change — children who succeeded in conservation tasks used *more* and *less,* whereas those that did not generally used *a lot* and *a little.*

Acquaintance with Chomsky's generative grammar led to linguistic theory being taken into account in our research and, like other psycholinguists, we first chose the passive voice as an object of experimentation (Caprez, Sinclair, & Studer, 1971; Sinclair & Ferreiro, 1970; Sinclair, Sinclair, & de Marcellus, 1971). Two parts of this lengthy study were original: First we studied not only comprehension but also elicited production, repetition and, with a small group of subjects, their (metalinguistic) reflections on the passive; second, we interviewed three groups of children speaking respectively French, English, and Swiss–German. An interesting result was that the same hierarchy of difficulties was found in all three languages, depending on the meaning of the verb (e.g., *the boy is pushed by the girl* was understood by children several years younger than those who understood *the boy is followed by the girl*). Barblan (1989), in a duplication and extension of C. Chomsky's (1969) experiments on *easy to see,* found that similar constructions in French with the verbs *hear, touch,* and *smell* were understood much earlier than constructions with *see.*

Comparisons between languages continued to be part of our research. Relative clauses were studied in French, English, and Spanish (Ferreiro, Othenin-Girard, Chipman, & Sinclair, 1976), and deletion problems by Rappe du Cher in English, French, German and Turkish (in Sinclair et al., 1976), with the results showing similarities and differences across the various languages. At the time, we were mainly interested in the differences noted across languages when the lexical meaning but not the structure was changed. To advance these studies, the next step would be a re-examination of differences in the results obtained with sentences of identical meaning across languages, such re-examination to be undertaken in the light of recent developments in generative grammar and comparative linguistics (cf. Rizzi, 1989).

Elicited production also continued to be part of our studies and often yielded more interesting results than comprehension tasks, for children's productions gave better clues to the underlying processes than the behaviors indicating understanding of proposed sentences. Grammatical acceptability judgments were sometimes also asked for (e.g., Ferreiro et al. 1976). Unexpected acquisition facts were revealed by production experiments in several detailed studies, allowing their authors to bring to light various mental processes by which children gradually construct subsystems of the grammar of their language (cf. Ferreiro, 1971; Karmiloff-Smith, 1979; Bronckart, 1976; Chipman, 1980).

In the meantime, we had gradually become aware that these experiments tapped children's language capacities at various levels of detachment from spontaneous verbal functioning. We often asked children to act out isolated sentences without any pragmatic or verbal context to justify the particular structure of the sentences; when trying to elicit such sentences we sometimes had to give instructions such as "Can you tell me once again what happened, but now start with X?" (X being for example the name of the boy doll that had been pushed by the girl). Fortunately there are many ways of complying with such instructions, which enabled us to point to some of the psycholinguistic processes leading to the production of the type of sentence aimed at. But some of our older subjects, from among those who succeeded, sometimes remarked: *"Yes, but you wouldn't really say it like that."*

This led to a series of studies that were explicitly aimed at exploring children's metalinguistic capacities. Berthoud-Papandropoulou (1976, 1978) was the first to devise such a study, exploring children's ideas about what a "word" is. Later, Zei (1979) studied children's awareness of phonemes, A. Sinclair (1986) their thinking about questions, and Christinat (1988) their thinking about sentences.

The explicitly metalinguistic studies showed that a high level of reflection (i.e., corresponding to that of the average educated but not expert adult) is not attained before the age of 10 or 11. In Berthoud-Papandropoulou's (1978, p. 63) study, children of that age conceptualize the "word" as having meaning as well as having an internal phonological and morphological structure in addition to functioning as a constituent element in a large unit (phrase or sentence). Conceptualization is of course not expressed in such terms, but becomes clear, for example, when children explain that *table* is a word, because "*Table* means a piece of furniture, *the* is what you put in front of it, it means the singular"; "One could say *tablesse,* that would be the wife of a table" (cf. Berthoud-Papandropoulou, 1976). In our very first metalinguistic experiment, the subjects who had correctly produced passive sentences in the production task were asked how a speaker of English would go about producing such sentences. Since they had first given descriptions of simple events in the active voice, their explanations were often based on how they changed the active sentence into the passive. At age 8, they would describe the passive sentence "The car is followed by the truck" as, for example, "Now the car is in front and the truck is in back." Around age 10, some children were capable of explaining that one changes the place of the agent and the patient in the sentence and that you also "have to change the words in the middle *is following* to *is being followed.*" Only when asked specifically about the word *by* do they agree that adding the preposition is also necessary. On the other hand, numerous examples of spontaneous reflection on some linguistic phenomena are found well before that age, often in comments on errors in word forms produced by younger children (cf. Kaper, 1959, who, to my knowledge, was the first to make a systematic study in this area; see also several chapters in A. Sinclair, Jarvella, & Levelt, 1978).

Further reflection about what kind of knowledge was revealed by these metalinguistic studies led us to yet another series of studies, aimed at discovering some precursors of metalinguistic capacities. Before children are able to reflect consciously on utterances and to verbalize their reflections, they are able to detach an utterance from its immediate context, from a specific speaker and a specific addressee, as well as from a specific time and place. They can repeat something another person said, and make fun of somebody's accent. Culioli (1976) coined the term epilinguistic activities for such verbal behavior and considered it to be the result of an as yet unconscious metalinguistic competence. Berthoud-Papandropoulou, Kilcher, and Veneziano devised methods for studying such epilinguistic capacities experimentally by using situations,

[i]n which the subjects are presented with utterances produced in a particular extra-linguistic context, and in which the task is such that subjects should neither function in the ordinary way, i.e. as initiators and addressees in a conversation, nor in a genuine metalinguistic mode, but somewhere in between. (1989, p. 17)

A good example of such a task is found in a study (Berthoud–Papandropoulou & Kilcher, 1987) where children from age 4 to 9 were asked to carry messages back and forth between two experimenters who were too far apart to communicate directly. In this situation, questions, commands and informative utterances become "objects made by somebody else" to be transported and transformed by the child, and various levels in the children's capacities to deal with this task were brought to light.

In a different field, that is, written language, Ferreiro (Ferreiro & Teberosky, 1979) inaugurated an extensive series of studies on children's gradual conceptualization of the alphabetic writing system. In all these studies, children who were already competent speakers engaged in various kinds of thinking about language; the results show that many reorganizations and higher-level constructions take place between ages 4 and 10.

Our most recent direction of research is also our first study of spontaneous verbal interaction in a natural setting and concerns the early acquisition of language (i.e., French). With the help of the *Fonds National Suisse de la Recherche Scientifique* we collected an extensive longitudinal corpus of the interactions of eight mother–baby pairs from the period when the baby produces a few isolated "words" to when the first multiword utterances appear. This period was chosen because of our interest in grammar, and secondarily because a corpus of systematic observations of early language in French was lacking. The results of these various studies led to our becoming aware of two phenomena, both of which seem to pertain to changes in focus and to abstraction in our subjects.

DIACHRONIC SIMILARITIES

In the first place, we noticed a surprising convergence between, on the one hand, answers given by 4- to 9-year-old children in various meta- and epilinguistic studies and, on the other, spontaneous two- and three-word utterances often produced before age 2. It became clear that mere inspection of a list of utterances such as *pied bébé, enfant carrousel, pantoufle maman, enfant tombé* (or *tomber*) (from our own records, adjusted to adult phonetic form), *cheveux couper papa* (from Bloch, 1924), or in English *pencil doggy, Mummy pumpkin, Sit chair? Adam fall toy* (from Brown, 1973) cannot tell us whether these are spontaneous early multiword utterances or responses from older children in some situation where they are asked to "reflect" on language. In the first publication of results from Berthoud–Papandropoulou's study on the word (Papandropoulou & Sinclair, 1974) we already speculated on a possible psychological link between early acquisition and later metalinguistic ideas. For example, when Berthoud–Papandropoulou asked her subjects to count the words in a sentence such as *"le garçon lave le camion"* (the boy washes the truck), they would say "two words," and asked what these words were they would answer *"garçon, camion"* or, slightly later, *"garçon, lave, camion"* (Berthoud–Papandropoulou, 1978). Ferreiro (1978), in one of her many studies of preschoolers' reconstruction of the alphabetic writing system, wrote short sentences while her subjects (4- to 6-year-olds) were looking on; she then uttered each sentence with normal intonation, following the written text with her finger in a continuous movement. The children were asked various questions about which words they thought were represented by the different segments of written text, where a particular word might be located, and so on. At a certain level, the children thought that only the elements of reality referred to in the utterance were represented (Ferreiro, 1978, p. 38). Thus, for the sentence *la neña come un caramelo* (the little girl eats a sweet), only *neña* and *caramelo* were thought to be written. Somewhat later, the verb is assumed to be represented, but only the children at the highest level accepted that the articles also were written. Similarly, in a group study of 4-year-old preschoolers, where the children were encouraged to propose "something you could try to write." Hardy and Platone (personal communication) noted proposals of two-word combinations without articles or auxiliaries, such as *maison brûler* (house burn or, *brûlée,* burned). For these surprising convergences between early spontaneous utterances and responses in tasks demanding some kind of reflection on language the term diachronic similarities is proposed.

Synchronic Differences

A second phenomenon was noted that recurs in various studies and seems to be just the opposite: Very different responses are given at approximately the same level, and sometimes even by the same subjects. Such synchronic differences were observed for example in Berthoud–Papandropoulou's count-the-words task (1978). Children who are at the level of counting as words only the tangible elements of reality may instead focus on the rhythmic and syllabic aspects of the spoken sentence and thus count the accented syllables, lifting a finger for each accent as they reproduce the proposed utterance. In another of Ferreiro's studies on the alphabetic writing system with Spanish-speaking children (1988, pp. 48–58), she discussed clear examples of two focuses that may lead to conflict. At the age of about 4 or 5, children work on the figurative form of the many examples of written language that they observe in their environment. They separate types of writing that are "good for reading" from those that are not, and establish certain conditions, including: to be "good for reading" there should be a minimum number of letter shapes, usually three, occasionally two, and the shapes should not be identical. These ideas are derived from a cognitive organization of the observed figural forms of environmental print. They may come into conflict with another idea (which is long in being constructed; cf. Ferreiro, 1988), derived from the search for a link between the graphical shapes and the meaning-carrying spoken words, especially proper names and common nouns. Spanish- and Italian-speaking children clearly entertain, at a certain level of development, a "syllabic hypothesis," according to which each letter stands for a spoken syllable. Monosyllabic content words—*sol* for example, but such words are rare in Spanish and Italian—may lead to a cognitive conflict, which will ultimately be resolved by the (basically correct) idea of phoneme–grapheme correspondence (cf. Ferreiro, 1988). At that level, French-speaking children still have to learn correct spelling, and Siegrist (1986) once again found differing focuses of attention; some children, for example, when trying to write a simple sentence, introduce only one segmentation, interestingly enough between subject and predicate; others separate each syllable.

An analysis undertaken by Veneziano on part of the data of our early language study, as well as other analyses of the same data (cf. H. Sinclair, 1989), also seem to show shifts in focus. Leaving aside many details, the following phenomena were noted (Veneziano, Sinclair, & Berthoud–Papandropoulou, 1990). In genuine two-word utterances, the two words are in some meaning relation one to the other (e.g., *Mummy pumpkin*) and they are uttered one after the other, with little pause and often in a single intonational contour. The temporal sequence of the words does not mirror a temporal sequence of events: The relations expressed are of many kinds, but generally hierarchical and not temporal. Veneziano showed that this basic feature of language, that is, its linearity, is constructed during the period of transition from one- to two-word utterances via a process of self-repetition. Temporal chaining of words and relating of meanings develop first separately and are later coordinated. That one-word utterances can be related in meaning without being chained was brought to light by other authors also (cf. Bloom, 1973; Scollon, 1979; Dore, Franklin, & Ramer, 1976; Ochs, Schieffelin, & Platt, 1979). Veneziano, however, reports examples of chaining without relatedness, and also found that the coordination of temporal chaining and meaning-relating was preceded by two self-repetition patterns. An example of the first is the following: the child first says: *pied,* while trying to put a shoe on the foot of a doll; after a pause she says: *pied pied bébé.* An example of the second pattern is a child saying: *ezène* (for *carrousel,* i.e., merry-go-round), and after a pause: *ezène enfant ezène.* In our view, this construction of the linearity of language opens the way to syntax. Word order cannot be constructed contrastively as a syntactical device without the notion that the temporal chaining of words expresses some kind of hierarchical relatedness. At the same time, another phenomenon is observed. The child, who until the age of 20 months said *pain* and *chien,* for example, begins to introduce weak vowels in front of such words, *epain* and *echien,* although this adds nothing to the communicative power of the utterance. At this point, words have not only acquired compositionality and are part of a lexicon that can be used contrastively, but the child now also seems to be capable of focusing on certain non-meaningful aspects of the form of words, thus opening the way to the beginnings of grammar.

We do not assume that at this point the child already has some notion of a noun class whose members are in French preceded by determiners (e.g., articles). The acquisition by the child of the various functions of articles undergoes a lengthy development even after the notion of noun class, verb class, and so on is already elaborated, as was clearly demonstrated by Karmiloff–Smith (1979). The point I want to make is that there appears to be a synchronicity of the construction of compositionality, that is, the idea of relations between words rather than between words and action schemes or communicative intentions, and of a focus on the form of certain words. In our view, this double construction is a first step toward grammatical organization with its syntax and morphology. The early two-word utterances themselves are not yet grammatical, a point on which we agree with Chomsky (1980, pp. 55–56), though they will soon be followed by utterances with clearly identifiable grammatical morphemes.

Summing up, one can say that the diachronic similarities show (a) considerable time lag between competent language use and reflection on language, and (b) a kind of return to basic elements of early spontaneous functioning when reflection on language is called for. The synchronic differences show that, at the same level, children are able to focus on different aspects of language phenomena, often on meaning and communicative intentions on the one hand, and on some observable elements of the form of utterances on the other.

Before discussing from a Piagetian, constructivist point of view in what way we consider these observations to be contributions to our understanding of children's elaboration of their language knowledge, I must introduce an important restriction on what is meant here by language knowledge.

I chose examples that allowed me to discuss grammar; I left aside studies more concerned with pragmatics or with the interplay between conceptual development and verbal expression (e.g., Berthoud–Papandropoulou &

Sinclair, 1978; Badaf, 1988). Knowledge of language in the broad sense is of course inextricably bound with other kinds of knowledge: of the world we live in, of interpersonal relations, of social custom, and so on. Nonetheless, without excluding the possibility that the deep-seated principles of language may be rooted in social interaction (Bruner, 1975) I believe that the specificity of language lies in its particular structure, that is, its grammar. This is also why my references to linguistic structures are mainly concerned with Chomskyan generative grammar. Similarly, I accept Piaget's postulate that it is the gradual construction of coherent reasoning that fundamentally fashions the ways children organize the world they live in—the world of people as well as the world of objects. Though Piaget's developmental theory and experimental studies rarely touch upon social interaction, the postulate of social interaction as a necessity for the construction of objective knowledge and the strict parallelism between inter- and intra-personal operations is often brought to the fore in his work. Furthermore, just as sensorimotor intelligence is supposed to provide the common basis for the acquisition of what later will become different domains of knowledge in which reasoning takes various forms without losing its commonality, I believe that language knowledge also has its source in this common base and that its acquisition will continue to show similarities with acquisitions in other fields of knowledge.

We have thus tried to find links between the acquisition of grammar—or morphosyntax—and Piaget's cognitive structures. As we concluded after our experiments on the passive:

> We postulate that general cognitive development influences, in different degrees, the language acquisition process. The development of sensorimotor intelligence provides the baby with enough suppositions about the nature of human language to start learning to speak and understand his mother tongue. Universal cognitive structures would thus determine the form and function of the universal first utterances, up to three or four elements per utterance. A general cognitive factor would also be at work in acquisition after this period: faced with examples of a specific pattern in one specific language, the child has to make inductive generalizations. His ability to do so would certainly seem to depend on general cognitive development. (A. Sinclair et al., 1971, p. 17)

In another paper (H. Sinclair, 1971, p. 205), I stressed the fact that our guiding principles were not reductionist: "We certainly do not think that language acquisition can be explained by the laws of cognitive development alone: the structure of language itself is a necessary part of the acquisition model."

THEORETICAL SPECULATIONS

At the time of our first experiments, we were thinking in terms of possible structural parallels, and the results of the studies on the passive provided such a parallel: Around age 6, children begin to succeed on conservation tasks, that is, they know that certain transformations leave certain quantitative properties invariant. In passive sentences, permutation of agent and patient (postponing the agent by means of the preposition by) results in a sentence with the same meaning as the corresponding active: The transformation leaves the semantic content invariant. The results of the experiments, especially in the production task, showed parallels in the way 6- and 7-year-old children constructed this type of semantic invariance and their construction of quantitive invariants.

As our experiments progressed, however, I came to doubt whether there indeed were genuine parallels in *structure,* and whether links between grammatical and operatory structures should be sought in their construction *processes.* My doubts were reinforced by changes that were taking place both in Piaget's work and in generative grammar.

In the 1970s, Piaget became increasingly interested in the mechanisms by which subjects form new constructions (cf. Piaget 1974a, 1974b, 1976, 1977, 1978, 1981). Gradually I realized that Piaget's abstract descriptions of certain privileged phases of cognitive development have to be seen as instrumental in a double sense. In Inhelder and de Caprona's (1990) terms, they are, for the epistemologist, "a method of analyzing cognitive progress," "flexible instruments in the study of thought," and "a means of understanding the epistemic subject." For the subject, "cognitive structures impose one mode of thinking rather than another . . . but the subject is usually unconscious of the structures that guide his thinking" (Piaget, 1976, p. 64). Inhelder (1989) gives the example of how in her study of adolescent reasoning (Inhelder & Piaget, 1955) she found a notable development of experimental strategies and the elaboration of systematic proofs, which converged with Piaget's abstract representation of formal logic, with which he was concerned at the time. Inhelder's subjects of course did not formulate their thinking in terms of lattices and Klein's groups, but Piaget's formal structure captured the underlying structure of their operations.

In Chomskyan generative grammar, a shift took place from rule systems to systems of principles. The principles belong to Universal Grammar and determine the possible variations across languages; choices among a restricted number of possibilities (parameter settings) occur when the subject is in contact with a particular language and yield the main grammatical rules of that language (its core grammar). Universal Grammar is considered to be a preprogrammed module with which all human infants are equipped. The goal of studies in generative grammar became more and more that of accounting for "a cognitive object, the knowledge of language (that) speakers share, and the acquisition of that knowledge" (Rizzi, 1989, p. 125).

Piagetian abstract formulations and generative grammar are comparable in their instrumental function for the epistemologist and psychologist. Competent speakers are no more capable than Inhelder's adolescent subjects of formulating the abstract principles and rules that underly their performances. When questioned about their judgments of grammaticality, they may theorize and make up linguistic rules, which often are clearly wrong, and usually concern only one particular case (Rizzi, 1989). This incapacity of nonexpert subjects to become aware of deep-seated principles and rules is one of the reasons why epistemologists and psychologists need abstract theories. Such theories often bring. to light unexpected relations between what appear to be isolated phenomena. This is what Piaget's operational logic did for the study of children's reasoning in many domains. Generative grammar also highlights such relations. For example, the fact that Italian and Spanish (in contrast to English and French) allow, and in certain cases impose, the construction of sentences without a subject is linked to differences between these languages in word order in certain passive sentences and in the use of pronouns in certain subordinate clauses. These systematic differences can be traced back to the theoretical construct called the null-subject parameter (cf, Rizzi, 1989). Another reason for the need of theories is that in many domains of knowledge the epistemologist–psychologist does not know what questions to ask or what experimental situations to design without theoretical guidelines. Revealing questions, crucial experiments and meaningful analyses of observations are derived from theoretical constructs in all scientific endeavors. Regarding the necessity and heuristic value of abstract representation, there thus seems to be clear convergence between Piagetian operatory logic and grammatical structures such as those proposed by generative grammar.

Concerning the other function of Piagetian structures mentioned herein, that of guiding the subject's thought while remaining unconscious, there also is agreement. Chomsky's (1986, p. 260) statement "Behavior is guided by rules and principles of a system of knowledge, and these are, in fact, generally not accessible to conscious awareness" echoes, almost word for word, Piaget's statement. These convergences should not make us forget certain important differences.

In the first place, Chomsky and his colleagues work backwards from the rule systems that account for the language behavior of competent adults to core grammars of various languages, and then hypothesize general principles that allow for a few basic differences between languages. Piaget's cognitive structures, though influenced by the work of logicians and mathematicians, were always grounded in experimental studies or observations of young children. To construct abstract representations of reasoning systems is a difficult task, even when studying the thinking of scientists: as Piaget and Garcia remark (1983, p. 37) "the observer has to understand the operations the subjects use in their actions, even if their awareness of these operations only bears on fragments which are sometimes deformed, incorrectly recorded and incomplete." At less developed levels, notably during the pre-operatory and sensorimotor periods, when there is only a logic of actions, the task is even more difficult. Nonetheless, Piaget and Garcia (1987) brought to light the existence, at early ages, of subsystems and "structural fragments" that are clearly precursors of the operations that will later form the integrated structure of formal thought. It is true that the hierarchical structures of universal, core, and peripheral grammar seem somewhat closer to the Piagetian abstract structures than earlier proposals in generative grammar, and that the theory, though not constructed from developmental data, is liable to be changed for various reasons, including "arguments from child language, language processing, aphasia and the like" (Rizzi, 1989, p. 128). Other linguists now also emphasize both the subject's activity and the links between principles, notions, or operations at various levels or in various subsystems of particular languages (cf. Seiler, 1989; Culioli, 1989): often the links are implicatory in the sense that the presence of one property implies that of another (Aitchison, 1989). Similarly, the latest cast of Piaget's operatory logic emphasizes the implications of meanings of actions and operations. Nonetheless, the formal descriptions of linguistic structure on the one hand and operatory logic on the other seem to be far apart.

The second difference between grammatical and Piaget's cognitive structures lies in fact that Piaget always combined his search for structures that reflect a discontinuity between levels of knowledge with a search for mechanisms that build these structures and that would account for the functional continuity of the growth of knowledge. Piaget and Garcia (1983) carried out an analysis of such mechanisms active in the progress of science and in the development of certain notions by the child: despite the very different structural levels, the mechanisms of progress were found to be common to both. Structures and mechanisms are brought together in Piaget's equilibration theory (cf. Piaget & Garcia, 1983, pp. 14–15; Piaget & Garcia, 1987, pp. 156–157). The main mechanism is considered to be that of abstraction, reaching back to biological mechanisms, which implies autoregulations and brings about differentiations as well as integrations of structures at all levels. Abstraction is at work at all levels, in spiral-like fashion, reorganizing coordinations of actions or of operations into structural fragments or subsystems (cf. Piaget & Garcia, 1987, p. 168) and, at higher levels, by abstraction of abstractions into ever more coherent and powerful systems. The way these systems are applied to different fields of knowledge varies increasingly with development, but the structuring mechanisms remain the same. Thus it would seem that parallels between language acquisition and acquisition in the various other domains of knowledge should be sought in the mechanisms of construction, and especially in abstraction.

To return to our examples, let us consider the idea that at a certain level the "words" of the very early utterances change their status. Piaget (1977, p. 305) gives an example of abstraction at the sensorimotor level, when the assimilation of several objects to one action scheme (as when the infant first rolls a little ball, and then a small cardboard cylinder) gives rise to an assimilation of the one object to the other, which constitutes the beginning of the construction of classes of objects that share certain properties such as the property of roundness. As discussed in Piaget and Garcia (1987, pp. 12–13) assimilation into an action scheme confers a meaning on the objects, and a succession of such assimilations leads to implications: Both ball and cylinder are rollable and round; each property comes to imply the other. Similarly, the child in our example focused on the regularity of vocalic elements preceding nouns in the adult language and assimilated these words to each other. This assimilation, due to abstraction, will later lead to the construction of word categories, such as that of nouns that are, in French, mostly preceded by an article or other determiner. At the same time, the child focused on the compositionality of words into multiword utterances. Just as she had not yet constructed word categories in the proper sense, she had not constructed word order according to the basic principles of French syntax. Further abstractions are necessary before even a small grammatical subsystem can be constructed. Nonetheless, the two different focuses open the way for a system in which word categories and word order are coordinated: There are indeed implications between categories of words and the constraints on their possible positions in sentences or phrases. Possibly, before such coordinations can take place, conflicts may arise. Many examples of abstraction at work on different aspects of a nascent system that engender conflicts are discussed in Inhelder, Sinclair, and Bovet (1974), as for example in a conservation-of-length study when children switched from focusing on the number of parts composing two roads to the observation that "one went further." The children in our examples of synchronic differences were reflecting on various subsystems of their language, either on the rhythmical phonological form and on the referents of utterances, or on the figural organization of written language and on the link between the written and the spoken words with their meanings; in the latter case, conflicts were observed that led to a reorganization and integration at a higher level.

It is, I believe, more difficult to interpret the examples of diachronic similarities at different levels of development and in different tasks. Certainly, there also, a gradual reorganization, a differentiation between form and content and their coordination, eventually took place. The older children were able to define "a word" as having both meaning, internal structure, and a place in a phrase or sentence; they became convinced that articles, though not content words, are also written, and they could explain how to construct a passive sentence. But why this return to very early constructions, which show little or no grammatical structure, in children who are already competent speakers? It is true that in other domains of knowledge early constructions are appealed to at ever higher levels of abstraction. An example is that of one-to-one correspondence, often observed in action by the age of 24 months (Sinclair et al. 1982), but this is a structural fragment derived from coordinations of action schemes by abstraction and will gradually be integrated into larger systems. It is, of course, possible that the type of metalinguistic questions asked in the experiments led the children to reflect on content rather than on form, but in several instances the same children also showed reflection on nonsemantic aspects of utterances. I do not think that this is the correct hypothesis, since the questions were very different from one experiment to the other, and the same phenomenon occurred. Another, more interesting possibility is that the chaining of meaning-related elements, established in communicative interaction with the adult and focused on shared meaning (cf. Veneziano, 1988) is as basic a pattern in language as one-to-one correspondence is in mathematics. If this is true, it would be an equally important structural fragment, which at different levels serves as an object for abstraction. The further developments observed can then be seen as abstractions of abstractions, on ever more coordinated objects of knowledge.

So far, I have used Piaget's postulate of abstraction as the main mechanism or process in the construction of knowledge. Within this general process, however, Piaget introduces distinctions that need to be made explicit for further speculation on language acquisition. He distinguishes two types of abstraction (1977, pp. 5–6). The first is called empirical abstraction and bears on observable properties of objects or material aspects of the subject's actions; empirical abstraction uses relations constructed previously (by the second type of abstraction) but leads to knowledge of physical causality, not to the construction of new logicomathematical knowledge. The second type of abstraction is called *abstraction réfléchissante* and bears on all cognitive activities of the subject (schemes, coordinations of actions and of operations, etc.). By this process the subject extracts certain characteristics of these activities and uses them for new goals (new adaptations, new problems, etc.). It is a process "that can either remain unconscious or give rise to awareness and conceptualization" (1977,

p. 303), and includes, first, what Piaget calls *réfléchissement,* that is, "on the one hand, the projection (as by a reflector) onto a superior plane of what is taken from an inferior plane (e.g., from action to representation) and, on the other, the reflection in the sense of a mental action of reconstruction and reorganization on the higher plane of what is transferred from the lower plane" (1977, p. 203). This *abstraction réfléchissante—* reflecting abstraction[1] — can be observed at all levels:

> At certain levels of sensori-motor activity the infant is able to abstract some coordinations from already established structures and to reorganize them in situations (s)he recognizes as new. At this level, we cannot know anything about the infant's awareness. At higher levels, when reflection is an act of thinking, it is necessary to introduce a further distinction: between reflection as a process and the subject's retroactive thinking about this process, as a reflection on reflection, in which case we will speak of *abstraction réfléchie—* reflected abstraction. (1977, p. 203)

Though it is difficult to transpose Piaget's theory of the development of logical structures and knowledge of physical causality to the acquisition of grammar, I would like to speculate on what I think are some of its important points:

1. From a very early age, the subject constructs relations between actions, and, later, between operations, in the form of implications. At first, these relations remain local and constitute only "fragments of structures" (Piaget & Garcia, 1987, p. 146), which are progressively coordinated into systems in the proper sense, such as that of concrete operatory logic. Structural fragments already possess an immanent psychological coherence, such that they allow certain implications and exclude others. These implications or relations will later form part of larger systems. In other words, subjects construct "rules" or "principles," which are not "aberrant" or "haphazard," but determined by the state of the system. To take once again the example of the passive, our 5- and 6-year-old subjects who declared it impossible to start with the name of Y when describing an event in which X pushes Y ("It would come out wrong. Y doesn't do it.") follow a word-order rule that is frequently valid in French, but not in the

---

[1] In English, both *reflecting* and *reflective* capture the two meanings Piaget intended by *réfléchissante:* a metaphorical meaning of the projection of something on a different plane by a reflecting or reflective surface and that of "going back in thought." *Reflective,* however, also means thoughtful (Concise Oxford Dictionary of Current English), which corresponds to the judgment of a native speaker of English that *reflecting* indicates an activity more clearly than *reflective,* which can indicate a state. Since Piaget emphasizes repeatedly that *abstraction réfléchissante* refers to a process, I prefer to translate it as *reflecting abstraction.*

passive. Similarly, children who consider that only content words are words have established a metalinguistic "principle," which is not aberrant: Many of what adults call words do have semantic content, but by no means all.

2. Increasingly powerful systems are built from local structural fragments by empirical and reflecting abstraction. The concept of the two types of abstraction is more difficult to transpose to the acquisition of grammar than that of the construction of systems from structural fragments. Children do not interact with utterances in the same way as they do with physical objects. They try to understand utterances produced by others, and they themselves produce utterances, which—for them—have meaning. I suggest, tentatively, that knowledge of grammar is also constructed by two different kinds of abstraction. Certain principles or rules of grammar are abstracted from relations the subject establishes between an utterance and its meaning: In French, many word order and pronominal rules are of this type. Others appear to be abstracted directly from phonological form, such as agreement between adjectives and nouns. Without proposing too close a parallel, I would link the latter type with empirical abstraction, and the former with reflecting abstraction. Thus, the example of the child who adds weak vowels to words such as *pain* and *chien* would be an instance of focus on form leading to something like empirical abstraction (depending, like all such abstractions, on the previous construction of a relation: in this case, a meaning relation). On the other hand, the child quoted by Bloch (1924), who in quick succession says *papa couper cheveux, cheveux couper papa,* and *couper cheveux papa* appears to be working on word order, reflecting on the meaning of utterances she hears and on utterances she produces herself in relation to a search for the "best" order her system can produce.

In conclusion, I think that the Piagetian notions of structural fragments, subsystems, and coordinated systems as products of a continuous process of two types of abstraction can help us to unravel further the intricate web of grammar knowledge and its acquisition. Certainly, these notions can contribute to the design of new experiments and to new analyses of spontaneous language behavior.

REFERENCES

Aitchison, J. (1989.) Hidden treasure: The search for language universals. In J. Montangero, & A. Tryphon (Eds.), *Language and cognition.* Geneva: Jean Piaget Archives Foundation.

Badaf, G. (1988) Psycholinguistique de mais. *Cahiers de l'Insitut de linguistique de Louvain, 14.* 3-4, 27-37.

Barblan, L. (1989). *Apports de la pragmatique, de la sémantique et de la syntaxe à la maîtrise du langage: Une étude psycholinguistique "difficile à conclure."* Doctoral dissertation, University of Geneva.

Berthoud-Papandropoulou, I. (1976). *La réflexion métalinguistique chez l'enfant*. Doctoral dissertation, University of Geneva.

Berthoud-Papandropoulou, I. (1978). An experimental study of children's ideas about language. In A. Sinclair, R. J. Jarvella & W. J. M. Levelt (Eds.), *The child's conception of language*. Berlin, Heidelberg, New York: Springer, pp. 55–64.

Berthoud-Papandropoulou, I., & Kilcher, H. (1987). Que faire quand on me dit de dire? *Archives de Psychologie, 55,* 219–239.

Berthoud-Papandropoulou, I., Kilcher, H., & Veneziano, E. (1989). What can children do with utterances? Linguistic and metalinguistic activities: Theory, methods and results. In J. Montangero & A. Tryphon (Eds.), *Language and cognition* (pp. 18–28). Geneva: Jean Piaget Archives Foundation.

Berthoud-Papandropoulou, I., & Sinclair, H. (1978). L'expression d'éventualités et de conditions chez l'enfant. *Archives de Psychologie, XLVI, 179,* 205–233

Bloch, O. (1924) La phrase dans le langage de l'enfant. *Journal de Psychologie, 21,* 18–43.

Bloom, L. (1973). *One word at a time*. The Hague, the Netherlands: Mouton.

Bronckart, J. P. (1976). *Genèse et organisation des formes verbales chez l'enfant*. Brussels: Dessart et Mardaga.

Brown, R. (1973). *A first language: the early stages*. Cambridge MA: Harvard University Press.

Bruner, J. (1975). The ontogenesis of speech-acts. *Journal of Child Language, 2*(1), 1–19.

Caprez, G., Sinclair, H., & Studer, B. (1971). Entwicklung der Passivform im Schweitzer-deutschen, Archives de Psychologie XLI, 161, 23–51.

Chipman, H. (1980). *Children's construction of the English pronominal system*. Bern, Stuttgart, Vienna: Hans Huber.

Chomsky, C. (1969). *Acquisition of syntax in children from 5 to 10*. Cambridge MA:MIT. Press.

Chomsky, N. (1980). *Rules and representations*. New York: Columbia University Press.

Chomsky, N. (1986) *Knowledge of language*. New York: Praeger.

Christinat, C. (1988). *La conceptualisation de la notion de phrase chez l'enfant*. Doctoral dissertation, University of Geneva.

Culioli, A. (1976). *Séminaire de DEA,* Unpublished manuscript, Université de Paris.

Culioli, A. (1989). Representation, referential processes and regulations. Language activity as form production and recognition. In J. Montangero, & A. Tryphon, (Eds), *Language and Cognition* (pp. 97–124). Geneva: Jean Piaget Archives Foundation.

Dore, J., Franklin, M. B., & Ramer, A. L. H. (1976). Transitional phenomena in early language acquisition. *Journal of Child Language, 3,* 13–28.

Ferreiro, E. (1971). *Les relations temporelles dans le langage de l'enfant*. Geneva: Droz.

Ferreiro, E. (1978). What is written in a written sentence? A developmental answer. *Boston University Journal of Education, 160*(4), 25–39.

Ferreiro, E. (1988). L'écriture avant la lettre. In H. Sinclair (Ed.), *La production de notations chez le jeune enfant*. Paris: Presses Universitaires de France.

Ferreiro, E., Othenin-Girard, C., Chipman, H., & Sinclair, H. (1976). How do children handle relative clauses? A study in comparative developmental linguistics. *Archives de Psychologie, XLIV, 172,* 229–266.

Ferreiro, E., & Teberosky, A. (1979). *Los sistemas de escritura en el desarrollo del niño*. Mexico, Spain, Argentina, Colombia: Signo ventiuno. English edition: (1982). *Literacy before schooling*. Exeter, NH, and London: Heinemann.

Inhelder, B. (1989). Bärbel Inhelder. In G. Lindzey (Ed.), *A history of psychology in autobiography, 8,* 209–243.

Inhelder, B., & de Caprona, D. (1990). The role and meaning of structures in genetic epistemology. In W. F. Overton (Ed.), *Reasoning, necessity and logic: developmental perspectives*. Hillsdale NJ: Lawrence Erlbaum Associates.

Inhelder B., & Piaget, J. (1955). *De la logique de l'enfant à la logique de l'adolescent*. Paris: Presses Universitaires de France. English edition: (1972) *The growth of logical thinking from childhood to adolescence*. London: Routledge & Kegan Paul.

Inhelder, B., Sinclair, H., & Bovet, M. (1974). *Aprentissage et structures de la connaissance*. Paris: Presses Universitaires de France. English edition: (1974) *Learning and the development of cognition*. Cambridge MA: Harvard University Press.

Inhelder, B., & de Caprona, D. (1990). The role and meaning of structures in genetic epistemology. In W. F. Overton (Ed.), *Reasoning, necessity and logic: developmental perspectives*. Hillsdale NJ: Lawrence Erlbaum Associates.

Kaper, W. (1959). *Kindersprachforschung mit Hilfe des Kindes*. Groningen, Netherlands: Wolters.

Karmiloff-Smith, A. (1979). *A functional approach to child language: a study of determiners and reference*. Cambridge, England: Cambridge University Press.

Ochs, E., Schieffelin, B. B., & Platt, M. L. (1979). Propositions across utterances and speakers. In E. Ochs & B. B. Schieffelin (Eds.), *Developmental pragmatics*. New York: Academic Press.

Papandropoulou, I., & Sinclair H. (1974). What is a word? Experimental study of children's ideas on grammar. *Human Development 17*, 241–258.

Piaget, J. (1974a). *La prise de conscience*. Paris: Presses Universitaires de France. English edition (1976): *The grasp of consciousness*. Cambridge MA: Harvard University Press.

Piaget, J. (1974b). *Recherches sur la contradiction*. Paris: Presses Universitaires de France. English edition (1980): *Experiments in contradiction*. Chicago: University of Chicago Press.

Piaget, J. (1976). The affective unconscious and the cognitive unconscious. In B. Inhelder & H. Chipman (Eds.), *Piaget and his school*. New York: Springer.

Piaget, J. (1977). *Recherches sur l'abstraction réfléchissante*. Paris: Presses Universitaires de France.

Piaget, J. (1978) *Recherches sur la généralisation*. Paris: Presses Universitaires de France.

Piaget, J. (1981) *Le possible et le nécessaire*. Paris: Presses Universitaires de France. English edition (1987): *Possibility and necessity*. Minneapolis: University of Minneapolis Press.

Piaget, J., & Garcia, R. (1983). *Psychogenèse et histoire des sciences*. Paris: Flammarion.

Piaget, J., & Garcia, R. (1987). *Vers une logique des significations*. Geneva: Murionde.

Rizzi, L. (1989). The new comparative syntax: principles and parameters of universal grammar. In J. Montangero & A. Tryphon (Eds.), *Language and cognition* (pp. 85–96). Geneva: Jean Piaget Archives Foundation.

Scollon, R. (1979). A real early stage: an unzippered condensation of a dissertation on child language. In E. Ochs & B. B. Schieffelin, (Eds.), *Developmental pragmatics*. New York: Academic Press.

Seiler, H. (1989). Universal linguistic dimensions, categories and prototypes. In J. Montangero & A. Tryphon (Eds.), *Language and cognition* (pp. 85–96). Geneva: Jean Piaget Archives Foundation.

Siegrist, F. (1986). *La conceptualisation du système alphabétique orthographique du français par l'enfant de 6 à 9 ans*. Doctoral dissertation, University of Geneva.

Sinclair, A. (1986). Children's ideas about the form and function of questions. In F. Lowenthal & F. Vandamme (Eds.), *Pragmatics and education*. New York: Plenum Press.

Sinclair, A., Jarvella, R. J., & Levelt, W. J. M. (Eds.). (1978): *The child's conception of language*. Berlin, Heidelberg, New York: Springer.

Sinclair, A., Sinclair, H., & de Marcellus, O. (1971). Young children's comprehension and production of passive sentences. *Archives de Psychologie, XLI* (161), 1–22.

Sinclair, H. (1971) Piaget's theory and language acquisition. In M. F. Rosskopf, L. P. Steffe, & S. Tabock (Eds.), *Piagetian cognitive development research and mathematical education*. National Council of Teachers of Mathematics, Reston VA.

Sinclair, H. (1989). Language acquisition: A constructivist view. In J. Montangero & A. Tryphon (Eds.), *Language and cognition*. Geneva: Jean Piaget Archives Foundation.

Sinclair, H., Berthoud-Papandropoulou, I., Bronckart, J. P., Chipman, H., Ferreiro, E., & Rappe du Cher, E. (1976). Recherches en psycholinguistique génétique. *Archives de Psychologie, XLIV* (171), 157–175.

Sinclair, H., & Ferreiro, E. (1970). Étude génétique de la compréhension, production et répétition des phrases au mode passif. *Archives de Psychologie, XL,*(160), 1–42.

Sinclair, H., Stambak, M., Lézine, S., Rayna, S., & Verba, M. (1982). *Les bébés et les choses.* Paris: Presses Universitaires de France. English edition (1989): *Infants and objects.* San Diego: Academic Press.

Veneziano, E. (1988). Vocal-verbal interaction and the construction of early lexical knowledge. In M. Smith & J. Locke (Eds.), *The emergent lexicon: The child's development of a linguistic vocabulary*. New York: Academic Press.

Veneziano, E., Sinclair, H., & Berthoud-Papandropoulou, I. (1990). From one word to two words: repetition patterns on the way to structured speech. *Journal of Child Language. 17,* 633–651.

Zei, B. (1979). Psychological reality of phonemes. *Journal of Child Language, 6,* 375–381.

10 The Narrative Construction of Reality

Jerome Bruner
New York University

Surely since the Enlightenment, if not before, the study of mind has centered principally upon how man achieves a "true" knowledge of the world. Emphasis in this pursuit has varied, of course: empiricists have concentrated upon the mind's interplay with an external world of nature, hoping to find the key in the association of sensations and ideas, while rationalists have looked inward to the powers of mind itself for the principles of right reason. The objective, in either case, has been to discover how we achieve "reality," that is to say, how we get a reliable "fix" on the world, a world that is, as it were, assumed to be immutable and, as it were, "there to be observed."

This quest has, of course, had a profound effect on the development of psychology, and the empiricist and rationalist traditions have dominated our conceptions of how the mind grows and how it gets its grasp on the "real world." Indeed, at midcentury, Gestalt theory represented the rationalist wing of this enterprise and American learning theory the empiricist. Both gave accounts of mental development as proceeding in some more or less linear and uniform fashion from an initial incompetence in the grasp of reality to a final competence, in one case attributing it to the working out of internal processes or mental organization, and in the other to some unspecified principle of reflection by which—whether through reinforcement, association, or conditioning—we came to respond to the world "as it is." There have always been dissidents who challenged these views, but conjectures about human mental development have been influenced far more by majoritarian rationalism and empiricism than by these dissident voices.

In more recent times, it was Piaget who became the spokesman for the classic rationalist tradition by arguing the universality of a series of invariant developmental stages, each with its own set of inherent logical operations that successively and inexorably led the child to construct a mental representation of the real world akin to that of the detached, dispassionate scientist. While he did not quite drive the empiricist learning theorists from the field (they have begun to take new life again through the formulation of "connectionist" computer simulations of learning), his views surely dominated the three decades following World War II.

Now there is mounting criticism of his views. The growth of knowledge of "reality" or of the mental powers that enable this growth to occur, the critics argue, is neither unilinear, strictly derivational in a logical sense, nor is it, as it were, "across the board." Mastery of one task does not assure mastery of other tasks that, in a formal sense, are governed by the same principles. Knowledge and skill, rather, are domain-specific and, consequently, uneven in their accretion. Principles and procedures learned in one domain do not automatically transfer to other domains. Such findings were not simply a "failure to confirm" Piaget or the rational premise generally (Segal et al., 1985). Rather, if the acquisition of knowledge and of mental powers is indeed domain-specific and not automatically transferable, this surely implies that a domain, so called, is a set of principles and procedures, rather like a prosthetic device, that permits intelligence to be used in certain ways, but not in others. Each particular way of using intelligence develops an integrity of its own — a kind of knowledge-plus-skill-plus-tool integrity — that fits it to a particular range of applicability. It is a little "reality" of its own that is constituted by the principles and procedures that we use within it.

These domains, looked at in another way, constitute something like a culture's treasury of tool kits. Few people ever master the whole range of tool kits: We grow clever in certain spheres, and remain incompetent in others in which, as it were, we do not become "hitched" to the relevant tool kit. Indeed, one can go even further and argue, as some have, that such cultural tool kits (if I may so designate the principles and procedures involved in domain-specific growth) may in fact have exerted selection pressures on the evolution of human capacities. It may be, for example, that the several forms of intelligence proposed by Howard Gardner (1983), which he attempts to validate by the joint evidence of neuropathology, genius, and cultural specialization, may be outcomes of such evolutionary selection. The attraction of this view is, of course, that it links man and his knowledge-gaining and knowledge-using capabilities to the culture of which he and his ancestors were active members. But it brings deeply into question not only the universality of knowledge from one domain to another, but the universal translatability of knowledge from one culture to another. For in this dispensation, knowledge is never "point-of-viewless."

This is a view that is very compatible with another trend that has arisen in the analysis of human intelligence and of "reality construction." It is not a new view, but it has taken new life in a new guise. Originally introduced by Vygotsky (1962, 1976), and championed by his widening circle of admirers (e.g., Cole, press, Stigler, Schweder, & Herdt, 1990), the new position is that cultural products, like language and other symbolic systems, mediate thought and place their stamp on our representations of reality. In its latest version, it takes the name, after Seeley–Brown and Collins (1988), of *distributed intelligence*. An individual's working intelligence is never "solo." It cannot be understood without taking into account his or her reference books, notes, computer programs and data bases, or most important of all, the network of friends, colleagues, or mentors on whom one leans for help and advice. Your chance of winning a Nobel Prize increases immeasurably if you have worked in the laboratory of somebody who has already won one, not because of pull but because of access to the ideas and criticisms of those who know better (Zuckerman, personal communication).

INTRODUCTION

Once one takes such views as seriously as they deserve, there are some interesting and nonobvious consequences. The first is that there are probably a fair number of important domains supported by cultural tool kits and distributional networks. A second is that the domains are probably differentially integrated in different cultures, as anthropologists have been insisting for some years now (Bruner, 1990; Geertz, 1983; Gladwin, 1970; Rosaldo, 1989). And a third is that many domains are not organized by logical principles or associative connections, particularly those that have to do with man's knowledge of himself, his social world, his culture. Indeed, most of our knowledge about human knowledge getting and reality constructing is drawn from studies of how people come to know the natural or physical world rather than the human or symbolic world. For many historical reasons, including the practical power inherent in the use of logic, mathematics, and empirical science, we have concentrated upon the child's growth as "little scientist," "little logician," and "little mathematician." These are typically Enlightenment-inspired studies. It is curious how little effort has gone into discovering how man comes to construct the social world and the things that transpire therein. Surely, such challenging recent works as E. E. Jones's magisterial *Interpersonal Perception* (1990) make it clear that we do not achieve our mastery of social reality by growing up as "little scientists," "little logicians," or "little mathematicians."

So while we have learned a very great deal indeed about how we come eventually to construct and "explain" a world of nature in terms of causes, probabilities, space–time manifolds, and so on, we know altogether too little about how we go about constructing and representing the rich and messy domain of human interaction.

It is with just this domain that I want now to concern myself. Like the domains of logical–scientific reality construction, it is well buttressed by principles and procedures. It has an available cultural tool kit or tradition on which its procedures are modeled, and its distributional reach is as wide and as active as gossip itself. Its form is so familiar and ubiquitous that it is likely to be overlooked, in much the same way as we suppose that the fish will be the last to discover water. As I have argued extensively elsewhere, we organize our experience and our memory of human happenings mainly in the form of narrative—stories, excuses, myths, reasons for doing and not doing, and so on. Narrative is a conventional form, transmitted culturally and constrained by each individual's level of mastery and by his or her conglomerate of prosthetic devices, colleagues, and mentors. Unlike the constructions generated by logical and scientific procedures, which can be weeded out by falsification, narrative constructions can only achieve "verisimilitude." Narratives, then, are a version of reality whose acceptability is governed by convention and "narrative necessity" rather than by empirical verification and logical requiredness, although ironically, we have no compunction about calling stories true or false (e.g., Bruner 1986, 1990; Sarbin, 1986).

I propose now to sketch out ten features of narrative, rather in the spirit of constructing an armature upon which a more systematic account might be constructed. As with all accounts of forms of representation of the world, I shall have a great difficulty in distinguishing what may be called the narrative mode of *thought* from the forms of narrative *discourse*. As with all prosthetic devices, each enables and gives form to the other, just as the structure of language and the structure of thought eventually become inextricable. Eventually it becomes a vain enterprise to say which is the more basic—the mental processes or the discourse form that expresses it— for, just as our experience of the natural world tends to imitate the categories of familiar science, so our experience of human affairs comes to take the form of the narratives we use in telling about them.

Much of what I have to say will not be at all new to those who have been working in the vineyards of narratology or who have concerned themselves with critical studies of narrative forms. Indeed, the ancestry of many of the ideas that concern me can be traced back directly to the debates that have been going on among literary theorists over the last decade or two. My comments are echoes of those debates now reverberating in the human sciences — not only in psychology, anthropology, and linguistics, but also in the philosophy of language. For once the "Cognitive Revolution" in the human sciences brought to the fore the issue of how "reality" is represented in the act of knowing, it became apparent that it did not suffice to equate representations with images, with propositions, with lexical networks, or even with such more temporally extended vehicles as sentences. It was perhaps a decade ago that psychologists became alive to the possibility of narrative as a form not only of representing but of constituting reality, a matter of which I shall have more to say presently. It was at that point that cognitively inclined psychologists and anthropologists began to discover that their colleagues in literary theory and historiography were deeply immersed in asking comparable questions about textually situated narrative. I think one can even date the "paradigm shift" to the appearance of a collection of essays on narrative in *Critical Inquiry,* later brought out in a book (Mitchell, 1981).

If some of what I have to say about the features of narrative, then, seem "old hat" to the literary theorist, let him or her bear in mind that the object is different. The central concern is not how narrative as text is constructed, but rather how it operates as an instrument of mind in the construction of reality. And now to the ten features of narrative.

TEN FEATURES OF NARRATIVE

Narrative Diachronicity.   A narrative is an account of events occurring over time. It is irreducibly durative. It may be characterizable in seemingly nontemporal terms (as a "tragedy" or a "farce") but such terms only summarize what are quintessentially patterns of events occurring over time. The time involved, moreover, as Ricoeur (1984) has noted, is "human time" rather than abstract or "clock" time. It is time whose significance is given by the meaning assigned to events within its compass. William Labov, one the greatest students of narrative, also regards temporal sequence as essential to narrative but he locates this temporality in the meaning-preserving sequence of clauses in narrative *discourse* itself (Labov, 1981; Labov & Waletzky, 1967). While this is a useful aid to linguistic analysis, it nonetheless obscures an important aspect of narrative representation. For there are many conventionalized ways of expressing the sequenced durativity of narrative even in discourse, like flashbacks and flash forwards, temporal synechdoche, and so on. As Nelson Goodman (1981) warns, narrative comprises an ensemble of ways of constructing and representing the sequential, diachronic order of human events, of which the sequencing of clauses in spoken or written "stories" is only one device. Even nonverbal media have conventions of narrative diachronicity, as in the "left-to-right" and "up-to-down" conventions of cartoon strips and cathedral windows. What underlies all conventionalized forms for representing narrative is a "mental model" that has its unique pattern of events over time that gives it its defining property. And to that we shall come presently.

Particularity. Narratives take as their ostensive reference particular happenings. But this is, as it were, their vehicle rather than their destination. For stories plainly fall into more general types; they are about boy-woos-girl, bully-gets-his-comeuppance, and so on. In this sense the particulars of narratives are tokens of broader types. Where the boy-woos-girl script calls for the giving of a gift, for example, the gift can equally well be flowers, perfume, or even an endless golden thread. Any of these may serve as an appropriate token or emblem of a gift. Particularity achieves its emblematic status by its embeddedness in a story that is in some sense generic. And, indeed, it is by virtue of this embeddedness in genre, to look ahead, that narrative particulars can be "filled in" when they are missing from an account. The "suggestiveness" of a story lies, then, in the emblematic nature of its particulars, its relevance to a more inclusive narrative type. But for all that, a narrative cannot be realized save through particular embodiment.

Intentional State Entailment. Narratives are about people acting in a setting, and the happenings that befall them must be relevant to their intentional states while so engaged—to their beliefs, desires, theories, values, and so on. When animals or nonagentive objects are cast as narrative protagonists, they must be endowed with intentional states for the purpose, like the Little Red Engine in the children's story. Physical events play a role in stories chiefly by affecting the intentional states of their protagonists. As Baudelaire put it, "The first business of an artist is to substitute man for nature."

But intentional states in narrative never fully determine the course of events, since a character with a particular intentional state might end up *doing* practically anything. For some measure of agency is always present in narrative, and agency presupposes choice—some element of "freedom." If people can predict anything from a character's intentional states, it is only how he will feel or how he will have perceived the situation. The loose link between intentional states and subsequent action is the reason why narrative accounts cannot provide causal explanations. What they supply instead is the basis for *interpreting* why a character acted as he or she did. Interpretation is concerned with "reasons" for things happening, rather than strictly with their "causes," a matter to which we turn next.

Hermeneutic Composability. A preliminary word of explanation is needed here. The word *hermeneutic* implies that there is a text or a text analogue *through* which somebody has been trying to express a meaning and *from* which somebody is trying to extract a meaning. This in turn implies that there is a difference between what is *expressed* in the text and what the text might *mean,* and furthermore that there is no unique solution to the task of determining *the* meaning for *this* expression. Such hermeneutic interpretation is required when there is neither a *rational* method of assuring the "truth" of a meaning assigned to the text as a whole, nor an *empirical* method for determining the verifiability of the constituent elements that make up the text. In effect, the best hope of hermeneutic analysis is to provide an intuitively convincing account of the meaning of the text as a whole in the light of the constituent parts that make it up. This leads to the dilemma of the so-called "hermeneutic circle," in which we try to justify the "rightness" of one reading of a text in terms of other readings rather than by, say, rational deduction or empirical proof. The most concrete way of explicating this dilemma or "circle" is by reference to the relations between the meanings assigned the whole of a text (say a story) and its constituent parts. As Charles Taylor puts it:

> [w]e are trying to establish a reading for the whole text, and for this we appeal to readings of its partial expressions; and yet because we are dealing with meaning, with making sense, where expressions only make sense or not in relation to others, the readings of partial expressions depend on those of others, and ultimately of the whole. (1989, p. 28)

This is probably nowhere better illustrated than in narrative. The accounts of protagonists and events that constitute a narrative are selected and shaped in terms of a putative story or plot that then "contains" them. At the same time, the "whole" (the mentally represented putative story) is dependent for its formation on a supply of constituent candidate parts. In this sense, as we have already noted, parts and wholes in a narrative rely upon each other for their viability (Ricoeur, 1984). In Vladimir Propp's (1968, 1984) terms, the parts of a narrative serve as "functions" of the narrative structure as a whole. But that whole cannot be constructed without reference to such appropriate parts. This puzzling part–whole textual interdependence in narrative is, of course, an illustration of the defining property of what is called the "hermeneutic circle." For a story can only be "realized" when its parts and whole can, as it were, be made to live together.

This hermeneutic property marks narrative both in its construction and in its comprehension. For narratives do not exist, as it were, in some real world, waiting there patiently and eternally to be veridically mirrored in a text. The act of constructing a narrative, moreover, is considerably more than "selecting" events either from real life, from memory, or from fantasy and then placing them in an appropriate order. The events themselves need to be *constituted* in the light of the overall narrative—in Propp's terms, to be made "functions" of the story. This is a matter to which we will return later.

Now let me return to "hermeneutic composability." The telling of a story and its comprehension *as* a story depend on the human capacity to process knowledge in this interpretive way. It is a way of processing that has, in the main, been grossly neglected by students of mind raised either in the rationalist or in the empiricist traditions. The former have been concerned with mind as an instrument of right reasoning, with the means we employ for establishing the necessary truth inherent in a set of connected propositions. Piaget was a striking example of this rational tradition. Empiricists, for their part, rested their claims upon a mind capable of verifying the constituent "atomic propositions" that comprised a text. But neither of these procedures, right reason or verification, suffice for explicating how a narrative is either put together by a speaker or interpreted by a hearer. This is the more surprising since there is compelling evidence to indicate that narrative comprehension is among the earliest powers of mind to appear in the young child and among the most widely used forms of organizing human experience (Nelson, 1989).

Many literary theorists and philosophers of mind have argued that the act of interpreting in this way is forced upon us only when a text of the world to which it presumes to refer is in some way "confused, incomplete, cloudy." (Taylor, 1985, p. 15). Doubtless we are more aware of our interpretive efforts when faced with textual or referential ambiguities. But I would take strong exception to the general claim that interpretation is forced upon us only by a surfeit of ambiguity. The illusion created by skillful narrative that this is not the case, that a story "is as it is" and needs no interpretation, is produced by two quite different processes. The first should probably be called "narrative seduction." Great storytellers have the artifices of narrative reality construction so well mastered that their telling pre-empts momentarily the possibility of any but a single interpretation— however bizarre it may be. The famous episode of a Martian invasion in the broadcast of Orson Welles's *War of the Worlds* provides a striking example (Cantril, 1940). Its brilliant exploitation of the devices of text, context, and *mis en scène* predisposed its hearers to one and only one interpretation, however bizarre it seemed to them in retrospect. It created "narrative necessity," a matter we understand much less than its logical counterpart, logical necessity. The other route to making a story seem self-evident and not in need of interpretation is via "narrative banalization." It is when we take a narrative as so socially conventional, so well known, so in keeping with the canon, that we can assign it to some well-rehearsed and virtually automatic interpretive routine. These constitute what Roland Barthes (1985) called "readerly" texts in contrast to "writerly" ones that challenge the listener or reader into unrehearsed interpretive activity.

In a word, then, it is not textual or referential ambiguity that compels interpretive activity in narrative comprehension, but narrative itself. Narrative seduction or narrative banalization may produce restricted or routine interpretive activity, but this does not alter the point. Readerly story interpretation or "hack" story constructions can be altered by surprisingly little instruction (Elbow, 1986). And the moment a hearer is made suspicious of the "facts" of a story or the ulterior motives of a narrator, he or she immediately becomes hermeneutically alert. If I may use an outrageous metaphor, automatized interpretations of narratives are comparable with the "default settings" of a computer: an economical, time- and effort-saving way of dealing with knowledge—or, as it has been called, a form of "mindlessness" (Langer, 1989).

Interpretation has a long history in biblical exegesis and in jurisprudence. It is studded with problems that will become more familiar shortly, problems that have to do more with context than text, with the conditions on telling rather than with what is told. Let me tag two of them better to identify them for subsequent discussion. The first is the issue of *intention:* "why" the story is told how and when it is, and interpreted as it is by interlocutors caught in different intentional stances themselves. Narratives are not, to use Roy Harris's (1989) felicitous phrase, "unsponsored texts" to be taken as existing unintentionally as if cast by fate upon a printed page. Even when the reader takes them in the most readerly way, he or she usually attributes them (following convention) as emanating from an omniscient narrator. But this condition is itself not to be overlooked as uninteresting. It probably derives from a set of social conditions that give special status to the written word in a society where literacy is a minoritarian prerogative.

A second contextual issue is the question of *background knowledge*—of both the storyteller and the listener, and how each interprets the background knowledge of the other. The philosopher Hilary Putnam (1975), in a quite different context, proposes two principles: the first is a Principle of Benefit of Doubt, the second a Principle of Reasonable Ignorance: the first "forbids us to assume that . . . experts are factually omniscient," the second that "any speakers are philosophically omniscient (even unconsciously)." We judge their accounts accordingly. At the other extreme, we are charitable toward ignorance and forgive children and neophytes their incomplete knowledge, "filling in" for them as necessary. Or Sperber and Wilson (1986), in their well-known discussion of "relevance," argue that in dialogue we typically presuppose that what an interlocutor says in replying to us is topic-relevant and that we most often assign an interpretation to it accordingly in order to make it so, thereby easing our task in understanding Other Minds. We also take for granted, indeed we institutionalize situations in which it is taken for granted that the "knowledge register" in which a story is told is different from the one in which it is taken up, as when the client tells the lawyer his or her story in "life talk" and is listened to in "law talk" so that the lawyer can advise about litigation (rather than life). The analyst and the analysand in therapy are comparable with the lawyer and client in legal consultation (Scheppele, 1989; Spence, 1982).

Both these contextual domains, intention attribution and background knowledge, provide not only bases for interpretation but, of course, important grounds for negotiating how a story shall be taken — or, indeed, how it should be told, a matter better reserved for later.

Canonicity and Breach.   To begin with, not every sequence of events recounted constitutes a narrative, even when it is diachronic, particular, and organized around intentional states. Some happenings do not warrant telling and accounts of them are said to be "pointless" rather than story-like. A Schank–Abelson (Schank & Abelson, 1977) script is one such case: It is a prescription for canonical behavior in a culturally defined situation — how to behave in a restaurant, say. Narratives require such scripts as necessary background, but they do not constitute narrativity itself. For to be worth telling, a tale must be about how an implicit canonical script has been breached, violated, or deviated from in a manner to do violence to what Hayden White (1981) calls the "legitimacy" of the canonical script. This usually involves what Labov (1981) calls a "precipitating event," a concept that Barbara Herrnstein-Smith (1978) puts to good use in her exploration of literary narrative.

Breaches of the canonical, like the scripts breached, are often highly conventional and are strongly influenced by narrative traditions. Such breaches are readily recognizable as familiar human plights — the betrayed wife, the cuckolded husband, the fleeced innocent, and so on. Again, they are conventional plights or "readerly" narratives. But both scripts and their breaches also provide rich grounds for innovation — as witness the contemporary literary-journalistic invention of the "yuppy" script or the formulation of the white collar criminal's breach. And this is, perhaps, what makes the innovative story teller such a powerful figure in a culture. He may go beyond the conventional scripts, leading people to see human happenings in a fresh way, indeed, in a way they had never before noticed or even dreamed. The shift from Hesiod to Homer, the advent of "inner adventure" in Lawrence Sterne's *Tristram Shandy,* the advent of Flaubert's perspectivalism, or Joyce's epiphanizing of banalities — these are all innovations that probably shaped our narrative versions of everyday reality as well as changing the course of literary history, the two perhaps being not that different.

It is to William Labov's (1981) great credit to have recognized and provided a linguistic account of narrative structure in terms of two components: what happened and why it is worth telling. It was for the first of these that he proposed his notion of irreducible clausal sequences. The second captures the element of breach in canonicity, and involves the use of what he calls *evaluation* for warranting a story's tellability as evidencing something unusual. From initial orientation to final coda, the language of evaluation is made to contrast to the language of clausal sequence – in tense, aspect, or other marking. It has even been remarked that in sign languages, the signing of sequence and of evaluation are done in different places in the course of telling a story, the former at the center of the body, the latter off to the side.

The breach component of a narrative can be created by linguistic means as well as by the use of a putatively delegitimizing precipitating event in the plot. Let me explain. The Russian Formalists distinguished between the "plot" of a narrative, its *fabula,* and its mode of telling, what they called its *sjuzet.* Just as there are linearization problems in converting a thought into a sentence, so there are problems in, so to speak, representing a fabula in its enabling sjuzet (Bruner, 1986). The literary linguist, Tzvetvan Todorov (1977), whose ideas we shall visit again later, argues that the function of inventive narrative is not so much to "fabulate" new plots as to render previously familiar ones uncertain or problematical, challenging a reader into fresh interpretive activity, echoing Roman Jakobson's (1960) famous definition of the writer's task, "to make the ordinary strange."

Referentiality.   The acceptability of a narrative obviously cannot depend on its correctly referring to reality, else there would be no fiction. Realism in fiction must then indeed be a literary convention rather than a matter of correct reference. Narrative "truth" is judged by its verisimilitude rather than its verifiability. There seems indeed to be some sense in which narrative, rather than referring to "reality," may in fact create or constitute it, as when fiction creates a world of its own – Joyce's "Dublin," where places like St. Stephen's Green or Grafton Street, for all that they bear familiar labels, are no less real or imaginary than the characters he invents to inhabit them. In a perhaps deeper sense, indeed, it may be that the plights and the intentional states depicted in successful fiction sensitize us to experience our own lives in ways to match. This suggests, of course, that the distinction between narrative fiction and narrative truth is nowhere nearly as obvious as common sense and usage would have us believe. *Why* common sense insists practically upon such a sharp distinction being drawn is quite another problem, perhaps related to the requirement of "bearing witness." But that lies beyond the scope of this essay.

What does concern us, rather, is why the distinction is intrinsically difficult to make and sustain. Surely one reason lies in what I earlier called the hermeneutic composability of narrative itself. For such composability creates problems for the conventional distinction between "sense" and "reference." That is, the sense of a story as a whole may alter the reference and even the referentiality of its component parts. For a story's components, insofar as they become its functions or captives, lose their status as singular and definite referring expressions. St. Stephen's Green becomes, as it were, a type rather than a token, a class of locales including the locus so named in Dublin. It is an invented referent not entirely free of the meanings imparted by the real place, just as a story that requires a "betrayal" as one of its constituent functions, can convert an ordinarily mundane event recounted into something that seems compellingly like a betrayal. And this, of course, is what makes circumstantial evidence so deadly and so often inadmissible in courts of law. Given hermeneutic composability, referring expressions within narrative are always problematical, never free of the narrative as a whole. What is meant by the "narrative as a whole"? This leads us to the so-called "law of genres," to which we turn next.

Genericness.   We all know that there are recognizable "kinds" of narrative: farce, black comedy, tragedy, the *Bildungsroman,* romance, satire, travel saga, and so on. But as Alastair Fowler (1982, p. 37) so nicely puts it, "genre is much less a pigeonhole than a pigeon." That is to say, we can speak of genre both as a property of a text or as a way of comprehending narrative. Mary McCarthy wrote short stories in several genres. She later gathered some of them together in an order of the increasing age of the chief female protagonist, added some interstitial "evaluation" sections, and published the lot as an autobiography entitled, *Memories of a Catholic Girlhood.* Thereafter (and doubtless to her dismay) readers interpreted her new stories as further installments of autobiography. Genres seem to provide both writer and reader with commodious and conventional models for limiting the hermeneutic task of making sense of human happenings — ones we narrate to ourselves as well as ones we hear others tell.

What are genres, viewed psychologically? Merely conventionalized representations of human plights? There are surely such plights in all human cultures: conflicts of family loyalty, the vagaries of human trust, the vicissitudes of romance, and so on. And it might even seem that they are universal, given that the classics can be done in "modern dress" and the tales of exotic peoples be locally translated. But I think that emphasis upon plights and upon their putative universality may obscure a deeper issue. For plight is only the plot form of a genre, its *fabula*. But genre is also a form of telling, its *sjuzet*. Even if genres specialize in conventionalized human plights, they achieve their effects by using language in a particular way. And to translate the "way of telling" of a genre into another language or culture where it does not exist requires a fresh literary-linguistic invention (Brower, 1959). The invention may, of course, be culturally out of reach. Language, after all, is contained within its uses. It is not just a syntax and a lexicon. The so-called "inward turn of narrative" in Western literature, for example, may have depended on the rise of silent reading, which is a rather recent invention. If the reflectiveness produced by silent reading was then intensified by the creation of new genres — the so-called modern and postmodern novels — we might well expect that such genres would not be easily accessible to the Western nonreader and even less so to a member of a nonliterate culture.

While genres, thus, may indeed be loose but conventional ways of representing human plights, they are also ways of telling that predispose us to use our minds and sensibilities in particular ways. In a word, while they may be representations of social ontology, they are also invitations to a particular style of epistemology. As such, they may have quite as powerful an influence in shaping our modes of thought as they have in creating the realities that their plots depict (Feldman, 1989; Heath, 1983; Ochs & Schieffelin, 1983; Ochs, Taylor, Rudolph, & Smith, 1989). So, for example, we celebrate innovations in genre as changing not only the content of imagination but its modus operandi: Flaubert for introducing a perspectival relativism that dethroned both the omniscient narrator and the singular "true" story, Joyce for slyly substituting free association to break the constraints of semantic and even syntactical conventionalism, Beckett for shredding the narrative continuities we had come to take for granted in storytelling, Calvino for converting postmodern antifoundationalism into classic mythic forms, and so on.

Narrative genre, in this dispensation, can be thought of not only as a way of constructing human plights, but as providing a guide for using mind, insofar as the use of mind is guided by the use of an enabling language.

Normativeness.   Because its "tellability" as a form of discourse rests upon a breach of conventional expectation, narrative is necessarily normative. A breach presupposes a norm. It is this founding condition of narrative that has led students of the subject, from Hayden White (1978) and Victor Turner (1982) to Paul Ricoeur (1984), to propose that narrative is centrally concerned with cultural legitimacy. A new generation of legal scholars (Cover, 1983; Scheppele, 1989), not surprisingly, has even begun to explore the implicit norms inherent in legal testimony, which, of course, is principally narrative in form.

While everybody from Aristotle to the so-called narrative grammarians, all agree that a story pivots on a breach in legitimacy, the differences in how the notion of breach is conceived are themselves revealing of differing cultural emphases. Take Kenneth Burke's (1945) celebrated account of the dramatic "pentad." The pentad consists of an Agent, an Action, a Scene, a Goal, and an Instrument, the appropriate balance between these elements being defined as a ratio determined by cultural convention. When this ratio becomes unbalanced, when conventional expectation is breached, Trouble ensues. And it is Trouble that provides the engine of drama, Trouble as an imbalance between any and all of the five elements of the pentad: Nora in *A Doll's House,* for example, is a rebellious Agent in an inappropriately bourgeois Scene, and so on. Precipitating events are, as it were, emblems of the imbalance. Burke's principal emphasis is on plight, *fabula.* It is, as it were, concerned ontologically with the cultural world and its arrangements, with norms as they "exist."

In the second half of our century, as the apparatus of skepticism comes to be applied not only to doubting the legitimacy of received social realities but also to questioning the very ways in which we come to know or construct reality, the normative program of narrative (both literary and popular) changes with it. "Trouble" becomes epistemic: Julian Barnes writes a stunning narrative on the *episteme* of Flaubert's perspectivalism, *Flaubert's Parrot;* or Italo Calvino produces a novel, *If on a Winter's Night a Traveller,* in which the issue is what is text and what context; and theories of poetics change accordingly. They too take an "epistemic turn." And so the linguist Tzvetvan Todorov sees the poetics of narrative as inhering in its very language, in a reliance on the use of linguistic transformations that render any and all accounts of human action more subjunctive, less certain, and subject withal to doubt about their construal. It is not simply that "text" becomes dominant but that the world to which it putatively refers is, as it were, the creature of the text (Suleiman & Crosman, 1980).

The normativeness of narrative, in a word, is not historically or culturally "once for all." Its form changes with the preoccupations of the age and the circumstances surrounding its production. Nor is it required of narrative, by the way, that the Trouble with which it deals be resolved. Narrative, I believe, is designed to contain uncanniness rather than to resolve it. It does not have to come out on the "right side." What Frank Kermode (1981) calls the "consolation of narrative" is not the comfort of a happy ending, but the comprehension of plight that, by being made understandable, becomes bearable.

Context Sensitivity and Negotiability.   This is a topic whose complexities we have already visited in an earlier discussion of "hermeneutic composability" and the interpretability of narrative. In considering context, the familiar issues of narrative intention and of background knowledge arise again. With respect to the first of these, much of literary theory has abandoned Coleridge's dictum that the reader should suspend disbelief and stand, as it were, naked before the text. Today we have "reader response" theory and books entitled, *The Reader in the Text* (Iser, 1989; Suleiman & Crosman, 1980). Indeed, the prevailing view is that the notion of totally suspending disbelief is at best an idealization of the reader and, at worst, a distortion of what the process of narrative comprehension involves. Inevitably, we assimilate narrative on our own terms, however much (in Wolfgang Iser's account, 1974) we treat the occasion of a narrative recital as a specialized and conventional speech act. We inevitably take the teller's intentions into account, and do so in terms of our background knowledge (and, indeed, in the light of our presuppositions about the teller's background knowledge).

I have a strong hunch, which may at first seem counterintuitive, that it is this very context sensitivity that makes narrative discourse in everyday life such a viable instrument for cultural negotiation. You tell your version, I tell mine, and we rarely need legal confrontation to settle the difference. Principles of charity and presumptions of relevance are balanced against principles of sufficient ignorance and sufficient doubt to a degree one would not expect where criteria of consistency and verification prevailed. We seem to be able to take competing story versions with a perspectival grain of salt, much more so than in the case of arguments or proofs. Judy Dunn's (1988) remarkable book on the beginning of social understanding in children makes it plain that this type of negotiation of different narrative versions starts early and is deeply imbedded in such practical social actions as the offering of excuses, not merely in storytelling per se. I think it is precisely this interplay of perspectives in arriving at "narrative truth" that has led philosophers like Richard Rorty (1979) and Charles Taylor (1989) to abandon univocally verificationist views of truth in favor of pragmatic ones. Nor is it surprising that anthropologists have increasingly turned away from positivist descriptions of cultures toward an interpretive one in which not objective categories but "meanings" are sought for, not meanings imposed *ex hypothesi* by an outsider, the anthropologist, but ones arrived at by indigenous participants immersed in the culture's own processes for negotiating meaning (e.g., Geertz, 1983; Rabinow & Sullivan, 1974; Stigler et al., 1990).

On this view, it is the very context dependence of narrative accounts that permits cultural negotiation which, when successful, makes possible such coherence and interdependence as a culture can achieve.

Narrative Accrual. How do we cobble stories together to make them into a whole of some sort? Sciences achieve their accrual by derivation from general principles, by relating particular findings to central paradigms, by couching empirical findings in a form that makes them subsumable under altering paradigms, and by countless other procedures for making science, as the saying goes, "cumulative." This is vastly aided, of course, by procedures for assuring verification though, as we know, verificationist criteria have limited applicability where human intentional states are concerned, which leaves psychology rather on the fringe.

Narrative accrual is not foundational in the scientist's sense. Yet narratives do accrue and, as anthropologists insist, the accruals eventually create something variously called a "culture" or a "history" or, more loosely, a "tradition." Even our own homely accounts of happenings in our own lives are eventually converted into more or less coherent autobiographies centered around a Self acting more or less purposefully in a social world (Bruner, 1990, chap. 4). Families similarly create a corpus of connected and shared tales and Elinor Ochs's studies in progress on family dinner-table talk begin to shed light on how this is accomplished. Institutions too, as we know from the innovative work of Hobsbawm and Ranger (1983), "invent" traditions out of previously ordinary happenings and then endow them with privileged status. And there are principles of jurisprudence, like *stare decisis,* that guarantee a tradition by assuring that once a "case" has been interpreted in one way, future cases that are similar shall be interpreted and decided equivalently. Insofar as the law insists upon such accrual of cases as "precedents," and insofar as cases are narratives, the legal system imposes an orderly process of narrative accrual.

There has been surprisingly little work done on this fascinating subject, although there are stirrings among anthropologists, influenced principally by Clifford Geertz (1988) and James Clifford (1988) and among historiographers, prodded by Michel Foucault's (1972) ground-breaking *The Archeology of Knowledge.* What kinds of strategies might guide the accrual of narratives into larger scale cultures or traditions or "world versions"? Surely one of them must be through the imposition of bogus *historical–causal entailment:* for example, the assassination of Archduke Ferdinand is seen as "causing" the outbreak of the World War I, or Pope Leo III's coronation of Charlemagne as Holy Roman Emperor on Christmas Day in 800 is offered as "a first step on the way toward" or as a precursor of the enactment of the European Community in 1992. There is a vast literature of caution against such simplicities by both philosophers and historians, but it has not in the least diminished our passion for converting *post hoc* into *propter hoc.*

Another strategy might be called, for lack of a better expression, *coherence by contemporaneity:* the belief that things happening at the same time must be connected. I made the wry discovery, writing my own intellectual autobiography several years ago, that once I had discovered in the *New York Times* index what else had been happening at the time of some personal event, I could scarcely resist connecting the lot into one coherent whole—connecting, not subsuming, not creating historical–causal entailments, but winding it into story. My first scientific paper (on maturing sexual receptivity in the female rat), for example, was published about the time Neville Chamberlain had been duped by Hitler at Munich. My original story before consulting the *Times* index was vaguely about a 19-year-old's first discovery, rather like a *Bildungsroman*. The post-index story, with Munich now included, was an exercise in irony: young Nero fiddling with rats while Rome burned! And by the same compelling process, we invent the Dark Ages, making everything all of a piece until, finally, the diversity becomes too great and then we invent the Renaissance.

Once shared culturally—distributed in the sense discussed earlier— narrative accruals achieve, like Emile Durkheim's (1965) collective representation or Carol Feldman's (1987) "ontic dumpings," exteriority and the power of constraint. The Dark Ages come to exist, and we come to cluck with wonder and admiration at the "exceptionality" of any nontraditional philosopher or deviant theologian who lived in its hypostatized shadows. I am told that the ex-President and Nancy Reagan sent a letter of sympathy to a nationally known soap opera character who had just gone blind—not the actor, but the character. But that is not unusual: Culture always reconstitutes itself by swallowing its own narrative tail—Dutch boys with fingers in the dike, Columbus Christianizing Indians, the Queen's honors list, the Europhilia that dates from Charlemagne.

What creates a culture, surely, must be a "local" capacity for accruing stories of happenings of the past into some sort of diachronic structure that permits a continuity into the present—in short, to construct a history, a tradition, a legal system, instruments assuring historical continuity if not legitimacy. I want to end my list of narrative properties on this rather obvious point for a particular reason. The perpetual construction and reconstruction of the past provide precisely the forms of canonicality that permit us to recognize when a breach has occurred and how it might be interpreted. The philosopher, W. T. Stace (1967) proposed two philosophical generations ago that the only recourse we have against solipsism (the unassailable view that argues that we cannot prove the existence of a real world, since all we can know is our own experience) is that human minds are alike and, more important, that they "work in common." One of the principal ways in which we work "mentally" in common, I would want to argue, is by the process of joint narrative accrual. Even our individual autobiographies, as I have argued elsewhere (Bruner 1990), depend on being placed within a continuity provided by a constructed and shared social history in which we locate our selves and our individual continuities. It is a sense of belonging to this canonical past that permits us to form our own narratives of deviation while maintaining complicity with the canon. Perhaps Stace was too concerned with metaphysics when he invoked this process as a defense against solipsism. We would more likely say today that it must surely be a major prophylactic against alienation.

THE ORIGINAL PREMISE

Let me return now to the original premise—that there are specific domains of human knowledge and skill and that they are supported and organized by cultural tool kits. If we accept this view, a first conclusion would be that in understanding the nature and growth of mind in any setting, we cannot take as our unit of analysis the isolated individual operating "inside one's own skin" in a cultural vacuum. Rather, we must accept the view that the human mind cannot express its nascent powers without the enablement of the symbolic systems of culture. While many of these systems are relatively autonomous in a given culture—the skills of shamanism, of specialized trades, and the like—some relate to domains of skill that must be shared by virtually all members of a culture if the culture is to be effective. The division of labor within a society goes only so far. Everybody within a culture must in some measure, for example, be able to enter into the exchange of the linguistic community, even granted that this community may be divided by idiolects and registers. Another domain that must be widely (though roughly) shared for a culture to operate with requisite effectiveness is the domain of social beliefs and procedures, what we think people are like and how they must get on with each other, what elsewhere I have called "folk psychology" and what Harold Garfinkel (1967) has called ethnosociology. These are domains that are, in the main, organized narratively.

What I have tried to do in this chapter is to describe some of the properties of a world of "reality" constructed according to narrative principles. In doing so, I have gone back and forth between describing narrative mental "powers" and the symbolic systems of narrative discourse that make the expression of these powers possible. It is only a beginning. My objective has been merely to lay out the ground plan of narrative realities. The daunting task that remains now is to show in detail how, in particular instances, narrative organizes the structure of human experience—how, in a word, "life" comes to imitate "art" and vice versa.

REFERENCES

Barthes, R. (1985). *The responsibility of forms: Essays on music, art, and representation.* New York: Hill & Wang.

Brower, R. (1959). *On translation.* Cambridge, MA: Harvard University Press.

Bruner, J. (1986). *Actual minds, possible worlds.* Cambridge, MA: Harvard University Press.

Bruner, J. (1990). *Acts of meaning*. Cambridge, MA: Harvard University Press.

Burke, K. (1945). *The grammar of motives*. New York: Prentice-Hall.

Cantril, H. (1940). *The invasion from Mars*. Princeton, NJ: Princeton University Press.

Clifford, J. (1988). *The predicament of culture*. Cambridge, MA: Harvard University Press. Manuscript.

Cole, M. (in preparation). *Culture in mind*.

Cover, Robert, "Nomos and Narrative: The Supreme Court 1982 Term," *Harvard Law Review, 97,* 1983.

Dunn, J. (1988). *The beginnings of social understanding*. Cambridge, MA: Harvard University Press.

Durkheim, E. (1965). *The elementary forms of the religious life*. New York: Free Press.

Elbow, P. (1986). *Embracing contraries: Explorations in learning and teaching*. New York: Oxford University Press.

Feldman, C. (1987). Thought from language: The linguistic construction of cognitive representations. In J. Bruner & H. Haste (Eds.), *Making sense: The child's construction of the world*. New York: Methuen.

Feldman, C. (1989). Monologue as problem-solving narrative. In K. Nelson (Ed.), *Narratives from the crib*. Cambridge, MA: Harvard University Press.

Foucault, M. (1972). *The archeology of knowledge*. New York: Pantheon.

Fowler, A. (1982). *Kinds of literature*. Cambridge, MA: Harvard University Press.

Gardner, H. (1983) *Frames of mind: The theory of multiple intelligence*. New York: Basic Books.

Garfinkel, H. (1967). *Studies in ethnomethodology*. Englewood Cliffs, NJ: Prentice-Hall.

Geertz, C. (1973). *The interpretation of cultures*. New York: Basic Books.

Geertz, C. (1983). *Local knowledge*. New York: Basic Books.

Geertz, C. (1988). *Works and lives: The anthropologist as author*. Stanford, CA: Stanford University Press.

Gladwin, T. (1970). *East is a big bird*. Cambridge, MA: Harvard University Press.

Goodman, N. (1981). Twisted tales. In W. J. T. Mitchell (Ed.), *On narrative*. Chicago: University of Chicago.

Harris, R. (1989). How does writing restructure thought. *Language and Communication, 9,* 99–106.

Heath, S. B. (1983). *Ways with words*. Cambridge, England: Cambridge University Press.

Herrnstein-Smith, B. (1978). *On the margins of discourse: The relation of literature to language*. Chicago: University of Chicago Press.

Hobsbawm, E., & Ranger, T. (Eds.). (1983). *The invention of tradition*. Cambridge, England: Cambridge University Press.

Iser, W. (1974). *The implied reader*. Baltimore: Johns Hopkins University Press.

Iser, W. (1989). *Prospecting: From reader response to literary anthropology*. Baltimore: Johns Hopkins University Press.

Jakobson, R. (1960). Linguistics and Poetics. In T. Sebeok (Ed.), *Style in language*. Cambridge, MA: MIT Press.

Jones, E. E. (1990). *Interpersonal perception*. San Francisco: Freeman.

Kermode, F. (1981). Secrets and narrative sequence. In W. J. T. Mitchell (Ed.), *On narrative,* Chicago: University of Chicago Press.

Labov, W. (1981). Speech actions and reactions in personal narrative. *Georgetown University Roundtable on Language and Linguistics,* pp. 219–247.

Labov, W., & Waletzky, J. (1967). Narrative analysis. In J. Helm (Ed.), *Essays on the verbal and visual arts*. Seattle: University of Washington Press.

Langer, E. (1989). *Mindfulness*. Reading MA: Addison Wesley.

Mitchell, W. J. T. (Ed.). (1981). *On narrative*. Chicago: University of Chicago Press.

Nelson, K. (Ed.). (1989). *Narratives from the crib*. Cambridge, MA: Harvard University Press.

Ochs, E., & Schieffelin, B. (1983). *Acquiring conversational competence*. London: Routledge.

Ochs, E., Taylor, C., Rudolph, D., & Smith, R. (Nov. 1989). *Narrative activity as a medium for theory-building*. Department of Linguistics, University of Southern California, Los Angeles.

Propp, V. (1984). *Theory and history of folklore*. Minneapolis: University of Minnesota Press.

Propp, V. (1968). *Morphology of the folktale*. (2nd ed). Austin: University of Texas Press.

Putnam, H. (1975). *Mind, language, and reality*. Cambridge, England: Cambridge University Press.

Rabinow, P., & Sullivan, W. (1974). *Interpretive social science: A reader*. Berkeley: University of California Press.

Ricoeur, P. (1984). *Time and narrative* (Vol. 1). Chicago: University of Chicago Press.

Rorty, R. (1979). *Philosophy and the mirror of nature*. Princeton, NJ: Princeton University Press.

Rosaldo, R. (1989). *Culture and truth: The remaking of social analysis*. Boston: Beacon Press.

Sarbin, T. (1986). *Narrative psychology: The storied nature of human conduct*. New York: Praeger.

Schank, R., & Abelson, R. (1977). *Scripts, plans, goals, and understanding*. Hillsdale, NJ: Lawrence Erlbaum Associates.

Scheppele, K. L. (1989). Foreword on legal storytelling. *Michigan Law Review, 87*(8), 2073-2098.

Seeley Brown, J., Collins, A., & Duguid, P. (1988). Situated cognition and the culture of learning. *Educational Researcher, 18*, 32-42.

Segal, J., Chipman, S., & Glaser, R. (1985). *Thinking and Learning Skills*. Hillsdale, NJ: Lawrence Erlbaum Associates.

Spence, D. (1982). *Narrative truth and historical truth: Meaning and interpretation in psychoanalysis*. New York: Norton.

Sperber, D., & Wilson, D. (1986). *Relevance: Communication and cognition*. Oxford, England: Blackwell.

Stigler, J. W., Schweder, R. A., & Herdt, G. (Eds.). (1990). *Cultural psychology*. Chicago: University of Chicago Press.

Stace, W. T. (1967). *Encyclopedia of philosophy* (Vol. 8, pp. 2-3). New York: Macmillan and Free Press.

Suleiman, S., & Crosman, I. (Eds.). (1980). *The reader in the text: Essays on audience and interpretation*. Princeton, NJ: Princeton University Press.

Taylor, C. (1985). Interpretation and the sciences of man. In *Philosophy and the Human Sciences* (Chap. 1). Cambridge, England: Cambridge University Press.

Taylor, C. (1989). *Sources of the self: The making of modern identity*. Cambridge, MA: Harvard University Press.

Todorov, T. (1977). *The poetics of prose*. Ithaca, NY: Cornell University Press.

Turner, V. (1982). *From ritual to theater: The human seriousness of play*. New York: Performing Arts Journal Publications.

Vygotsky, L. (1962). *Thought and language*. Cambridge, MA: MIT Press.

Vygotsky, L. (1978). *Mind in society*. Cambridge, MA: Harvard University Press.

White, H. (1978). *Tropics of discourse: Essays in cultural criticism*. Baltimore: Johns Hopkins University Press.

White, H. (1981). The value of narrativity in the representation of reality. In W. J. T. Mitchell (Ed.), *On narrative*. Chicago: University of Chicago Press.

V CONSTRUCTING SOCIETIES

11 The Developmental Origin of Human Societies

Hans G. Furth
Catholic University of America

THE DEVELOPMENTAL-CONSTRUCTIVIST APPROACH

This chapter deals with society as an object of children's thinking, or more precisely, the prerequisite psychological competencies children must have in order to "think" society. The approach proposed here goes behind culture-specific practices of what is commonly called socialization and addresses the developmental origin of society as a notion in the child's psychology—an inchoate, barely conscious thinking, but a beginning nevertheless, a core mental scheme to which societal experiences can be assimilated. This approach faces many serious obstacles, not the least of which is the ambiguity surrounding the concepts of society and of socialization.

Society has a peculiarly paradoxical status. In one sense it can be treated as the most abstract concept among the limitless multitude of human artifacts and constructions, in another sense as the most concrete instance of human agency, from the most particular individual to the most general collective actions. On closer inspection this tension between abstract construct and concrete constructing, between outside object and inside subject, lies at the heart of nearly all of human psychology. Nevertheless, the approach I present here claims as one of its virtues, not only that it accepts this tension as a given but beyond that, traces the origin of this tension to characteristically human aptitudes that develop both in history and individually as each person grows from infancy to adulthood. In other words, the tension between instituted and instituting with regard to society is not a problem to be avoided by a misplaced focus on one or the other aspect, but is the expected result of particular competencies lying at the psychological origins of human societies. It will be argued that developmental description of these aptitudes should go some way toward a more adequate explanation of the nature of human societies and cultures.

A short, introductory comment on the concept of socialization is pertinent in a chapter concerned with the psychological origins of society. Socialization purports to describe the learning process through which children become active participants of the society in which they live. Assuming that society is at first outside the child, socialization is likened to an internalization of social values, norms, routines. The focus is on how children learn, adjust, or adapt to instituted practices and how certain learning environments are more or less conducive to that end. Society and its practices are treated as an interdependent network of functional relations such that the total system is in a state of a tolerable balance. From a developmental viewpoint this approach has two principal shortcomings due to an implicit overemphasis on the instituted objectively given and its corresponding neglect of the two features of any genuine instituting— namely, the active concrete agency on the part of the assimilating subject at the receiving end of socialization and second, genuine change and novelty in the final product of the process.

As I propose to follow through with a radical developmental–constructivist approach, along the lines pursued by Jean Piaget relative to the child's logical development, I am making a personal plea to avoid purely scholastic disputes on interpreting or correlating the writings of various authors. Naturally, no one in the field can avoid taking a personal stand on such authors as Freud, Marx, Piaget, and Lorenz, in addition to a multitude of largely unknown authorities summarily taken as accepted tradition. Is it yet possible to focus our interest on the concrete situation, that is, the child growing up in a historically particular society, rather than arguing that one or another interpretation of an author is or is not correct? Ultimately for my purpose, we should care little for a specific author, but rather for understanding to the best of our historically limited ability the actual phenomenon the author studied.

Human societies exist; plausibly they came into existence at the same time as our modern species, at a certain period in the evolutionary history of humanization. Even though there is much room for divergent opinions and a lack of direct empirical evidence, keep this picture in mind. Whatever opinion we hold on the evolutionary origin of human society, the story must be framed in such a way that it is psychologically real, concrete, and possible. And nothing is more real in human psychology than the development of the child. How infants make psychological contact with the society of which they are a part from the moment of conception is the question I will explore in this chapter. In whatever manner society started in prehistorical times, it certainly started—as it does today—in infancy. The developmental question obviously is more amenable to empirical investigation than prehistory. So I shall note and use what Piaget and Freud have studied concerning the psychological development of infants and relate it to the instituting of societies. My focus is on concrete psychological possibilities relative to this issue, not on imposing my interpretation of specific authors as evidence. I invite you to follow my exposition in this positive constructive spirit.

Two assumptions of the developmental approach can be spelled out briefly. First, there is a bias against accepting innate completeness while at the same time rejecting an unconstrained malleableness vis-à-vis the environment. Innate dispositions (or tendencies) are fully endorsed, but they must be worked on by human agents in order to develop into operative psychological competencies.

Second, the focus is on general aptitudes. They are recognized as species-specific, hence adaptive constraints or possibilities. The basic ethological posture is kept in mind that asks: In response to which concrete situations have human psychological universals evolved? (Furth, 1987, chap. 5). At the same time a radical historical relativism is implied regarding all nonuniversal aptitudes and even more strongly and pervasively all historically concrete and particular psychological situations.

TWO APTITUDES UNDERLYING HUMAN SOCIETIES

What could be the meaning of my claim that two psychological aptitudes underlie, or are at the origin of, human societies? This is indeed a bold claim and has the faint aroma of purely speculative, if not dogmatic, pronouncements on a fixed human nature, the very thing I seemed to have rejected from the start as contrary to a developmental–constructivist approach. These are not arbitrary aptitudes taken from a list of possible characteristics supposedly unique to humans or human societies; rather they are cognitive–logical and emotional–motivational prerequisites to ground personal agency and make genuine newness possible. Generally you would not find them explicitly mentioned in the psychological literature, for they are foundational aptitudes, not specific know-how. To the reflecting adult they are indeed a priori in a true Kantian sense, to the developing child they are concrete experiences and constructed developmental achievements. Whereas I speak of two aptitudes, one cognitive, the other motivational, in concrete reality they are inseparable. One without the other does not make sense. I call the two aptitudes *the logic of the object* and *the desire of the object* and point to Piaget and Freud as the respective originators of these concepts. I must note, however, that neither author explicitly referred to the mutually necessary connection between these two aptitudes, which I postulate as a basic precondition for the functioning of either.

In an earlier essay (Furth, 1987) I attempted to show that Piaget's logic of the object is empty without Freud's desire of the object and vice-versa. I presented these as developmental achievements beginning around 2 years of age and culminating around 6 years of age in what Freud called the collapse of the infantile Oedipal world. Freud referred to the unconscious conservation of this world as due to primary repression while Piaget noted the first formation of adequate conscious logical operations. I proposed that the desire of the object (the primordial "want-my-object" of children: "want-my mummy, daddy, toy, etc.") underlies all future sublimated achievements of adults, not merely as a potentially disturbing factor but, on the contrary, as its necessary and foundational component. I tried to connect this "object" with society by insisting that the object wanted by the children is the pleasure of interpersonal relations in which they engage from the time of birth.

I had some misgivings about the interpersonal–societal connection, since I became more and more convinced that interindividual and societal relations are qualitatively two different things. With this problem in mind I began to observe the symbolic role play of children. In connection with imaginary play and fantasy I asked some basic evolutionary–developmental questions of why and for what purpose. Could it be that these universally spontaneous and ubiquitous activities are related to the constructing of a societal framework?

About the same time I encountered the writings of Castoriadis (1987). It took the occasion of reflecting on the meaning of *l'imaginaire radical* (IR) — the foundational aptitude Castoriadis postulated for making sense of human societies — to make me realize that there is no smooth psychological bridge from a face-to-face to a societal collectivity. On the one hand, interindividual attachment cannot by itself provide the growing child with the cognitive and emotional experience of living as a member of a society. On the other hand, the traditional learning processes of socialization do not seem to be entirely adequate to explain a child's societal understanding. The question remains: How do children come to comprehend and participate in the societal world?

Castoriadis refers here to the human aptitude of IR, a concept he says is fleetingly mentioned by Aristotle and Kant, but then mysteriously neglected by these philosophers in favor of the more popular notion of the reproductive imagination. IR and imagination are different competencies and the surface similarity of the two words is more confusing than enlightening. Unfortunately other than in French traditions the concept of IR has almost no meaning. In France it is possible for Lacan to differentiate *le symbol* from *l'imaginaire* in the sense of the rational collective symbol (e.g., societal language) versus the irrational private image. This distinction between language and image, though seemingly obvious to some, is singularly unhelpful in comprehending the nature of IR insofar as it projects an adult conceptualization into the psychology of the young child.

According to Castoriadis, IR is the psychological base of societal experience. It determines in large part what is real or not real for a given society, what can or cannot be said, what is or is not valued, what can or cannot be thought. It encompasses and in this sense is prior to all particular psychological–social experiences and makes them possible in the first place. These experiences include the self, consciousness, rationality, language. In itself IR is said to be irrational (perhaps better: prerational) and disconnected from biological or instrumental ends.

Castoriadis probably introduced IR to counteract the prevailing structuralist tendency to describe society in overly rational and instrumental ways, regardless of whether this is done in a positivistic, functional, or Marxist persuasion. To these impersonal forces IR opposed the personal impulse of human agencies in all their chaotic diversity and indefinite openness. Here I emphasize two aspects that point to an amazing convergence between the society-oriented IR of Castoriadis, the emotion-oriented unconscious of Freud, and the reality-oriented logic of Piaget.

First, there is the unconscious, or better, preconscious quality of IR, which is operative to a large extent in the unconscious psychology of the person. Whereas Freud explored a person's unconscious as it affects the personal life of the individual, IR may be seen as the unconscious as it affects the life of the society of which the individual is a member. "To affect" is a weak verb; if in its place we put "to institute" we see at once the relevance of the unconscious as a concrete psychological agency for society as well as for personhood. Unfortunately, the unconscious is not a generally accepted or well-defined concept in psychology. An adequate answer to the problem of how the unconscious comes to be could contribute toward some consensus on that crucial part of human psychology.

A second characteristic of IR is even more controversial as well as more obscure in its meaning. IR is said to be disconnected from the given reality, at least to the extent that it is creative and reality making rather than merely reality accommodating. This constructive power is of course the reason why IR is at the core of instituting society. But, as said before, unless we can describe developmentally how this aptitude for creating newness comes to be, we cannot expect a consensual understanding of IR or, insofar as IR foundationally relates to society, of society. On this point Piaget's logic of the mental object is pertinent and potentially enlightening. For the object, being action-disconnected, is open to change and genuine newness. Reflecting on Piaget's developmental theory of the object and the symbol and on Castoriadis's IR, I came to the conclusion that the connection between the object and society is not one that requires any external mediation. I suspected that *the mental object in and of itself is such that it has a societal character.*

My thesis can be succinctly stated. The object is a mental construct on the part of the actively developing child, based on past and present concrete action experiences; it has from its first beginnings, around 2–3 years of age, a societal form. Consequently in children's mental objects, as in societies, we find generalizations, rule making, values and norms, unanalyzed assumptions, customs and traditions, history and societal communication (language). Also, there are roles of age, gender, class, and race, the desire to be respected by peers, concern with power status, and most strikingly, the interpersonal use of the reality-making power of imagining in the service of pleasure and interpersonal egocentric advantage. In the following two sections I shall provide theoretical support for this thesis and in the last section suggest some direct empirical evidence. Further, I propose that object formation as presented here is largely identical with Castoriadis's IR. I expect that setting side by side IR and the object of Freud and Piaget will be an enriching exercise in relating IR to its biological–developmental base and the theories of Freud and Piaget to the obligatory societal content of human psychology. This could lead to a more adequate understanding of the psychology–society connection as exemplified in meaningful empirical research and constructive political action.

IN DEFENSE OF ACTION KNOWLEDGE

As an introduction to this theme I invite you to consider with me the vicissitudes of Freudian psychology regarding infants' mentality. Freud did not concern himself seriously with children younger than 2- or 3-years-old and he posited the Oedipal situation with its dramatic conflictual resolution (the "collapse") as the major determinant of an individual's psychology. Against what was considered a too negative and instinctual assessment on the part of Freud, ego and object relations therapists emphasized the healthy positive contributions toward a harmonious ego; they referred to conflict-free zones of a person's psychology. Along these lines were Freudian scholars who considered repression and unconscious forces as accidental, alien elements introduced from outside; indeed, societies of people without these conflict-related attributes could be envisioned. All this can of course be seen as falling within the Utopian tradition of which the Marxist–Leninist version is but a recent illustration, reminding us how easily a theory can be misused with devastating consequences.

Against this tendency to immunize and neutralize Freudian theory and in order perhaps to get chaos back into the psyche Melanie Klein reintroduced conflict, fear, splitting and madness right into the psyches of newly born infants. In Klein's and others' (such as Lacan's) interpretation, the pre-Oedipal family situation was considered crucial in psychological development with the subsequent Oedipal situation being relegated to a secondary drama, to a large extent determined by what preceded it. Now what is striking in the reception of Klein's position is the eagerness with which cognitive scholars welcomed the presence of adult-like knowledge in newborn infants. Indeed, the cognitive literature is full of studies that claim to demonstrate that infants of the most tender age understand spatial coordinates, quantitative invariance, linguistic structures, imitation of actions not observable on their own body, and so on (e.g., Mandler, 1990). Klein's proposal of innate, or almost innate psychodynamic structures fits into this picture.

Why is it that Klein's speculation, not to mention Jung's inherited symbolism, Chomsky's built-in language structures and cognitive psychology's innate mental equipment, are so appealing? Apart from a reaction against past dogmatic assertions about children's incompetencies, the innate position relieves psychologists of having to explain how these cognitive or emotional structures enter into the child's psychology, which really means they need not be explained at all, they are simply given and are treated as part of the answer.

Whereas developmental investigators like Freud or Piaget attempt to explain adult aptitudes in developmental–constructivist terms, for innatists there is nothing to explain. Questions about development that can and do substantially affect the understanding of the final construct are never asked or researched. But when that object of study is conceptually and empirically not well determined, how can psychology ever reach a consensual position on what it is supposed to study? How, for instance, can we study symbolism, intelligence, language, the unconscious, if conflicting and fluctuating definitions and differing concrete instances of these concepts are constantly forthcoming? A strong theory is needed to anchor these concepts in an overall conceptual framework that goes beyond the ad hoc use of everyday language or particular cultural situations. Unfortunately, strong comprehensive theories are, prima facie, suspect for today's empirical scholars. Criticism is cheap and rewarding, whereas constructive assimilation is branded as unoriginal and not "with it," that is, not with the latest of the fast-changing fashions in the social sciences.

All this may appear somewhat peripheral, yet is actually pertinent to the main concern of this section, which postulates an action psychology chronologically and developmentally prior to an inner, mental psychology. This action psychology has no need of inner images or representations in order to learn, to remember, to recognize, no need of inner language in order to communicate or interpret, no need of internal symbols in order to signify. In short, there is sensorimotor logic and intelligence in the coordination of actions and perceptions (which in infants are demonstrably action-related) but there is no inner mental world that is known and experienced as such. Piaget in his biological perspective assumed the existence of this sensorimotor intelligence from birth. By means of a wealth of systematic observations, he demonstrated the passage from less to more comprehensive sensorimotor structures. He found that children around 2 years of age achieve a qualitatively new way of using logic. He referred to this new competence as the action-separated and, as such, the permanent object. I have called it here the "logic of the object," in contrast to the preceding sensorimotor "logic of action." Piaget traced the development of object logic from its exceedingly unstable status at first (despite the remarkable degree of stability obtained in action coordination) to the preliminary closure of concrete operations in children around 6 years old. These are operations on concrete or concretely imaginable actions and after some years lead to the more encompassing closure of formal operations through which we can internally reason and operate on formal propositions (see Kuhn, this volume).

Piaget's formulations will make sense if you are prepared to accept on its own terms a logic of action as different from a logic of objects and operations. Sensorimotor knowing is the key to understanding Piaget's theory. Without it, the theory has no *raison d'être*. There is richness and stability (with corresponding flexibility) accruing to one's conceptual instrumentarium if one can explain—both theoretically and empirically—how an object signifier (symbol) differs from an action signifier (signal), how object memory (recall) differs from action memory (recognition), how object communication (language) differs from action communication, how mental desire differs from bodily need. In sum, the logic of the object makes for the possibility of internal, mental actions (e.g., thinking, imagining). Mentation finds its cognitive, endogenous explanation in its own active construction on the basis of previously constructed sensorimotor action schemes.

Another issue related to sensorimotor development concerns logical necessity and universals. Today's recalcitrance against accepting logic as necessary and universal is historically comprehensible as a reaction against a previously prevailing dogmatism and idealism. But having discovered historical and cultural relativism, does it make sense to assume a crazily relativistic universe where anything goes? How can there be openness to possibilities and genuine newness unless there is an unchanging anchor of stability and invariance against which a measure of personal freedom and creativity can make its mark? For Piaget (1971, pp. 313–317) the necessity inherent in the logic of operations is this ultimate anchor of logical coordination and flexible stability; it is the crowning achievement of sensorimotor and object development and unthinkable without it.

Piaget argued against the proposition that logical necessity can be innate or that it can be the contingent result of an evolutionary or individual adaptation to external contingencies. For him the growth of logical structures is the paradigmatic case of constructive development. Not being instinctual or innate, logical operations must be acquired and in this sense require action within a meaningful environment. Yet they draw their enriching substance not from the external object of action but from the logic of the action coordination itself. In other words, for Piaget, logical operations do derive from experience, but from logical experience within, not from empirical experience without (see Beilin, this volume).

PSYCHOLOGICAL CHAOS AND THE DESIRE OF THE OBJECT

In the previous section I recalled the psychoanalytic tradition of Melanie Klein, which posited a chaotic fantasy life in newborn infants. As a developmentalist I find the notion of an innate fantasy psychologically unreal, even as the attribution of inherent conflict appears biologically unconvincing. How could a species evolve with an innate drive toward conflict and disarray and what could be this drive's evolutionary purpose? In Piaget's view there is no fantasy life, for the simple reason that fantasy requires the logic of the object and this does not develop before infants are around 2 years old. Prior to this developmental milestone, infants can experience a first period unencumbered by the potential pitfalls of a mental object world. They live and learn in the rich action world of sensorimotor knowing and feelings and actively grow in the logic of action, perception, and interpersonal relation.

Children achieve the logic of action-disconnected objects around 2 years of age. At this point the cognitive aptitudes for forming symbols, including internal images, imagination, and fantasy, become gradually available. These various aptitudes have indeterminate and individually fluctuating meanings; however, what they have in common is precisely that they are action-disconnected object signifiers (in contrast to preceding sensorimotor signals, which are signifiers in action). To simplify my exposition, I refer to all object signifiers by the term "symbol," leaving room for further differentiation between various types of symbols, such as external versus internal, representative versus constructed, socially shared (conventional) versus idiosyncratic. Piaget's contribution in tracing the developmental origin of the symbolic power and linking it cognitively to object logic is unique among the multitude of scholars past and present who use the concept of symbol in their discourses without perceiving any need to explain its action-disconnected signifying power. It is assumed to be a natural fact, something given. The contrast between Piaget and others is strikingly indicated if you realize that for Piaget the logic of the object explains the symbol whereas for others the symbol is generally used to explain what Piaget calls object and operations.

However, what is lacking in Piaget's theory of symbol formation, or simply assumed, is the motivational force that impels children to form action-disconnected signifiers. The object is but an empty framework, the cognitive prerequisite to the formation of the symbol, while the symbol is disconnected and arbitrary, satisfying no biological need. A hungry 4-year-old child would not fantasize food but would, in good sensorimotor fashion, search for food or cry for attention. The only psychologically real motivating force behind the symbol is Freud's *Lustprinzip,* the pleasure in fulfilling a desire. Desire and object mutually imply each other, as Kierkegaard (1843/1987, p. 80) long ago observed: "Only when there is an object is there desire; only when there is desire is there an object. The desire and the object are twins, neither of which comes into the world one split second before the other."

Underlying the symbol, from a cognitive perspective, there is the object, but from a motivational perspective, there is desire. Remember, these are not formal semantic propositions, but concrete experiences beginning gradually around age 2 and becoming increasingly frequent and intense in subsequent years. Note that desire too, just like object and symbol, carries the stamp of disconnectedness. Whereas object is action-disconnected know-how, desire is action-disconnected libido. Disconnectedness characterizes the two novel competencies, which I have proposed as being at the psychological origin of human societies and that I have linked to the IR of Castoriadis. The pretend play of children illustrates this double disconnectedness, as will be pointed out in the concluding section.

When desire is fulfilled in the object there is the psychological experience of symbol; in Freud's language, a symbol—of whatever type—is an object to which libido is attached. Here then is the birth of the mental world in which all humans eventually come to live. I have indicated earlier that I now recognize that this mental world from its very beginning has a societal framework.

How would I see conflicts and chaos entering human psychology without either postulating instinctual drives in that direction or making conflicts entirely dependent on the environment such that propitious contingencies could conceivably preclude conflictual states altogether? In my view conflict and chaos are indirect results of the state of affairs peculiar to human psychology, especially in the period from about 2 to 6 years of age; they are inherent in the biology-disconnected object which in its constructive use always requires a precarious balance between logic and desire. Having achieved the power to construct a world of symbols, children still lack at first, the most elementary instruments to put order into this inner world. As a consequence, glaring inconsistencies and illusions are bound to occur as desires change from moment to moment and become articulated in corresponding images and fantasies. Only around 6 years of age with the achievement of concrete operations, will children for the first time be able to make reasonably firm judgments based on logical criteria. Before that everything is bound to be in a twilight zone where objective reality and private image blur.

Then consider the difference between bodily *needs* that motivate action knowledge with its given physiological, physical and social constraints and bodily–mental *desires* that construct their own mental objects in a world of no physical constraints and potentially limitless openness. Add to this the body states of good, bad, and ambivalent emotional experiences consolidated during the first 2 years in sensorimotor habits that now become articulated and thereby intensified in fantasy and internal image. The result is a chaos of conflicting emotions and images. As new experiences are assimilated to this available chaotic mental framework, chaos feeds on itself in a cumulative manner. Mental mechanisms of defense, splitting, displacement, and repression come into play if only for the sake of mental economy. In short, starting after 2 years of age a multilayered, conflicting mentality of various shades of consciousness comes into being. Potential disequilibrium and cognitive and emotional conflict abound, and reality is by no means a well-determined coherent or even privileged region.

I have used the word "chaos" deliberately to point to a situation where a linear predictive logic fails and superficially disorder prevails. However, as in the physical theory of "order out of chaos," logic and order are by no means absent. On the contrary, this childish mental world is the developmental source from which flow directly all future social and individual achievements, constructive happiness as well as destructive selfishness and cruelty, and in between the common human misery psychoanalysts know so well. This child's chaotic world is so precious to the adaptive purposes of humanization that its core remains conserved in each adult's psyche: This is the emergence of the unconscious in the Freudian sense. Freud stressed the collapse of the Oedipal world through what he called "primary repression," a process children complete around 6 years of age, the very time when for the first time conscious logical operations are adequately available to them. Unconscious material, says Freud (1918/1955 p. 120), is protected from the onslaught of conscious development.

The developmental perspective on human mentality I have proposed fully accepts the core of Freudian and post-Freudian psychodynamic insights (Furth, 1992) but insists that the concrete action psychology of the growing child is respected and that adult psychology is not needlessly projected into the infant. Only in this way can speculative opinions become amenable, if not to empirical verification, at least to a convincing degree of plausibility.

Human mentality is but another name for human psychology as it develops after around 2 years of age, when the threshold of the disconnected object and disconnected libido is reached. This development, I propose, has in all its instances a logical and libidinal component. What is commonly called the irrational part of the psyche is not bereft of logic, while the most objective and factual knowledge is always connected to the peculiar subjectivity of libidinal desire. Sublimation therefore is not the elimination of desire but merely its partial attunement to socially accepted objects. Primal repression as the conservation of the child's mentality in the unconscious is here seen as the counterpart to social sublimation. Children around age 6 complete primal repression just as they begin to work toward sublimation. Both processes are developmentally linked to the first emergence of adequate conscious logic (Piaget's concrete operations).

CONCLUSION: CHILDREN CONSTRUCT A SOCIETAL FRAMEWORK

It is hardly controversial anymore to propose that evolution has adapted human psychology along social lines (Byrne & Whiten, 1988). This chapter has attempted to flesh out the social lines in two respects: (a) the societal character of human relations is noted; (b) the psychological competencies are specified that have to be actively developed in early childhood so that societal dimensions become possible. This position does not mean that society is innate; on the contrary, it treats society as a developmental construct. In this constructive sense it is claimed that, long before each different culture has succeeded in socializing its children, they already live mentally in a society; that as soon as children have the power to construct a mental object and articulate a mental desire, the object and the desire already include society; that the creativity afforded by the logic of the object is spontaneously directed toward the instituting of society just as the desire of the object spontaneously makes the child attached to society. With the development of a symbolic mental life around 2 to 3 years of age, face-to-face, interindividual relationships and interactions spontaneously take on a new, societal quality. Phenomenologically speaking, children begin to live in a societal world. Given the "want-my-object" attitude of Freud's *Lustprinzip,* the object in its most general meaning is therefore society, that is, "want-my-society" serves a much more plausible evolutionary purpose than an empty "want-my-pleasure."

On account of the developmental transformation beginning around 2 years of age, the child's action communication becomes *societal* language, the child's individuality becomes the *societal* role of a girl or a boy and the role of a child belonging to a particular adult *society,* the child's learning and doing take on the form of a particular *societal* culture, the child's pleasures and emotions become attached to specific *societal* values and ideologies. The chaotic Oedipal world is steeped in this societal framework. The repression of this world by around 6 years of age is then primarily the unconscious conservation of the child's first and most intense attachment to societal values and ideas. This is what I call the societal unconscious, which like Castoriadis's IR is the psychological base of all adult societies; it is that to which, in children's socialization, the adult society is assimilated and which is capable of bringing about newness and change in that very society. Finally, the child's cognitive and emotional immaturity surrounding the psychological origin of society is the only convincing explanation why human generations have been able, if not eager, to embrace millennia of apparently humanly degrading institutions and generally suffer silently the discontents of civilization.

All the theories that posit external institutions and social contingencies as being ultimately responsible for a disturbed or disintegrated psyche miss the point that the chaos of society reflects the chaos of the psyche rather than the other way around. Society is the chief construct of a human psychology that has societal instituting as its primary evolutionary task. Society partakes of the same mixture of open-ended logic and driven desire as found in a person's mental life. Young children are driven to play societal roles as if their life depended on it — as indeed it does, because without society there is no ego, no person.

Children's social pretend play is one of the chief activities in their evolving mental life. It has the advantage of being observable and of including concrete interactions with peers. The concrete social interactions of the play are held together by the symbolic ideas and values of the shared pretend construction. Now if you substitute in the previous sentence "culture" for "play" and "reality" for "pretend," you have a fair description of adult society: The concrete social interactions of the *culture* are held together by the symbolic ideas and values of the shared *reality* construction. This would seem a surprisingly convincing indication that children's pretend play is indeed the construction of a childish societal world or, if you like, that adult society is modeled after young children's pretend play. Also note how in these two sentences "pretend" and "reality" have a similar status of being psychologically constructed, a far cry from the view (Leslie, 1987) that contrasts pretend as subjectively fabricated with reality as objectively given.

My collaborator Steven Kane and I (Furth & Kane, 1992, Kane & Furth, 1992) have recently analyzed a specific dramatic role play of three girls, 5 years of age, lasting just under an hour. We could readily identify the various components of a societal framework — that is, values, norms, roles, and so on. The interpersonal use of pretending for egocentric advantage was particularly impressive and reminded us of the Marxist notion of ideology and false consciousness. It was hard to decide whether, for the players, their symbolic pretenses or their concrete interactions were more important. Indeed, these two dimensions were as tightly interwoven in the girls' play as they are in what we adults call our social reality.

Consider the following interchange concerning use of a necklace between two girls, A and B, getting dressed for a royal ball:

B: Since I found this first, can I use it?

A: If you want this you can use it at the royal ball — the second royal ball. 'Cause at the first one I wear it; and the second one you wear it; and the next one I wear it. We take turns. But this time I wear it.

B wants to justify her use by the norm of finders keepers. But being the younger she asks A for approval. This is at first granted, only to be modified immediately by A's invention of a pretend future and the promise of the norm of turn taking. So we have a complex interweaving of competitive roles, search for approval, pretend formation, historical narrative, social norms.

In the following excerpt a pretend reality is invented to stake an ownership claim during the pretend play:

B: Oh, since I got this first, let's pretend, um, this was(1) my telephone and we used it for pretend(2). I used it for real(1), except [=such that] it was my telephone and you used it for pretend(2).

A: I could use it for real(3) life too.

B: OK. OK. But, um, let's pretend(1, 2) . . . remember this telephone is mine(1), but you could only use(2) it.

Three senses of reality are here mentioned, (1) the private pretend reality of B, (2) the shared pretend play, (3) the "real," adult world. Action disconnectedness is evident in all play but especially here in B's invention of a "pretend reality" (1) (a classical oxymoron) — and her wish (1, 2) to relate the shared pretend play (2) to this invention (1) rather than to "real life" (3).

Elements of the play (with its plot and subsidiary themes) no doubt derive from the U. S. middle-class environment, which encourages such activities; but the spontaneous use the girls made of these elements in the service of their interpersonal relations indicate a genuine co-constructing of a shared societal reality. In other cultures symbolic play may well be different. Nevertheless, the internal play of imagination and inner language is ubiquitous and continues throughout life. There is no reason to doubt that internal play has similar societal tendencies as social play, with subjective constructions even more unconstrained and free to invent newness. That children "play society" is hardly controversial; why they play has so far not been answered satisfactorily. Since the only reasonable conclusion remains that without the psychological prerequisites of childhood play there would be no societies, it may be no exaggeration to assert that the aptitudes that impel play — the logic of the object and the desire of the object — are basic to the instituting of society.

REFERENCES

Byrne, R. W., & Whiten, A. (Eds.). (1988). *Machiavellian intelligence: Social expertise and the evolution of intellect in monkeys, apes, and humans.* Oxford, England: Oxford University Press.

Castoriadis, C. (1987). *The imaginary institution of society.* Cambridge, MA: MIT Press.

Freud, S. (1918/1955). History of an infantile neurosis. *Standard Edition,* vol. 17, 1–123. London: Hogarth Press.

Furth, H. G. (1987). *Knowledge as desire: An essay on Freud and Piaget.* New York: Columbia University Press.

Furth, H. G. (1992). Psychoanalysis and social thought: The endogenous origin of society. *Political Psychology, 13,* 91–104.

Furth, H. G., & Kane, S. R. (1992). Children constructing society: A new perspective on children at play. In H. McGurk (Ed.), *Childhood social development: Contemporary perspectives.* Hove, England: Lawrence Erlbaum Associates.

Kane, S. R., & Furth, H. G. (1992). Children constructing social reality: A frame analysis of social pretend play, *Human Development, 35.*

Kierkegaard, S. (1843/1987). *Either/Or. Part I.* Princeton, NJ: Princeton University Press.

Leslie, A. M. (1987). Pretense and representation: The origins of theory of mind. *Psychological Review, 94,* 412–426.

Mandler, J. (1990). A new perspective on cognitive development in infancy. *American Scientist, 78,* 236–243.

Piaget, J. (1971). *Biology and knowledge: An essay on relations between organic regulations and cognitive processes.* Chicago: University of Chicago Press.

12 Social Construction In Piaget's Theory

James Youniss
The Catholic University of America

William Damon
Brown University

Piaget's views on the role of social relations in the individual construction of knowledge are less known than his position on the child's construction of logical thought. This may be due to the timing of Piaget's reintroduction into American psychology. In the late 1950s, psychologists were seeking a new model of the human subject who would be an active agent and bring reflective powers to the task of controlling the external environment (Bruner, Goodnow, & Austin, 1956). Piaget's emphases on construction and the development of logical thinking provided some first steps toward this desired model; as a consequence, his theory and findings spread quickly through the American psychological scene (Flavell, 1962).

At this time in Piaget's own theory building, however, his efforts were focused on elaborating the structures of logical thought (Inhelder & Piaget, 1958). His moral judgment work was almost three decades behind him, and his other "sociological" studies—finally collected as a group in the mid-1960's—would never be published in English (Chapman, 1986). In America, Piaget would forever be seen as an investigator of "cold cognition," a theorist who viewed the child as a scientist discovering intellectual insights in splendid isolation.

After a burst of interest lasting almost two decades (admittedly a long life by the faddish standards of contemporary American social science), Piaget's approach has been largely discarded as too cognitive, too structural, and too universalist in its claims. It has been replaced by more process-oriented, more affective, and more contextualist approaches. The theory's connotative imprint was stamped at the time of its second entry into American psychology, and the theory is still read primarily as a statement about the individual's ability to control physical reality through logical means. To this day, it retains the indelible trademark of the apocryphal child who discovers formal properties of things, such as number, while playing alone with pebbles on the beach.

We do not deny that there are grounds for such a depiction. Sources for it can be found in Piaget's extensive writings. Yet there is an equally clear, though less frequently articulated side that we believe deserves serious attention. In our view, Piaget's ideas about social construction are integral to his general epistemology and have important implications not just for social and moral knowledge, but for his theory in general (Dean & Youniss, 1991; Youniss, 1983). We do not consider his ideas on social construction to be a minor theme or afterthought. Rather, they provide a serious account of the knowledge process that entails co-constructive exchanges between children and other persons as much as between children and physical objects.

In the present chapter, we elaborate on a particular theme that is central to the theory but has not been adequately noted by Piagetian scholars. We refer to the concept of the *culture-acquiring child,* which denotes children's identification with and desire to be part of the culture they know through interacting with other children and adults. Damon (1983) proposes that psychologists must address two issues in explaining social development. One is how children become individuals with unique personalities and senses of self. The second is how children become members of society who think, like, and share knowledge with other members. Most developmental theories have been directed to the former issue in the sense of accounting for individual differences among children.

The aim of this chapter is to describe Piaget's account of how children adopt cultural patterns of interacting and, in the process, identify with these patterns and the culture they represent. We shall describe Piaget's position, show its roots in Piaget's distinctive epistemological stance, note some points of resistance to this position among contemporary psychologists, and link the position to other social constructivist work on culture and development.

PIAGET'S EARLY WRITINGS

We begin by reviewing an essay that Piaget wrote as a speech for the New Education Fellowship (Piaget, 1932a). The NEF was an association of European scholars who were devoted to reforming post-World War I European politics through educational reform. They viewed the war as a product of reactionary forces that were based in financial self-interest and cultural nationalism. Rather than attacking political structures directly, these scholars chose to reform politics through the education of a new kind of citizen. They sought to create citizens who were committed to cooperation and open to cultural diversity. Persons' views would necessarily be based on particular experience, but each person would try to coordinate his or her views with those of other individuals. Piaget introduced the problem as follows:

> Contemporary society is an extremely recent phenomenon when compared to the history of mankind. Social occurrences take place today on a new scale, a new plane. All important events in the modern world are international. What happens at one point on our planet has an immediate repercussion all over the world. This interdependence has gradually established itself in every sphere of life. The economics of isolation, purely internal politics, intellectual and moral reactions limited to one group, no longer exist. (p. 4)

It is clear that Piaget's interest was shared by other intellectuals of his day. According to Heilbroner (1970), the post-World War I period witnessed a renewal of the liberal perspective. Mid-19th-century surges of democracy were met with late-century reaction and ultimately with the fractionation that led to nationalistic confrontation in a devastating war. The new liberalism called for a perspective that acknowledged interdependence of nations and engendered a spirit of respect for cultural diversity. Throughout his essay, Piaget was as concerned about adults' adaptation to the problem as he was about children's adaptation. Piaget said that even informed scholars were uncertain of how to proceed beyond traditional boundaries of national, ethnic, and religious truths. In his words, "We are like children faced by the grown-up world" (p. 6).

Piaget's solution is interesting because it expresses for the first time what was to became a lifelong concern in his work. He suggested that educators should try to instill in children, not information, but a "tool" or "intellectual instrument" by which they could begin to develop coordinated knowledge. For this task he chose the model of science that he thought possessed this instrument and was responsible for its monumental successes. Piaget was contrasting 19th-century progress in science to 19th-century chaotic fluctuations in political affairs. Since he understood this instrument to be simultaneously intellectual and moral, the analogy between science and politics fit his argument neatly.

Piaget outlined three explicit benefits of the scientific attitude:

1. It would help diminish egocentric thinking by helping children to see their own intellectual and moral positions in coordination with other positions.
2. It would free children from the social coercion of tradition that imposes beliefs without regard to others' possible beliefs. The

scientific attitude would encourage serious consideration of diverse beliefs and coordination among them.
3. It would bring children into reciprocal relations with other positions.

Piaget elaborated on this point as follows: "Each of us must come to see that his own individual, group, or national world is only one among many other possible worlds. It is this method of confronting points of view which appears to be . . . analogous to the scientific method of coordination" (pp. 12–13).

Piaget then proceeded to consider education as the means by which this instrument might be developed. He proposed that it be formed not "by the old-fashioned school . . . of master and pupil, that is the relation of an inferior who passively obeys to a superior . . ." (p. 24). Rather, the new education would stress: "Group work, common study, self government, etc." This is because "Only a type of education founded upon a social relationship which is of a kind to succeed in uniting adults, will allow of the development of sane moral and international attitudes, and make of our children a finer generation than ourselves" (p. 25).

This essay emphasizes five critical aspects of Piaget's thinking, many of which are usually covert in his writings (Piaget, 1932 a and b). First, it reveals his political stance, which was liberal in the classic sense of that term. Second, it shows him to be a product of his intellectual times in that he shared with other NEF members a stance against the late-19th-century reactionary attempt to replace democracy with enlightened state-regulated capitalism (Heilbroner, 1970). Third, and more to the point of developmental psychology, the essay embodies an early form of Piaget's interest in peer socialization insofar as he argued for its advantages over master–pupil teaching. Fourth, it shows that, at this early date, Piaget understood science to be a social and not an individual enterprise. The operations of science were precisely those that countered the narrowness that came from individualistic thinking. And fifth, it provides a rough draft of his elaborated argument that social communication, reciprocity, and cooperation are the basic means for achieving balanced—later called equilibrated—intellectual and moral knowledge.

It is important to note that this essay does not stand as an isolated piece in the Piagetian corpus. The basic ideas can be found elsewhere, such as in the better-known work on "moral judgment" also published in English in 1932 (Piaget, 1932b). One sees in his conceptualization of moral development an even sharper argument regarding the importance of cooperative relationships. Beginning with young children's commitment to understand the interactions in which they are partners, Piaget builds a systematic case for two streams of development, one emerging from relations of unilateral authority and the other emanating from cooperation among peers. We have covered this argument in detail in previous work (Damon, 1983; Youniss, 1980).

In describing the autonomous moral agent that would ensue from cooperative relations, Piaget (1932b) took explicit care to deny the position that, today, is often attributed to him. He consciously took issue with Kant, who based autonomy on rational calculation so that when pressed for justification, an individual would take recourse in the logical derivation of a principle. Piaget countered that view by arguing for a morality based on mutual respect in which each person would feel both responsible to *justify* his or her position to another person and would, reciprocally, *listen* to the other person's views.

SOCIALIZATION IN PIAGET'S THEORY

In this section we review aspects of Piaget's writings that form a sketch of his theory of socialization. Our main sources for this section are Piaget's (1932b) study of moral judgment and his (1970) review of his general theory. We suggest that it helps for the moment to set aside the usual view that social experience is a means to promote individual development. While Piaget argues for this, he also describes social experience as a means for the child's introduction into and identification with an existing social order. It is the latter that we want to emphasize.

Basic Elements.   Socialization occurs through normal, everyday interactions, wherein the child's actions meet resistance and need to be adjusted to the actions of other persons, as other persons adjust their actions in relation to the child. This point is found throughout Piaget's (1932b) monograph and is emphasized to combat the view that children develop in cognitive isolation from other persons. When the point is coupled with the fact that knowledge is a construction, one sees the broader implications of the theory. First, the main premise of traditional approaches to socialization becomes radically altered. Adults cannot directly transmit ideas to children because their ideas must be reconstructed by the child. Reconstruction fundamentally changes whatever the adult brings to the interaction and transforms it into an understandable scheme in the child's cognitive reality. Second, because ideas are presented in an interactive format, the child's schemes necessarily take account of the adult's position. In this manner, children's schemes are socialized at the point of communicative contact through a normal process of the child's actions meeting resistance when the objects they affect, react, and provide reciprocal effects.

A basic element in Piaget's theory is that children seek order in the realm of the action by abstracting formal invariances from real actions. The process of constructing order necessarily requires that children deal with interactions and not just their own actions. The invariant properties that children abstract would be properties of interactions. Piaget (1932b, p. 360) proposes that the psychological individual cannot exist in isolation from other individuals.

We realize that this point stands in opposition to those commentaries that stress that children are naturally egocentric and must work their way toward the realization that there are other views of reality. Piaget, however, is unambiguous in his argument. If the central task is to construct order from actions, then children must at a very early age realize that other views exist. This is because their actions necessarily run into the actions and intentions of their interactive partners. According to Piaget (1932b), children already at 2 years of age recognize intentions. His argument is that children would concretely experience numerous occasions when their intentions were thwarted by the intervention of intentions from other persons. Hence, they would be maladaptive in believing that their own intentions and actions could alone create results in social situations (Dean & Youniss, 1991).

Role of Relationships.   In his writings during the 1930s, Piaget was adamant about the distinct roles played by different interpersonal relationships in the knowledge acquisition process (Piaget, 1932a, 1932b). He proposed that relationships of unilateral authority generated respect for the views espoused by the authoritative figure. However, such respect lacked a grounding in communicative understanding, because it was not open to development in the classic Piagetian meaning of that concept. This is because construction is one-sided with the result that the child cannot accommodate adequately to the authority figure's initiatives. While children understand that adults bring points of views to interactions, and while children try to grasp adults' views, they end up failing to comprehend adults' perspectives and distort the views toward their own schemes (Piaget, 1932b, p. 36). Piaget subsequently came to call this "sociocentrism" (Piaget, 1970, p. 724).

Piaget contrasted relationships of unilateral authority sharply to relationships of cooperation. In the latter, children act as partners with other persons to co-construct knowledge. Cooperation begins in symmetrical reciprocity, whereby any person can contribute to an interaction with the same act the other person has or will initiate. This elemental fact ultimately leads to exchanges of ideas in processes by which children jointly construct reality. In contrast to unilateral authority, cooperation implies that neither person would hold to a view without attending to the view offered by the other. Hence, the tendency is for each person to build on the other's ideas while explaining his or own ideas to the other. As will be shown later, cooperation thus leads to mutual understanding and contrasts to the alienation of views that tends to result from unilateral authority.

Peers.   Damon (1983) has outlined Piaget's position with respect to the role of peers in the knowledge process and in socialization. In his 1932 writings, Piaget depicted children's relationships with peers as the ideal context for cooperation. His reasoning was that peers would, on the average, have to cooperate to get along since their relationship was based on symmetrical reciprocity. This means that any initiative from one child could be matched by a different initiative from another peer. Hence, peers would tend to be at loggerheads if they were to operate solely according to the principle of symmetry. It is precisely in trying to overcome stalemate that peers would need to develop procedures of cooperation so that each would express points of view that would be heard, and so that each would learn to respect the points of view expressed by others.

In his 1932 monograph, Piaget (1932b) argued strongly that in the process of discovering and practicing procedures that mediate peer cooperation, children form a common sense of social solidarity. This is based on two specific components. The first is reliance on processes that require the cooperation of others. An illustrative process would be arbitrating disputes over rules of games. In order to cultivate democratic procedures, such as debate, discussion, and majority rule, children have to cooperate. Piaget's argument is that continued practice of such procedures would engender a sense of solidarity as a by-product. The second is based in mutual understanding that results from children's communicative exchanges of ideas. As children rely on each other for feedback about ideas, they would come to know one another's views because they were parties to a mutual construction. Thus mutual understanding would produce solidarity in the very ways children came to interpret reality. Not only would experience be shared, but the meaning of the experience would be the product of joint construction.

Morality.   Piaget (1932b) proposed that morality was based on respect for persons rather than respect for tradition or rules. One can see this proposal as the consequence of his broader theory of socialization. Respect for persons is grounded in the processes of human interaction by which knowledge is co-constructed. In keeping with his theory of relationship, Piaget distinguishes between kinds of respect. Unilateral relationships engender respect of authority, but it is precarious because it lacks the ultimate grounding in mutuality. Should competing views between authorities arise, children would lack the procedural calculations by which these views could be analyzed and reassessed. Respect based on cooperation, however, allows views to be submitted to procedures that must follow the norms of reciprocity and discussion.

Throughout the socialization process, children believe that the interaction patterns they find as orderly, are in fact necessary patterns that all other persons share. Piaget illustrated the point by reporting children's beliefs about the origin of rules for games. To paraphrase the typical child: Rules are learned from older children who learned rules from their fathers who, in turn, learned rules from their fathers. Piaget proposed that children want to learn these rules because they believe that in doing so, they themselves become like adults and get closer to seeing reality as adults see it. In this regard, Piaget's socialization process leads to acquiring culture and identification with what children believe to be the root of culture—adults' views of it.

The final point in our analysis is that for Piaget, culture is not a static entity but consists in ways of interacting by which persons co-construct knowledge. Piaget makes this point quite powerfully when he describes the characteristics of the autonomous moral individual. We are aware that this hypothetical individual has already been depicted in the literature as the person who can think logically and, in moments of dispute, can turn to reason to justify his or her position. This depiction does not accurately reflect Piaget's own view on the matter. To show what that view is, we allow Piaget (1932b) to speak for himself: The autonomous self "takes up its stand on the norms of reciprocity and objective discussion, and knows how to submit to these in order to make itself respected" (pp. 95–96). Autonomy entails learning how "to understand the other person and be understood by him" (p. 95) and is based on "the norm of reciprocity in sympathy" (p. 107).

POINTS OF RESISTANCE

Reaction—and resistance—to Piaget's moral theory has been replete with ironies of distortion and misapprehension. The strangest of these ironies is that many of those who have considered themselves Piagetians—most notably Kohlberg and his followers—have approached moral development in a diametrically opposite manner from Piaget. A more aggravating irony is that other work, springing from a more empiricist tradition, has been so misdirected as actually to discredit Piaget's moral theory without accurately representing it in the first place. This is because many of the experimental research programs intended to test Piaget's moral judgment theory were directed at phenomena that were largely peripheral to Piaget's major claims, or in some cases even directed at claims that Piaget never really made.

To his credit, Kohlberg did more than any other individual to resuscitate

Piaget's moral judgment work from the obscurity to which it had fallen by the late 1950s. In fact, in many ways Kohlberg's bold and seminal work recaptured the entire area of moral development for the field of psychology. Once Kohlberg published his ground-breaking dissertation, the empirical study of people's moral beliefs and the growth thereof again became a legitimate topic for scientific researchers. It has remained so ever since. Kohlberg (1963, 1969) considered himself a Piagetian and placed his own studies squarely within the Genevan tradition. The immediate popularity of Kohlberg's work gave new life both to Piaget's theory and to the topic of moral development.

In this context, however, it must be noted that Kohlberg presented his dissertation — as well as the 1963 *Vita Humana* (now *Human Development*) article that reported it — as a repudiation of Piaget's central thesis in *The Moral Judgment of the Child*. Piaget had based his developmental position on the notion that children live within two moral worlds, the one arising from their relations with adults and the other arising from their relations with peers. Kohlberg rejected this notion entirely and set out to disprove it.

On the surface, Kohlberg's argument with Piaget may seem like a minor dispute within the coherent "cognitive–development approach" (Kohlberg's [1969] term, significantly, not Piaget's). Yet in actuality the difference is not a minor one at all. It represents radically separate views about what moral judgment is, where it comes from, how it changes during ontogenesis, and how it is linked to social action.

Simultaneous but Separate Spheres. For Piaget, the child's values are functionally tied to the social contexts in which the child is embedded. Children operate in two main spheres, with adults and with peers. These two spheres engender — and demand — different sorts of values. To live within the adult world, children need to acquire respect for authority, social tradition, and the established order of things. To live within the peer world, children need to acquire mutual respect for one another, an ability to cooperate with equals, and a sense that rules and other social standards may be negotiated and modified through agreed-upon procedures of fairness. *Both* sets of values are required for adaptation to the childhood social universe. They can, and do, coexist during the main part of childhood; and the child's gradual shift to the peer-oriented values is more a result of changing life circumstances than stage-like cognitive transformations.

Like other American social scientists of the late 1950s, Kohlberg no doubt read Piaget's moral judgment work in light of Piaget's structuralist writings on logical reasoning — the most formalistic of which, the book on formal operations, had just been published in English (Inhelder & Piaget, 1958). (The book had been translated, to complete the ironies, by the renowned chronicler-to-be of postchildhood heteronomous morality, Stanley Milgram). To Kohlberg, Piaget's insistence on two simultaneous sets of moral values in one child must have seemed like a simple early-career error by the Swiss structuralist-to-be. How could a child juggle such conflicting ideas without quickly trying to resolve them? Kohlberg believed that a mind could not be divided against itself for long.

Kohlberg's own resolution was that there was only one dominant childhood structure of morality, a structure that resembled Piaget's heteronomy: Adult-centered, blindly obedient to authority, rigidly loyal to those in charge. All other forms of morality, Kohlberg believed, bore a strictly developmental relation to this original authoritarian view. Later in life, other forms arose from this primitive one and went beyond it both structurally and functionally. The forms of mutual respect and peer fairness that Piaget described, therefore, showed up in Kohlberg's stage descriptions only after childhood had passed.

Empirically, Kohlberg's position proved problematical, as work by Damon (1977), Eisenberg (1982), and Youniss (1980) showed. Even at a very early age, children express—and act on—rich and robust notions of kindness, sharing, fairness, reciprocity, and other peer-oriented moral standards. They hold these notions at the same time that they avow deep respect for authority and traditional rules (Damon, 1980). It is not at all uncommon to hear a child say in one breath that he would always do whatever Mom tells him, and then in the next breath that he would share his bike with his friend even if Mom said not to, because his friend had always been generous with him (Damon, 1983).

Practical and Theoretical Modes.   But even more problematical than the empirical anomalies of Kohlberg's position were its theoretical vulnerabilities. Because of its extreme holism and cognitivism, Kohlberg's approach lost much of the explanatory power of Piaget's original formulation. At the same time, ironically, these very choices that Kohlberg made as a departure from Piaget's original treatise cast doubt on Piaget's own approach. Once Kohlberg had appropriated the "cognitive–developmental" position for his own particular view of things, implausible claims and assumptions about moral behavior forever became associated with Piagetianism in the public mind.

An illustration of this can be found in how the two theorists handled the judgment–conduct relation. The relation between judgment and conduct is of course at the center of most psychologists' concern with moral judgment. Generally, statements of moral belief are seen as interesting only insofar as they reveal propensities toward actual social conduct. Piaget did not wrestle with this problem *per se,* but his account of children's rule following in a marbles game makes clear that he approached judgment and conduct as inseparable systems of action. Rather, Piaget distinguished between practical and theoretical modes of behavior: The practical occurs on the plane of direct action, the theoretical on the plane of consciousness. Piaget proposed a developmental relation between the two. First the child works out the conception of rules in the course of actual play with peers, then later the child grasps in consciousness a symbolic representation of this once-practical conception. For Piaget, therefore, the origins of both judgment and conduct are to be found in the child's behavior within social relations. The child's theoretical and hypothetical reasoning about morality comes later, a developmental product of the earlier practical activity.

Kohlberg drew the distinction differently and turned Piaget's proposed developmental relation on its head. Rather than contrasting practical to theoretical moral activity, Kohlberg (1971) contrasted judgment to action. Although closer to our commonsense way of viewing morality, the judgment/ action split is impossible to conceptualize with any clarity. Does a verbal statement (say, Patrick Henry's "Give me liberty or give me death!") represent judgment or conduct? Are the two ever really separated in reality? Even in the throes of embattled action, is there not judgment? Even in the solitude of reflection, is there not action? Piaget avoided this problem by focusing on modes of action (practical versus theoretical) that are closely attached to distinct contexts of behavior (real-life vs. hypothetical).

Kohlberg's view of the relation between the two (which he generally conceptualized as "reasoning" vs. "action") presented even more difficulties. His methods of interrogation and analysis, of course, were entirely dedicated toward identifying a subject's stage of reasoning about hypothetical moral issues. The problem for Kohlberg then became determining how well this reasoning stage would predict how the subject behaved in "real life" (that is, outside the interview situation). Inevitably this led Kohlberg to a model of prediction that gave priority to reasoning as the primary agent in the construction of moral behavior.

The original Kohlbergian assumption was that people acquire moral beliefs as part of their intellectual development. Moral reasoning was closely linked to other intellectual achievements — particularly logic and role taking, both of which were seen as necessary though not sufficient for higher stages of moral judgment. The process of moral growth in Kohlberg's eyes was a process of "figuring out" the right thing to do. The problem of "real-life" moral behavior, then, became simply a problem in application: Would subjects apply the moral principles that they had "figured out" to their own conduct in various life circumstances? In his early writings, Kohlberg assumed that, in the long run, they would; because it is a human tendency (à la cognitive dissonance theory) for people to resolve internal contradictions among their own beliefs and acts. There may be momentary gaps between reasoning and action (as when fear prevents persons from "living up to" their moral principles). But eventually there will be coherence, either through adoption of more noble behavior or through distortion and forced regression in one's moral reasoning.

Too many inconclusive experimental results, plus an extended foray into the real-world cauldron of educational reform, led Kohlberg to rethink his views on reasoning and action. Clearly the children and adults he had observed were not behaving in a manner that could be directly predicted from their moral stages. In a somewhat patchwork fashion, Kohlberg added Durkheimian notions such as societal perspective and moral atmosphere to his explanatory model. But he never retreated from his belief in the priority of an individual's reasoning. He saw this as the best entry point for intervention as well as the true causal agent in an individual's moral conduct. Parameters of the social context remain situational factors that could facilitate or hinder the application of the individual's moral beliefs about what is right.

It is not, of course, possible to know exactly how Piaget would have addressed the whole complex of issues surrounding moral conduct. His treatment of these issues was limited to the developmental account that he sketched in his one book on the matter. But Piaget's own approach, however limited, avoided many of the pitfalls created by Kohlberg's revised "cognitive–developmentalism."

For one thing, Piaget's theory assumes no fundamental split between reasoning and action: Thought is a form of action, derivative of praxis-based forms, but with a capacity to operate on the plane of mental representation. Thus it is meaningless to split moral reasoning and moral conduct in order to discuss their "relation." Instead, it becomes possible to speak of the reasoning elements — such as intention, evaluation, choice — that are an essential part of any moral act.

For another thing, Piaget's theory places absolutely no priority on reasoning over any other component of moral behavior. If anything, at least developmentally, Kohlberg's priority on reasoning reverses Piaget's. Practical activity, writes Piaget, precedes and shapes the intellectualized consciousness that grows out of it.

Individuals in Society.   But most importantly, Piaget's moral work sets moral development and moral behavior firmly in the social relations that engender morality. For Piaget, individual moral judgment is always adaptive to social situations. As the child's primary social situation moves from the family to the peer group, the child develops a new form of morality in response. There are key cognitive processes that are implicated in this development; but these cognitive processes always go hand in hand with the child's shifting social circumstances, *because their function is to adapt to these circumstances.* Piaget's view of intelligence-as-adaptation prevented him from disconnecting the moral reasoner from the moral actor, or the individual moral agent from the social context. In this regard, he was far closer to Durkheim than to Kohlberg; although of course Piaget argued vehemently against Durkheim's singular focus on the constraining and authoritative elements of morality. For Piaget, unlike Durkheim, morality grew out of not one but two social relations in childhood; and the child played an active role in constructing moral meaning out of this bifurcated social experience. Piaget's "moral child," therefore was less socially isolated than Kohlberg's and more mentally active than Durkheim's.

Misdirected Research.   Piaget's social-relational position was lost not only on Kohlberg but on most of the psychological research community. The most dramatic examples of this were the host of experiments on moral intentionality carried out after the publication of Piaget's moral judgment book in English. By far the most famous experimental finding in the book was the intentions/consequences sequence suggested by Piaget's "15 broken cups" dilemma. Children's judgments that were based on considerations of intentions ("he did worse because he was trying to steal jam") represented what Piaget called "subjective responsibility." Piaget reported that these subjective judgments usually appeared later in a child's life than "objective" judgments that are based on consequences ("he did worse because he broke more cups"). Piaget's report of children's actual judgments, however, clearly revealed that even young children understood both intention and consequences as potentially operative factors in judgment (Dean & Youniss, 1991).

Moral intentionality became the "conservation" of the moral development field. It provided psychologists with a means of testing (and criticizing) Piaget's theory by seeing whether they could get a higher-level response from children who were supposedly too young to provide such according to Piaget. As in the conservation literature, the experiments were carried out in hundreds of different ways, some quite foreign to anything that Piaget had in mind when he described the phenomena. And, as in the conservation literature, an uninterpretable *mélange* of findings were produced over a decade or so of intense experimentation. Some researchers replicated Piaget's reported findings. Others, by altering situational variables in the dilemma, managed to get very young children to make judgments based on considerations of intentions.

The problem for this whole literature was that Piaget never intended to locate the shift from objective to subjective responsibility solely in the child's intellectual abilities. Rather, commensurate with Piaget's entire position, he located this shift in the gradual transformation taking place within the child's social world.

Demands of Social Construction. As the child spends more and more time in peer interaction, different sorts of social necessities come to the fore. Unlike the child's relations with adults—where adults need to be obeyed, no matter what—the peer relation requires negotiation, compromise, a continual "meeting of the minds." In this kind of setting, the child becomes forced to take others' intentions into account. Enough experience in such settings does indeed facilitate the development of a new cognitive perspective, more attuned to the inner mental life; but Piaget did not make the claim that such insights about others' thinking could not appear at an earlier time. In Piaget's moral book—unlike in his earlier work on language or his later work on space—it is social, rather than mental, decentration that is portrayed as the main mover of judgmental change during the childhood years. So it is not surprising—and not at all a critical test of Piaget's theory—that, by altering key situational variables, contemporary researchers could get children to make intentional moral judgments. Piaget was interested in moral intentionality not as a milestone of mental progress but as a feature of social relationships, a feature that, in the peer world at least, children must mutually coordinate for optimal adaptation.

In the course of managing features of social interaction such as the intentions of others, children construct their social and moral intelligence. This is the heart of Piaget's position on social construction and for us the most profound distinguishing mark of Piaget's approach.

Again, the contrast to Kohlberg could not be more dramatic. For Kohlberg, intellectual development was a relatively self-contained process. Just as he gave priority to the relation between "judgment" and "action," so too he gave priority to intellectual reasoning in the process of developmental change. Moral judgment, he believed, derived developmentally from insights about role taking, which in turn derived from logical skills—all of which stood in a kind of nesting relation with one another, with logic being necessary but not sufficient for role taking and role taking being necessary but not sufficient for moral judgment. Kohlberg, of course, also saw some role for social influence. He wrote of social dimensions such as the complexity of social systems, as well as social experiences such as education and work, as spurs to moral growth (Kohlberg & Higgins, 1987). But the primary driving force in Kohlberg's developmental scheme was the individual's reasoning, a process of "figuring out" what is right.

In Piaget's position, we have found a more promising way of looking at social influence and developmental change. Piaget begins with the relationship, determines its qualities, identifies the opportunities that these qualities offer its participants as well as the constraints that they place upon them, and from there draws conclusions about the relationship's developmental impact. Of course, Piaget was by no means a social determinist, and he never lost sight of the individual's construction of meaning within the relationship. But, at least in his moral judgment book (as well as in his untranslated essays on sociology), he gives the social relationship a prior and operative role in the individual's development (Chapman, 1986; see also Chapman, this volume).

It is this relational perspective that we have emphasized in this chapter, partly because this is a part of Piaget that is little known and partly because we both have drawn heavily on Piaget's fertile position in our own work (Damon, 1977, 1983; Damon & Colby, 1987; Youniss, 1980, 1981, 1987). For us, Piaget's account of social construction is all the more valuable because he did manage to balance it with an account of the individual's role in the meaning-making process.

There are not many developmental theorists who have been able to navigate between the opposing hazards of extreme individualism and extreme social determinism. Vygotsky is certainly another and the virtues of his approach are well appreciated at present (Vygotsky, 1978; Wertsch, 1987). Perhaps because Vygotsky wrote so much less than Piaget, his theory has not met with the resistance that Piaget's has. Ironically, Piaget's theory has met with quite contradictory points of resistance. There are those, such as the social learning theorists and the radical social constructivists, who have found the theory hopelessly cognitive and universalistic; and there are those, such as Kohlberg, who have found it not enough oriented toward global structures of individual thought. We, however, have taken a different message from Piaget's moral judgment work, and have found in this message a good starting point for understanding the role of social construction in development.

A CONTEMPORARY VIEW ON PEER CULTURE

In his writings during the 1930s, Piaget addressed the neglected importance of peer interaction and the sense of solidarity that resulted from the practice of cooperation. He did not use the term peer culture, but his description is similar to that found in contemporary writers. For present purposes, we review the work of Corsaro (1985), who has conceptualized peer culture in an insightful way. It is interesting that Corsaro (Corsaro & Eder, 1990; Corsaro & Rizzo, 1988) views his work as perhaps at odds with Piaget's major emphasis. We obviously, differ with regard to this aspect of his thinking because we see agreement on fundamental issues. In particular, Corsaro believes that Piaget proposed that the primary function of inter-personal experience was to promote "individual development." Whatever truth this view contains, we believe that Piaget was also concerned with the function of interpersonal experience in promoting cultural identity. This possible difference aside, we propose to describe the points on which

Corsaro's contemporary thinking extends ideas that Piaget proposed in his early work.

First, Corsaro, emphasized the importance of peer experience in children's social development. Peer experience is not viewed as an "apprenticeship for adult society" but is seen as the means for establishing peer culture in its own right. In this regard, Corsaro, like Piaget, stands apart from the mainstream of socialization theorists who view peer experiences either as teaching the rudiments of adult society or as a potential source of deviance from adult society's norms.

Second, Corsaro proposed that children's socialization is a collective process that occurs in public rather than an individual process that takes place in private reflection. A chief task of childhood is to construct knowledge, not primarily for oneself, but for a community of persons who share the same sense of culture (Corsaro & Eder, 1990, p. 199). Knowledge is not constructed for its own or the individual's sake but is directed to mutual understanding with other persons (Cook–Gumperz & Corsaro, 1977).

Third, Corsaro proposed that "By interacting and negotiating with others [children] establish understanding that become fundamental social knowledge on which they continually build" (Corsaro & Eder, 1990, p. 200). In this regard, children create a culture in which they co-construct the procedures by which meaning can be socially created and re-created. And fourth, children do not become socialized by internalizing adult culture. Rather, they "become part of adult culture and contribute to its reproduction through their negotiations with adults and their creative reproduction of a series of peer cultures with other children" (p. 201).

We propose that Corsaro's analysis agrees with Piaget's on three fundamental points and carries them a step further than Piaget toward a more complete view of negotiation.

Knowledge is co-constructed through interactions and is negotiated in the interactive process. It can be argued that Piaget's writings on social development were ignored in part because his view of the knowledge process clashed so sharply with those of standard socialization theories, which emphasized transmission of items and their internalization. In a constructivist approach, items are reconstituted in the process of interaction so that they become negotiated into new items apropos the schemes of the persons involved.

Corsaro and Piaget would agree that meaning is constructed by the procedures being used and, Piaget would add, by the structure of the relationship between the persons. In a sense, the content of the items recedes in importance relative to the mutuality of meaning that is established. While content remains important, the key to identification is more the procedures that allow the persons to continue to produce meaning while remaining within a common framework. This fact takes account of the close connection between the generative character of social knowledge and the social means by which it is reproduced. "The structural properties of social systems are both medium and outcome of the practices they recursively organize" (Giddens, as cited by Corsaro & Eder, 1990, p. 200).

Peer experience is not incidental to "primary" socialization but is part of the child's overall socialization.   Corsaro, as Piaget, proposes that peer socialization is primary and constitutes an important domain that contributes uniquely to children's social development. Corsaro focuses on the fact that peer interaction has patterns that pertain to it and may not be evident in interactions with adults. Rather than stressing their differences from adult patterns, however, Corsaro emphasizes that in adopting these patterns, children learn how to co-construct reliably with other persons in a shared social system. For instance, children learn about the procedures that mediate sharing, participation, dealing with concerns publicly, and resisting adult authority.

There is little doubt that the peer aspects of Piaget's writings were a deterrent to their being recognized as relevant to concerns of major socialization theorists. In many theories, peer experience was construed as a source of deviance from adult, normative socialization. Corsaro, as Piaget, has tried to demonstrate that recurrent patterns of peer interaction are not "deviant" but replicate norms that adults would want to convey. As Piaget, Corsaro recognizes that peers, compared with adults, may be better able to produce these norms because they are in a reciprocal relationship. An example is seen in pretend play during which children cooperatively co-construct story lines, being individually creative while they also take account of the other person's contribution to their evolving construction (Garvey, 1977; Cook–Gumperz & Corsaro, 1977).

Peer and adult cultures are not separated by a barrier that needs special remedial work for reconciliation.   Corsaro has proposed that peer culture is a separate construction from the culture that is constructed through adult–child interactions. However, there is not a single peer culture that is created once and retained thereafter. Rather, children are pictured as continuously involved in reconstructing peer cultures in a time series running from the preschool through the adolescent years. The practical consequence is that the patterns one finds, let us say, in very young children, are not fixed for life but are themselves open to reconstruction in a developmental fashion. Piaget recognizes this point in arguing that children develop procedures in a progressive manner in order to help them sustain cooperative relationships. Tit-for-tat exchanges may be adequate for a peer relationship between 5-year-old children, but that form must be transformed to allow for compromise and negotiation when disputes arise between adolescent friends (Youniss & Smollar, 1985).

Corsaro also recognizes the presence of two worlds and addresses their relation by showing how peer culture is bridged with adult culture. Corsaro (1985) recognizes that children experience peer interactions at the same time they experience interactions with adults. It would be unimaginable that children keep the respective experiences totally apart. Corsaro suggests that many properties of one culture are brought into the other. For instance, children may transport notions of age, size, and intelligence into the peer culture, when they otherwise would not consider them important for peer interactions. Since coexistence with peers and adults persists through time, the crossing between them must be continuous. It is noted, however, that crossing entails reconstruction as data from one domain are adapted to the other domain. The long-range effect is that the original separation becomes permeable and content from the two relations may interact over the course of development.

CONCLUSION

In this chapter, we have made the case that Piaget's approach to social construction was both more farsighted and more revolutionary than many have realized. It took seriously the origins of thought in social interaction while not veering as far toward social determinism as Durkheim had done previously, or as the American social learning theorists and social constructivists were to do subsequently. Although Piaget's theory had been misrepresented by its followers such as Kohlberg as well as by its legion of detractors, it offers an unusually plausible account of how persons construct meaning in the course of their social transactions. With the single exception of Vygotskian theory, it stands alone among developmental approaches in its capacity to explain how the quality of particular social experience influences the nature of the ideas and values that arise from that experience. For this reason, Piaget's theory remains valuable for those, such as ourselves, who are interested in the social construction of knowledge, as well as for those, such as Corsaro, who are interested in the social construction of culture. Our hope is that, when properly understood, Piaget's theory can be exploited to its full potential.

REFERENCES

Bruner, J. S., Goodnow, J. J., & Austin, G. A. (1956). *A study of thinking.* New York: Wiley.
Chapman, M. (1986). The structure of exchange: Piaget's sociological theory. *Human Developmental, 29,* 181–194.

Cook-Gumperz, J., & Corsaro, W. A. (1977). Social ecological constraints on children's communicative strategies. *Sociology, 11,* 411–434.

Corsaro, W. A. (1985). *Friendship and peer culture in the early years.* Norwood, NJ: Ablex.

Corsaro, W. A., & Eder, D. (1990). Children's peer cultures. *Annual Review of Sociology, 16,* 197–220.

Corsaro, W. A., & Rizzo, T. A. (1988). *Discussione* and friendship: Socialization processes in the peer culture of Italian nursery school children. *American Sociological Review, 53,* 879–894.

Damon, W. (1977). *The social world of the child.* San Francisco: Jossey–Bass.

Damon, W. (1980). Patterns of change in children's social reasoning. *Child Development, 51,* 1010–1017.

Damon, W. (1983). *Social and personality development.* New York: Norton.

Damon, W. (1988). *The moral child: Nurturing children's natural moral growth.* New York: Free Press.

Damon, W., & Colby, A. (1987). Social influence and moral change. In W. M. Kurtines & J. L. Gewirtz (Eds.), *Social interaction and sociomoral development.* New York: Wiley.

Dean, A. L., & Youniss, J. (1991). The transformation of Piagetian theory by American psychology: The early competence issue. In M. Chapman & M. Chandler (Eds.), *Criteria for competence.* Hillsdale, NJ: Lawrence, Erlbaum Associates.

Eisenberg, N. (Ed.). (1982). *The development of prosocial behavior.* New York: Academic Press.

Flavell, J. H. (1962). Historical and bibliographic note. In W. Kessen & C. Kuhlman (Eds.), *Thought in the young child. Monographs of the Society for Research in Child Development,* V 27 (Serial No. 83).

Garvey, C. (1977). *Play.* Cambridge, MA: Harvard University Press.

Heilbroner, R. L. (1970). *Between capitalism and socialism.* New York: Vintage Books.

Inhelder, B., & Piaget, J. (1958). *The growth of logical thinking from childhood to adolescence.* New York: Basic Books.

Kohlberg, L. (1963). The development of children's orientations toward a moral order: I. Sequence in the development of moral thought. *Vita Humana, 6,* 11–33.

Kohlberg, L. (1969). Stage and sequence: The cognitive–developmental approach to socialization. In D. A. Goslin (Ed.), *Handbook of socialization theory and research.* Chicago: Rand McNally.

Kohlberg, L. (1971). From is to ought: How to commit the naturalistic fallacy and get away with it in the study of moral development. In T. Mishel (Ed.), *Cognitive development and epistemology.* New York: Academic Press.

Kohlberg, L., & Higgins, A. (1987). School democracy and social interaction. In W. M. Kurtines, & J. L. Gewirtz (Eds.), *Social interaction and sociomoral development.* New York: Wiley.

Piaget, J. (1932a). Social evolution and the new education. *Education Tomorrow,* No. 4. London: New Education Fellowship.

Piaget, J. (1932b). *The moral judgment of the child.* London: Routledge & Kegan Paul.

Piaget, J. (1970). Piaget's theory. In P. H. Mussen (Ed.), *Carmichael's manual of child psychology.* New York: Wiley.

Vygotsky, L. (1978). *Mind in society: The development of higher psychological processes.* Cambridge, MA: Harvard University Press.

Wertsch, J. V. (1987). *Vygotsky and the social formation of mind.* Cambridge, MA: Harvard University Press.

Youniss, J. (1980). *Parents and peers in social development.* Chicago: University of Chicago Press.

Youniss, J. (1981). An analysis of moral development through a theory of social construction. *Merrill–Palmer Quarterly, 27,* 384–403.

Youniss, J. (1983). Piaget and the self constituted through relations. In W. F. Overton (Ed.), *The relationship between social and cognitive development.* Hillsdale, NJ: Lawrence Erlbaum Associates.

Youniss, J. (1987). Social construction and moral development: Update and expansion. In W. M. Kurtines & J. L. Gewirtz (Eds.), *Social interaction and sociomoral development.* New York: Wiley.

Youniss, J., & Smollar, J. (1985). *Adolescent relations with mothers, fathers, and friends* Chicago: University of Chicago Press.

13

Restructuring and Constructivism: The Development of American Educational Reform

Frank B. Murray
University of Delaware

After the launch of Sputnik in 1957 and throughout the crises over civil rights in the 1970s, Piagetian theory dominated the discourse about educational research and practice. This dominance is puzzling for two reasons. First, Piaget and his collaborators actually wrote very little over the years about either education or schooling (e.g., Ginsburg, 1981; Murray, 1979). Second, subsequent researchers have found correlations between schooling and individual performance only among some of the higher-level Piagetian tasks (e.g., Goodnow & Bethon, 1966). Nevertheless, because Piaget and his collaborators in Geneva were virtually the only psychologists before the 1960s to write about how children understand concepts that are actually parts of school curricula, educators and others quickly turned to them whenever education and schooling were thought to be in crisis.

THE SPUTNIK CRISIS (1960s) AND THE CIVIL RIGHTS CRISIS (1970s)

The driving principle behind some educational reforms proposed in the 1960s and early 1970s was perceived by Bruner (1961) and others as a direct implication of Piaget's theory: Any academic subject can be taught to any child of any age in some intellectually honest form. This sweeping inference led to the so-called spiral curriculum approach in which every subject worthy of an adult's attention was thought to be teachable throughout the school years in ways that reflect the particular constraints and powers at each stage of intellectual development.

Ironically, the hypothesis that any subject can be taught at any age with integrity could just as well be seen as incompatible with Piaget's theory, insofar as the postulated discontinuities between each stage, or the qualitative changes that legitimatize the declaration of a new stage, threaten the integrity and honesty of the discipline. The links between engaging, for instance, in preschool geo-board activities and understanding the theorems of Euclid, or between learning, say, the letters of the alphabet and comprehending *The Scarlet Letter* or *The Letter Purple,* are too distant to support an intellectually valid — or even a developmentally interesting — set of connections between the former kind of learning and the latter. Yet other links, which seem equally strained on first appearance, may be rooted strongly enough in cognitive development to justify, in fact, the spiral curriculum approach. According to Piagetian theory, thematic links do exist between the sequential stages of learning. Earlier stages do provide necessary bases, even if insufficient ones, for learning that occurs later on. These links, sometimes referred to as the *vertical décalage,* support the construction of a spiral curriculum. For example, a complicated notion such as density has its conceptual underpinnings in the conservations of weight and volume, which in turn have their footings in the ideas of identity, correspondence, and object permanence.

Like the patterns of earlier reforms, those based in the 1960s on the tests and measurements made by the Genevan group inadvertently left out — or deliberately ignored — poor children and children from minority groups. Children from these sectors were overrepresented in special education, school dropouts, and suspensions; they were underrepresented in gifted programs and college attendance (e.g., Howe, 1990; Irvine, 1990; Goodlad & Keating, 1990). Over the decades, such educational policies as tracking, ability grouping, and supporting school finances on local property taxes have built up, singly (or in some combination), a legacy that now serves only to reduce educational opportunities for some minority pupils (Oakes, 1985).

Piaget's theory of intelligence showed some promise in the 1970s for the education of children who had not profited from traditional schooling. His theory held that the structure of intelligence and intellectual development is universal and relatively insensitive to cultural and social differences. In addition, because his theory seemed to focus on what the child *could* do as opposed to what he *could not* do, it also proved an attractive ideological alternative to the prevailing psychometric approach of organizing instructional groups (summarized in Maccoby & Zellner, 1970; Hooper & DeFain, 1974; Schwebel & Raph, 1973; Hunt, 1961). As a result, many planners selected, sometimes hastily, the basic cognitive tasks of Piagetian theory when they searched for teachable skills for preparatory and compensatory education projects. The open-education plan of the British Infant School Movement had already been rationalized in terms of Piagetian theory. Thus, the calls to transplant an open-education plan to American preschool and primary education served only to reinforce calls for further applications of Piagetian theory.

Unfortunately, the slow introduction of the spiral curricula in the 1960s and the focus on training in basis skills during the 1970s were both accomplished at the expense of some gains made by the progressive education movement, which was credited with the state of educational decline that had made Sputnik possible (see Cremin, 1961). While the progressive recommendations of child-centeredness and the pupil's active discovery fared well in the Piagetian-inspired reforms, the Dewey emphasis on collaboration and cooperation in learning, and the recognition that the pupil's *genuine* interest is a prerequisite condition for learning and development, lost ground in the immediate post-Sputnik reforms (Stedman & Smith, 1983). The critical role of collaboration and cooperation in Piaget's account of the child's intellectual development was needlessly overlooked or minimized by educational reformers and other commentators (see, for example, Cohen, 1983, and Murray, 1985a). With the noticeable exception of the social interaction training techniques (for a review, see Murray, 1986), the "Piagetian" reformers devised pedagogical techniques that assigned pupils to work alone in discovering or inventing the principles at the core of logic and science.

THE NATION-AT-RISK CRISIS

By 1981 the nation could no longer ignore the fact that performance on the SAT (The Scholastic Aptitude Test) had been declining steadily each year since the end of the schoolyear in 1963. This decline and the relatively poor performance of the nation's best high school students in international comparisons (Ogle & Alsalam, 1990), bolstered by the nation's weakened economic position, led a special federal commission to conclude that the quality of schooling was unacceptably low and the entire nation was thus at risk. They, and the authors of scores of subsequent reports, called for yet another reform and restructuring of American schools (Elmore & Associates, 1990).

In Piagetian terms, this time the American educational system's *assimilation* of the major new reform ideas required an *accommodation* or *restructuring,* in place of the "nondevelopmental" innovations that usually characterize educational reform (Goodlad, 1990). Because very little in the schools can be simply increased or decreased productively, a new "stage" in the development of American schooling, a new "equilibrated state," was advocated for schools, even though the **Nation-at-risk** reformers initially thought the schools could remain pretty much at their current stage and meet the nation's needs simply by increasing the amount of time available for instruction. **Restructuring** in both the political and Genevan senses was called for because the very form or structure of education had to be changed. Not only did a full and diverse range of pupils, massive amounts of new curricular information, and new missions need accommodating but so did the centrality of the newly "empowered" teacher who had earlier been displaced by the "teacher-proof" aspects introduced into the classroom through many of the spiral curricula.

The current American educational crisis, unlike the earlier Sputnik and civil rights crises, was defined almost entirely by the poor performance of American students on standardized tests of academic information and skill. The poorest performance on the National Assessment of Educational Progress tests (NAEP) was on those items that required the student to use higher levels of cognitive functioning. Scores on the basic skills items were good by comparison. Nearly every school district in the nation was performing above average, the so-called Lake Wobegon effect, in comparison with the normed results of basic skills tests a decade earlier (Linn, Graue, & Sanders, 1990; Shanker, 1989).

Apparently the schools were succeeding in the areas of basic skills. These areas, the easiest to teach and evaluate, were the ones emphasized in the headstart programs and early childhood interventions of the late 1970s. However, other areas, addressed in the post-Sputnik reforms and subsequently ignored in the reforms of the 1970s, now stood out as the very areas of greatest educational weakness (Educational Testing Service, 1990).

Given these circumstances, can Piaget's theory again provide guidance to educational reformers as it had in the 1960s following the Sputnik crises and throughout the 1970s during the civil rights crises when the nation addressed the same weaknesses in schooling?

CONSTRAINTS ON THE IMPLICATIONS OF PSYCHOLOGICAL THEORIES FOR EDUCATION

Our ability to derive educational practices from theoretical propositions depends on three factors: our ability to think clearly and make valid deductions; the truth of the theoretical proposition under review; and the truth of the educational practice linked to that proposition. We have a measure of control over two of these factors — our ability to make proper deductions and our ability to determine empirically whether a practice accomplishes what it is supposed to accomplish.

The truth of theoretical propositions is always in doubt because it is possible to derive sound practices from both true and false theoretical propositions (Murray, 1989). Thus, we cannot establish the truth of a theoretical proposition by demonstrating that an educational practice works even when the practice can be derived unambiguously from a proposition in the theory. On the other hand, a theoretical proposition can be disproved, or found to be false, should a properly deduced practice prove to be unsound.

We can expect, as a result, that many sound educational practices, like discovery learning, can be derived validly from propositions in Piagetian theory and from those in other theories such as Skinner's or Vygotsky's, which, in other respects, are clearly incompatible with certain Genevan propositions about the development of intelligence. Montessori school practices are, for example, compatible with Piaget's theory (Elkind, 1976; Gardner, 1966), even though the theories of Montessori and of Piaget are quite different. Progressive education, for example, made as much sense as an outgrowth of Dewey's account of thinking as it did as an implication of Piaget's view of intelligence (Seltzer, 1977).

Owing to the vagueness in the propositions of many psychological theories, including Piaget's, we can expect different, sometimes contradictory, educational practices being derived from the same theoretical principles. What, for example, is the role of language in schooling based on Piaget's theory? How should the role change in each successive developmental stage? Several possibilities could be considered; they range from giving language a minor role, particularly in the primary grades (e.g., Furth, 1978), to giving it the major role it currently has as teacher talk dominates the classroom (Hawley & Rosenholtz, 1984).

J. McVicker Hunt (1961) argued, in this connection, that the *match* between the pupil's stage of cognitive development and the demands of the curriculum are implied in Piaget's theory for schooling. Hans Alebi (cited in Flavell, 1963), on the other hand, took Piaget's theory to mean that the pupil, regardless of grade level, needs to have curriculum material presented in a way that recapitulates the entire set of prior stages. Recently, Granott (1991) has also provided evidence that microdevelopment follows the lines of macrodevelopment. For Hunt, the teacher of adolescents can thus presume that the student's formal operational competence can be addressed directly in the lesson. For Alebi and Granott, the teacher of adolescents needs to begin the lesson with some sensorimotor representation, followed by a figural representation of the lesson's content, and so forth until the lesson can be approached in the way that the teacher who accepts Hunt's perspective had already assumed in the first place.

By far the most serious constraint on the usefulness of Piaget's theory for educational practice, apart from the uncertainty in the logical link between theoretical propositions and the practices implemented in their name, is its narrow focus. Piaget's theory is really about a very limited span of the school curriculum, namely, about information that is true by necessity and those possibilities that can be made true by necessity. Of all the possibilities that are true, only a small number is true by necessity, and Piaget's theory is about the development of that small, but vitally important, segment of what, over the life-span, we come to know as necessarily true. (For an explication of the connection between operativity and necessity, see Murray, 1990.)

The theory is also exclusively about the *epistemic subject,* the pure knower, whose competence as a "knower" is unaffected by any other factor that influences cognition in real life. Thus, the theory is about the optimal school situation in which the pupil, as an epistemic subject, engages the curriculum without regard to the inevitable limitations that accrue through a real pupil's inattention, failure to recall prerequisite information, and any of the other factors that depress the pupil's mastery of school tasks.

The theory appears to be clearer in *proscription* than in *prescription.* For example, the theory holds that preoperational or concrete operational pupils will not succeed in understanding lessons about the product–moment relationships in the beam balance even though they may learn the jargon and formula associated with the relationship, and even though they may have noted each separate factor in the relationship and scored well on some school tests of the relationship. But, the theory is not as clear about what lessons the preoperational child should take in place of the beam balance lesson. The so-called Neo-Piagetians, most notably Case and his colleagues (e.g., Case, 1985, 1988), have been able to devise sequences of school lessons that lead the pupil to understand the beam balance relationships and other concepts that are central to the elementary school.

THE POST-NATION-AT-RISK WAVES OF REFORM: PROPOSED SOLUTIONS

Despite these qualifications and the fact that Piaget was not mentioned in the report entitled *A Nation at Risk* are there still lessons from Piaget's theory for the 1990s as there were decades ago, first for the Sputnik and then for the civil rights crises? The current efforts to reform the schools and the areas in which Piaget's theory can provide some guidance are nicely captured by Carroll's model of school learning (Carroll, 1989):

degree of learning = f (time spent/time needed for learning).

Here **time** *spent* in learning is a function of the **time** the pupil is willing to work on the school task (perseverance) or the **time** the teacher allocates for the lesson (allocated time), whichever is less. The **time** *needed for learning* is a function of the pupil's ability, which in turn is taken as the **time** the pupil needs to learn the task on his or her own, minus the **time** the pupil saves as a result of instruction (or in some unfortunate cases, the **time** that is *added* owing to low-quality instruction).

In sum, the time the pupil needs to learn the lesson is a function of two general factors—the pupil's ability, as measured by unassisted learning time, and instructional quality, as measured by time the pupil saves as a result of the school's and teacher's efforts.

FIRST SOLUTIONS: INCREASING THE TIME FOR SCHOOLWORK

The national efforts to raise the degree of learning, especially those inspired by the report entitled *A Nation at Risk,* were limited initially to the numerator of Carroll's model. They focused on fairly crude ways to increase the time allocated for schoolwork, either through lengthening the schoolday beyond 6 hours and the schoolyear beyond 180 days, and in some cases by increasing the number of years the pupil attends school (Barrett, 1990).

The attempts to increase the amount of time the pupil actually spends on mastering the lesson, once the time has been allocated by the teacher and the school, have not been influenced very much by Piaget's account of development (Ben–Peretz & Bromme, 1990). Instead, they have been inspired by straightforward programs of research that analyze the relationships between the time the teacher allocates (a surprisingly small amount in some instances), the amount of time the pupil is actually engaged in attempting to learn the lesson, and the brief interval in which the pupil actually learns what the lesson requires. The key factor in determining the pupil's perseverance appears to be the success the pupil has in the initial attempts to grasp what the lesson calls for (Berliner, 1990).

SECOND SOLUTIONS: DECREASING THE TIME TO LEARN THE LESSON

As the time spent in learning will always be determined by the smallest value in the numerator, and as the curriculum is expanding rapidly, modern reformers have come to see that the greatest changes in school learning are likely to come from the factors that comprise the time the pupil needs to learn the lesson. Of course, educators have always seen that the pupil's ability and the quality of instruction significantly determine the outcome of a lesson. The question is whether Piaget's theory has anything new to add at this time.

The Pupil's Ability.   The full power of Piaget's theory has not been realized in this regard, but the extensions of Piaget's theory by the so-called "neo-Piagetian" researchers does provide a more comprehensive account of the child's developing intellectual performance (Demetriou, 1988).

The basic cognitive building block in the Genevan account is the child's growing ability to invent the opposite of any event, action, or attribute the child has in mind. Two forms of opposite occur: In the simplest— negation—the child conceives of the undoing of the attribute, event, or action; in the more complex—the reciprocal—the child must invent another idea, attribute, or event that has the effect of undoing or canceling the original notion. The entire mental system of necessary and possible links and connections that stands at the heart of logic, mathematics, physics, and so forth, depends on the child's ability to form and discriminate a possible entity, imagine its being undone, inventing yet another way to cancel it, and then seeing that these two means of reversing or undoing the attribute are themselves bound together in a system of mutual implication. In time the child thus understands that an area can be made larger, for example, by increasing its width and that the area can be returned to its original size by decreasing its width, or that it can be returned to its original size by conceiving of another attribute, height, that can be altered to restore the area to its original size. More importantly, the child, through these inventions of width, height, and so on, comes to see that they are necessarily related, insofar as the possibility of width implies the idea of height, just as the idea of "three" implies the existence of the other numbers, and just as the notion of "addition" implies "subtraction."

The task of intellectual development throughout the life-span is the formation of ideas that are necessary; this rests on an ability to imagine the *possibility* of an opposite for whatever we have in mind. That most of what we know to be true fails to be true by necessity is rooted in the fact that it is so difficult for us to construct or imagine a negation and reciprocal of many of our most interesting ideas.

Because the Genevan account does not provide for individual differences in pupils (because the epistemic subject has no individual characteristics), the teacher's attention is drawn to the features of the school task, not the pupil's inherent ability, as a more important feature of the school's work. A slogan of the current reform movement, *all children can learn,* can also be derived from the Genevan perspective and means that the school curriculum is well within the grasp of all but the seriously damaged child. Consequently, because all regularly enrolled pupils should be expected to master the curriculum, the school cannot excuse school failure on the grounds that the pupils were not able, did not try, had the wrong background, and so forth (Goodlad & Keating, 1990; Holmes Group, 1990). When the school tasks have the characteristics Case (1988) and others have specified, the pupil, at the appropriate stage, has the competence to do the work required in the school.

The Genevan perspective is also in line with another of the current reform slogans, namely the calls for **understanding,** not just learning. The year-by-year comparisons of the national tests of the school's accomplishments (e.g., **NAEP**) indicate that pupils learn a great deal each year (Murray, 1985b). The problem is that pupils understand very little of what they have learned (Educational Testing Service, 1990). The *structure d'ensemble* construct in Genevan theory confers understanding via necessity on mental events because all elements in the formal operational cognitive system are connected by necessity to all other elements in the system and derive their meaning and sense from those connections.

In sharp contrast to other developmental theories, Piaget's theory is precisely about how we come to understand what we know. Thus, the theory is ideally suited to provide the guiding rationale for contemporary school reformers who have set as their goal each and every pupil's understanding and use of the mind to make sense of what is learned in school as well as the other puzzling phenomena that are encountered in everyday life. The goal of modern school reformers is to have pupils, like the children in the Genevan experiments, plunge successfully into a problem armed only with their ability to use their minds well.

One of the lessons of Inhelder and Piaget's seminal book, *The Growth of Logical Thinking from Childhood to Adolescence* (1958), was that pupils' school learning did not always serve them well when they had to confront novel versions of the same problem they had learned about in school. They had to draw on other resources, quite apart from specific lessons, to solve these problems at an operational level. Concrete operational thinking is in fact quite resistant to schooling effects, at least as schooling is currently conducted, while schooling as such appears to have some connection to formal operational thought (Murray, 1978).

In summary, Piaget's theory has strong claims to make about the intellectual competence of schoolchildren and how that competence can be expected to vary by age and grade level. In addition, the theory tends to shift the pedagogical issues from the consideration of the child's competence to the characteristics of the school task itself.

Even though Piagetian theory is clearly about the first term of the denominator in the Carroll model of school learning, namely, *pupil ability,* the importance of this factor is minimized by the goals of universal schooling because the schools are required to succeed with the pupils they receive regardless of their respective abilities. Consequently, the burden of reform has shifted to the second term in the denominator, *time needed for learning,* which depends, in turn, on the **quality of instruction** (Elmore & Associates, 1990).

Reformers, as well as traditional school people, have, of course, always addressed the constraints imposed on school learning by the pupil's ability when they delay instruction in some topics so that pupils of greater ability, or further development, are assigned the more difficult school tasks, or when they segregate the school's pupils on measures of intellectual ability, especially when it is done on the basis of mental age, which is positively associated with the Genevan stages and levels (Brown, 1973).

The Quality of Instruction.   Piaget wrote almost nothing about pedagogy other than to endorse generally the discovery methods that were the standard feature of progressive education (Ginsburg, 1981). The theory, however, gave rise to three instructive decades of research on teaching procedures that might speed the advance of a child from one stage to another. In addition to their invention of training procedures, each with its own rationale and link to a developmental theory, developmental psychologists have uncovered scores of variables that influence whether a child or adolescent gives evidence that he or she *understands* a concept.

A number of task variables (the *horizontal décalage* factors) have been discovered, and each presents itself as a candidate upon which some pedagogical method can be devised because the variable affects the probability that the concept or relationship in question will be understood. Murray (1981) reviewed a comprehensive set of task variables that affect whether the child will give evidence that the conservation relationship has been understood, for example. While the manipulation of these variables can be quite helpful in promoting understanding, or evidence of operativity, the variables also signify conceptual errors that must be corrected at some point. Thus, in a good school, the errors (or misconceptions) of childhood constitute a scaffold of imperfect understanding that can "spiral" toward fuller understanding.

In tasks involving the conservation of amount it makes a difference, for example, whether the substance whose amount is to be conserved is discontinuous (sand or pebbles) or continuous (water). The discontinuous material is often, but not always, found to be easier for children. This difference has been featured in attempts to teach conservation to preoperational children (e.g., Murray, 1978, 1981). On the other hand, the child at some point comes to understand that the continuity or discontinuity of the materials is irrelevant and in no way influences whether the amount of sand or water changes, for example, when it is poured into a differently shaped vessel.

As it happens, since 1961 about 180 carefully executed attempts to **teach** young children to understand the conservation relationship have been published. Rarely do these studies reveal any motivation to improve the schools; rather they show a desire to test a claim in Genevan theory, usually the alleged immutable character of the Genevan stages. The claim is that learning and experience, the benefits of the "Vygotsky" social milieu, and maturation — while necessary for cognitive development — are not separately or collectively sufficient for it. The results of the "training" literature, as it is called, are still instructive for the design of pedagogical strategies because each provides reasons for the preoperational child's error and a remedy for it.

The results of these training studies are remarkably consistent, on the whole, although there is evidence of cohort effects in that the children in the late 1970s onward learned their lessons more easily than those in the 1960s. Nevertheless, overall, only half the children in these laboratory experiments changed in any significant way, and they made only half the gains that could have been made in the lesson. Not surprisingly, children who had some grasp of the concept in question, as assessed by a pretest, invariably made greater gains than those who were genuine novices (Beilin, 1971, 1977; Brainerd, 1973; Glaser & Resnick, 1972; Peill, 1975; Strauss, 1972, 1974/1975).

These are not encouraging results for the schools insofar as the concepts would not be considered difficult. Even in fairly ideal teaching situations (small groups and few distractions), only about half the class actually learned something along the lines of what was intended. Some children, of course, scored perfectly on tests of what they were taught and some could solve similar problems, and even other problems that were quite different from those that were explicitly taught.

Over the 30-year period, there emerged several generic methods for teaching the conservation concepts and each has wide applicability in education because conservation is a feature of every curricular concept, not just those examined by Piaget and others. In fact conservation can be seen as a prototypical test of the understanding of any concept because it requires a high level of understanding to know whether a concept has changed fundamentally when some attributes associated with the concept have changed. The Platonic dialogues, for example, which probed the meaning of important concepts, such as justice, virtue, law, love, and so forth, were invariably a kind of conservation exercise in which a situation that represented a concept was set out and modified in some small way to see if there had been a change in justice or virtue or love or whatever. Consequently, teaching methods that were directed toward the child's understanding of the conditions under which any concept is, or is not, altered could become an important part of teacher education. Even though these strategies were developed in another academic tradition and for other reasons, many of them were clearly in line with how classroom teachers would approach teaching the concepts in question and provide the teacher with a productive way of thinking about the pupil's misconceptions.

THE QUALITY OF INSTRUCTION AND TEACHER EDUCATION

If the empowered teacher is central to the "second wave" of school reform, the teacher's view of the discipline, and what it means to understand it, is critical for restructuring schooling in the "third wave."

The Case for Genetic Epistemology

Piagetian theory's greatest role in the current "crisis" may well be in the field of teacher education insofar as the study of *genetic epistemology* could provide the prospective teacher with precisely the kind of understanding that educational reformers imagine when they point out that pedagogical technique is domain specific (Shulman, 1986, 1987).

This discipline-based pedagogy option entails the study of the developmental psychological literature from the perspective of the development of the concepts that make up the curriculum. In this approach the student learns the relevant developmental constraints upon the pupil's acquisition of the curriculum and also learns, as an unavoidable part of the discussion, the nature of the subject itself. The story of how the young child develops the notion of number, for example, is valuable in its own right, but also reveals salient parts of number theory, the arithmetical algorithms, and other aspects of mathematics. Similarly, the account of the child's moral development reveals the principal issues in moral philosophy and political theory, for example.

It would not be possible to study the development of the child's concept of weight, for example, without studying the same notion as it appears in Newtonian mechanics and other branches of physics. The young child, for example, can be shown to operate with the following "equation" for weight (Murray & Johnson, 1970, 1975):

> Weight = f[the object's mass, size, shape, texture, temperature, hardness, continuity, label, but not the object's horizontal or vertical position in space]

The elementary schoolteacher needs to be aware of the young child's view of weight because it is based upon a consistent child-logic that conceals many misconceptions about weight. These misconceptions have implications for pedagogy and curriculum design (Murray, 1982; Murray & Markessini, 1982).

Adolescents and many adults operate with the following simpler and to some degree more sophisticated "equation":

Weight = f[the object's mass]

In other words, the only way adults can think of to change an object's weight is to alter its mass, that is, add something or take something away from the object. The young child can imagine many other ways for altering weight — all, unfortunately, incorrect.

The educated person operates with another expression, namely,

Weight = f[mass of the object × mass of the planet / square of the distance between their centers].

In addition the educated person may be able to convert the expression into a genuine equation by using a value, [g] for the gravitational constant, which permits algebraic manipulation of the terms in the expression. At this point, other factors may be introduced into the expression to treat certain buoyant forces, variations in the earth's g, and so on.

There is a similar developmental progression for the child's understanding of the beam balance in which the young child's understanding of "weighing" is controlled solely by the effects of adding or subtracting weight from a beam balance pan without regard to the influence of any other factor (Siegler, 1981). Later, the distance of the balance pan from the fulcrum is gradually factored into the child's scheme for the operation of the balance, and after several more developmental steps we see the product-moment law in place in the adolescent's thinking.

All concepts and relations in the curriculum can be profitably approached from this perspective. The approach also has face validity in teacher education because it contains the kinds of information that prospective teachers accept as clearly relevant for their future work.

The prospective teacher's study of genetic epistemology, however, is more than a device by which students in teacher education might learn their academic disciplines. It goes to the core of the kind of knowledge the teacher needs, namely, generative ways of organizing information and knowledge. It entails the search for structures, ways of representing the subject matter, and analogies and metaphors that will take *each* pupil well beyond what can be held together temporally and spatially through rote memorization. Pedagogical content knowledge (Shulman, 1986, 1987) is fundamentally about the structures of genetic epistemology that confer some appropriate level of understanding, and it is ultimately about those structures that actually advance our understanding (see Murray & Fallon, 1989).

To take another example, the young elementary schoolchild will be taught one of the algorithms for subtraction. There are several options for taking 67 from 95, for example. The two numbers in the problem can be regrouped and represented as (60 + 7) taken from (80 + 15), by a strategy known as *decomposition,* or the numbers in the problem may be represented as (70 + 7) taken from (90 + 15), by a strategy known as *equal additions,* or more elaborate and equally correct algorithms can be taught in which the correct answer, 28, is had by making different combinations of calculations that are also sound and academically sensible.

On what basis should the teacher choose an algorithm, since mathematically there is no basis for selecting one algorithm over another, except perhaps on elegance or parsimony? Kamii (1989), for example, offers an alternative from her study of genetic epistemology. She finds that young children will invent yet other strategies that are a more natural outgrowth of the young child's understanding of number than are the usual school-taught algorithms of decomposition or equal additions.

The teacher's knowledge, however, needs to extend also to an area that is sometimes thought to be of a different order from subject-matter understanding, namely the teacher's knowledge of pedagogical technique. The lessons from Piagetian theory, however, are equally powerful in this domain because procedural knowledge, like sensorimotor knowledge, is a fundamental component of all conceptual understanding. The research on the differences between novice and expert teachers has just begun (Berliner, 1988; Black, 1989). The Genevan contribution to the literature on procedural knowledge is focused on how the procedures become organized into a coherent system that eventually has formal operational properties.

Virtually every reform report (e.g., Holmes Group, 1986, 1990) endorses cooperative learning as a modern teaching strategy or procedure that is superior to traditional methods. The strategy has clear links to Genevan theory and to other accounts of mental functioning and may provide yet another area for the utility of Piagetian scholarship in education.

The Case of How Cooperative Learning is Understood

The term, *cooperative learning,* refers to a family of instructional practices in which the teacher gives various directions to groups of pupils about how to work together. It is a teaching practice rarely employed by novices as it has very little in common with the novice methods of "telling the truth publicly" and individual pupil seat-work assignments. In a cooperative learning exercise, the class is divided into groups of four to six children usually of the same age, but differing in ability, ethnicity, and sex. The directions the teacher gives are designed, one way or another, to have the children work together as a team on some academic task. The children, of course, must learn to cooperate to follow the teacher's instructions, but cooperation itself, while a worthy educational objective, is not the principal objective in cooperative learning instruction. The claim of cooperative learning advocates, one that is usually supported in field research, is that ordinary school learning is enhanced considerably when children, following one or another of the cooperative learning procedures, learn in groups rather than on their own or in competition with other pupils.

Basically, the various kinds of cooperative instructions teachers give to their pupils are grounded in four theoretical perspectives: social learning theory, Vygotskian theory, the newer cognitive science research on experts and novices, and Piagetian theory.

Social Learning Theory.   Practices derived from the tradition of social learning are the most widely used in the schools. They are based on the common principle that pupils will work hard on those tasks for which they gain a reward and will fail to work on tasks that either yield no reward or yield punishment. In cooperative learning instruction, the teacher employs the approval of other pupils and the expectations of the group and relies heavily on the ability of the pupil to imitate the academic behavior of others. Thus it is critical that the teacher reward a pupil *only* when all members of the group succeed in learning the assignment or, in the case where the teacher assigned the pupils different parts of a complicated task, only on the basis of the group's overall achievement and not according to the merit of any individual pupil's contribution to the group's effort. These are the tools of the cooperative learning teacher. If the teacher merely instructs the pupils to work together and to help each other, the academic gains are generally no greater than had the pupils worked alone on the task (Johnson, Maruyama, Johnson, Nelson, & Skon, 1981; Slavin, 1986)

Vygotskian Theory.   Even though few educators are aware of it, the most compelling theoretical rationale for cooperative learning comes, not from John Dewey, but from L. S. Vygotsky, who claimed that our distinctively human mental functions and accomplishments have their origins in our social relationships. Mental functioning in this view is the internalized and transformed version of the accomplishments of a group. The theory gives great weight to a group's common perspectives and solutions to problems as they are arrived at through debate, argument, negotiation, discussion, compromise, and dialectic. This collaboration by a community of learners is seen as indispensable for cognitive growth; its role is more than a mere facilitator of events; it is the means by which such growth occurs and a provision for it must be made in schooling. Researchers and teachers often find that the dyad can solve a problem where individuals working on their own cannot solve it. There is a distance, called *a zone of proximal development* by Vygotsky, between what the pupil can do on his own and what the child could achieve were the child to work under the guidance of teachers or in collaboration with more capable peers. Thus, teachers who wish to maximize what the child can accomplish will minimize the time the child works alone on school tasks.

Research in this tradition (for a review, see Forman & Cazden, 1985) has not resulted so far in novel practices in the schools, but it has provided a demonstration of the growth in individual children's problem solving when the problems are approached collaboratively and when the teacher sees the other children in the class as indispensable parts of the lesson and not as a barrier to each pupil's accomplishments.

Cognitive Science.   The characteristics of ideal learning environments from the cognitive science perspective (Collins, Brown, & Newman, 1986) follow closely many features that are embedded in the common cooperative learning formats, all of which make provisions for modeling, coaching, and scaffolding, for example. However, some novel cooperative learning procedures, like *reciprocal teaching,* have been developed by cognitive scientists for classroom instruction (Palinscar & Brown, 1984). Both laboratory and classroom studies have demonstrated that the *reciprocal teaching method* is effective in significantly raising and maintaining the reading comprehension scores of poor readers (Collins et al., 1986; Symons, Snyder, Cariglia–Bull, & Pressley, 1989).

Basically the method is thought to be successful because the pupil gradually, but solidly, develops a new conceptual model for the skill and couples it with specific strategies that are used by expert readers. The cooperative learning features of these expert–novice teaching procedures lead the pupil to integrate the multiple roles that the successful problem solver inevitably masters. Thus, student writers are helped as a writers when they read and critique other pupil's work and when they have their own work read by others, and so on. By taking turns writing and reading, they acquire a larger view of the writing task, a new conceptual model for it, a model closer to that possessed by the expert writer.

Tutoring, when it is viewed from the perspective of the benefits that accrue to the tutor, is also a form of cooperative learning, although it is difficult to know to what to attribute the benefits to the tutor — the tutoring act itself, the preparation for tutoring, or the kind of study the tutor engages in when preparing the lesson (Hufnagel, 1984).

Piagetian Theory Revisited.   Teachers, working within the Piagetian tradition, use cooperative learning lessons to accelerate the pupil's intellectual development by forcing the child to confront systematically another child who holds an opposing point of view about the answer to some school task. Basically, the teacher places two pupils who disagree about the answer to a problem in a group and tells them to work together until they can agree or come to a common answer, at which time the lesson will conclude. Once the pupils agree, usually in about 5 minutes, the teacher tests the children alone and usually finds that the pupils who initially do poorly on the problem now, on their own, solve the problem in a way that is indistinguishable from the way a correct problem solver solved it in the first place (for a review of this literature, see Murray, 1986).

In some instances teachers may also instruct the pupils simply to imitate a correct problem solver, and on other occasions the teacher may instruct one child, in the presence of the other, to pretend to reason in a mature way. In other words, the teacher places the pupil in some social situation where he or she is forced to take a viewpoint that conflicts with his or her own point of view. The practice works best if the teacher ensures that one pupil understands the task, but some cognitive growth occurs when neither child knows the correct answer to the problem but only when each initially offers an incorrect answer that contradicts the other's answer.

Overall, these social interaction or cooperative learning effects, documented consistently in some 30 studies, are limited to mental tasks that have strong relationships with age, but they do occur across a wide variety of such tasks and with groups of various sizes (2-5), Grades (K-5), and ethnic and social diversity. These developmental tasks, nevertheless, are important parts of the school curriculum because they are about information that is necessarily true. These social interaction versions of cooperative learning, apart from being effective ways to promote cognitive growth, are also more effective for developmental tasks in the school curriculum than traditional instructional practices that are based upon direct teaching or conditioning.

These various theories or perspectives help explain how the cooperative learning innovations produce their impressive results. They also guide the teacher in ways of dealing with novel problems presented in the lesson. Over and above accomplishment on school tasks, cooperative learning—between pupils and pupils, and between pupils and teachers—may be the essential means, as both Vygotsky and Piaget claimed, by which the mind constructs knowledge and invents meaning. Thus, in grasping the reasons behind a successful teaching strategy, even if it is counterintuitive, like cooperative learning, the teacher will be guided to the core of education, namely, to developing the child's mind and his or her ability to use it well.

Teacher's Theoretical Reasoning

Unfortunately, we know very little about how teachers actually think about their teaching. This fact yields a final arena for a Piagetian approach to an educational reform issue, the assessment of teachers' competence. What, for example, do teachers really think they are doing when they implement cooperative learning techniques?

Like subjects in a Piagetian investigation, they could be asked their reasons for doing what they do. Could there be a way to determine whether some reasons were better, more mature, more sophisticated than others? The Kohlberg scale of moral development, despite its widely documented limitations, provides an instructive and prototypical case for the assessment of the teacher's knowledge about teaching insofar as there are no a priori correct answers to, or conclusions about, any of the moral dilemma problems posed in the Kohlberg or Genevan assessments. (There is no definitive way, for example, to conclude that Heinz should not steal the otherwise unavailable drug that would save his wife's life or that he should steal it.) There is a way, however, to determine that some responses are more sophisticated or maturer than others. Kohlberg-type scales are scored solely in terms of the sophistication of the supporting reasons for the decision to steal or not to steal, for example, not in terms of the decision itself. Similarly, one would be interested in the teacher's reasons for implementing cooperative learning, not whether it or some other technique was employed in the classroom to solve a particular pedagogical problem.

Unfortunately, there is no equivalent scale of pedagogical development like the scales of moral judgment, although, following the Genevan line of thinking, the ingredients are potentially available. Ammon and Hutcheson (1989), for example, have speculated about a five-level sequence of teacher conceptions about behavior, development, learning, and teaching. Any number of generic teaching dilemmas or cases could be posed in a way that could reveal the *structure* of the teacher's reasoning about teaching and schooling. The **structure** would be assessed, not the specific content or information, but rather its form and adequacy. How well does the teacher understand and explain any professional problem or event, such as cooperative learning?

Presumably, better explanations systematically introduce more relevant and discriminable factors and at the same time have a way to integrate these separate factors into a structured whole that has wide applicability. The form or structure of the explanation, as in all Genevan accounts of cognitive development in some domain, would be the central focus of this line of research.

INFLUENCE OF SCHOOLING ON GENEVAN THEORY

While the implications of Piagetian theory are as strong for education as they were at any other time, they remain unrealized in the main. It is wrong to conclude, however, that the relationship between schooling and Piagetian scholarship is a unidirectional path that benefits only the schools. It is not widely appreciated that cooperative research projects, between developmental psychologists and teachers, have advanced the field at a theoretical level.

Throughout the 1960s and early 1970s, for example, it was widely held that one implication of Piagetian theory was that the young child (below the age of 7) was structurally incapable of taking a cognitive point of view different from his own (Cox, 1980). Researchers all over the world confirmed the young child's stubborn egocentrism in scores of laboratory studies, and the extensions of the fact of egocentrism were found in curriculum and instructional designs that accepted the immutability of the young child's limited competence.

When teachers and mothers researched these issues, however, based on their own unique familiarity with children and as part of their own graduate research training in the 1970s, they quickly devised experiments that showed that young children were able to take the point of view of others in many situations (Cox, 1980). These experiments led to substantial modifications in the prevailing interpretations of the child's cognitive competence that in turn supported the invention of pedagogical techniques, such as cooperative learning and reciprocal teaching, that now presuppose the young pupil's competence to take the point of view of another pupil. It would not be hard to document other cases where the unique perspectives of schoolteachers and specialists have shaped academic research projects that in turn led to significant modifications in the prevailing learning and developmental theories.

These modifications, it is to be hoped, will provide both an improved developmental psychology and a truly professional teaching force of reflective practitioners who can carry out the next stages in the development of teaching (Fosnot, 1989; Holmes Group, 1990). A true profession of teaching, in other words, awaits a pedagogy that has formal operational properties.

REFERENCES

Ammon, P., & Hutcheson, B. (1989). Promoting the development of teachers' pedagogical conceptions. *Genetic Epistemologist, XVII*(4), 23–29.

Barrett, M. (1990). The case for more school days. *Network News and Views, IX*(12), 25–37.

Beilin, H. (1971). The training and acquisition of logical operations. In Rosskopf et al. (Eds.), *Piagetian cognitive-development research and mathematical education.* Washington, DC: National Council of Teachers of Mathematics, Inc.

Beilin, H. (1977). Inducing conservation through training. In G. Steiner (Ed.), *Psychology of the 20th century: Piaget and beyond* (Vol. 7). Bern, Switzerland: Kinder.

Ben-Peretz, M., & Bromme, R. (1990). *The nature of time in schools: Theoretical concepts, practitioner perceptions.* New York: Teachers College Press.

Berliner, D. (1988). Implications of studies of expertise in pedagogy for teacher education and evaluation. *New directions for teacher assessment: Proceedings of the 1988 ETS invitational conference* (pp. 39–68). Princeton, NJ: Educational Testing Service.

Berliner, D. (1990). What's all the fuss about instructional time? In M. Ben-Peretz & R. Bromme (Eds.), *The nature of time in schools: Theoretical concepts, practitioner perceptions.* New York: Teachers College Press.

Black, A. (1989). Developmental teacher education. *Genetic Epistemologist, XVII*(4).

Brainerd, C. J. (1973). Judgments and explanations as criteria for the presence of cognitive structures. *Psychological Bulletin, 79,* 172–179.

Brown, A. (1973). Conservation of number and continuous quantity in normal, bright, and retarded children. *Child Development, 44,* 376–379.

Bruner, J. (1961). *The process of education.* Cambridge, MA: Harvard University Press.

Carroll, J. (1989). The Carroll Model: A 25-year retrospective and prospective view. *Educational Researcher, 18*(1), 26–31.

Case, R. (1985). *Intellectual development: Birth to adulthood.* New York: Academic Press.

Case, R. (1988). Structure and process of intellectual development. In A. Demetriou (Ed.), *The neo-Piagetian theories of cognitive development: Toward an integration* (pp. 65–101). Amsterdam: Elsevier Science Publishers.

Cohen, D. (1983). *Piaget: Critique and reassessment.* New York: St. Martin's Press.

Collins, A., Brown, J., & Newman, S. (1986). Cognitive apprenticeship: Teaching the craft of reading, writing, and mathematics. In L. Resnick (Ed.), *Cognition and instruction: Issues and agendas* (pp. 1–41). Hillsdale, NJ: Lawrence Erlbaum Associates.

Cox, M. (1980). *Are young children egocentric?* New York: St. Martin's Press.

Cremin, L. (1961). *The transformation of the school.* New York: Vintage Books.

Demetriou, A. (1988). *The neo-Piagetian theories of cognitive development: Toward an integration.* Amsterdam: Elsevier Science Publishers.

Educational Testing Service. (1990). *The educational reform decade.* Princeton, NJ: ETS Policy Information Center.

Elkind, D. (1976). *Child development and education: A Piagetian perspective.* New York: Oxford University Press.

Elmore, R., & Associates. (1990). *Restructuring schools: The next generation of educational reform.* San Francisco: Jossey-Bass.

Flavell, J. (1963). *The developmental psychology of Jean Piaget.* New York: Van Nostrand.

Forman, E., & Cazden, C. (1985). Exploring Vygotskian perspectives in education: The cognitive value of peer interaction. In J. V. Wertsch (Ed.), *Culture, communication and cognition: Vygotskian perspectives* (pp. 323–347). New York: Academic Press.

Fosnot, C. (1989). *Enquiring teachers, enquiring learners: A constructivist approach for teaching.* New York: Teachers College Press.

Furth, H. (1978). Reading as thinking: A developmental perspective. In F. Murray & J. Pikulski (Eds.), *The acquisition of reading: Cognitive, linguistic, and perceptual prerequisites* (pp. 43–54). Baltimore: University Park Press.

Gardner, R. (1966). A psychologist looks at Montessori. *Elementary School Journal, 67*(2), 72–83.

Ginsburg, H. (1981). Piaget and education: The contributions and limits of genetic epistemology. In I. Sigel, D. Brodzinsky, & R. Golinkoff (Eds.), *New direction in Piagetian theory and practice* (pp. 315–330). Hillsdale, NJ: Lawrence Erlbaum Associates.

Glaser, R., & Resnick, L. (1972). Instructional psychology. In P. H. Mussen & M. Rosenweig (Eds.), *Annual Review of Psychology.* Palo Alto, CA: Annual Reviews.

Goodlad, J. (1990). *Teachers for our nation's schools.* San Francisco: Jossey-Bass.

Goodlad, J., & Keating, P. (1990). *Access to knowledge: An agenda for our nation's schools.* New York: College Entrance Examination Board.

Goodnow, J., & Bethon, G. (1966). Piaget's tasks: The effects of schooling and intelligence. *Child Development, 37,* 573–582.

Granott, N. (1991). *From macro to micro and back: On the analysis of microdevelopment.* Paper presented at the 21st annual symposium of the Jean Piaget Society, Philadelphia, PA.

Hawley, W., & Rosenholtz, S. (1984). Good schools: What research says about improving student achievement. *Peabody Journal of Education, 61*(4).

Holmes Group. (1986). *Tomorrow's teachers,* East Lansing, MI: Holmes Group.

Holmes Group. (1990). *Tomorrow's schools: Principles for the design of professional development schools.* East Lansing, MI: Holmes Group.

Hooper, F., & DeFain, J. (1974). *The search for a distinctly Piagetian contribution to education.* Theoretical Paper No. 50. Madison: Wisconsin Research and Development Center.

Howe, H. (1990). Thinking about the "Forgotten Half." *Teachers College Record, 92,* 293–305.

Hufnagel, P. (1984). *Effects of tutoring on tutors.* Unpublished doctoral dissertation, University of Delaware.

Hunt, J. (1961). *Intelligence and experience.* New York: Ronald Press.

Inhelder, B., & Piaget, J. (1958). *The growth of logical thinking from childhood to adolescence.* New York: Basic Books.

Irvine, J. (1990). *Black students and school failure: Policies, practices, and prescriptions.* New York: Greenwood Press.

Johnson, D., Maruyama, G., Johnson, R., Nelson, D., & Skon, L. (1981). Effects of cooperative, competitive, and individualistic goal structures on achievement: A meta-analysis. *Psychological Bulletin, 89,* 47–62.

Kamii, C. (1989). *Young children continue to reinvent arithmetic—2nd grade.* New York: Teachers College Press.

Linn, R., Graue, A., & Sanders, T. (1990). Comparing state and district test results to national norms: Interpretations of scoring "above the national average." *Technical Report 307,* Los Angeles: Center for Research on Evaluation, Standards, and Student Testing, UCLA.

Maccoby, E., & Zellner, M. (1970). *Experiments in primary education.* New York: Harcourt Brace Jovanovich.

Murray, F. (1978). Teaching strategies and conservation training. In A. M. Lesgold, J. W. Pellegrino, S. Fokkema, & R. Glaser, (Eds.), *Cognitive psychology and instruction* (pp. 419–428). New York: Plenum.

Murray, F. (1979). The generation of educational practice from developmental theory. *Educational Psychologist, 14,* 30–43.

Murray, F. (1981). The conservation paradigm: Conservation of conservation research. In I. Sigel, D. Brodzinsky, & R. Golinkoff (Eds.), *New directions and applications of Piaget's theory* (pp. 143–176). Hillsdale, NJ: Lawrence Erlbaum Associates.

Murray, F. (1982). The pedagogical adequacy of children's conservation explanations. *Journal of Educational Psychology, 74*(5), 656–659.

Murray, F. (1985a). Was Piaget Too Successful? Review of the D. Cohen's "Piaget: Critique and Reassessment." *Contemporary Psychology, 30*(8), 645–646.

Murray, F. (1985b). Paradoxes of a university at risk. In J. Blits (Ed.), *The American university: Problems, prospects and trends* (pp. 101–120). Buffalo, NY: Prometheus Books.

Murray, F. (1986). Micro-mainstreaming. In J. Meisel (Ed.), *The consequences of mainstreaming handicapped children* (pp. 43–54). Hillsdale, NJ: Lawrence Erlbaum Associates.

Murray, F. (1989). Explanations in education. In M. Reynolds (Ed.), *Knowledge base for the beginning teacher* (pp. 1–12). New York: Pergamon Press.

Murray, F. (1990). The conversion of truth into necessity. In W. Overton (Ed.), *Reasoning, necessity and logic: Developmental perspectives* (pp. 183–204). Hillsdale, NJ: Lawrence Erlbaum Associates.

Murray, F., & Fallon, D. (1989). *The reform of teacher education for the 21st century: Project 30 year one report.* Newark: University of Delaware.

Murray, F., & Johnson, P. (1970). A note on using curriculum models in analyzing the child's concept of weight. *Journal of Research in Science Teaching, 7,* 377–381.

Murray, F., & Johnson, P. (1975). Relevant and some irrelevant factors in the child's concept of weight. *Journal of Educational Psychology, 67,* 705–711.

Murray, F., & Markessini, J. (1982). A semantic basis of nonconservation of weight. *Psychological Record, 32,* 375–379.

Oakes, J. (1985). *Keeping track: How schools structure inequality.* New Haven, CT: Yale University Press.

Ogle, L., & Alsalam, N. (1990). *The condition of education 1990: Vol. 1. Elementary and secondary education.* Washington, DC: U. S. Department of Education.

Palinscar, A., & Brown, A., (1984). Reciprocal teaching of comprehension-fostering and monitoring activities. *Cognition and Instruction, 1,* 117–175.

Peill, E. J. (1975). *Invention and discovery of reality: The acquisition of conservation of amount.* New York: Wiley.

Schwebel, M., & Raph, J. (1973). *Piaget in the classroom.* New York: Basic Books.

Seltzer, E. (1977). A comparison between John Dewey's theory of inquiry and Jean Piaget's genetic analysis. *Journal of Genetic Psychology, 130,* 323.

Shanker, A. (1989). The social and educational dilemmas of test use. *The uses of standardized tests in American education.* Princeton, NJ: Educational Testing Service.

Shulman, L. (1986). Those who understand: Knowledge growth in teaching. *Educational Researcher, 15*(2), 4–14.

Shulman, L. (1987). Knowledge and teaching: Foundations of the new reform. *Harvard Educational Review, 57*(1), 1–22.

Siegler, R. (1981). Developmental sequences within and between concepts. *Monographs of the Society for Research in Child Development, 46*(No. 189).

Slavin, R. (1986). Small group methods. In M. Dunkin (Ed.), *The International Encyclopedia of Teaching and Teacher Education* (pp. 245–327). New York: Pergamon Press.

Stedman, L., & Smith, M. (1983). Recent reform proposals for American education. *Contemporary Education Review, 2,* 85–104.

Strauss, S. (1972). Inducing cognitive development and learning: a review of short-term training experiments: I. the organismic–developmental approach. *Cognition, 1,* 329–357.

Strauss, S. (1974/1975). A reply to Brainerd. *Cognition, 3,* 155–185.

Symons, S., Snyder, B., Cariglia-Bull, T., & Pressley, M. (1989). Why be so optimistic about cognitive strategy instruction? In C. McCormick, G. Miller, & M. Pressley (Eds.), *Cognitive strategy research: From basic research to educational applications* (pp. 1–32). New York: Springer–Verlag.

VI FINAL COMMENTARY

14 In Conclusion: Continuing Implications

Harry Beilin and Peter B. Pufall

Conclusion, as in the title of this chapter, trades on two meanings. In the traditional sense, we bring the book to an end exercising our editorial prerogative one last time. We selectively and interpretively sum up the ideas offered by our colleagues in the preceding chapters. In the other sense, we use this review as a forum within which to judge whether Piaget's ideas could have a continuing and constructive influence on developmental theory and research. Any who have arrived at this point by reading this volume from the beginning must share our conclusion that the scholars contributing to this work reveal the ongoing vitality of Piaget's theory and less directly his research. As confident as we are in concluding that Piaget's influence will not end, it is equally clear that our conclusion is not shared by some developmentalists.

Among Genevans, there are two positive attitudes these days to Piaget's theory (Inhelder, de Caprona, & Cornu-Wells, 1987). One view, some might associate with *paradigmatic* science, holds that there are many ideas implicit and explicit in the theory that have never been adequately explored and developed. Those following this route into the future will devote themselves to extracting and developing the implications of Piaget's theory as it existed at the time of his death. This strategy would serve Piaget's theory and scholarly fields concerned with knowledge and development, as it serves well any major scholar in any scientific field whose theory is rich and complex.

The other strategy may appear to some as more valuable and forward looking, and could be construed more as the route of the true *constructivist*. It holds that Piaget's theory must be revised where it is found wanting and extended to new domains, some of which Piaget may have never imagined, such as how human knowledge develops, interacting with and constructing microworlds (e.g., Forman & Pufall, 1988), as well as those he noted but never explored systematically, such as affectivity (see the Case & Furth contributions to this volume). The *paradigmatic* approach is normally applied to philosophical, historical, and literary works, less so to scientific theories; nevertheless, in our view, much is to be gained from applying this strategy to developmental research. The *constructivist* approach is more common and is necessary, or else theories still vital, like Piaget's, end as objects of historical curiosity, at best.

Both strategies are exemplified by the contributors to the present volume, who collectively are more sympathetic to Piaget than any randomly drawn set of developmentalists. Among the non-Piagetians in the field, views range from respect for the theory to outright hostility with the journey from one pole to the other passing through indifference. There is more than one non-Piagetian in the volume. Some are former Piagetians whose theoretical allegiance is at present elsewhere. Others have only had a glancing relationship with Piaget's theory. They are included here because it has been the expressed policy of the Jean Piaget Society, almost from its start, to encourage the presentation of views different from Piaget's, on the assumption that scholarly progress is most likely to occur in an atmosphere of challenge, and even confrontation among competing ideas. In this respect, the society is less like a church and more like what a university should be.

UNDERSTANDING SELF-ORGANIZING SYSTEMS AS EQUILIBRATING SYSTEMS: GARCIA, CHAPMAN, AND CASE

Rolando Garcia first sets Piaget's genetic epistemology against the backdrop of the epistemological dilemma facing early 20th-century physics. If all that is knowable is structure, how then does experimental science constrain competing theories and how does intuition constrain the knowledge of reality? He unequivocally concludes that Piaget's genetic epistemology of mind constructed through adaptive actions successfully resolves this thorny issue.

Then, Garcia examines adaptive construction within the context of contemporary physics describing and explaining how complex systems, of which cognitive systems are one kind, undergo organized change as a consequence of perturbations induced by variations in external forces. The issues with which he is concerned lie at the heart of a general theory of natural developmental change, whether that change is in the realm of mental or physical structures. It is by virtue of the presumed parallelism of the mental and physical that Garcia adopts dynamic systems theory to account for cognitive development. Prigogine's theory of dissipative structures is employed, not as a metaphor for change, but as an explanation of mechanisms "that govern both the growth of knowledge and change of structure." It is fundamental to this proposal to consider cognition within the framework of a system, consistent with Piaget's holism, and parallel with Quine's meaning holism. There is considerable debate in the philosophy of mind over holism; Garcia's characterization of how systems undergo change as holistic entities adds a scientific dimension to the debate that is often buried in philosophical analysis more concerned with language than with physical "reality." His illuminating analysis of self-regulating mechanisms furthers our understanding of equilibration as a natural principle.

Without seeming to contradict Piaget's attitude toward social and other environmental forces in the acquisition of knowledge, Garcia alludes to social dimension as significant in restructuring the interaction between subject and object. Just as he did in *Psychogenesis and the History of Science* (Piaget & Garcia, 1989), Garcia joins those who criticize Piaget for giving no or too little heed to social dynamics. Garcia suggests that social dynamics are to cognitive systems what external forces are to physical systems. The parallel, while inviting, must be considered as preliminary at best. In our view the kinds of social factors to which he alludes are only metaphorical, not real forces, and may be more accurately understood as *informational structures*. These informational structures fail to meet criteria of being dimensionalized and unitized, as external forces are in thermodynamic systems. They are often chaotic, or at least ambiguous, implying many degrees of freedom for adaptation or self-organization.

On another issue, Garcia states that, "the cognitive system is neither continuous nor linear process. The existence of stages is an expression of these two facts." We are more in accord with a more integrated analysis of linear and nonlinear aspects he and Piaget (Piaget & Garcia, 1991, pp. 138–139) offer elsewhere, "when we say 'whole system' we refer of course to the structural aspects of the system, not the functional aspects. . . . But the discontinuity is structural not functional. Cognitive development is thus characterized by structural discontinuity and functional continuity."

Chapman's intellectual history of Piaget's continuous refinements and transformations of equilibration leaves no doubt that Piaget's theory itself was changing throughout Piaget's lifetime, and that equilibration is the first among equals as a core construct in Piaget's theory. Chapman's careful analysis and clear presentation will serve those of a paradigmatic persuasion who cannot help but be informed by his writing. At the same time he constructively extends Piaget in two ways. One, by examining equilibration within the context of recent discussions in theoretical physics and biology about self organizing systems. He, like Garcia, notes the enticing parallels between Piaget's position with respect to the developing mind and characterizations of physical systems as holistic and metastable, which when they reach criticality, reorganize (see Bak & Chen, 1991, for an overview). By the same token he does not fully accept the parallel. He is well aware that the "minor events" creating catastrophes and reorganization in physical systems have different properties from those creating similar effects in cognitive systems.

This realization contributes to the second extension, his proposal to expand Piaget's epistemic dyad of subject and object to an epistemic triad embodying subject, object of knowledge, and others (interlocutors). In this sense the social forces in Garcia's system are defined as intersubjective transactions creating disequilibria necessary to the developmental process in Piaget's theory.

At issue with respect to Chapman's proposal is the extent to which its fundamental claims can be said to differ from Piaget's, and, if they do whether they can lead us to a new conceptualization of equilibration. Chapman avoids a trivial extension that would suggest that triadic transactions simply differentiate objects of knowing into physical and social. Rather, he suggests that human interactions, argumentation for example, yield disequilibria different in kind from those created by the resistances of physical objects. The dialogic triadic system changes the nature of the object to a representational and, therefore fundamentally, theoretical object; that is, they are always "about" reality.

We question another feature of Chapman's proposal. On the one hand while clearly constructive in kind, it has the potential of fundamentally distorting Piaget's position that development is intrasubjectively regulated by reflective abstraction. Thus, we view Chapman's extension of equilibration theory, within an intersubjective social framework, as posing a challenge to Piaget's theory. It is a challenge added to a chorus of voices declaring that an adequate theory of cognitive development requires a systematic account of social causation beyond that which Piaget provided.

Case's nonpolemical critique of Piaget's theory preserves the original intent of neo-Piagetian scholars to integrate classic Piagetian concepts with various versions of information-processing theory. Within his chapter, Case identifies tenets of Piaget's theory that he believes to be broadly shared by neo-Piagetian theorists. They are easily as foundational to the credo of those who remain simply Piagetians.

One extension of Piaget's theory contained in Case's chapter, the cyclical recapitulation of structural sequences may be more of a paradigmatic elaboration than a constructive extension of Piaget's theory. It appears to be a much-needed specification of Piaget's general, but late-appearing, idea that cognitive development is spiral and not linear. That is, while we become more adaptively attuned to our world through structurally reorganized operations that more effectively construct reality, the steps in that reorganization may be constructed by simple procedures deployed again and again as self-regulative responses to perturbations.

Other extensions are clearly more constructive, as Case maps out the complementary relation between Piagetian and neo-Piagetian assumptions. He, as others, incorporates cultural/social theory. His position on cultural/ social causation is a forthright challenge to Piaget's position for the following reasons. First, he characterizes Piaget's logic as only one of many possible cultural inventions structuring the nature of cognitive development. This view shifts logic from a construction ultimately tied to tested reality to a culturally constructed instrumentality of mind. Second, Case assumes that social and institutional processes are equal in importance to endogenous factors in development. Third, there is the unmistakable assumption that children reconstitute the intellectual systems they inherit from their cultures. Thus, there is a strong undercurrent of at least a weak form of cultural relativism in Case's position.

In Case's view, one of the continuing and critical differences between neo-Piagetian theories and Piaget's is their rejection of Piaget's logical (symbolic) modeling of natural thought. He proposes instead, a method of analyzing the level and complexity of thought independent of content that is not axiomatically logical, but stresses formal complexity and levels of hierarchical integration in an alternative definition of "structure." This new structure is linked with notions of expanding memorial and attentional capacity to forge constraints on development. The resulting conception attempts to retain the idea of intra-individual consistency in performance (the *structure d'ensemble*) notion, without the logical architecture, and without an apparent theoretical equivalent of equilibration, within a framework of domain specificity and modularity. Introducing nonlogical procedures into self-organizing systems is one way of accounting for spiral developmental processes. However, in this context it appears to be introduced for additional reasons. It permits hypothesizing further developments in adult thought than Piaget had, and allows the theory to be generalized into other domains, such as affectivity.

Finally, in discussing these matters, Case identifies areas waiting to be examined empirically within this framework. The body of empirical work generated by neo-Piagetians has always been impressive and they have used it effectively to buttress claims for various versions of their general theory.

THEORY OF MIND: EXAMINING REPRESENTATION IN THOUGHT; FLAVELL AS WELL AS PERNER AND ASTINGTON

Flavell's chapter, along with Perner and Wilde–Astington's, bear upon central issues concerning the children's understanding of their own and other's mind, or as it is currently described, their having a "theory of mind." Flavell's chapter is a personal intellectual history woven around a continuing quest to understand perspective taking and that particularly intrasubjective quality of mind, egocentricity. In this regard his work seems paradigmatically Piagetian. This is especially evident in his observation that egocentricity is embedded in the fact that we are the knower and therefore know our own view first, and perhaps best. This has led him to see his life's work retrospectively as an examination of how we develop the capacities to compensate for our fundamental and continuing egocentricity.

Perhaps his study of role taking, at the beginning of this quest, is of special note because of its historical relation to social cognition. That work, and it seems to us a significant part of the current work on theory of mind, is more concerned with socially significant facts about pretense and false belief, than it is concerned with how social interactions with other minds is causally linked to the development of mind, the concern central to Chapman, Kuhn, as well as Youniss and Damon. Flavell's interest, in particular, is in understanding mind as object, and understanding mind as process.

Flavell's examination of these interests shows him to be a developmentalist in the Piagetian tradition in his emphasis on qualitative ontogenetic change, consistency across tasks, and his theory of levels. However, the theory he constructs takes him away from the Piagetian tradition. It is evident in the safe distance he maintains from a structuralist strategy, making no reference to logical model building, while relying more on functionally specified processes such as cognitive connections and representations to differentiate cognitive stages. Moreover, Flavell's speculations about the processes of development are primarily situated in both social exchange and self-reflection, which have the potential to perturb the organism setting the stage for equilibration. This final reference to equilibration is then tempered when Flavell confides that he is often convinced by conversations with Level 1 children that they will not be *made to* but must *mature to* understand that we have different representations of reality.

Flavell's description of his research on the child's theory of mind shows a willingness to draw parallels between and perhaps even integrate the "theory" about theory of mind with the Piagetian perspective. Not so *Josef Perner* and *Janet Astington*. They see incompatible theoretical differences, hence their place with respect to Piaget's theory may be better thought of as *reconstructive* than constructive.

The key to their theory rests on the meaning, nature, and applications of representation. Perner and Astington's basic claim appears to be that true representation exists only when the child *understands* the mind as representational, usually at about 4 years of age. Prior to that time, what appears to Piaget and others as representational is explained in other terms, such as, the child engages in hypothetical reasoning (a cloth *could be* a pillow) that does not implicate representation per se (understanding a cloth *represents* a pillow).

Aside from being counterintuitive, we believe the claim goes too far. The fundamental definition of representation that something stands in the place of something else different in kind (together with the glosses discussed by Perner/Astington) is not different from Piaget's definition of symbolic representation. It is certainly possible to debate whether Jacqueline understands the cloth to be a representation, but it seems hardly possible to deny that in carrying out cognitive functions such as imagery and language, the 2-year-old child is engaging in mental representation. For similar reasons, representational theorists of mind (e.g., Fodor, Pylyshyn) place nondevelopmental propositional forms of representation in mind as early as possible. Even Piaget sees the need for the start of representational process in the sensorimotor period (with signals). Perner's characterization of children as "situational theorists" able to "represent alternative situations" is consistent with the widely shared view that representation develops well before age 4.

What Perner and Astington appear to be doing is adding a stringent condition, namely *understanding* that the mind is representational, onto the ordinary criteria specifying what constitutes a representation. As we see it, the solution to the question of why children do not understand misrepresentations until age 4 is not to deny representation to the 2-year-old. Rather it is theoretically more coherent to propose two levels in the development of representation. The first level entails *making* things stand in the place of other things, and is achieved between 18 and 24 months. This level of representation embodies Perner and Astington's "situation theorists" and Piaget's basic conceptualization of symbolic representation. The second level entails *understanding* that the mind is representational is achieved around age 4. At this level of representation children can work their way through challenges of misrepresentation such as "false belief" and the "appearance–reality" distinction.

In all, there is something paradoxical in the attempt of cognitive theorists to see representational processes instated as early as possible in child cognition (see Mandler, 1983), and the theory of mind theorists in general (with Chandler the acknowledged exception) attempting to place it relatively late in development. The Piagetian developmental position appears as an intermediate formulation. In our view, this position is not incompatible with the child's theory of mind position, and as Boden makes clear, not incompatible with the position taken by cognitive scientists, or further, with (philosophical) representational theory of mind theorists, except, and most importantly, that it is developmental.

SEEKING TRUTH AND MEANING: LOGIC AND SCIENTIFIC
REASONING; BRYNES AND KUHN

To anyone minimally knowledgeable about Piaget's theory, it comes as no surprise that two areas of principal interest were those of logical and scientific thought. Piaget's concerns with reasoning and logic were of two sorts. First, to delineate and account for the development of natural logical thinking, as such, and second, to model all rational thought by means of logical theory, principally, with truth-functional logic. Beilin's chapter examining Piaget's New Theory makes clear that Piaget made some of the most radical changes in his logic theory of rationality in the last years of his life.

Brynes, providing a constructive perspective, responds to both of Piaget's concerns, detailing current directions in research and theory often going beyond the strict logicist models applied to natural logical thinking. The new path taken by Piaget placed greater emphasis on meaning (intensional logic) and less on truth testing (extensional truth-table logic) while remaining within a logical framework. From Brynes's account much of the current work on logical theory is outside a Piagetian frame directed as it is toward linguistic modeling in a variety of forms. These range from theories that emphasize rule-governed language production and comprehension (the prototypical case being early Chomskyan linguistics) to the pragmatic theories that minimize formal structure and emphasize semantic and contentful properties of language. In this regard, the latter logic theories reflect both a shift toward functional analysis, a shift paralleling the change in Piaget's later work, and in a different way, a shift toward a social structuring of formal systems (linguistic or rational thought) through communicative activity.

Brynes himself is loath to adopt formal models of mind, except in their weakest form. In part, his minimalist view of the value of logical analyses of rationality may be due to his sensitivity to the seduction of the *formal fallacy,* examined in the first part of his chapter. In our view, however, investigators should not so quickly abandon Piaget's fundamental dictum that there is "no form without function and no function without form." An adequate account of logical and rational thought within a developmental frame requires theory that embraces both logical form as well as semantic content and function.

The analysis of rational thought by Kuhn takes a quite different tack from Brynes, searching out the forms of reasoning that characterize and developmentally link the "child scientist" and the everyday "adult scientist." These two forms can be described as explanation and argumentation, respectively. The former seems to us to be what Piaget called the *search for reasons* in his later theory, a motivational aspect of mind impelling human rational activity. This conception is broader than Kuhn's, encompassing exploration, the central feature of thought in her view of the child scientist but lost, or at least languishing, in the adolescent and adult. While we are charmed by Kuhn's familial anecdote vivifying this discouraging characterization of development, we are unwilling to accept Kuhn's general conclusion that adult scientific reasoning entails an alternative model of thought categorically different from the child's. Rather, we see argumentation as the *something more* of adult rationality. In any case, what is critically wanting is an understanding of how either a cognitive alternative or enhancement develops from the exploratory, procedural type of understanding of early childhood.

Kuhn's alternative view of science as argument simultaneously moves her away from a logical modeling of thought and toward a social and linguistic pragmatics stressing practices of interpersonal and social discourse. Structural analysis in this framework includes rhetorical and dialogic categories of discourse as units of analysis, a position similar to Chapman's.

In her chapter, Kuhn does not explore the nature of causal theories embodied in her subject's thinking; she emphasizes the structure of argumentation made to support those theories, and in particular their understanding of the differentiation and integration of theory and evidence. Though there is some indication of domain specificity within her work, more importantly, Kuhn shows that forms of reasoning tend to transcend the content areas about which each subject argued. The relative consistency within subjects is balanced by the considerable variability in forms of argumentation across subjects, at every age level, and across categories of expertise. This variability is reduced when subjects are grouped by their level of formal education and even by their intention to attend college. From this research it is impossible to decide whether educational goals are facilitated by cognitive skills or whether the educational goals foster their development. As difficult as it is to answer to that question, it is vital to seek it out because it is germane to Piaget's assumption that natural logic is not culturally relative but species general.

Given that the question of cultural relativity remains an open question, it is not surprising that it is not evident how the scientific novice acquires the skills of argumentation central to scientific reasoning. However that occurs, the critical accomplishment, according to Kuhn, is reflectively coordinating present theories with the evidence those theories generate in real and thought experiments. This position is part of a growing body of evidence that humans have difficulty reasoning rationally in contexts that require it. Irrationality is an aspect of scientific reasoning Piaget is said to have underestimated in his search for the universal parameters of rational thought. This is not to say that Kuhn embraces mental life as fundamentally irrational. On the contrary she explicitly acknowledges that argumentation exploits Piaget's position that reflectivity is basic to rationality and that exploration and argumentation are equally necessary to the development of a better-educated citizenry capable of "higher-order thinking."

LANGUAGE, CULTURE, AND THOUGHT: SINCLAIR AND BRUNER

The chapters by Sinclair and Bruner are both devoted to the enduring question of the relation between language and thought; and both could not be more different in their basic assumptions and theoretical goals. *Hermina Sinclair* provides, first, an overview of the history of the paradigmatic language studies undertaken in Geneva by herself and her students, long after Piaget himself gave up the study of language. Their studies did not revive his earlier perspective on language but rather were structured by Piaget's logic models of mental development that were current in Geneva as Sinclair and her colleagues began their developmental linguistic work.

She makes clear that Genevan language studies were then, as now, concerned principally, though not exclusively, with syntactical development paralleling the development of mental structures of general interest to Piagetians. At once this chapter should debunk two myths. One, the continued predilection to identify the Genevan position on language with Piaget's largely bypassed views of the 1920s and 1930s. Two, the tendency to concentrate on, and thereby exaggerate, the differences between the Piagetian and Chomskyan research programs while failing to note their affinities (Beilin, 1975).

The second focus of her chapter is more constructive and forward looking while maintaining the Piagetian tradition of exploring theoretical and empirical relations between language and operational development. Sinclair's reviews of synchronic linguistic developments offers evidence of the spiral nature of development noted in our discussion of Case. In her words, "the structuring mechanisms [empirical and reflective abstractions] remain the same" but are applied to different language domains. She stipulates that restructuring linguistic properties such as phonological markings of pronominal agreement may be regulated by empirical abstraction while grammar may be reconstructed through reflective abstraction. However, Sinclair makes it clear that this hypothesis is offered tentatively, as she notes, "Children do not interact with utterances in the same way as they do with physical objects." In offering this qualification, she appears to join forces with Garcia, Chapman, and Kuhn in acknowledging that social and physical entities may play different roles in the subject–object relationship.

Despite Sinclair's acknowledgment that social and interpersonal forces play a significant role in shaping language, her emphasis is on intrapsychic mechanisms that drive language development. *Jerome Bruner's* current view turns this emphasis upside-down, and in doing so he constructs an epistemology with only tentative links, at best, to Piaget's perspective.

In the course of his exposition he perpetuates a number of myths about Piaget's theory. First, is the assertion that Piaget holds development to be unilinear. Piaget, particularly in his later work, argued against this view, a point reiterated in our discussion of Garcia. Second, is the claim that mind is derivational in a logical sense (again, see Garcia, as well as Youniss & Damon in this volume) and "across the board" (see Chapman, 1988, for a thorough analysis of this point).

This caveat aside, Bruner's cultural framework for studying the origin of mind and an understanding of reality emphasizes almost exclusively the social origins of language and thought. "Cultural products, such as language and other symbolic systems, mediate thought and place their stamp on our representations of reality," he writes. While a position similar to this can be construed in Piaget's early writings on language, Bruner's narrative model of mind goes well beyond Piaget's early position. His perspective is the outcome of a trend started in language studies with the attack, anchored in theories of pragmatics (speech-act theory, etc.) on syntactically based theory, principally Chomsky's. Its origins can be traced further back in the philosophical thought of the modern era to Nietzsche and the general dictum "life is text, text is life." As Bruner puts it, "It is not simply that 'text' becomes dominant but that the world to which it particularly refers is, as it were, a creature of the text." Mediated through recent semiotic, hermenuetic, deconstructionist, and related poststructuralist means of analysis, the ideas inherent in these positions may well be said to dominate current theory in the humanities, with increasingly greater inroads in the social sciences. Through the influence of anthropology and sociology these ideas have linked up with culture theory and are manifest not only in narrative analysis but in the discourse analyses seen in Kuhn's and Chapman's chapters.

Bruner claims that in understanding ourselves and our reality, "we organize our experience and our memory . . . mainly in the form of narrative. . . ." Further, narratives are "a version of reality whose acceptability [not truth] it is to be noted is governed by convention . . ." These ideas have been vigorously attacked as relativistic in philosophy (Laudan, 1990), the humanities, and the social sciences. The impetus for Bruner's view comes from, as he puts it, "doubting the legitimacy of received social realities [and] questioning the very ways in which we come to know or construct reality." This doubting began with the attack and ultimate demise of logical positivism. An important consequence has been the shift from causal forms of explanation to an emphasis on meaning and the uses of interpretation, a shift particularly evident in the social sciences.

Bruner is not alone in this epistemological shift in science. Beilin's chapter in this volume and our discussions of Garcia and Brynes make clear that Piaget himself was influenced by the same intellectual trends in developing his theory of meaning at the end of his career. However, his new theoretical stance differs from Bruner's in that, throughout the refinements he introduced, Piaget maintained his emphasis on the intrapsychic self-regulating forces of mental life.

Against Piaget's basic universalism and individualistic principles of the Enlightenment stands Bruner's alternative view of human minds that work in common through "the process of joint narrative accrual . . . within the context of a shared culture." Whether the world and reality are most appropriately understood according to narrative principles, structural and functional principles of Piaget, or the causal theories of connectionists cannot be decisively adjudicated at this time and certainly should not be carried out at the level of argumentation alone. While we differ significantly with Bruner's epistemology, there is no denying that he offers a clear and unmistakable alternative to Piaget's position. It is the kind of challenge that makes a vigorous contribution to the current debate.

CONSTRUCTING SOCIETIES: FURTH, YOUNISS & DAMON, AND MURRAY

Furth, Youniss, Damon, and Murray unambiguously adopt a constructivist stance with respect to Piaget's theory, and do so by exploring the developing child within a societal perspective. In contrast to Bruner, and his rather explicit cultural determinism, Furth, as well as Youniss and Damon, distance themselves from radical social and cultural determinism. They share Piaget's version of constructivism, rather than a position in which society imposes itself on the child, shaping development through societal contingencies. In their perspective, individual constructive acts are not fully understood unless they are construed in relation to society. Murray's examination of cooperative learning is conceptually sympathetic with Youniss and Damon's argument that peer cultures present special opportunities for development and Furth's classically Piagetian stance on the centrality of logic to mental development.

Furth continues to develop the relation between Piaget's and Freud's contributions to our understanding of the developing child he began in *Knowledge as Desire*. He extends this analysis by arguing that the origin of society is anchored in the development of two aptitudes: the logic of object

(Piaget's component) and the desire for object (Freud's component). When children develop beyond the logic of action of sensorimotor intelligence and the search for immediate gratification of biological needs to disconnected logic of objects and psychological desires, mental life is transformed to "reality making" in the service of pleasure.

Reality making is necessarily subjective and symbolic, a position that is completely consistent with Piaget's but it is also, according to Furth, fundamentally societal. Its societal orientation is not exclusively or even most importantly linked to the fact that our central symbolical activity is to adopt the language of our culture, as Bruner would hold, but that the objects of desire and satisfaction are embedded in social relations, in society. He exemplifies his point by analyzing the fantasy play of children, showing that in their play children are constructing societal relations, not merely imitating specific societal roles.

There is much provocative beyond this in Furth's proposition that children institute society in their fantasy. Perhaps the boldest proposal is his speculative hypothesis that the chaotic world constructed in the pre-Oedipal and prelogical period, and then repressed, accounts for our willingness to "suffer silently the discontents of civilization." On the other hand, for Furth, as Beilin, logic constructed from action is central to intellect; logic both brings order out of the chaos of our wishes and the diversity of our social reality, and protects mental life from being exclusively formed by culture, from being culturally relative.

Without nostalgia or sentiment, Youniss and Damon yearn for the developmental perspective embodied in Piaget's early writings emphasizing interpersonal interactions as significant in the construction of knowledge in general and social development in particular. Absent from their insightful historical account of Piaget's thoughts in the 1920s and 1930s is any reflection on why Piaget abandoned this perspective when he entered his formal structural period and why this earlier perspective was never fully reinstated in his last writing when functional and social aspects of mental life and its development were once again considered.

Their perspective of society and development, when set side by side with Chapman's and Kuhn's analysis of dialogue as a societal constraint on reasoning, makes clear the diversity of views that are at the same time constructive, in the Piagetian sense, and subsumed under the rubric of social influences on development. Youniss and Damon's understanding of societal constraints goes well beyond the structural and functional aspects of "argumentation." Moreover, their account of social influences is not to be confused with a Vygotskian accounting of society's role in developing mind from the interpersonal to the intrapersonal.

As in previous work, their accounts are sociological, anthropological, and even historical in scope. Their quest can be broadly cast as "what are the structures which child and culture co-construct?" In this sense, development is an adaptive relation between organism and others in a societal context that is mutually determined. Societal contexts embody intersubjective procedures of interacting, for example, negotiating and arguing, which in turn foster the intrasubjective construction of personal qualities, for example, sharing and participation. Finally, explicit in their perspective is their characterization of the two social spheres within which we develop, authority (adults) and mutuality (peers) as permeable or open to one another and developmental, not exclusive and destructive.

Following World War I, Piaget was active in educational programs designed to foster peace. As Youniss and Damon suggest in their chapter, Piaget thought science could make a significant contribution to public affairs. He made a number of proposals, based on his own research, largely concerning child care and education that he felt would lead to a generation that valued reciprocity and the construction of mutual benefits rather than national separateness, which fostered hostility and aggression. After World War II, although he served on some United Nations commissions, his belief in the potential of science for ameliorating the world's ills seems to have changed. As Murray points out, with few exceptions, Piaget's writings suggest that he was loath to apply his now more formal theory in any specific manner to either child care or education.

Murray's historical account of educational reformers in the United States during the 1960s indicates they were less circumspect than Piaget in making major curricular changes, such as the new mathematics curriculum, and we would add, instituting compensatory education programs, on the basis of their interpretations of Piagetian principles. Murray carries this tradition forward in response to the present crisis in American education, and in the face of indifference to Piaget's theory among most other reformers.

In his analysis, Piaget's genetic epistemology is offered as a framework within which to understand pedagogy, not as a model for curricular change. Given this perspective, Piaget's theory could give a clearer interpretation of and justification for contemporary educational constructs such as "understanding" and "cooperative learning," even though they have emerged independent of Piaget's ideas. Seeing cooperative learning as consistent with Piagetian principles puts him in the company of Chapman and Kuhn, although his account is theoretically more general, emphasizing as it does the potential for intrasubjective disequilibria generated by discussions. At the same time it is more practical, indicating the need to involve interlocutors who are at different levels of development with respect to the focal task rather than exploring dialogic procedures independent of developmental level. More futuristically, he muses at the potential for developing educational programs *if* the teacher were to apply reflectively genetic epistemology, that is, to analyze systematically the structure of one's own pedagogic activities, to test the principles and to adapt continually those principles in the light of that testing.

CONCLUSIONS

We end by returning to the first chapter of this volume, written by one of us (H. B.). It is both *paradigmatic* and *constructive* in its review of Piaget's theory as it was emerging at the time of his death, and setting forth the direction Piaget intended his own theory to take, at least in its next phase of development. It states four issues that might be conceived of as the core of Piaget's *New Theory*. We have chosen to repeat them here both as a way of generally recapitulating what we believe to be major themes within the volume, and also as a final way of examining the potential of Piaget's theory for the future pursuit of knowledge and its development. They offer a map, not drawn in sharp relief, but vivid enough to provide a sense of direction.

First, within the *New Theory,* there is a commitment to examining mental life as rational, with an underlying logical structure that is both intensional and extensional. The current commitment to meaning (intension) should not blind us to the continuing commitment Piaget had to truth testing (extension).

Second, procedural knowledge is developmentally prior to operational knowledge with the implication that possibility, the opening of new avenues of knowledge, takes precedence over the constraints imposed by necessary relations. Possibility is thus the critical adaptive property of mental development.

Third, equilibration remains the driving force in development and provides the rationale for an understanding of cognitive development as a constructive process.

Fourth, social and historical forces are critically involved in the process of development, but they do not pre-empt the priority of individual self-regulating mechanisms in the construction and organization of knowledge.

These issues in consort with the unique contributions of our colleagues in these chapters, leave little uncertainty that Piaget's theory remains a vigorous contender in the arena of ideas, and is likely to be so for some time. The theory is by its very nature dynamic, and it is as inevitable that it will be transformed as it was throughout Piaget's lifetime. In the end, there is no conclusion, only implication and possibility.

REFERENCES

Bak, P., & Chen, K. (1991). Self-organized criticality. *Scientific American, 264*(1), 46–53.
Beilin, H. (1975). *Studies in the cognitive basis of language development.* New York: Academic Press.

Chapman, M. (1988). *Constructive evolution: Origins and development of Piaget's thought.* Cambridge, MA: Cambridge University Press.

Forman, G., & Pufall, P. B. (1988). *Constructivism in the computer age.* Hillsdale, NJ: Lawrence Erlbaum Associates.

Inhelder, B., de Caprona, D., & Cornu-Wells, A. (1987). *Piaget today.* Hove/London: Lawrence Erlbaum Associates.

Laudan, L. (1990). *Science and relativism.* Chicago: University of Chicago Press.

Mandler, J. M. (1983). Representation. In J. H. Flavell & E. Markman (Eds.), *Manual of child psychology* (Vol. 3). New York: Wiley.

Piaget, J. & Garcia, R. (1989). *Psychogenesis and the history of science.* New York: Columbia University Press.

Piaget, J., & Garcia, R. (1991). *Toward a logic of meanings.* Hillsdale, NJ: Lawrence Erlbaum Associates.

Author Index

Subject Index